Mass Suicides on
Saipan and Tinian, 1944

Mass Suicides on Saipan and Tinian, 1944

An Examination of the Civilian Deaths in Historical Context

ALEXANDER ASTROTH

McFarland & Company, Inc., Publishers
Jefferson, North Carolina

LIBRARY OF CONGRESS CATALOGUING-IN-PUBLICATION DATA

Names: Astroth, Alexander, 1992– author.
Title: Mass suicides on Saipan and Tinian, 1944 : an examination of the civilian deaths in historical context / Alexander Astroth.
Description: Jefferson, North Carolina : McFarland & Company, Inc., Publishers, 2019 | Includes bibliographical references and index.
Identifiers: LCCN 2019004703 | ISBN 9781476674568 (paperback : acid free paper) ∞
Subjects: LCSH: Saipan, Battle of, Northern Mariana Islands, 1944. | World War, 1939–1945—Campaigns—Northern Mariana Islands. | Mass suicide—Northern Mariana Islands—Saipan. | Mass suicide—Northern Mariana Islands—Tinian. | Civilian war casualties—Northern Mariana Islands—Saipan. | Civilian war casualties—Northern Mariana Islands—Tinian. | World War, 1939–1945—Casualties—Northern Mariana Islands—Tinian. | World War, 1939–1945—Casualties—Northern Mariana Islands—Saipan.
Classification: LCC D767.99.S3 A88 2019 | DDC 940.53/967—dc23
LC record available at https://lccn.loc.gov/2019004703

BRITISH LIBRARY CATALOGUING DATA ARE AVAILABLE

ISBN (print) 978-1-4766-7456-8
ISBN (ebook) 978-1-4766-3516-3

© 2019 Alexander Astroth. All rights reserved

No part of this book may be reproduced or transmitted in any form or by any means, electronic or mechanical, including photocopying or recording, or by any information storage and retrieval system, without permission in writing from the publisher.

Front cover: a woman hugs her child as she walks along the beach to the stockade, Saipan, June 1944, USMC #83998 (National Archives); back cover: two children sit on a stretcher amid the rubble of Saipan, July 1944, TR#10212 (National Archives); cover design inspired by Michael Spizzirri

Printed in the United States of America

McFarland & Company, Inc., Publishers
Box 611, Jefferson, North Carolina 28640
www.mcfarlandpub.com

Acknowledgments

Many individuals helped improve this book. The author is thankful to Haruko Taya Cook, Nicole Dombrowski-Risser, Wakako Higuchi, Bruce M. Petty, Scott Russell, Don A. Farrell, Boyd Dixon, Mike T. Carson, Darlene Moore, Rosalind Hunter-Anderson, David Atienza de Frutos, Alexandre Coello de la Rosa, Carlos Madrid Alvarez-Piner, Francis X. Hezel, Melba Veloso, Stephanie Mawson, Katharyn Tuten-Puckett, Robert Hunter, Beatrice Trefalt, Oleg Benesch, Janice Matsumura, James Francis Warren, Yuriko Nagata, Keiko Tamura, Mayu Kanamori, Nobuko Adachi, Robert Huey, Stewart Curry, Julia Bullock, Hyeok Hweon Kang, Evelyn W., Ray E. Boomhower, Gerald Meehl, Philip E. Preston, Colonel Christopher Woodbridge, NARA Archivist Nathaniel Patch, CNMI Archivist John Cook, NYSMM Archivist Jim Gandy, Veterans History Project Reference Specialist Megan Harris, and librarians Tamara Zielinski, Vanette Schwartz, Christina Special, and Benjamin Stone. The author is grateful to Saipan-Tinian Veteran Robert B. Sheeks and his son Robert H. Sheeks and the families of Saipan-Tinian Veteran Frederic A. Stott and Saipan correspondent Robert L. Sherrod, as well as many other veterans' next of kin consulted. The author is responsible for any errors in fact or interpretation.

The author greatly appreciates the staffs of the National Archives and Records Administration, American Folklife Center at the Library of Congress, Defense Technical Information Center, National Museum of the Pacific War, New York State Military Museum, Wisconsin Veterans Museum, Veteran Voices of Pittsburgh Oral History Initiative, Northern Marianas Humanities Council, CNMI Archives at Northern Marianas College, Micronesian Seminar, Center for Pacific Islands Studies at the University of Hawaii at Manoa, University of Hawaii at Manoa Library, University of Illinois at Urbana-Champaign Library, University of Chicago Library, Field Museum of Natural History in Chicago, Marine Corps Gazette, Saipan Tribune, and Marianas Variety. McFarland did an exceptional job in preparing and printing the book. George Feifer's book *Tennozan: The Battle of Okinawa and the Atomic Bomb* (1992), which discusses the experiences of Okinawan civilians in 1945, was a major inspiration to the author. This work was made possible because of the support and encouragement of the author's family. It is dedicated to his cousin Eric Robert Seely (April 18, 1995–December 3, 2017) of Monee, Illinois.

Table of Contents

Acknowledgments v
Preface 1
Introduction 3

Part 1: Before 1944

1. Prehistory and European Colonization 15
2. Japanese Takeover of Saipan and Tinian 30
3. Cultures and Societies of Saipan and Tinian 44
4. The Asia-Pacific War and Islands' Militarizations 62

Part 2: 1944

5. Saipan and Tinian Invasions 73
6. Mass Civilian Suicides 85
7. Causes of the Mass Civilian Suicides 105
8. Non-Suicide Deaths 127
9. Civilian Internment Camps 153
10. Number of Civilian Deaths and Suicides 164

Aftermath 169
Chapter Notes 179
Bibliography 199
Index 211

Preface

Akiko Kikuchi admired Saipan. In the late 1930s and early 1940s, when she was a young woman, sugarcane farms on the volcanic-limestone island stretched from the coasts to the jungles and mountains. Salt-scented winds and the sound of swaying cane were ever-present. The varicolored sunrises and sunsets over the sea and the many coconut palms and tropical flowering plants were unfailingly beautiful. The towns on the island were well developed and vibrant. Ships and boats were always coming and going at the harbor, while people were busy working in the nearby fields, factories, and shops. Akiko loved her family, and her life was structured and calm. In June 1944, however, the Americans bombarded and invaded the Japanese-controlled and -defended island. Saipan and the neighboring island of Tinian to the south were devastated by bombs, naval and artillery shells, and flame weapons.

During the battle, Akiko hid in dense vegetation and dark, unsanitary caves filled with excrement and blood for weeks. She was dehydrated, malnourished, and sick like many other civilians. When on the move and looking for water, she saw and smelled the decomposing bodies of men, women, and children. Many people died from diseases and wounds from Japanese and American weapons. Some were murdered in atrocities committed by Japanese troops. In July, Akiko fled to the northern end of Saipan. There, on top and near the cliffs, a number of civilians were committing suicide and murder-suicide because they were told by Japanese troops and other noncombatants that the Americans would rape, torture, and slaughter them. Additionally, a number of Japanese troops were forcing civilians to commit suicide or murdering them before killing themselves. Akiko was frightened and jumped off a cliff.[1] Fortunately, she survived the fall and was rescued by the Americans. She was put in the civilian internment camp in southwestern Saipan and was later repatriated to Japan after the surrender of the empire. Akiko's family members died during the battle and it left a sadness inside her for the remainder of her life.

Many people have heard about the mass civilian suicides on Saipan in which Akiko was involved. Popular World War II documentaries, such as *Victory at Sea* (1952–1953), *The World at War* (1973–1974), and *World War II in HD* (2009), briefly show American military footage of some of the suicides on the island. Though their occurrence is well known, English-language historical scholarship on the Saipan mass suicides is limited. Historian Haruko Taya Cook wrote excellent articles about the Japanese media's sensationalization of the Saipan suicides in the months after they occurred, but no other scholars have conducted research and published English-language works specifically on the topic. The Tinian suicides are little known and have been neglected by historians and anthropologists. There are several Saipan and Tinian battle narratives, but these mainly focus on the fighting between American and Japanese troops. American military records containing information about the mass suicides on both islands were declassified and made available to the public by 1980, but few of the documents have been examined, used, or cited in publications since then. Most of the records are held and preserved in the United States National Archives at College Park, Maryland.

Mass Suicides on Saipan and Tinian, 1944 took four years to research and write. Information was obtained from a range of primary sources, including archival documents, period newspaper articles, memoirs, and interviews. The author draws heavily on the Northern Troops and Landing Force (NTLF) Saipan and Tinian operations reports that were created in the Pacific in 1944 and presently reside in Record Group 38 at the National Archives (the NTLF was the American force that invaded Saipan and Tinian). The author also relies on testimonies from the oral history collections at the American Folklife Center at the Library of Congress, National Museum of the Pacific War, New York State Military Museum, and other institutions. This book includes a great number of excerpts from the NTLF reports, as well as civilian, war correspondent, and troop firsthand accounts of the mass suicides to explain "what" happened on Saipan and Tinian. The original documents and eyewitness accounts also help us better understand "why" the mass suicides happened. The author tried to limit paraphrasing as much as possible so that readers can view and contemplate the documents' texts and veterans' and civilian survivors' testimonies in their own words. There is some author commentary that accompanies the excerpts, but this is not a sociological examination of the mass suicides. Sociological terminology and analytical methods, such as those put forth by Emile Durkheim and later academics, are not employed. The author does not examine other mass suicides in world history as a comparative study, nor does he devote every chapter to the mass suicides on the two islands. The civilian experiences on the two islands were not limited to collective suicides; there is far more to their stories.

This book is about the peoples of Saipan and Tinian from prehistoric times to the present, with an emphasis on the civilians who died and survived in 1944. It starts at prehistoric times and proceeds chronologically and thematically so that readers obtain a better understanding of the islands, their inhabitants, and the historical events and developments that led to Japanese rule, the two battles, and civilian deaths. The work includes more than 25 United States Marine Corps, Navy, and Army archival photographs of civilians on Saipan and Tinian from Record Groups 111-SC, 127, and 208 in the National Archives.

Introduction

"The Japanese garrison and civilians died virtually to the last man, woman and child."[1] The Battle of Saipan, 1944—*The Cambridge History of the Second World War* (2015)

The civilian deaths, including mass suicides, on Saipan and Tinian in 1944 are commonly misunderstood happenings of the Asia-Pacific War. They are often misunderstood because of the lack of good scholarship on them. It is a myth that virtually all or most of the civilians died during the Battle of Saipan (June 15-July 9, 1944) and the Battle of Tinian (July 24-August 1, 1944). The myth has and continues to be told, particularly about the civilians of Saipan, however. John Toland wrongfully asserted in his Pulitzer Prize-winning book *The Rising Sun: The Decline and Fall of the Japanese Empire 1936-1945* (1970), "Almost 22,000 Japanese civilians—two out of three—perished needlessly" on Saipan.[2] More than fifteen books published after Toland's work stated that almost, at least, or more than 22,000 civilians died on the island.[3] A military history writer claimed in 2005, "Only a few Japanese civilians [on Saipan]...fell into American hands alive."[4] The *Library of Congress World War II Companion* (2007) stated, "More than 20,000 civilians died on Saipan."[5] Another myth repeatedly told is that the majority of the civilians on Saipan committed suicide.[6] Historian Shunsuke Tsurumi stated in 1982, on Saipan, "the majority of the 25,000 Japanese civilians, including women and children, committed suicide."[7] Social scientist David R. Beisel wrote in 2007, "20,000 Japanese civilians threw themselves off a cliff in Saipan."[8] An American political scientist wrote in 2007, "Most civilians on the island [Saipan] killed themselves rather than surrender."[9] An American historian stated in 2016, during the Battle of Saipan, "more than 20,000 civilians lost their lives, chiefly by suicide."[10]

The dearth of scholarship on the civilian deaths has led authors of secondary works to give many different figures concerning the number of noncombatants who died in the mass suicides on Saipan, including "hundreds,"[11] 1,000,[12] 8,000,[13] 10,000,[14] 18,000,[15] and 20,000[16] people. Others asserted the number of suicides is higher. An American archaeologist stated, "an estimated 22,000 civilians committed suicide."[17] A British historian wrote, "in Saipan ... on 7 July 1944, 25,000 Japanese civilians committed suicide rather than be taken prisoner."[18] The tenth edition of the textbook *The American Past: A Survey of American History* (2014), stated, "Of 35,000 Japanese on Saipan, including civilians, all but 1,000 fought to the death or committed suicide."[19] One writer claimed, "Here, upwards of 40,000 Japanese, mainly civilians, leaped to their deaths rather than be captured by the approaching American forces."[20] Another wrote, on Saipan, "actual numbers are not known, but estimates run from 25,000 to 60,000 Japanese civilians, including men, women, and children, killed themselves."[21] The Tinian suicides are usually ignored or not known.

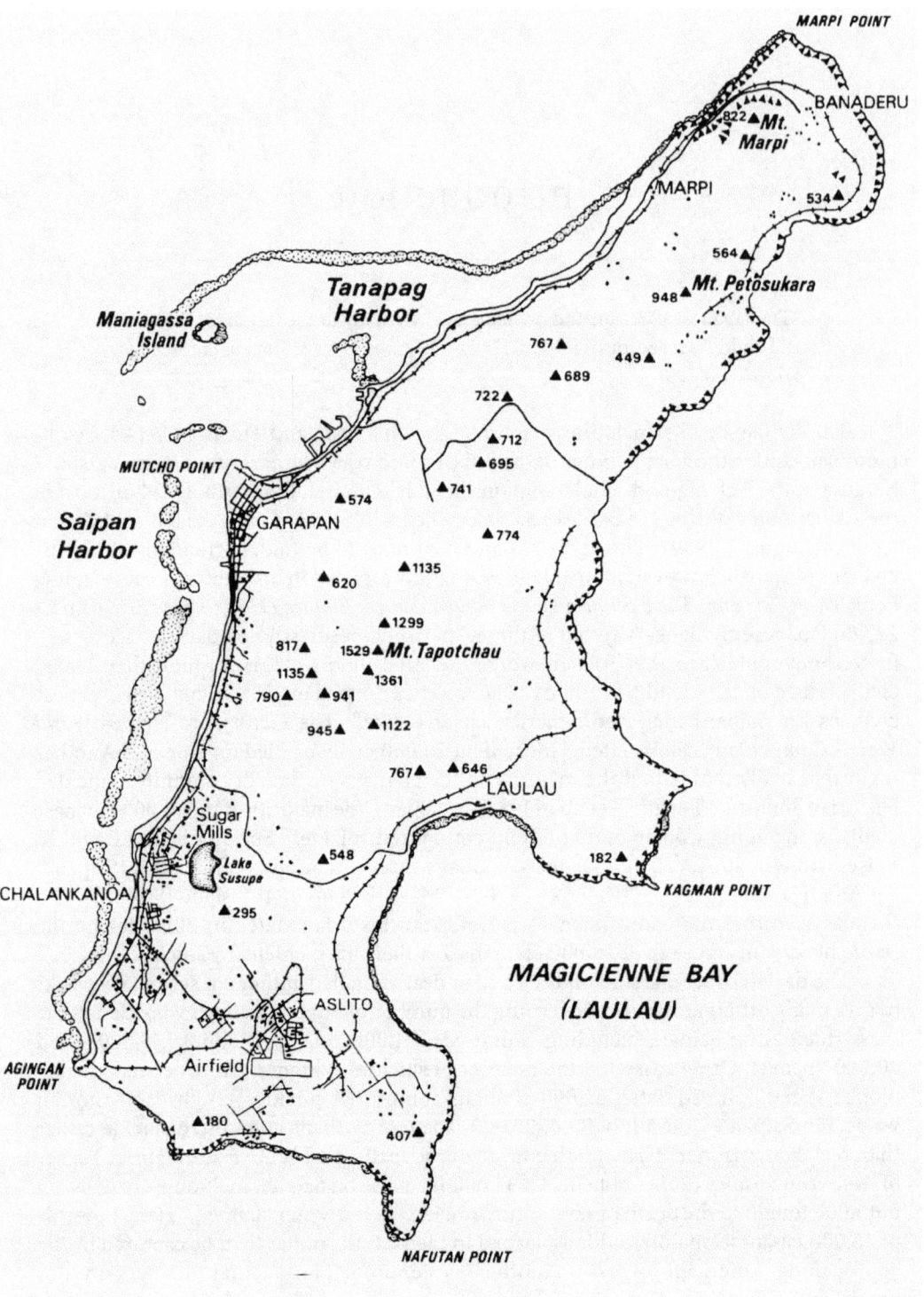

Saipan Island in the late 1930s. Drawn by cartographer Noel Diaz. Reprinted from Mark R. Peattie's *Nanyo* (1988). Courtesy University of Hawaii Press.

The primary sources reveal that the number of civilian deaths, including suicides, on Saipan was much lower than most claims in the secondary literature. In June 1944, before the battle began, the civilian population on the island was approximately 28,663 people. Of that number, approximately 18,227 civilians survived and 10,436 died from all causes on Saipan (Chapter 10). Nearly two-thirds of the population survived the Battle of Saipan and internment. On Tinian, the civilian population was approximately 14,371 people. Of that number, approximately 11,761 civilians survived and 2,610 died. These numbers exclude the 4,238 civilians (2,580 from Saipan and 1,658 from Tinian) who were evacuated by the Japanese Navy before June 1944[22]; hundreds of them, unfortunately, died at sea from American submarine attacks or later in American firebombings on the mainland. According to eyewitnesses, the number of civilians who took their own lives on both islands was in the hundreds. The number of noncombatants who died from suicides and murder-suicides on Saipan and Tinian combined was likely less than 2,000. The suicides and murders did not happen all at once but over weeks, especially during the final days of the battles and the mop-up operations. They took place in areas other than the cliffs as well, including the islands' caves, fields, and jungles. Most of the civilian deaths were caused by diseases and from being caught in the fighting. More than 2,000 civilians died from malnutrition, diseases, and days and weeks old wounds in the American stockades and internment camps on Saipan and Tinian during and in the months following the battles (Chapter 9).[23] The Japanese garrisons did not die "to the last man" on Saipan and Tinian as well. Over two thousand Japanese troops and Korean military laborers surrendered or were captured on the two islands.[24]

Why did the mass suicides happen? United States military, Northern Troops and Landing Force (NTLF) reports, as well as troop, war correspondent, and civilian firsthand accounts, reveal that the civilian suicides on Saipan and Tinian were primarily the result of fear and coercion (Chapters 6 and 7). Civilians feared the invading Americans. The Japanese government and media disseminated propaganda during the war that portrayed the enemy as "demons." Moreover, Japanese Army and Navy troops on Saipan and Tinian, as well as civilians, spread rumors that the Americans would rape, torture, and murder noncombatants. Many civilians fled to the northern end of Saipan and the southern end of Tinian after the American amphibious landings. They were trapped at the edges of the islands near the ends of the battles. They either had to fall into the hands of the Americans or die. Some attempted to hold out in the caves and jungles; a number of these holdouts, however, died from diseases and dehydration or were killed in American mop-up operations after the islands were secured. Civilians also feared Japanese troops. A number of Japanese troops prevented civilians from surrendering, forced them to commit suicide, and committed atrocities and murder-suicides. Some Japanese troops also conducted "mercy killings" with the permission of noncombatants or at their bequest so the Americans would not get to them.[25] Sadly, they did not know that most Americans did not want to hurt civilians. Mercy killings were consensual, whereas murder-suicides were not. Some civilians also killed their family members, friends, and strangers because they were forced to do so by Japanese troops or did not want their loved ones to be harmed by American or Japanese troops. There were also rumors told among troops and civilians that even if the islands fell, the Japanese Navy would retake them eventually.[26] Some feared if they surrendered, that they would be considered "traitors" and possibly executed after the reoccupation or return to Japan. The psychological and physical stressors of being in a combat zone for weeks undoubtedly took their toll on the minds of those struggling to

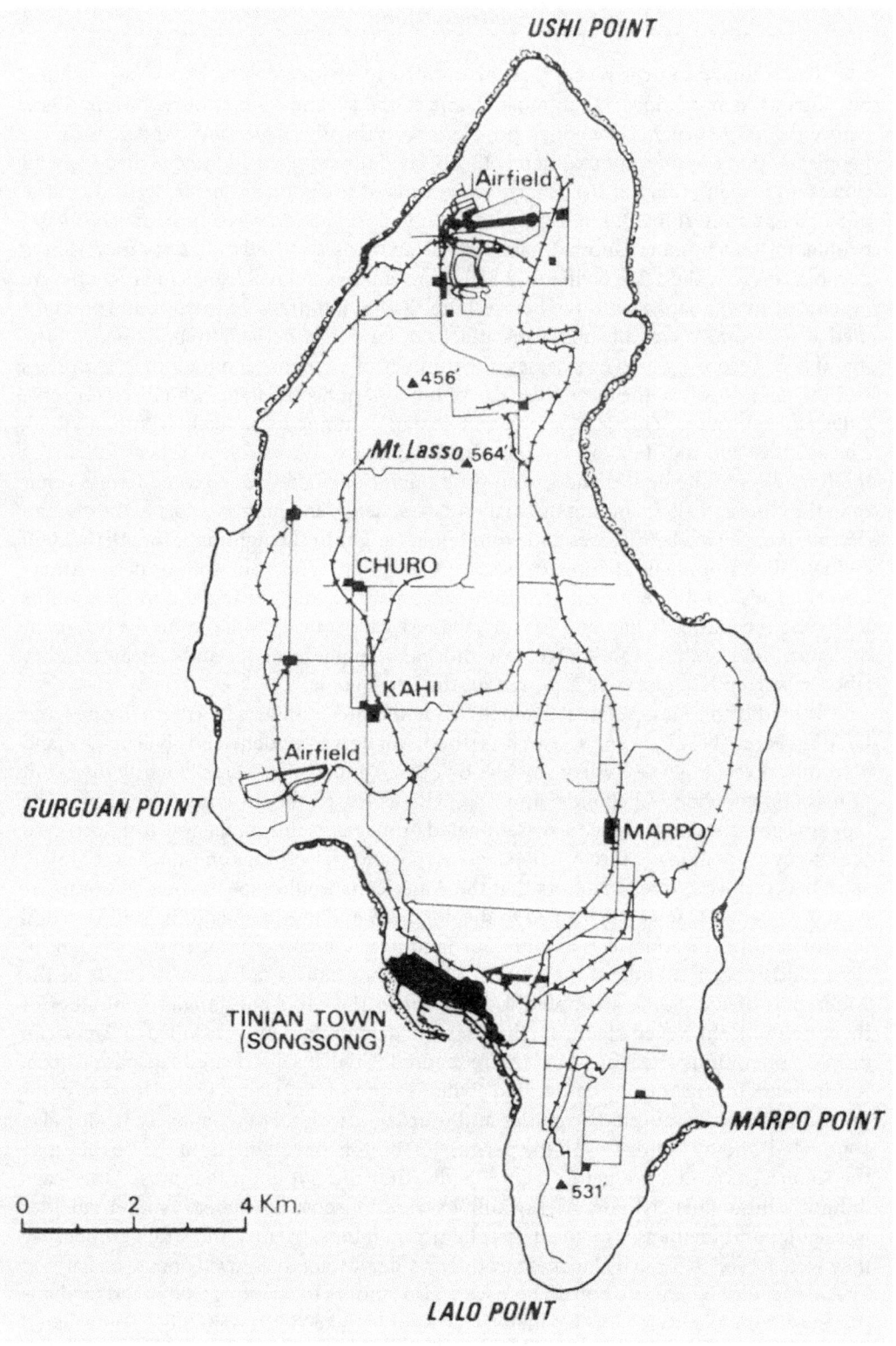

Tinian Island in the late 1930s. Drawn by cartographer Noel Diaz. Reprinted from Mark R. Peattie's *Nanyo* (1988). Courtesy University of Hawaii Press.

survive. Civilians and the overwhelmed Japanese troops on the islands were suffering from a lack of water, food and cleanliness, as well as from trauma and sleep deprivation. Under these conditions and circumstances, preexisting fears were exacerbated, and new ones arose. There is nothing striking or unique about fear of the enemy. American troops fighting on the islands had fears about their Japanese counterparts as well. They heard about what Japanese troops did to surrendering combatants and civilians in China and the Philippines, and many had no intentions of surrendering if their units were overrun in counterattacks or of being dragged behind enemy lines to face possible torture for intelligence. It must be stated that not all Japanese officers and enlisted men on the islands committed atrocities or believed civilians needed to die on Saipan and Tinian. Many imperial troops left noncombatants alone or allowed them to surrender. Had this not been the case, civilian deaths on the islands would have been greater.

Suicides committed because of fear, and not by coercion, were deliberate. However, they were not done willfully or eagerly because of patriotism and nationalism. Suicides committed because of coercion from Japanese troops or other civilians were not deliberate and not really acts of "suicide," which the Merriam-Webster Dictionary defines as "the act or an instance of taking one's own life voluntarily and intentionally."[27] According to historian Janice Matsumura, coerced suicides during the Pacific War "should be more accurately described as acts of compulsory self-destruction or murder at the hands of military authorities."[28] Some scholars have used the terms "compulsory mass/group suicide" (*kyoseiteki shudan jiketsu*), "mass deaths" (*shudanshi*), and "forced collective deaths" (*kyosei shudanshi*) to describe the coerced deaths of civilians that Japanese troops were responsible for in Okinawa Prefecture in 1945.[29] In this work, the term "mass suicides," which appears in some of the primary sources, is broadly used to denote coerced or compulsory suicides, murder-suicides, mercy killings, and suicides from fear of American and Japanese troops.

There is not complete personal data about the Japanese, Okinawan, and Korean civilians who died on Saipan and Tinian. Many of their names, ages, birthplaces, educational backgrounds, occupations, organization affiliations, and so on are unknown.[30] Many Japanese and Korean records concerning this information were destroyed or discarded. Furthermore, some civilian diaries, letters, and other writings burned up in the battles, while others never kept any.[31] Without these records and intimate writings, we do not know the civilians' innermost thoughts and convictions. Furthermore, the Americans did not conduct a thorough civilian body count or investigate the identities of civilian dead. Even if they did, they would not be able to tell apart, in most cases, a suicide and murder to determine the manner of death. We cannot carry out a systematic study to determine motivations for civilians' decisions if we do not have the written materials for content analysis and do not even know the identities of those who willfully committed suicide during the battles. Anthropologist Emiko Ohnuki-Tierney and Social Scientists Tomonori Morikawa and John Orbell were able to produce scholarship about the motivations of Kamikaze pilots in the war because we have the numerous writings these men left behind.[32] Their works about the Kamikaze pilots give us some insights into the mentality of Japanese military men, but the civilians of Saipan and Tinian were not in the military.

The Oxford Companion to World War II (1995) stated that Saipan civilians committed suicide because they were "faithful to the Japanese cause."[33] This assertion about the civilians' motivations is conjecture; there is little to no evidence that civilians willfully committed suicide because of loyalty to the emperor or the empire and its war effort. Again, the primary sources and written materials we do have, the NTLF reports and testimonies of American and Japanese troops and East Asian and Micronesian civilians who survived the battles, reveal that a number of Japanese troops murdered and coerced civilians and that there was widespread fear of American and Japanese troops amongst the civilian populations of the two islands. These accounts also show that most civilians did not commit suicide or take up arms against the Americans and die fighting as paramilitary personnel, and, therefore, tell us that most civilians on Saipan and Tinian did not truly follow any patriotic/nationalistic philosophies or loyalty codes whatsoever that called for their deaths. Tens of thousands of civilians committed *mass surrender* or allowed themselves to be captured rather than mass suicide on Saipan and Tinian.

There were no mass civilian suicides in mainland Japan in the months before and after the surrender of the empire in September 1945. Nearly all Japanese people, including the emperor, empress, and their children, "went on with their lives."[34] In Manchuria (Manchukuo), however, a number of Japanese civilians died from suicides and murder-suicides preceding and following the surrender.[35] But why there and not in Tokyo or elsewhere in the Japanese mainland? Japanese civilians in Manchuria feared the invading Russians, the Chinese, and Korean guerrilla fighters. A number of civilians killed themselves and their family members because they believed the enemy would harm them. Many others were coerced to commit suicide or murdered by Japanese troops and local leaders.[36] Anthropologist Mariko Asano Tamanoi explains, in Manchuria, survivor testimonies suggest that "compulsory group suicide involved several layers of power relationships."[37] The armed male leaders, who believed suicide was necessary, had power over the women and unarmed men; the younger and stronger individuals had power over the elderly; parents had power over their children. Like in Okinawa Prefecture, "the decision to commit suicide was made by only a few individuals, never *collectively*."[38] There were no mass suicides in mainland Japan because there were no fear-inducing invasions by the United States and the Soviet Union or circumstances for Japanese troops and civilian leaders to murder or coerce civilians to commit suicide as was the case on Saipan and Tinian and in Okinawa Prefecture and Manchuria.

It is estimated that more than ten thousand civilians died from non-suicide causes (Chapter 8), including diseases and wounds, on Saipan and Tinian combined. These deaths have largely been disregarded and unexamined because of myths about the mass suicides and the focus on combatants in secondary books. Who were the peoples on the islands who died from suicides and from non-suicide causes? What were their lives before the battles? The author attempts to answer these questions in Part 1 while discussing the larger historical events that impacted their lives. There was more to these peoples' existences than what they faced as noncombatants trapped on battlefields. This book discusses their lives, and not just their deaths, to honor them and their memory and bring their story out of obscurity.

We cannot grasp who these people really were or when and why the non-indigenous peoples ended up on the islands by starting the narrative in 1944. We must go back to the times of the prehistoric Chamorros and European colonization (Chapter 1) and the Japanese takeover in 1914 (Chapter 2) to obtain crucial context about the peoples. The

Opposite: **The Mariana Islands. Courtesy CNMI Division of Historic Preservation.**

MARIANA ISLANDS

- Farallon de Pajaros
- Maug
- Asuncion
- Agrihan
- Pagan
- Alamagan
- Guguan
- Sarigan
- Anatahan
- Farallon de Medinilla
- SAIPAN
- TINIAN
- Aguijan
- ROTA
- GUAM

0 10 20 30 40 50
STATUTE MILES

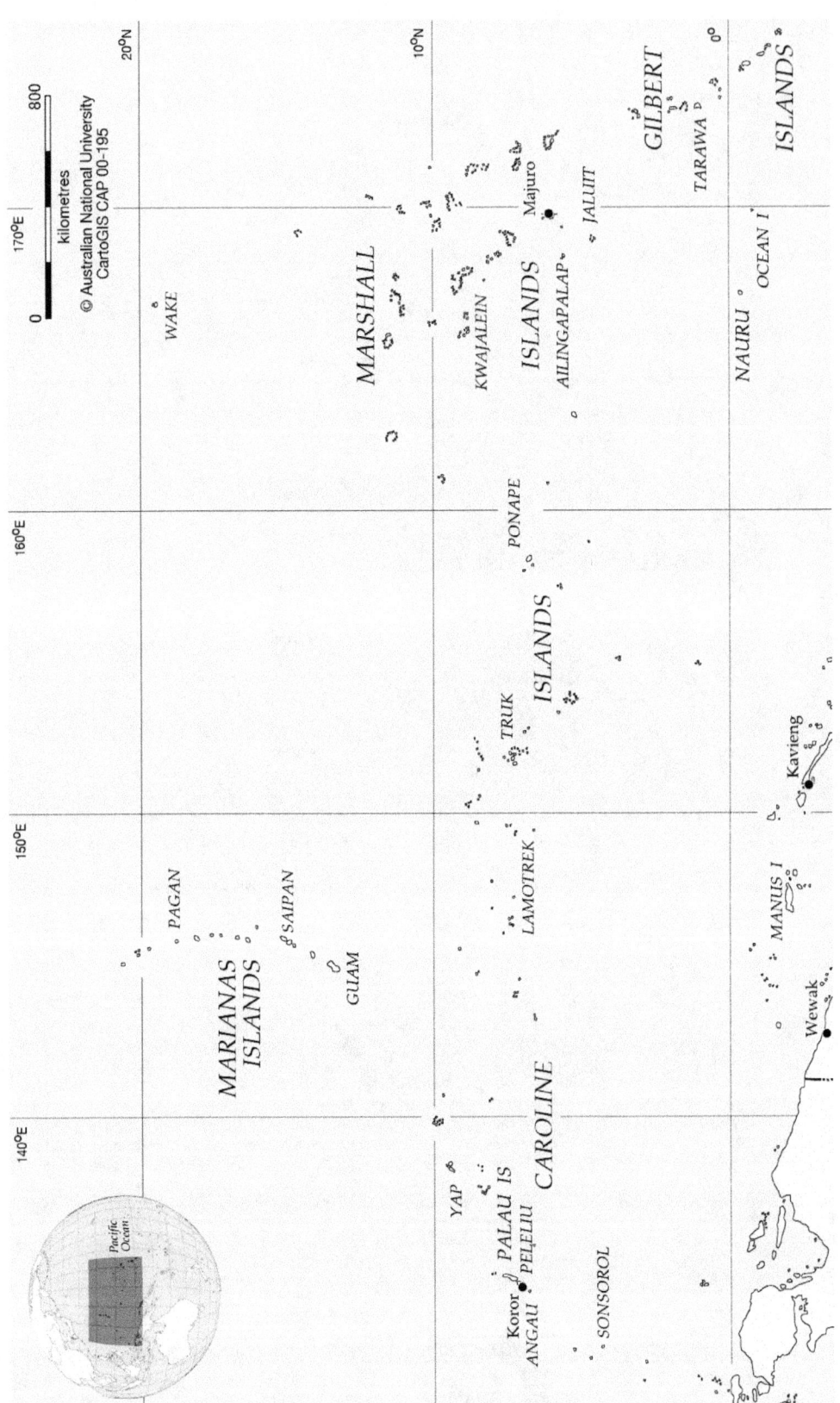

Micronesia. Courtesy CartoGIS Services, College of Asia and the Pacific, Australian National University.

indigenous Chamorros and the Carolinians lived on Saipan, while less than 30 Micronesians resided on Tinian. There were Japanese, Okinawan, and Korean civilians on Saipan and Tinian in 1944. The Chamorros and Carolinians still practiced and maintained much of their prehistoric and European colonial era cultures and customs under Japanese rule (1914–1944). Any Chamorro or Carolinian elder, who was age 45 or older in 1944, was born during the late years of the Spanish Colonial Period (1521–1899) and lived through the German Colonial Period (1899–1914) on Saipan. They were the parents and grandparents of Chamorro, Carolinian, and Micronesian-East Asian civilians who were born in the first half of the twentieth century. They interacted with Japanese, Okinawan, and Korean migrants, most who arrived between 1914 and 1941, and East Asian children born in the islands during the pre-war years. They died or survived with them in the battles and some witnessed the mass suicides. While most suicides were carried out by the Japanese and Okinawans, a number of Chamorros, Carolinians, and Koreans died in murder-suicides and atrocities that were part of the overall phenomenon of the mass suicides. There were also some Japanese-Chamorro, Japanese-Carolinian, and Okinawan-Chamorro/Carolinian children who died from suicides.

This book has ten chapters between the introduction and the aftermath. It is divided into two parts. Part 1 (Chapters 1 through 4) is about the islands' peoples and historical events and happenings before 1944, while Part 2 (Chapters 5 through 10) is about the islands' civilians in 1944. Chapter 1 summarizes Saipan and Tinian's natural histories, the prehistoric period (c. 1500 BCE–1521 CE), and the Spanish and German colonial periods. The chapter describes who the indigenous Chamorros and the Carolinians on the two islands were and what they experienced under European colonial rule before the Japanese takeover in the second decade of the twentieth century. Chapter 2 discusses Japanese expansion into Micronesia between the 1880s and 1920s. It covers why and how the Japanese obtained control of Saipan and Tinian in 1914 and their establishment of the South Seas Government in 1922. Also covered is the rise of the Japanese sugarcane and fishing industries in the 1920s and 1930s; the arrival of great numbers of Japanese, Okinawan, Korean migrants; and the growth and development of towns and villages on the two islands. Chapter 3 examines the religions and cultures of the Japanese, Okinawan, and Korean people on the two islands. It also covers Japanese assimilation policies, the discrimination non–Japanese people experienced, and the lives of women on the two islands. Chapters 4 examines the roots of the war in which the mass suicides occurred. Additionally, it discusses the militarizations of Saipan and Tinian in the late 1930s and 1940s and the hardships the peoples of the islands experienced, including forced labor and the lack of food. Prostitutes, sex slaves, "comfort women," and Korean military laborers on Saipan and Tinian are also briefly discussed.

Chapter 5 in Part 2 describes the American strategic plans, bombardments, and invasions of Saipan and Tinian. The author provides concise overviews of the Battles of Saipan and Tinian. Chapter 6 includes a great number of firsthand accounts about the mass suicides. The troop, war correspondent, and civilian survivor accounts describe civilian deaths on Saipan and Tinian on different days and in different areas or from different vantage points. The chapter also provides information about American troops' interactions with civilians, their reactions to the mass suicides, and efforts to save noncombatants. Chapter 7 discusses the causes of the mass suicides and why a number of Japanese troops murdered civilians. Chapter 8 clarifies how civilians died from many causes other than suicides, including diseases and wounds from Japanese and American weapons. Chapter 9 covers the awful conditions of the American stockades and civilian internment camps between June and November 1944. Chapter 10 examines the number of civilian deaths and suicides during the battles. Here, the author, using primary source data, contests the high estimates of civilian deaths given by some scholars and writers. The conclusion explains the mythologization of the mass suicides, the reparation of East Asian civilian survivors to their homelands, the American colonial period, and the memorialization and commemoration of the suicides.

In this work, surnames appear in the order they were written in the source documents or given in oral testimonies. No diacritical marks have been used for non–English

The Empire of Japan in 1942. Courtesy CartoGIS Services, College of Asia and the Pacific, Australian National University.

words. Regarding the reliability of the writings and testimonies drawn on and used in this book, the author acknowledges that some could be biased based on numerous factors, including nationalism, ethnocentrism, and racism. The complexities and vagaries of memory are also acknowledged. It must be humbly accepted that the veterans and civilian survivors who spoke or wrote about the events on Saipan and Tinian said what they thought was important or right at the time in which they did so. We can look at who is saying what, how many people are saying the same thing, and corroborate some of it with photographs, footage, and military reports to make more solid interpretations about what happened and why.

PART 1: BEFORE 1944

1

Prehistory and European Colonization

Saipan and Tinian are two of the fifteen tropical islands that form the crescent-shaped Mariana Archipelago, also known as the Mariana Islands or the Marianas. The archipelago is part of the Izu-Bonin-Mariana Arc, a system that stretches from the Japanese main islands to Guam. It is in the western North Pacific Ocean at the eastern end of the Philippine Sea and is an island group in Micronesia, a subregion of Oceania. Other major island groups in Micronesia include the Carolines, Marshalls, and Kiribati (Gilberts). The Marianas vertically span over 460 miles and are split into two arc groups. In the geologically older southern arc, consisting of six islands, are Guam, Rota, Aguiguan, Tinian, Saipan, and Farallon de Medinilla. In the younger and volcanically active northern arc, consisting of nine islands, are Anatahan, Sarigan, Guguan, Alamagan, Pagan, Agrihan, Asuncion, Maug, and Farallon de Pajaros. The islands sit directly west of the Marianas Trench, the deepest part of the world's oceans.

The Marianas are part of the Pacific "Ring of Fire." Saipan and Tinian are raised limestone islands that formed through volcanic activity. The islands began as underwater volcanoes approximately 42 million years ago.[1] The submarine volcanoes grew from intermittent eruptions over millions of years and eventually rose above the ocean's surface and became mountainous islands. Exposed coral reefs on the new islands' surfaces dried out, died, and became layers of limestone above the volcanic rock. The reefs that remained submerged and grew around the islands were rich sea life habitats. During and following the formation of Saipan and Tinian, typhoons, tropical storms, and earthquakes eroded their surface rock into soil, which collected in the valleys. Periodic eruptions broke through the limestone and added mineral-rich ash and rocks to the soils. Decayed plant and animal matter further enriched the volcanic, limestone earth. Birds from Island Southeast Asia, Melanesia, and other Pacific Island groups traveled to the Marianas and deposited the seeds of a diverse number of tropical tree, shrub, vine, and grass species that were in their guts and plumage. Fruit bats carrying seeds also flew to the archipelago. Humans later introduced non-endemic animal and plant species to the islands.

Saipan

Saipan is the second largest island in the Marianas after Guam. It is approximately 12.5 miles long, 5.5 miles at its widest point, and has a land area of 47 square miles.[2] The island is approximately 3 miles north of Tinian, 135 miles north of Guam, 1,460 miles south of Tokyo, 1,650 miles east of Manila, and 3,700 miles west of Honolulu. Saipan is a rugged island with numerous mountains and hills with jungles and caves. Pacific War correspondent Robert Sherrod described the island as a "low-lying prehistoric monster, whose spine rose in the center to 1,554-foot Mt. Tapochau."[3] The island's distinct shape is formed by several land masses and minor peninsulas projecting out to the ocean. These projections include Agingan Point in the southwest, Nafutan Point in the southeast, Kagman Peninsula in the central-east, Mutcho Point in the central-west, and Marpi Point in the far north. Lake Susupe, a landlocked brackish-water lake surrounded by swamp, is situated in southwestern Saipan north of Agingan Point.[4] Maniagassa Island (Managaha Island), a sandbar islet, is located off Saipan's west-central shore. Bird Island or "Moon Viewing Island" is a small cliff island just off the northeast coast of Saipan.[5] There are two bays on Saipan's eastern shore: Magicienne Bay (Laulau Bay) in the south and the smaller Fanonchuluyan Bay in the north.[6] Tanapag Harbor is located in the west directly north of Mutcho Point. Just south of Saipan, pass the narrow Saipan Channel, is Tinian.

Tinian

Tinian, the third largest island in the Marianas, is 3 miles south of Saipan. The island is approximately 12 miles long and 6.5 miles wide and has a land area of 39 square miles.[7] In the north-central and southern segments of the island are mountains and ridges with caves. Prominent mountains in the north-central area include Mt. Lasso (564 ft) and Mt. Maga (390 ft). Mt. Kastiyu (614 ft), located in the southeastern end, is the highest point on Tinian. In the island's center is the lush and fertile central plateau and Marpo Valley. Tinian's shape is formed by Ushi Point in the north, Asiga Point in the northeast, Gurguan Point in the central-west, Masalog Point in the central-east, and Marpo and Lalo Points in the south. Sanhalom Harbor (Sunharon Harbor) is located in the southwest. Humans arrived on Saipan and Tinian after millions of years of geological and ecological processes.

The Prehistoric Chamorros

The first peoples to reach Saipan and Tinian were ocean voyagers who came from Island Southeast Asia to the Marianas before 1,500 BCE.[8] They were among the earliest peoples to enter "Remote Oceania," the area in the Pacific with islands isolated by the open sea north and east of New Guinea, the Bismarck Archipelago, and the Solomons in "Near Oceania."[9] The exact date and specifics of their arrival and establishment of permanent settlements are unknown.[10] The voyagers likely traveled in sailing canoes and relied on the stars, currents, wind patterns, seabird flight pathways, and other means to locate the islands.[11] They probably went to the islands because of resource and land scarcity or warfare in their homelands.[12] Many centuries later, more Island Southeast Asians and small numbers of peoples from other island groups in Micronesia, also voyaged to the Marianas. The prehistoric Chamorro ethnic group eventually emerged.

The Chamorros farmed banana, bamboo, breadfruit, coconut, duckweed, fadang nuts, pandanus, sugarcane, taro, yams, and rice.[13] The Marianas marked the eastern limit of rice cultivation in the Pacific Islands in prehistoric times.[14] The Chamorros also grew and chewed betel nut like other Pacific Islanders and Island Southeast Asians.[15] Seaweed was collected and consumed as well.[16] They used manual agricultural practices and soil enhancement methods, including shifting cultivation, similar to those practiced throughout Remote Oceania.[17] There were farm plots and managed forests, but no terrain-changing agricultural earthworks, such as terraces and mounds.[18]

The Chamorros also had no working animals and never introduced and raised cattle or pigs. Rats were in the islands before European contact.[19] Islanders caught and ate seafood, including reef and pelagic fish, clams, conches, crabs, eels, lobsters, mussels, octopus, oysters, sea cucumbers, seaweed, shrimp, snails, squid, and turtles.[20] They also consumed freshwater eels, fruit bats, wild ducks, and seabirds and their eggs for proteins, fats, and minerals. They often cooked their food with earthenware pottery over fires and in pit ovens. Food was also consumed raw or preserved by sun drying and salting.[21] Despite the diverse foods available, life in the islands was hard. Analyses of prehistoric human remains in the Marianas indicate that the population suffered from high infant and maternal mortality rates and low life expectancies.[22] Periodic typhoons, earthquakes, and tsunamis and resulting famines from crop failure and reef damage caused many deaths.

The Chamorros built grass, leaf, and frond huts and wooden posts houses. Some lived in caves during certain periods. They also constructed wooden structures on top of *latte* stones, which were large, vertical stone foundation pillars with hemispherical capstones on the top.[23] The Chamorros made a variety of tools and implements from bone, shell, stone, volcanic rock, and other local materials for the construction of their homes and canoes, agriculture, fishing, food and medicine preparation, and other purposes.[24] Plant materials from coconut palms, bamboo, breadfruit, hibiscus, and pandanus were utilized for many functions. They created pottery from clays and coral sand. The Chamorros also constructed many different weapons and periodically warred amongst each other. Islanders were fully or partially nude, as the climate and life along the coasts did not necessitate clothing. At times, they wore tropical grasses and leaves and adorned themselves with flowers and turtle shell, bone, and seashell ornaments and jewelry. They also practiced tooth staining and etching.

The Chamorros had customs and rituals regarding all cycles of life, including birth, the transition to adulthood, marriage, and death. They practiced ancestor worship, animism, magic, and shamanism. The dead were buried under or near their homes, often with shell grave goods.[25] The skulls of ancestors were kept in homes or special huts.[26] The Chamorros regularly chanted and recited the histories, legends, and myths of their ancestors and created cave pictographs and petroglyphs of humans, animals, and symbols.[27] They consulted shamans and sorcerers to communicate with the spirits and obtain blessings for agriculture, fishing, and health, while healers and herbalist were called on to treat the ill and injured with natural products.[28]

Chamorro society was organized into matriclans.[29] Chiefs, the sons of high-ranking women, led clans. A clan had one or more villages and was linked to the other clans in the islands through trade, resource sharing, land accessibility agreements, and marriages. The Chamorro way of life revolved around interdependence, reciprocity, and community. Land tenure arrangements were based on the fulfillment of subsistence needs and the procurement of essential products.[30] Clans often gathered for feasts, marriages, funerals, and other events. Men frequently convened in communal huts and discussed clan affairs, while women cared for and established special bonds with their children.[31]

The Chamorro population grew over the centuries. The older generations passed down knowledge about their people and surviving on the islands. Islanders were spared from many of the diseases that ravaged the peoples of Asia, Africa, and Europe because of the remoteness of the Marianas. The Chamorros were not completely isolated from the outside world, however. They occasionally traded with visiting peoples from the Carolines. The traders from the south introduced some new social and cultural ideas, as well as fishing and agricultural skills and technologies.[32] The Chamorros were an adaptive and dynamic people who were not static and unchanging. They were not a perfect, flawless people; the Chamorros were human beings and thus periodic kin-group and inter-village disputes, warfare, and violence were a reality in the Marianas during prehistoric times.[33] Despite some adverse internal happenings, they built a small, but stable agricultural and sea-based civilization in the Pacific. Unfortunately, diseases from Europe and elsewhere came beginning in the sixteenth century and killed great numbers of Chamorros.

The Spanish Colonial Period (1521–1899)

In 1521, the Spanish located the Marianas as the conquest of Mesoamerica was underway. The Spanish initially called the Marianas "the Islands of Thieves" (*Las Islas de los Ladrones*) after they misinterpreted Micronesian gift exchanges and reciprocity customs on their vessels off one of the islands as robbery.[34] The Spanish retaliated by landing an armed party ashore, burning huts, pillaging, and killing a small number of Chamorros.[35] Following the year of the first contact, the Spanish periodically visited the islands for the reprovisioning and watering of their ships. They traded iron implements and other goods for island products.[36] During this time, some Spanish subjects were shipwrecked off the islands and lived among the Chamorros.

In 1565, Spain claimed *Los Ladrones* as a possession after a detachment from a Pacific expedition landed on the island, planted a cross, and posted a declaration. There were some violent encounters, but the detachment did not stay long and left for the bigger prize of the Philippines. The Chamorros thus remained in control of the islands.[37] In the 1590s and 1600s, some of the first Catholic proselytizers, mostly castaways and ship jumpers, arrived in the archipelago. They only stayed for short periods, however, and were unsuccessful in their isolated conversion efforts.[38] In the seventeenth century, a number of Spanish and people from other countries in Europe, primarily Catholic missionaries and bureaucrats, desired to christianize the Chamorros and bring them into the dominion of the Catholic Spanish Empire as was done to the peoples in the Americas and elsewhere.

The Spanish believed the islands were of strategic value. They thought the Ladrones could serve as "stepping-stones" to Japan and other islands in the Pacific, which had not been conquered and christianized.[39] Additionally, following the Spanish conquest of the Philippines in the late sixteenth century, the islands became a resupply port of call for galleons between the Americas and Island Southeast Asia.[40] In the 1560s, the Spanish initiated the Manila-Acapulco galleon commerce to trade colonial commodities and natural resources for valuable Asian goods. Westbound galleons carried men, correspondence, supplies, and most importantly mined silver from the Americas to the Philippines.[41] Eastbound Manila–based galleons shipped silk, drugs, jewels, porcelain, rugs, spices, textiles, and other products, as well as slaves, from Asia to the Americas.[42] Many of the Asian goods were then transported from New Spain to the Iberian Peninsula where they were traded and sold throughout Europe. The Spanish knew the Chamorros' islands had no precious metals and limited land for agriculture but recognized that they could be used as forts to support and defend the trans-Pacific galleon trade that was vital for financing their colonial project and conversion efforts in the Philippines.[43]

Catholic missionaries from Spain, its colonies, and other European countries, had their own agendas that were not always in line or compatible with those of the colonial machine. Most of them were far more concerned about bringing "spiritual salvation" to people of the islands than supporting the galleon trade.[44] According to anthropologist David Atienza de Frutos, "Colonial political forces and empires always carry a particular ideology that justifies their expansion; but neither we can analyze these colonial forces as a compact group with no complexities and internal paradoxes and contradictions, nor we can analyze the occupied culture and actors with the opposite unify interests and motivations."[45]

In 1668, a small group of missionaries and lay helpers, with the backing of the Spanish Crown and royal funds, landed on Guam, the southernmost island in the Marianas and largest island in Micronesia.[46] The missionaries, who were protected by a number of Chamorro chiefs and clans and aided by shipwrecked Spanish subjects who learned the indigenous language, peacefully established a mission on the island and converted many islanders. However, their efforts to eliminate much of the indigenous Chamorro religion and a number of cultural practices, which they believed were "the work of the Devil," created tensions that led to violence.[47] According to historian Alexandre Coello de la Rosa, "The missionaries heavy-handedly dismissed Chamorro religious, cultural, and social norms, considering them too barbaric or inferior to merit a deeper understanding.... When the natives resisted or rebelled, the missionaries did not revise their model, but continued *imposing* Christianity and its legal-moral order, which led to the outbreak of widespread rebellion and killing."[48] Misunderstandings and rumors also caused the violence and uprisings.[49] The Chamorros thought the holy water and oil used by the missionaries were poisoned and killed their family members, particularly infants, though it was really the microorganisms unknowingly spread by the Spanish and other factors that caused the deaths.[50] Some Chamorros began killing missionaries and their lay helpers out of vengeance and hoped to stop the deaths and religious and cultural suppression.[51]

The Spanish, at the insistence of the missionaries, eventually brought in soldiers of different ethnicities from their colonial possessions to quell the "rebellions" and facilitate the conversion of the islanders.[52] They conducted intermittent, punitive "pacification" campaigns in the Marianas in the last three decades of the seventeenth century.[53] Pro–Spanish, christianized Chamorro kin-groups helped the soldiers fight against anti–Spanish Chamorro kin-groups.[54] A number of the kin-groups warred against each other before the Spanish even located the island. Some partnered with the Spanish solely to strengthen their power and influence, while others did so out of fear.[55] According to scholar Frank Quimby, "There was no island-wide unified armed resistance.... The Islanders' decentralised politics, with inter-village and inter-island rivalry and shifting networks of kin, village and district alliances, some of which sought to exploit the Spanish presence for advantage, virtually precluded a centralised, coordinated response."[56]

The violence in the campaigns escalated with the passing of the years and growing desires for revenge on both sides. Multi-ethnic, Spanish-led forces gained control of Guam first and then set upon Saipan, Tinian, and the other islands to the north. They executed some "rebel" chiefs, destroyed Chamorro crops and food stores, burned villages, and sometimes killed a small number of inhabitants, including women and children.[57] On Saipan, one missionary wrote that a number of villages "were laid waste with iron and fire."[58] The conquerors took and exploited Chamorro land. They cut down trees, which the Chamorros harvested fruit from or obtained materials for cultural and subsistence practices, and used the wood to construct or repair stockades and forts, churches, government buildings, ships, and more.[59] Some soldiers and officials, who were Spanish Criollos and Peninsulares, Filipinos, Indigenous Americans, and Mestizos, raped Chamorro girls and women, took "war brides," paid for sex, and spread venereal diseases.[60] Spanish missionary Father Manuel de Solorzano wrote in 1681, the soldiers "crimes are too long to recount. They ... violated the Indian women."[61] Many of the soldiers were peasants, vagrants, or ex-convicts who were underpaid for their participation in the conquest. They took their frustrations out on the indigenous population and at times even mutinied and rebelled against their commanders.[62]

The Spanish, who had superior technology and stronger immunities to global diseases, defeated or converted all the Chamorro clans and conquered the islands. The Chamorros experienced a tremendous population decline during the period. The conquerors did not carry out genocidal or exterminatory policies, but diseases spread before, during, and after the campaigns caused the near extinction of the Chamorro people.[63] According to scholar Francis X. Hezel, "Depopulation during this era is an indisputable fact, but most of the fatalities were not the result of violence.... The lethal effects of the illnesses that the Spanish brought far outweighed the damage done by their muskets and swords."[64] The population also decreased from suicides, "the flight of some indigenous people that decided not to live their lives under the European control," and a "negative natality rate." Some Chamorro women could not have children because of diseases, malnutrition, and injuries. Other women, however, did not want to have children because of the "colonial impact" or they wanted to "resist" the administration and missionaries, who desired population growth through more marriages and births.[65]

Following the pacification campaigns, the Spanish forcibly transferred most of the Chamorros on Saipan, Tinian, and the smaller islands of the archipelago to Guam and concentrated them into towns.[66] This was done to "palliate" the "demographic collapse" in the archipelago from diseases, keep the Chamorros subjugated, and ensure the survival of the mission.[67] Sadly, some Chamorros never reached Guam; they were lost at sea en route to the island.[68] Infectious diseases spread easily in the clustered towns on Guam. The Spanish administration was apathetic about the deplorable public health situation on the southernmost island in the archipelago and sent few medical practitioners there. Periodic famines caused by natural disasters also caused deaths after the campaigns.[69] The Chamorro population in the Marianas, in the tens of thousands prior to the Spanish arrival, shrunk to around a few thousand under Spanish rule.[70] There were a number of individuals among the Spanish-led forces and missions who were saddened by Chamorro deaths. Spanish and later German, Japanese, and American perceptions of the Chamorros were not uniform and varied from person to person. There were diverse personalities, character traits, and points of view in the colonizer populations from the seventeenth century and onward.

The Chamorros and their islands were the firsts in the Pacific to be colonized by a European power. The Spanish annexed the archipelago and made it part of the Viceroyalty of New Spain. Agana, Guam was designated the capital of the islands. They renamed Saipan to San Joseph and Tinian to Buenavista, while the entire fifteen island archipelago was rechristened "*Las Islas Marianas*" in honor of the Virgin Mary and Mariana of Austria (1634–1696), the Queen Regent of Spain and patroness to the first mission in the islands.[71] The Empire of Spain based its claim of the islands on the Treaty of Tordesillas (1494) and Treaty of Zaragoza (1529), both signed with Portugal, which "authorized" the crown's control over Oceania and the Americas, save for Eastern Brazil.[72]

The Council of the Indies, a colonial administrative body that served the King of Spain, held supreme command over all Spanish overseas possessions.[73] Under the council, the Viceroy of New Spain in Mexico City ruled as the monarch of all Spanish colonies in the Americas and Pacific north of the Isthmus of Panama.[74] A governor directly administered the Marianas from Guam.[75] The Marianas governors had tremendous autonomy and ruled the faraway "frontier" islands as they pleased.[76] The Royal Spanish Treasury in New Spain funded administrative, military, and religious operations in the Marianas through the royal subsidy that was shipped to Guam on galleons.[77] The Marianas were subject to the Laws of the Indies, which were decrees for Spain's colonial territories issued by the Council of the Indies.[78]

The Spanish administrators did not eradicate the pre-contact Chamorro power structure. Rather, they incorporated it into the Marianas colonial system.[79] They relied on loyal christianized Chamorro chiefs and collaborators, as well as some Filipino and Mestizo soldiers who served with distinction, to oversee village and district affairs on Guam, head the indigenous militia, and police the island. The low-level officials enforced laws, collected taxes, and organized public works. The Spanish gave these local officials special titles, church honor seats, and, most importantly, land grants. A Chamorro upper or elite hereditary class, known as the *principalia*, developed. The principalia and even lower class Chamorros were important actors and participants that "pragmatically engaged the colonial regime itself, negotiating for a measure of autonomy."[80] According to anthropologist David Atienza de Frutos, the Chamorros were not a "passive and submissive population that was totally in the hands of the colonial power." There was "indigenous agency" and "adaptive resistance" and the Chamorros shaped the "historical development of their islands."[81]

The Spanish administrators, with the aid of Chamorro collaborators and European and ethnic subjects, imposed draconian and exploitative policies and edicts on Guam. They placed the island under martial law and forced islanders to swear oaths of allegiance to the crown. Ancestral and communal lands were claimed as government lands, bestowed to the church, or broken up into private estates and properties.[82] The Spanish forced the Chamorros to work on farms and ranches and construct churches, buildings, and roads.[83] Some islanders were pressed into service on Spanish ships to perform lowly and dangerous tasks. The colonizers "justified Chamorro enslavement based on their physique as well as their natural environment."[84] The forced labor was so grueling at times that a number of Chamorros died from exhaustion and sickness and some committed suicide.[85] Spanish demands for contributions of produce and livestock inevitably led to malnutrition and disease. Some women were said to have sterilized themselves, aborted, and committed infanticide "to free their children from subjugation to the Spanish."[86] Head taxes were later introduced and put further strain on families.[87] A number of Spanish government officials were corrupt; they exploited the indigenous population and embezzled royal subsidy funds intended for the betterment of the colony and its peoples to fill their own coffers.[88] Sexual violence against Chamorro women and girls committed by power holders of all ethnicities was a recurring problem.[89] Many incidents of rape and abuse were likely never discovered or recorded.

The colonial administrators and missionaries brought the Chamorros "under the bells" (*bajo las campanas*) of the Catholic Church on Guam. There were churches in all the village districts. Agana, the main population center, was the first European-style town in Oceania with a Catholic cathedral. The Spanish did away with much of the indigenous religion or absorbed it into Marianas Catholicism in the late seventeenth and eighteenth centuries. They destroyed ancestral shrines and bone and shell amulets, burned "idols," and buried or shattered skulls kept in homes.[90] They mandated that Chamorros baptize their children; attend compulsory daily masses, devotions, prayer vigils, and rosary services; receive the sacraments; and celebrate saint feast days and holy days of obligation such as All Saints' Day, Christmas, and Easter. The Chamorros were also required to marry and bury their dead in the Catholic tradition. According to historian Alexandre Coello de la Rosa, "Chamorro everyday culture had been invariably transformed by the imposed rituals and customs of Catholicism."[91]

Spanish colonization metamorphosed the Chamorros. The large matriclans were replaced with an ambilineal nuclear family structure.[92] European dance, decorum, clothing, hairstyles, games, and social customs were popularized.[93] The Spanish introduced tobacco, liquor, metals, dogs and cats, and New World vegetables, such as corn, beans, peppers, and tomatoes. They also brought in European and Asian livestock, including cattle, pigs, goats, quail, deer, horses, and carabao.[94] Many Chamorro children attended mission schools and Spanish, Filipino, and Latin words entered the Chamorro lexicon, while the Roman alphabet was adopted. The Chamorros assumed Spanish names and surnames. According to anthropologist Alexander Spoehr, the Chamorro culture transformed into a "Hispanicized Oceanic hybrid" with influences from the Iberian Peninsula and the Spanish-controlled territories of the Americas and Philippines.[95] Additionally, merchants, privateers, pirates, blackbirders, beachcombers, castaways, and whalers from all over the world stopped in the Marianas and introduced elements of their cultures to the Chamorros.[96] Chamorro enmity toward their foreign overlords decreased because of acculturation. A number of Chamorros, even non-principalia, were grateful that the Spanish brought Catholicism to them and islanders helped maintain the mission.

During the Spanish colonial period, the prehistoric Chamorro ethnic group faded away and the new or modern Chamorros, a global people of mixed Chamorro, European, Indigenous American, and Island Southeast Asian ancestry, emerged.[97] Spanish and global sociocultural influences on the Chamorros, while substantial, were not absolute. The Chamorros retained a number of their traditional customs concerning agriculture, ancestral veneration, feasts, myths, and song. Their language, although altered, was preserved.

It was mostly mothers, esteemed givers and maintainers of life, who were responsible for perpetuating and passing on the indigenous culture and language to their children in the privacy of their homes.[98] According to scholar Robert F. Rogers, "Most racial admixtures of outsiders with Chamorros originated by foreign men fathering children with local women of Chamorro ancestry."[99] Additionally, elements of Chamorro matrilineality and matrifocality persisted through women's roles in managing and participating in many family affairs, such as death rituals and funerals.[100] Traditions of admiration and respect for mothers also continued and coincided with devotion and obligations to the Virgin Mary.[101] Components of the clan system survived as well. Chamorro residence shifted to nuclear patterns, but extended families maintained strong ties through gatherings at Catholic masses, sacrament rites, fiestas, and other events.[102] According to one scholar, "Chamorro tradition has to be considered in a general sense as a syncretic and dynamic culture" with Catholic rituals "intertwining, interacting with and layering on top of Chamorro rituals."[103] Farming, which pulled islanders away from the Spanish influences of the towns into a somewhat more independent and liberating environment, further contributed to the preservation of elements of the prehistoric culture.[104] According to anthropologist David Atienza de Frutos, "Without a doubt, the colonial impact was tragic for the inhabitants of the Marianas," but there still was "a continuity of the Chamorro cultural experience."[105] According to historian Alexandre Coello de la Rosa, "Colonialism is an ambivalent and fluid process that involves appropriation, cultural borrowing, and effective resistance on the part of the colonized. As a result, Chamorros' cultural patterns not only survived after the arrival of Spanish colonizers, they were integrated, adapted, or reinterpreted to the new Christian symbols and codes as a way to preserve their own customs and traditions in a wholly Chamorro syncretism."[106]

In the early nineteenth century, the Spanish stopped sending galleons to the Marianas because of war and economic turmoil in Spain, the Wars of Independence in the Spanish Americas, and the opening of new trade and supply routes through the Indian Ocean.[107] Afterward, the Marianas were incorporated as a province into the Spanish East Indies Territory headquartered in Manila.[108] The Spanish eventually allowed the Chamorros to return to the islands to the north.[109] Many Chamorros went to Saipan, but few migrated back to Tinian. A number of Chamorro principalia were given land grants on Saipan. Some Chamorros traveled abroad and migrated to other islands in the Pacific; a small Chamorro community formed on Yap in the Carolines.[110] The Spanish attempted to reduce administrative costs and make the Marianas more self-sufficient through agriculture projects, but the endeavors were largely unsuccessful. They decided to use the Marianas as a penal colony and transferred hundreds of political exiles and criminals, mostly Filipinos, to the islands. Tinian was also used as a leprosy colony. In 1856, a smallpox epidemic killed a great number of people in the Marianas.[111] In the 1860s, a small number of the first Japanese migrants arrived in the islands and many of them married into local families.[112] Some Chinese immigrated to the islands and integrated into the population as well.[113] In the last century of Spanish rule, the Carolinians (Refaluwasch), another Micronesian people, also made the Marianas their home.

The Caroline Islands (*Las Islas Carolinas*), south of the Marianas, received little attention from Spain, except for missionary activities, until the late nineteenth century when other maritime powers, including Germany, the United Kingdom, Japan, and the United States, grew interested in the islands. The Carolinians established sailing routes to the Marianas and had trade relations with the Chamorros in prehistoric times. In the nineteenth and early twentieth centuries, typhoons devastated many atolls and islands in the Carolines. Hundreds of Carolinians migrated to the Marianas with Spain and later Germany's permission.[114] The colonial administrations desired to increase the population of the Marianas and use the Carolinians for agricultural labor, particularly livestock husbandry and butchering.[115] The Carolinians primarily settled on the central-west coast of Saipan just south of Tanapag Harbor. They named the settlement Arabwal, the Carolinian name for the tropical, creeping vine bayhops (beach morning-glory).[116] The Chamorros called the settlement Garapan. A small number of Carolinians made their way to Tinian and resided in the southwestern fishing village of Sanhalom, which was later renamed Tinian Town.[117] The Chamorros and Carolinians established other small villages on the two islands during the period.[118] The population on Saipan was significantly larger than Tinian.

The Carolinians were skilled fishers, farmers, and carvers and were mostly organized into matriclans headed by chiefs.[119] They had an economy based on the production, distribution, and trade of agricultural, sea, and handcrafted goods.[120] They fished the reefs and planted taro, yams, and other tropical crops on Saipan and Tinian. The Carolinians also raised Spanish-introduced livestock.[121] They occasionally traded coconuts, beef, sea products, coffee, and tobacco to Europeans and Japanese traders in Micronesia for metal tools, rice, and other foreign goods.[122] The Carolinians, unlike the Chamorros, did not experience the conquest and acculturation period. They rarely came in contact with the Spanish administration centered in Guam and thus retained much of their ancestral culture into the twentieth century. The Carolinians wore woven loincloths and leaf, bast, and grass wraparound skirts.[123] They adorned their bodies and sometimes faces with tattoos and paints and had ornaments and jewelry made of coconut, fish bone, shell, and other natural products.[124] The new arrivers to the Marianas practiced animism, ancestor worship, oracle reading, shamanism, and sorcery. They both revered and feared a number of gods, spirits, and ghosts.[125] Clans held large fish and sometimes pork or beef feasts following special ceremonies and rituals. They shared stories and chanted often. The Chamorros and Carolinians lived together in peace on the islands and shared the common bond of Micronesian ancestry and identity under foreign rule. A number of Carolinian-Chamorro families formed and thrived.

In the late nineteenth century, the Spanish Empire, weakened by decades of warfare, internal revolts, and economic downturn in the Iberian Peninsula and its colonial possessions, was drawing its last breaths in the Pacific. In 1898, the United States defeated the empire in the Spanish-American War. Spain ceded the Philippines, Puerto Rico, and Guam to the young and mighty industrial power as war reparations in the 1898 Treaty of Paris. The United States could have taken Saipan, Tinian, and the smaller islands to the north in 1898, but it did not see any reason for doing so at the time. Consequently, the Marianas were divided. The Spanish, having lost their administrative centers in the Philippines and Guam, were no longer able to govern Micronesia effectively. In 1899, Spain sold their remaining territories in the Carolines, Marshalls, and Marianas, which included Saipan and Tinian, to the German Empire. Of course, the Chamorros and Carolinians were not consulted about the exchange. Spain transferred a garrison of approximately 270 Filipino soldiers and their families, as well as administrators, to Saipan to manage the island until the transfer. The Filipino soldiers reportedly committed a number of crimes against the Chamorros and Carolinians during their brief stay.[126]

The German Colonial Period (1899–1914)

In the 1850s, the German trading house J.C. Godeffroy & Sohn began a copra (dried coconut meat) enterprise in the Samoan Islands in Polynesia.[127] Within a decade, the company was active throughout the South Pacific and Micronesia. Concurrently, the firms F. & W. Hennings and Hoffschlaeger & Stapenhorst started trading operations in Fiji and the Marshalls, respectively.[128] The companies at first relied on trade with the indigenous populations to obtain the tropical goods they exported globally. In the 1860s, German firms established coconut plantations in the islands for copra production, as well as smaller cotton, indigo, pineapple, sugarcane, and tobacco farms. Copra was the leading commodity in the Pacific in the nineteenth century. Copra oil was used in numerous industrial applications and products in Europe, the United States, and Japan. Coconuts enabled the Germans to expand their commercial activities in the Pacific. In the 1870s, the firm Robertson & Hernsheim set up trade operations in the Carolines and the Bismarck Archipelago, while Adolph Capelle & Company built coconut plantations on Agrihan and Pagan in the Marianas.[129] In the 1880s, the Jaluit Company established itself in the Marshalls and banking magnate Adolf von Hansemann's New Guinea Company rose in northeastern New Guinea.[130]

The German Empire (1871–1918), in its early years, supported private trading companies in the Pacific on a small-scale.[131] In the late 1870s and early 1880s, Imperial German Navy warships conducted reconnaissance in the region to protect German economic interests. German naval officers negotiated treaties with the indigenous chiefs and rulers of several islands in order to build a network of coaling stations for their steam-powered vessels in the Pacific.[132] In the last two decades of the nineteenth century, German firms in the Pacific pressured their government to colonize islands in the faraway region. The trading companies wanted increased military protection and sought greater exploitation of the scattered islands and archipelagos they already had operations in. Land claims were a major source of geopolitical contention among the foreign powers in the Pacific because of the profitability of the plantation system. In the 1880s, land ownership quarrels in the Samoan Islands, where Germany, the United Kingdom, and the United States all had interests, were so heated that they almost precipitated a war.

German trading companies were supported in their appeals for Pacific colonization by domestic expansionist groups, such as the German Colonial Society.[133] The unification and consolidation of Germany into an empire in 1871 spawned a patriotic fervor among the population that engendered expansionist sentiments.[134] German nationalists desired an empire commensurate to the British Empire and coveted new territories in Oceania and elsewhere for glory and prestige. German economists and politicians sought new markets, raw materials, and capital for their burgeoning empire. Policy makers and social scientists called for increased migration and overseas settlement to counter overpopulation. Naval officers desired new coaling stations and communication points, while missionaries wanted to save the souls of "pagan heathens" in the islands.[135]

Although many German actors and institutions favored expansion into Oceania, there was some opposition. The empire's leading statesmen desired German hegemony in continental Europe and initially gave little thought to grabbing up small and little-known specks of land in the far-flung waters of the Pacific. They supported the global extension of German influence through private commercial activities and trade and believed colonial projects would threaten German commerce and foreign relations with other European powers, particularly the United Kingdom.[136] The statesmen were eventually influenced by expansionist groups and elites, however, and the government authorized the colonization of the Pacific Islands.

The mid-1880s was an auspicious time for German colonial expansion into Micronesia and Melanesia. Spain was in decline and could not exert its authority in the region. France was concerned mostly with Indochina, West Africa, and eastern Polynesia. The United States was still fixated on "winning the west" of the North American continent. The United Kingdom, the leading power in the Pacific at the time, was tied up in the Mahdist War (1881–1899) in northeast Africa, monitoring Russian extension in Central and East Asia, and focused on the colonization of Burma, which sat directly east of British India. The British Empire did not want to spend money and resources challenging Germany in the low-priority region.[137]

The Germans, taking advantage of favorable international conditions, initiated their colonial foothold in the Pacific with the takeover of northeastern New Guinea and the Bismarck Archipelago in 1884. They proceeded to take the Marshalls and northern Solomons in 1885, Nauru (Pleasant Island) in 1888, and Western Samoa in 1900.[138] In 1897, Germany obtained Jiazhou (Kiautschou) Bay, Shantung Peninsula, China and, soon thereafter, developed their Asia-Pacific naval base there.[139] In 1899, it purchased all the islands in the Carolines and Marianas, except Guam, from the Spanish Empire. Enewetak and Ujelang in the Marshalls and the Polynesian outlier islands of Kapingamarangi and Nukuoro were included in the purchase as well.[140] The Germans made nearly all Spanish and Filipinos leave the islands. The colonial government of German New Guinea (*Deutsch-Neuguinea*), headquartered in Kokopo, New Britain, administered all imperial possessions in the Pacific, except for the protectorate of German Samoa. In 1910, the headquarters was relocated to Rabaul, New Britain. Germany's Micronesian possessions in German New Guinea were termed the "Islands Territory" (*Inselgebiet*).[141] The Colonial Section, part of the German Foreign Office, supervised German New Guinea until 1907. From 1907 to 1914, the German Colonial Office oversaw the colony.[142] German New Guinea was also known as the German Pacific Protectorate (*Deutsches Sudsee Schutzgebiet*).

A governor administered German New Guinea. A vice-governor in Ponape (Pohnpei) oversaw the Islands Territory below the governor.[143] District officers directed the districts within the Islands Territory.[144] The district officers had great autonomy because they were far away from New Britain and Berlin and communications by sea took much time. There were three districts in German Micronesia: the Marianas District (based in Saipan), the Eastern Carolines District (Ponape), and the Western Carolines District (Yap). The Marshall Islands were administered under a different framework, with the assistance of private trade firms, until 1907 when the Marshalls District (Jaluit) was created.[145]

In the Marianas District, the Germans mostly respected Chamorro and Carolinian private land rights but seized "unused" communal lands and took over Spanish government properties.[146] They built administrative buildings, elementary schools, medical facilities, new roads, and some maritime infrastructure. The schools, which taught German and Micronesian languages, among other subjects, were meant to turn students into compliant, self-supporting agricultural laborers and tradespeople under German leadership and management. Some special schools and institutes, beyond the elementary schools, existed for men to study and train to become policemen, interpreters, and local officials. Catholic missionary schools also operated in the Marianas.[147] The Germans conducted anthropological and linguistic research and village and community development initiatives that islanders participated in as well.[148]

The Germans, like the Spanish, relied on low-level Micronesian administrators. The Marianas District officer appointed indigenous mayors and district overseers to run villages and village districts on the islands, respectively. These men handled local affairs and directed tax collection, public works, and the population register.[149] The Marianas District chief of police hired Micronesians to police the archipelago because of the small number of German nationals in the islands. The Micronesian police or local militia, who were required to study the German language, served as brokers for the foreign rulers.[150] They enforced colonial laws and assisted the mayors and overseers in tax collection and public projects.

The court system in the colony consisted of the local Magistrate Court, which handled misdemeanors and minor offenses, and the District Court, which dealt with criminal offenses and appeals. The German New Guinea Imperial High Court was the highest court in the colony.[151] The Germans built no military installations in the Marianas and did not station troops there.[152] The Chamorros and Carolinians of Saipan and Tinian did not protest their new ruler's occupation; an indigenous resistance movement or uprising against German rule, such as the bloody Sokehs Rebellion (1910–1911) on Sokehs Island off Ponape, never occurred in the Marianas. Many of the Chamorro neo-principalia landholders backed the Germans who, for the most part, did not touch their holdings. Some upper-class Chamorros, who had farming operations, learned German business practices and made connections that made them wealthier.

The Germans did not seize neo-principalia land on Saipan largely because there were few German immigrants or firms on the island that needed it. The Marianas were at the very bottom of their colonial possession hierarchy in the Pacific. The Germans valued the land they had in northeastern New Guinea and the Bismarck Archipelago, as well as their large coconut plantations in the Marshalls and mining operations in the Palaus and Nauru. There were no industries and economic activities of great importance in the Marianas, however. There were exotic feather and plume collecting operations and some bountiful coconut plantations in the remote northern islands, but typhoons and the coconut beetle reduced copra production on Saipan and Tinian. Tinian, which was sparsely populated, only really supported livestock operations, particularly beef and hide production, run by the Tinian Gesellschaft. The Marianas were little more than a midway resupply station for merchant and naval vessels traveling from the western to eastern Pacific and back.[153] There was a sizeable administrative deficit in the German Marianas. In 1907, the Germans dissolved the Marianas District and downgraded it to a station because of a lack of revenue. The Marianas were made part of the Western Carolines District in Yap.[154] A station master on Saipan oversaw the Marianas for the remainder of German rule.

While the Germans were disappointed with their holdings in the Marianas, the whole of German New Guinea was regarded as a backwater segment of the empire. German colonization efforts in Oceania were marginal compared to those in Africa. Moreover, German commerce during the early decades of the twentieth century was concentrated in Europe and not in its colonies.[155] According to historian Sebastian Conrad, "trade with the Pacific colonies made up less than 0.15 percent of total German foreign trade" in 1909."[156] Aside from coconuts, there were no crops that brought in substantial profits and the mining operations in a couple of island groups only brought in so much. The Germans did not seriously undertake commercial fishing or marine industries. They did not establish a market for their domestic goods in the colony because of the small populations and limited buying power of islanders. Regarding trade, the Germans were outperformed by the Japanese. The Japanese, who were much aided by close geographic proximity, had a virtual monopoly on freight by 1908. They unseated German firms and took the lion's share of commercial profits in the western North Pacific.

Micronesia did not become a settler colony for German nationals. In 1912, only 232 German citizens lived in the Carolines, Marianas, and Marshalls.[157] The Pacific Islander population increased during German rule, however. The Germans resettled hundreds of Carolinians whose islands were devastated by typhoons to Saipan. They also forcibly relocated Carolinians who were seen as threats to their administration in the two Carolines districts to the Marianas.[158] Additionally, they established a penal colony on Saipan with prisoners from German-controlled islands throughout the Pacific.[159] The United States Navy deported many "uncooperative" Carolinians in Guam, whom they called "savages," to Saipan with Germany's permission in the first decade of the 1900s as well.[160] A number of Chamorros from Guam, who were concerned about the Americans' cultural and religious suppression policies and offered free farmland and transportation by the Germans, migrated to Saipan too.[161] During the same time, a small number of Japanese and Samoans, who were mostly involved in trade or farming, moved to the Marianas.

The German resettlements and land grants were not based so much on humanitarianism, but long-term economic strategy. The islands north of Guam were depopulated during the Spanish colonial period. The Germans needed larger populations in the islands to counter labor shortages and eventually create and maintain plantations. In 1911, the population of the German Marianas was 3,146. On Saipan, the population was just over 2,500, with 1,254 Chamorros, 1,211 Carolinians, 35 foreigners, and only a small handful of Germans. On Tinian, the population was a mere 27 people, with 12 Chamorros and 15 Carolinians. The remainder of the population was scattered on Rota and the islands to the north.[162]

A number of Germans, like their Spanish predecessors and the Americans on Guam, believed the Chamorros and Carolinians were inferior peoples and used several ethnophaulisms to label and disparage Micronesians. They attempted to legitimize their rule in Micronesia, as in their other colonial possessions, as a "civilizing mission" intended to elevate the indigenous population.[163] According to historian Gerd Hardach, the Germans

> justified colonial rule on the presumption of "white" superiority and "coloured" inferiority. Colonialism was inherently racist. Racism was not necessarily displayed in prejudices, insulting language or aggressive behavior against indigenous peoples. There were other more sophisticated colonialist ideologies that were no less discriminatory: the settler ideology of industrious traders and plantation owners who put indolent "natives" into gainful employment; the favourite administrative self-portrait of patriarchal officials and responsive children; the Christian image of benevolent missionaries and simple-minded heathens; and its secularized version, acceptable to liberals and even to socialists, of enlightened colonizers who led the colonized onto the road of civilization. And finally, there were the legislators, bringing law and order to primitive people.[164]

Micronesians were denied German citizenship and the rights that accompanied it. They were classified as colonial subjects (*Schutzgebietsangehorige*) as opposed to imperial subjects (*Reichsangehorige*). The Germans placed Micronesians under a different and inferior legal sphere and did not allow them political self-determination and suffrage.[165] Furthermore, Micronesian workers and traders were paid less than their European counterparts.[166] German business, export, and import taxes and duties, as well as private loan prohibitions for Micronesians, also made it difficult for islanders to start and operate profitable companies.[167] Islanders had to pay cash, commodity, and labor poll taxes and complete temporary compulsory labor on farms and for public works projects.[168]

The Germans restricted interracial marriages between Micronesians and Europeans.[169] Few European women migrated to the islands, however, and, as a result, the colonizers set up brothels with Chamorro and Carolinian prostitutes for residents and visitors.[170] There was a rise in venereal diseases in the islands, particularly gonorrhea and syphilis, between 1899 and 1914.[171] The Germans did little to change the deplorable public health situation they inherited from the Spanish. Health facilities were substandard, and the administration did not post a government doctor in the Marianas until 1909. Immunization campaigns to prevent a smallpox epidemic and water purification projects were conducted, but little more was done.[172] The resettled Carolinians, who had weaker immunities than the more globalized Chamorros, particularly suffered. According to historian Dirk H. R. Spennemann, there was a "high number of deaths among the Carolinian immigrant community due to exposure to new strains of diseases and a lack of resistance against them."[173]

Whereas Spanish rule in the Marianas persisted for over two centuries, "German Times," *Tiempon Aleman* as the Chamorros called it, ended in less than two decades. In 1914, the First World War extended to Saipan and Tinian's shores. Japan, a country that rapidly established itself as a world power during the Meiji Era (1868–1912), bloodlessly seized the undefended Marianas north of Guam and other island groups in Micronesia in the early Taisho Era (1912–1926).

2

Japanese Takeover of Saipan and Tinian

The Empire of Japan (*Dai Nippon Teikoku*, 1868–1945) emerged during a time when the western industrial powers were conducting overseas national expansion. In 1868, the United States, following the bloody Civil War, was pursuing its "Manifest Destiny," an aggressive continental expansion campaign aimed at consolidating control over all American Indian land "from sea to shining sea." Manifest Destiny was achieved through ethnic cleansing, forced deportations (Indian removals), and conquests during the Mexican-American War (1846–1848), American Indian Wars (1776–1924), and other military campaigns. United States expansion was not limited to the North American continent. After the Guano Islands Act of 1856 was passed, the United States claimed a number of atolls and small islands in the Pacific, including Baker Island, Howland Island, Jarvis Island, and Johnston Atoll. Midway Atoll was taken in 1867. The American frontier was no longer in the Americas.

In 1893, the Americans overthrew the Kingdom of Hawaii, and five years later, in 1898, the Hawaiian Islands were incorporated as a United States territory. That year, the United States also defeated the Spanish Empire in the Spanish-American War and took the Philippines, Guam, and Puerto Rico as war spoils with the signing of the Treaty of Paris (1898). Wake Island was made part of America in 1898 too. The United States consolidated its power in the Philippines by defeating independence forces and killing great numbers of Filipinos, including civilians, in the Philippine-American War (1899–1902). The eastern Samoan Islands were added to the "American Empire" with the conclusion of the Tripartite Convention of 1899 between Germany, the United Kingdom, and the United States. In 1903, the Panama Canal Zone became an unincorporated territory of the United States, and Guantanamo Bay was perpetually leased from the newly independent nation of Cuba. In 1912, Alaska, which had been in American hands since 1867, was incorporated as a territory. The United States also occupied several Caribbean and Central American countries during the Banana Wars (1898–1934), including Cuba, the Dominican Republic, Haiti, and Nicaragua. The British, Dutch, French, Germans, and Russians all had possessions in the Pacific and or Asia.

Japanese expansionism arose predominantly out of a sober fear of western expansionism.[1] Japan was forced open by the United States and was pressured into signing unequal treaties with the industrial powers, including the Kanagawa Treaty with the United States and Anglo-Japanese Friendship Treaty with the United Kingdom in 1854, the Treaty of Shimoda with the Russians in 1855, the Ansei Five-Power Treaties in 1858, and the Prussian-Japanese Treaty of Friendship, Commerce, and Navigation in 1861. The Japanese feared their nation was going to be further manipulated or even carved up like China. Japan was also concerned with the presence of a foreign military power in Korea. According to historian Jun Uchida, "Separated from the archipelago by only 120 miles, the Korean peninsula, as the Meiji leaders repeatedly declared, was a 'dagger thrust at the heart of Japan.'"[2] Japan regarded Russia, which was expanding into Manchuria, as the main threat to Korea and its own sovereignty. Historian Roy Hidemichi Akagi wrote in *Japan's Foreign Relations 1542–1936: A Short History* (1936), "The maintenance of Japan's national security, one of the fundamental aspirations of the Island Empire, necessitated the elimination of all foreign control, especially Russian domination, in Korea and Manchuria."[3] Japan, who closely studied the rise of America and sent men to study in the United States, was well aware of the Monroe Doctrine policy, which held that the United States would not permit European colonization in the Americas. The island nation similarly wished to stop colonization activities in the Asia-Pacific region. Of course, Japan's expansionist ambitions were not entirely based on national defense concerns. With conquest and colonization comes treasure. Many Japanese statesmen, industrialists, and militarists coveted Korea's and other countries' natural resources and fertile lands that would bring them and their empire riches.

Between the late 1860s and 1890s, the Empire of Japan rapidly industrialized and built a formidable military to protect itself and extend its power and influence in East Asia and the Pacific. In 1895, Japan defeated China in the First Sino-Japanese War (1894–1895) and gained Taiwan and the Pescadores (Penghu) Islands; Korea came under Japanese influence. A decade later, in 1905, Japan defeated the Russian Empire in the Russo-Japanese War and obtained the southern half of Sakhalin Island, a long-term lease on the southern tip of the Liaotung Peninsula (Kwantung Leased Territory or *Kantoshu*), and economic interests in Manchuria. Korea was made a protectorate (*hogokoku*) and formally annexed five years later in 1910 as the colony (*shokuminchi*) of Chosen. The other Pacific powers did not contest Japan's annexation of Korea. The United Kingdom and Japan had signed the Anglo-Japanese Alliance in 1902, and Germany and France had priorities elsewhere. The United States and Japan came to a mutual understanding about their claims in the Philippines and Korea, respectively, through the Taft-Katsura Memorandum of 1905, the Root–Takahira Agreement in 1908, and later treaties.

The Japanese supported two main expansionist platforms, the Asian continental advance (*hokushin*) and southward advance (*nanshin*). Between 1882 and 1942, the *nanshin* was carried out by the Japanese government, military, and private companies. As early as 1862, while the Tokugawa Shogun was still in power, the Bonin Islands, an archipelago of over 30 subtropical and tropical islands southeast of Kyushu, were claimed by Japan. In 1876, the Empire of Japan officially annexed the Bonins and renamed them the Ogasawara Islands.[4] Three years later, in 1879, the empire annexed the Ryukyu Islands and established Okinawa Prefecture. It claimed the Volcano Islands (Kita Iwo Jima, Iwo Jima, and Minami Iwo Jima) less than a decade later. In the 1880s, the Japanese set their sights on Micronesia. They were determined to penetrate the "South Seas" despite a foreign presence in all the island groups in the region.

In 1882, while Spain still ruled much of the western North Pacific, the Imperial Japanese Navy (*Dai Nippon Teikoku Kaigun*, IJN) entered Micronesian waters for the first time. The era of maritime Japan (*kaikoku Nippon*) in the South Seas began. For the next six decades, the sunburst naval ensign (*kyokujitsuki*) was a regular site off the Marianas,

Carolines, and Marshalls. Pro-nanshin advocates believed the advance into and colonization of Micronesia would display Japan's might, foster lucrative tropical trade and industries, decrease overpopulation burdens by providing new lands for settlement, and ultimately give Japan strategic bases for national defense and future expansion into Island Southeast Asia and Melanesia. During the 1880s, Japanese civilian writers, explorers, and naturalists, who were eager to see the islands, booked passage on IJN warships conducting training and reconnaissance missions in Micronesia and Melanesia. A body of literature concerning the region emerged in late nineteenth century Japan, which included works such as Shiga Shigetaka's *Conditions in the South Seas* (*Nanyo Jiji*, 1887), Komiyama Tenko's *The Great King of the Pacific* (*Boken Kigyo: Rento Daio, 1887*), Hattori Toru's *Japan in the South Seas* (*Nihon no Nanyo*, 1888), Yano Ryukei's *The Story of the Floating Castle* (*Ukishiro Monogatari*, 1890), and Suzuki Tsunenori's *Customs and Landscapes in the South Seas* (*Nanyo fubutsushi*, 1893).[5] These literary works presented a romanticized image of the South Seas that sparked the imagination of the Japanese public. Meiji-era newspapers, magazines, and political pamphlets also ran articles about the nanshin and the tropical islands to the south. An "obsession for the southward advance" (*nanshin netsu*) permeated Japan.[6]

In the 1890s, private Japanese trading companies entered Micronesia. They traded domestic Japanese goods, including canned foods, liquors, firearms, and sundries, to Europeans and indigenous inhabitants for tropical products. Many of the trailblazing companies went bankrupt from Spanish commercial restrictions and the loss of ships, men, and cargo in tropical storms and typhoons. Despite numerous failures, the floodgate for Japanese trade was open. In 1893, the Hiki South Seas Trading Company Limited (*Nanyo Boeki Hiki Goshi Gaisha*), one of the most successful trading companies in Micronesia prior to the First World War, was established. Hiki built plantations and commercial stores in the Marianas and Carolines and became the first Japanese company to regularly bring the tropical products of the South Seas to the Japanese home islands. Meanwhile, in 1898, Japan annexed Marcus Island (Minami-Torishima), an island about 830 miles northeast of the Marianas.[7]

The Japanese were not hindered by Spain's successor in Micronesia in the 1900s and early 1910s. The Germans profited from land lease payments and business taxes on Japanese companies and increased economic activity and shipping networks in their colony. In 1901, the Murayama South Seas Trading Company Unlimited (*Nanyo Boeki Murayama Gomeigaisha*), the leading competitor of the Hiki Company, was established and traded in the Carolines. Hiki and Murayama were unremitting in their commercial endeavors, and, by 1906, approximately 80 percent of all trade in German Micronesia was conducted by Japanese firms.[8] In 1908, Hiki and Murayama merged. The new enterprise was named the South Seas Trading Company (*Nanyo Boeki Kabushikigaisha*, NBK) or "Nambo." The company's activities, in addition to tropical goods trading, included commercial fishing, inter-island mail, freight, and passenger transportation services. Nambo was the vanguard of Japanese expansion into the equatorial Pacific.

Traders with Nambo and other Japanese companies in Micronesia, despite receiving relatively good pay and being held in esteem as frontiersmen who helped expand the empire's borders, led difficult lives. According to historian Mark R. Peattie, "These were not easy years for these Japanese commercial pioneers. The great distances, the cramped quarters, the monotony of weeks at sea, the sudden squalls, the constant hazards of reef and rock, must have made life aboard their small ships arduous, wretched, and not a little dangerous. For those who remained on the islands and lonely atolls to mind the small stores and warehouses that were the distribution points for Japanese wares and the collection places for island cargoes to be sent back to Japan, the months of solitude without news from their homeland, the enervating heat and humidity, and the sense of extreme isolation, must have often mattered far more than the breathtaking beauty of their surroundings."[9] Few Japanese women went to the South Seas around the turn of the century. Japanese men, desiring companionship and seeking to build trade relationships with the islands' indigenous inhabitants, often took Micronesian wives. The isolated trader lifestyle did not last long, however. Circumstances for the Japanese in Micronesia changed drastically during and following the First World War.

On August 4, 1914, the United Kingdom declared war on Germany in response to the German invasion of neutral Belgium. Japan, which signed the Anglo-Japanese Alliance in 1902 with the United Kingdom and coveted German territories and economic interests in East Asia and the Pacific, followed by declaring war on Germany on August 23, 1914. The Japanese had a superior military force in the Asia-Pacific region. During September and October 1914, the IJN seized German possessions in the Carolines, Marianas, and Marshalls without bloodshed. On October 14, the IJN Second South Seas Squadron captured Saipan.[10] Japan ruled Micronesia. It was the empire's largest imperial possession and stretched "about 2,700 miles across from west to east, and about 1,300 miles from south to north."[11] The total sea and land area, approximately three million square miles, was about the size of the contiguous United States. To the north, in November 1914, the Japanese defeated the Germans at the Siege of Tsingtao and occupied their concessions in the Shantung Peninsula, China. Over the following years, Japan provided monetary and material support to the Allied powers in Europe and the IJN conducted escort and anti-submarine operations against the Germans.

On December 28, 1914, the Japanese established a naval administration in Micronesia, under the authority of the Navy Ministry, with the promulgation of the "Regulations for the Interim Defense Troop in the South Sea Islands."[12] The IJN Second South Seas Squadron was transformed into the IJN Provisional South Sea Islands Defense Force (*Rinji Nanyo Gunto Bobitai*) and assumed control of the "newly occupied territories" (*shinsen-ryochi*) in Micronesia through 1922.[13] The defense force, headquartered in Truk (Chuuk), established six naval districts (Jaluit, Palau, Ponape, Saipan, Truk, Yap), which were administered by IJN commanders and lieutenant commanders who oversaw troop detachments.[14] The Saipan Naval District consisted of all islands in the Marianas except for Guam, which remained in American hands. The naval district officers were eager to prove themselves and permanently establish Japan's position in Micronesia. They conducted censuses and surveys, promoted agriculture and education, and directed small development and infrastructure projects. They were aided by Nambo agents and old trade hands who shared valuable knowledge about the islands and their peoples. The transition of rule was peaceful; nearly all German nationals were quietly expelled from the islands, and an indigenous independence or resistance movement against the Japanese did not develop like in Japan's other colonial possessions.[15] Nevertheless, a number of Chamorros and Carolinians were dissatisfied with the entrenchment of another colonial power.[16]

On November 11, 1918, Germany signed the Armistice of Compiegne, thus accepting defeat and ending the fighting in the First World War. The war officially ended with the signing of the Treaty of Versailles on June 28, 1919. The League of Nations, an intergovernmental organization founded to "promote international cooperation and to achieve international peace and security," was established less than two years later on January 10, 1920. On December 17, 1920, the League of Nations, acknowledging Japan's assistance to the Allied powers, formally recognized the occupation of the Islands Territory of German New Guinea (Marianas, Carolines, Marshalls) and transferred their ownership to the empire as a Class "C" mandate as outlined in Article 22 of the Covenant of the League of Nations. The mandate was named the Japanese South Sea Islands Mandate or South Seas Mandate (*Nanyo inin tochiryo*).[17] Regarding the other German possessions in the Pacific, Australia and the United Kingdom were granted Nauru and the Territory of New Guinea, which included northeastern New Guinea, the Bismarck Archipelago, and the northern Solomons. New Zealand was given Western Samoa. Japan, as with the other powers, was prohibited from establishing military bases and fortifications in its mandate and was required to end the naval administration of the islands.

The transition from a naval administration to a civilian-administered colonial mandate in Japanese Micronesia was not precipitous. Between 1915 and 1918, Tokyo sent civil servants to the islands to assist IJN officers in administering them.[18] On July 1, 1918, the Navy Ministry established the Department of Civil Administration or Civil Affairs Bureau (*Minseibu*) in the Carolines, which was operated by civilians. A number of the military and civil administrators were not as friendly and accepting of indigenous customs as some of the earlier Japanese traders. According to historian Yumiko Imaizumi, "Reports presented by staffs of Japanese government and Navy repeatedly mentioned problems with garrison and civilian government personnel displaying overbearing attitudes towards local people and using violence against them."[19] There were written statements that IJN personnel raped and impregnated women in the Marianas during the naval administration.[20] In late 1921, many of the IJN administrators and troops withdrew from Micronesia while the Civil Affairs Bureau was preparing to be replaced by a colonial government.[21]

On March 31, 1922, the South Seas Bureau or South Seas Government (*Nanyocho*), headquartered in Koror, Palau in the western Carolines was established with the promulgation of Imperial Ordinance No. 107.[22] It assumed control of approximately 623 islands scattered throughout Micronesia and had three departments: the Interior Department (Local Affairs Section, Police Affairs Sec.); Financial Department (Budget Sec., Accounting Sec., Engineering Sec., Field Office); and Colonization Department (Industrial Sec., Land Survey Sec., Communication Sec.).[23] Seitaro Yasutake, an official in the Tokyo Liaison Office of the South Seas Government in the late 1930s and early 1940s, stated, "the functions and status of the South Sea Bureau and prefectural governments in Japan were nearly identical," though the Nanyocho had more authority and administrative independence.[24] The South Seas Government's emblem was a "circlet of palm fronds enclosing a cherry blossom" and it flew the imperial "circle of the sun" flag (*Hinomaru*).[25] The government was under the Japanese Office of Colonial Affairs (*Takushoku jimu kyoku*) from 1922 to 1929, the Ministry of Colonization (*Takumusho*) from 1929 to 1942, and finally the Ministry of Greater East Asia (*Daitoasho*) from 1942 to 1945.[26] The Japanese, as instructed by the League of Nations, wrote official annual reports concerning the administration of their mandate and sent representatives to the League of Nations Permanent Mandates Commission based in Geneva, Switzerland.[27]

The South Seas Government was headed by a director or governor (*chokan*) who administered the mandate under the authority of the Prime Minister and ministries of Japan.[28] Below the governor were branch governors (*shichokan*) who directed the mandate's six branch governments (*shicho*), which included the Saipan District (Mariana

Islands), Jaluit District (Marshall Islands), Ponape District (Eastern Carolines), Truk District (Central Carolines), and Yap and Palau Districts (Western Carolines).[29] The Saipan District was headquartered in Garapan. An administration building with a clock tower was constructed on a small hill in the town at the same location of the old German administration building and government school.[30] Positions in the South Seas Government were highly selective. The branch governors and men chosen to serve under them were among the most educated and experienced in the empire. Many were graduates of Japan's most prestigious universities and had prior service in the colonial governments of Korea, Taiwan, Manchuria, and Karafuto or the concessions in China. These men directed the districts' agriculture, commerce, education, and public health, among other responsibilities.

In 1922, the South Seas Government promulgated the "Rules for Native Village Officials," which mirrored the village (*mura*) administrative system in mainland Japan. The Japanese, like their Spanish and German predecessors, hired and bribed Chamorro and Carolinian leaders and chiefs as middlemen functionaries to maintain the town and village systems and facilitate Japanese-Micronesian relations.[31] These local officials directed tax collections and population surveys, served as translators, and disseminated information about laws and other matters from the colonial administrators to fellow islanders.[32] The Japanese police also hired Micronesian patrolmen or constables (*junkei*) to assist them in law enforcement, and schools hired non–Japanese assistant teachers (*hojo kyoin*).[33]

The Civil, Criminal, and Commercial Codes of the Empire of Japan, in addition to imperial ordinances and special South Seas Government laws and regulations, were enforced in the mandate.[34] The main court in the Saipan District was the Saipan Local Court of the South Seas Government. The Higher Court of the South Seas Government in Koror, Palau handled appeal cases.[35] The South Seas Government Police Section (*Keimuka*), which operated based on the Police and Penal Regulations of the South Sea Islands (*Nanyo gunto keisatsu shobatsu rei*), was modeled on the colonial Taiwan police system and headed by a superintendent (*keishi*). Police inspectors (*keibu*) and assistant inspectors (*keibujo*) served under the superintendent and managed policemen (*junsa*).[36] At the bottom, were the Micronesians constables and messengers. The Japanese built police stations and jails in all the major islands.[37]

The South Seas Government, upon its formation, claimed all former German government properties and unused and undeveloped land in the Marianas and other Micronesian island groups.[38] Much of the "undeveloped" land taken was communal land that Chamorros and Carolinians used for hunting, fishing, foraging, livestock grazing, logging, and other cultural and subsistence agriculture activities. Japanese imperial subjects initially were not allowed to own land. Only the government could lease private properties and farms from Micronesians. In the 1920s, the government conducted land surveys and sometimes pressured or tricked Chamorros and Carolinians to renounce ownership rights or enter into rental contracts.[39] It, in turn, leased the land to government-subsidized companies and businesses.

It was easy for the colonial government to take what it wanted in the Marianas because the Spanish and Germans did not conduct full land surveys or maintain adequate records. A number of islanders had no written records of the land they received or inherited and farmed during the prior two colonial regimes. They based their claims on oral agreements and often marked boundaries with natural features or stones. Many old

Chamorro principalia families, who held some influence or were able to prove their holdings, happily leased their land to the Japanese, however, and made handsome profits. The neo-principalia had business relationships with Japanese traders, mostly concerning farming operations, preceding the naval occupation in 1914. Some learned Japanese as early as the turn of the century to strengthen relations. The government obtained most of the good land on Saipan within a decade. By 1932, the government owned 22,679 of Saipan's 28,951 acres and almost all of the island's arable land.[40] The entirety of Tinian, where only a small number of Micronesians lived, was in Japanese hands. Between 1931 and 1940, the South Seas Government allowed Japanese imperial subjects to lease or purchase land directly from Micronesians.[41]

The South Seas Government heavily promoted agricultural, sea, and trade enterprises. In 1923, it established the Tropical Industry Laboratory (*Nanyocho Nettai Sangyo Shikenjo*) to advance industrial research and economic development in the mandate.[42] Between 1895 and 1914, the Japanese established a lucrative sugar industry in their Taiwan colony. During the First World War, some Japanese entrepreneurs believed they could make a fortune in sugar outside of Taiwan following the IJN's capture and occupation of Micronesia. In 1916, two companies, the Nishimura Development Company (*Nishimura Takushoku*) and the South Seas Production Company (*Nanyo Shokusan*), began planting in the south and north of Saipan, respectively, with the backing of the IJN.[43] The companies recruited more than 1,000 people from rural Japan, Korea, Okinawa Prefecture, and the Bonins and rushed into operation.[44] Both lacked knowledge in the art and science of sugar planting, harvesting, and manufacturing, however. According to historian David C. Purcell, Jr., "No one among the workers knew what to do with the juice after it had been extracted from the cane, and when it was boiled down, nothing was produced. The juice was poured into a tank in hopes that it would ferment and produce a low-grade alcoholic drink, but this too failed, and the juice was ultimately poured into the sea."[45]

Additionally, productivity was reduced by labor disputes, tropical disease outbreaks, and fires. Koreans experienced discrimination, and there were quarrels between Japanese and non–Japanese workers.[46] Field supervisors were also embezzling funds and wasting money on lavish company dinners and parties. Unsurprisingly, the companies failed after only a few years. The workers were abandoned on the island with no means to support themselves and could not return to their homelands. They survived by "bartering eggs and coconuts for small quantities of rice and cooking oil at the local NBK station on Saipan."[47] Meanwhile, Japanese sugar operations were foundering on other islands throughout Micronesia. The Suzuki Brothers Trading Company (*Suzuki Shokai*), for example, incurred substantial financial losses and had to give up their sugar venture on Ponape after insects and flooding ruined their canefields.[48]

In 1920, Matsue Haruji, a prominent sugar industrialist, visited Saipan and Tinian. Matuse was born in 1876 in Aizuwakamatsu, Fukushima Prefecture, into a former samurai family. He graduated from Tokyo Industrial College in 1899 and studied at Louisiana State University under the world's leading sugar agricultural scientists. Following university, he directed sugar factories in Japan and Taiwan and prospered as a businessman.[49] Matuse was certain, after sampling Saipan and Tinian's soils and hiking their coasts, valleys, and jungle-covered ridges for weeks, that the islands were prime locations for sugarcane planting. He knew exactly why the companies on Saipan, Ponape, and other places failed and would not make the same blunders. He desired to prove wrong the big Taiwan sugar corporations, such as the Japan Sugar Company (*Dai Nihon Seito Kabushiki Kaisha*),

Meiji Sugar Company (*Meiji Seito*), and Ensuiko (*Ensuiko Seito*), who declared that the Mariana Islands were too small, mountainous, and "primitive" to establish profitable operations.[50] After touring the Marianas, Matuse returned to Japan and convinced several investors, including the Oriental Development Company (*Toyo Takushoku Kabushiki Kaisha*), a corporation deeply involved in the colonization of Korea, to provide the funds needed for establishing a sugar production company. After securing the necessary capital, Matsue purchased the assets of the two failed Saipan companies and paid all their debts, including back wages owed to the abandoned workers.[51] While some of the workers returned to their homelands, many admired Matsue's determination and remained on Saipan to work for him.

In 1921, Matsue established the South Seas Development Company (*Nanyo Kohatsu Kabushiki Kaisha, NKK*), also known as "Nanko." The South Seas Government granted the Nanyo Kohatsu agricultural subsidies and land on Saipan.[52] The company recruited peasants and factory workers from Okinawa Prefecture, mainland Japan, the Satsunan Islands in Kagoshima Prefecture, and Korea. The populations in these places were rapidly increasing, and many households were destitute from crop failures, unstable rice and silk prices, and social unrest.[53] Okinawans were seeking to escape the poverty and famines of the time, colloquially referred to as "poisonous sago palm eating hell" (*sotetsu jikoku*), and readily sought to work overseas.[54] Chodo Matsujiro, an Okinawan who migrated to Saipan at age eighteen in 1922, recounted, "At the time, my family was poor. Since they could not afford to send me to upper school, I yearned to make a name for myself in some undeveloped land."[55] Large-scale sugarcane farming had been taking place in Okinawa since the Satsuma invasion in the early seventeenth century and, therefore, many Okinawans employed by the Nanyo Kohatsu had experience farming the crop.[56] The company also recruited thousands of Koreans, many who were displaced by Japanese changes to the land-tenure system or impoverished by other social and economic upheavals in their colonized peninsula.[57]

Migrants traveled to Saipan by sea on cargo and passenger ships. Their fare and housing were covered by the company that recruited them or the government. Many of them were in second-class accommodations or steerage on the voyage to the southern end of the Japanese empire. The conditions below deck ranged from excellent to appalling depending on the ship and crew. On some ships, poor sanitation and overcrowded conditions led to the spread of infectious diseases. It was hot and humid, and for many passengers, it was their first time at sea. Seasickness was common, and some women even gave birth on board. When ships sunk from severe weather or accidents, the passengers in steerage often perished.

Migrants were welcomed, processed, settled in, and then started work. They were employed as salary contract laborers (*sagyofu*) or tenant farmers (*kosakunin*). The tenant farmers leased land from the company and paid fees in the form of harvested cane.[58] There were a small number of Chamorro and Carolinian sugarcane producers who owned the land they farmed and sold their harvested cane to the Nanyo Kohatsu.[59] Sugar agriculture was arduous; workers toiled from sunrise to sunset, day in and day out, in the canefields and factories in the humid, tropical heat of the Marianas. They earned side income by cutting wood, making charcoal, raising livestock, and growing castor oil plants, cassava (tapioca), coconuts, coffee, cotton, papaya, pineapples, and other small crops on their homesteads and unused land.[60] Immigrant guidance centers and residents' associations provided relief and social services for new settlers.[61]

The Nanyo Kohatsu was hard hit by several setbacks in its early years. Between 1922 and 1923, it was on the verge of bankruptcy because of a decline in global sugar prices, delayed shipments of factory equipment from Europe, bad weather, and damage to crops by cane borer beetles.[62] In September 1923, the Tokyo warehouse holding the company's first major shipment of sugar burned down by a fire caused by the Great Kanto Earthquake (*Kanto Daishinsai*). Company leaders, undaunted by the misfortunes, acted decisively. They obtained a pest-resilient variety of sugarcane from Taiwan, had Formosan koa and ironwood trees planted at the edges of canefields to guard crops against tropical storms, and introduced the tachinid fly and Taiwan blackbird, natural enemies of the cane borer, to Saipan.[63]

The Nanyo Kohatsu's reforms in 1923 and 1924 were highly effective, and sugarcane production on Saipan greatly increased following their implementation. In the mid-1920s, the company began turning major profits and enlarged its activities on the island. It continually expanded its large sugar factory in Chalan Kanoa, as well as a narrow-gauge railway that was specifically designed for the transportation of cane and laid around the perimeter of the island.[64] An alcohol distillery was built to utilize the leftover molasses from the sugar manufacturing process. Caterpillar bulldozers were imported from the United States and used to clear difficult terrain for planting.[65] The company also held prize competitions among cane harvesting teams, which increased camaraderie, care, and yields.[66] Sugar quickly became the leading export and most profitable commodity in the South Seas Mandate, surpassing copra, mined phosphate, and sea products.

In the late 1920s, the Nanyo Kohatsu leased nearly all of Tinian from the South Seas Government for sugarcane planting.[67] Japanese, Okinawans, and Koreans already on Saipan and new migrants were sent to the island to clear and plant it. Rota followed soon thereafter. Eventually, even the more remote islands of the Marianas, including Anatahan, Alamagan, Pagan, and Agrihan, had canefields. In the 1930s, Tinian, which had an island-wide sugarcane farm "master grid plan," surpassed Saipan in sugar production. Tinian had ethanol production plants and two sugar mills.[68] East Asians continued to immigrate to the islands in large numbers and have children. Sugarcane planting acreage increased annually. Dr. Paul Hibbert Clyde, an American historian who toured the Japanese Mandate in 1934, stated, "No jungle can survive the onrush of these pioneers, and in Saipan, Tinian, and Rota, Japanese energy is taxing every foot of soil for a great industry."[69] In 1925, the population of the Saipan District, according to the South Seas Government, was 8,800 people (5,299 Japanese, Okinawans, Koreans; 2,578 Chamorros; 915 Carolinians; 8 foreigners).[70] In 1935, the population was 44,043 people (39,731 Japanese, Okinawans, Koreans; 3,274 Chamorros; 1,023 Carolinians; 15 foreigners).[71] In 1941, the total population of Saipan, Tinian, and Rota was 53,753 people (48,923 Japanese subjects, including Okinawans and Koreans; 4,808 Chamorros and Carolinians; 22 foreigners).[72] There were more than 4,000 Koreans on Saipan and Tinian combined in the early 1940s. Okinawans were the largest ethnic group on Saipan and Tinian and greatly outnumbered Japanese from the mainland.[73]

The Japanese Ministry of Overseas Affairs reported that over 90 percent of the arable farmland on Saipan and Tinian was devoted to sugarcane agriculture by 1941.[74] Tens of thousands of tons of raw sugar and gallons of alcohol were produced there annually.[75] Despite the islands' exiguous sizes compared to Taiwan and Japan's importation of sugar from foreign nations, approximately one in every twenty tons of sugar consumed in the empire came from the Marianas.[76] The cane grown in the Marianas was of high-quality,

Sugarcane farmers and their families in Japanese Marianas, c. 1930s. Courtesy Don A. Farrell.

and Nanyo Kohatsu scientists and laborers were skilled at removing the sugar from it. Hisao Kabayama, an official in the Agriculture and Forestry Section of the South Seas Government, stated, "The sugarcane extraction rate on Saipan was much more than on Taiwan."[77] Willard Price, an American writer who traveled to the islands in the 1930s, wrote, "One of the finest sugar canes in the world has been developed here. Java cane was formerly used. Unsatisfied scientists blended it with other canes from all over the world, producing endless varieties. The final result ... a blend of Java and Formosa, which thrives in the soil of Saipan. It grows to great size and has high sugar content."[78]

Sugarcane farming and manufacturing were not simple processes. In the Marianas, Nanyo Kohatsu workers conducted seven essential steps for sugarcane farming: (1) land clearing; (2) planting; (3) cultivation; (4) irrigation and fertilization; (5) canefield burning; (6) harvesting; (7) transportation from field to factory. In step one, Saipan and Tinian canefarmers cleared, plowed, harrowed, furrowed, and ditched the valleys and jungles of the islands with hand tools and mechanized equipment. In step two, they planted and sowed stalk cuttings from the previous harvest. In step three, the land was cultivated by weeding, hoeing, and hilling up the soil around the base of the new plants.[79] Step four involved irrigation and fertilization during crop growth. The canefields were fertilized with nitrate of soda, burnt canestalk ash, filter-press cake (a by-product of sugarcane manufacturing rich in nitrogen and phosphorus), and manure (both animal waste and night soil).[80] The canes' dead and withered leaves were removed to enhance growth and used as fertilizer. In step five, completed just before the harvest, the canefields were burned. Burning the cane, which did not destroy the sugar juice in the internode joints, made it easier for laborers to cut the bare stalks, decreased unnecessary byproducts in the manufacturing process, and reduced the time and costs of clearing the fields for the next planting.[81] Step six involved cutting the cane stalk at two points; the first cut was at the top internodes, which were low in sugar and used for future planting, and the second cut was at the base to release the plant from the roots.[82] Cane cutting was a long, tedious task. Dr. William Carter Stubbs, one of the world's leading sugar agriculturalists in the early twentieth century and a director of the Louisiana Sugar Experiment Station, wrote, "cane is cut by hand labor, each stalk receiving the same attention. The cutter seizes the cane near the top, with his left hand, strips it of its foliage with the back of his cane knife, tops it, and the severs the stalk at the ground and throws it to the heap, which is made for the convenience of loading, on every third row. A good cutter in good cane will average about three tons of cane per day."[83] In step seven, laborers hauled heavy bundles of cut stalks to the railways. The cane was then loaded on railcars and transported to the factory for processing.

At the large sugar refineries in Chalan Kanoa and Tinian Town, which ran day and night during the harvests, the cane bundles were pulled from the railcars by mechanical unloaders and dropped onto slow-moving carriers that went to the crushers. The manufacturing process, carefully carried out by factory workers, involved five principal steps: (1) extraction of the sugar juice, (2) clarification of the juice, (3) concentration of the juice to syrup, (4) boiling of the juice in vacuum pans, (5) purging the sugar in centrifugal machines.[84] In step one, the cane stalks holding the sugar juice were crushed by revolving steel rollers, and the expelled sugar juice ran into receptacle tanks. Unnecessary byproducts and impurities, including gums, waxes, and salts, were removed from the juice in the tanks. Bagasse, the fibrous, woody parts of the cane leftover from the crushing, were dried, transported to the boilers, and burned to generate steam-electric power for factory operations.[85] In step two, lime was added to the juice. The mixture was boiled and then ran into large settling tanks. Once the cloudy mixture settled, all scum, filter-press cake "mud," and other remaining impurities were removed, and the juice was sent to evaporator receiving tanks. In step three, the juice was boiled in the evaporators, turned into syrup, and pumped to vacuum pan receiving tanks.[86] In step four, the syrup was boiled at low temperatures and reduced pressures in the vacuum pans until masses of sugar crystals and thick molasses formed. In the final step, most of the molasses was removed from the sugar in centrifugal machines. The sugar was dehydrated with dry steam until the final product was achieved.[87] It was bagged, weighed, boxed, stored, and lastly shipped to mainland Japan or elsewhere. The Nanyo Kohatsu hired Japanese chemists, engineers, and other scientists from the mainland and all over the world, including Taiwan, Hawaii, and Cuba, to oversee and perfect the manufacturing process.[88] Nanyo Kohatsu sugar was shipped by the South Seas Trading Company and other Japanese companies.

The South Seas Trading Company (*Nanyo Boeki Kaisha*, NBK) or "Nambo," which was the merged corporation of the old Hiki and Murayama trading firms, had a monopoly on trade, freight, and mail services in Micronesia beginning in the early twentieth century. The company, with the support of the IJN, grew appreciably during the First World War and invested in new ships, warehouses, and stations throughout the South Seas. By 1917, its operations reached San Francisco, California.[89] Nambo agents were well-versed in geography, goods exchange, and indigenous relations and among the most experienced in the Pacific. They built their company into the largest copra trader in Micronesia. Following the First World War, Nambo was joined by the preeminent Japan Mail Steamship Company (*Nippon Yusen Kaisha, NYK*) and the South Sea Marine Transportation Company (*Nanyo Kaiun Kaisha*) in managing sea transportation in the region.[90]

Nambo trade stations were conspicuous manifestations of Japanese ascendancy in the islands in the early decades of the twentieth century and they generated new ways of life. According to Mark R. Peattie:

> Typically, the station consisted of a combination house, store, and warehouse, with a customhouse and bathhouse in the rear. The building usually sat on a concrete foundation just inland from the beach, its walls of whitewashed lumbar, its corrugated tin roofs painted red, and "NBK" emblazoned in large letters on the side facing the lagoon. From the shelves of this tiny emporium came miso paste, soy sauce, rice, biscuits, cigarettes, clothes, watches, towels, pots, pans, dishes, tobacco, kerosene lamps, sewing machines, fishing gear, sugar, tea, hardware supplies, and all manner of wares that came to shape the tastes and lifestyles of the villagers whose palm-thatched houses clustered nearby. Once every three months—every four on some of the remoter atolls—the Nambo steamer would drop anchor off the beach to unload a fresh supply of such goods and to pick up the waiting cargo of copra, dried bonito, trepang, and tortoiseshell—a trade cycle that seldom varied.[91]

Nambo established commercial fishing fleets and fish processing facilities on Saipan after Micronesia became a Japanese mandate.[92] The Nanko Marine Production Company (*Nanko Suisan Kabushiki Kaisha*), a subsidiary of the Nanyo Kohatsu that later became part of the semi-governmental South Seas Colonization Company (*Nanyo Takushoku Kabushiki Kaisha*), also operated out of the Marianas and became the largest fishing company in Micronesia during the Japanese Colonial Period.[93] The South Seas Government subsidized Japanese fisheries in Micronesia and implemented the "Regulations for Encouragement of Fishery Industry in the South Sea Islands" (1922) and later the "Regulations on Financial Assistance to Fishery Management" (1937).[94] In the mid–1930s, the Japanese Ministry of Overseas Affairs budgeted millions of yen for the promotion of fisheries and marine research in Micronesia in a ten-year development plan. It also encouraged the expansion of fishing grounds into Melanesia and Island Southeast Asia.[95]

The South Seas Government made maritime infrastructure development in the colony one of its highest priorities. Civil engineering projects were undertaken on Saipan beginning in the 1920s. In 1926, the government dredged Tanapag Harbor and built two concrete jetties and a wharf to accommodate larger vessels.[96] Over the next five years, loading terminals, storage and processing facilities, canneries, and ice plants popped up on the island. Tinian's Sunharon Harbor experienced similar development. Within a decade, both Saipan and Tinian had modern ports. The ports took in cargo, including rice, machinery, textiles, wood, oil, wax, liquor, and cigarettes, from Yokohama and Osaka, Busan and Mokpo (Korea), Takao (Taiwan), and elsewhere. From the Marianas, the imports were dispersed throughout the South Seas Mandate.

The Saipan District became a base of operations for commercial fishing throughout the western Pacific. Thousands of tons of bonito, tuna, mackerel, shark, sea cucumber, and lobster were processed in the Saipan District yearly.[97] The fishing industry enabled the people of Saipan and Tinian to purchase high-quality sea products from fishermen and companies certified by the South Seas Government before it was exported. According to historian Wakako Higuchi, "the Japanese residents in the islands consumed fresh fish such as horse mackerel, Spanish mackerel, striped mullet and other reef fish (*meyasu*, *sunakuchi, kamasu,* and *itoyon*)."[98] Luxury foods and medicinals, such as shark fins, shark liver oil, and turtle, were enjoyed by the islands' elite and shipped to buyers in East Asia. Dried bonito (*katsuobushi*) from the Marianas and other Micronesian island groups was prized throughout the empire and was the second leading export in the mandate behind sugar.

Fishermen and longshoremen from the north, like farmers, were actively recruited by Nambo, Nanko Suisan, and other fisheries.[99] Upon returning from sea with their catch, Saipan and Tinian fishermen were assisted by company workers and their wives and children in cleaning and processing the fish. Fishermen were respected for their role in advancing and feeding the mandate. Those who sailed into the harbor with a particularly large catch received the admiration of the community. Citizens cared deeply for the fishermen's safety and women offered them locks of their hair, small dolls, face powder, and lip rouge to appease *Funadama*, the guardian kami of fishers and ships, as well as other gods. The Japanese Marianas was a family-oriented society deeply tied to the profitable sugar and fishing industries. The canefields and ocean were at the heart of the people's way of life and great sources of profit.

The South Seas Mandate prospered from the success of the sugar and marine industries in the Marianas. It gained substantial revenue from port clearance dues and customs duties, particularly on Nanyo Kohatsu sugar and Nambo fish.[100] In the mid–1930s, the colonial government intensified infrastructure development on Saipan and Tinian. Garapan and Tinian Town, small fishing villages with less than fifty Japanese in 1914, were transformed into the largest population centers in Micronesia in less than two decades.[101] They were modern, booming towns with power plants, factories, hospitals, schools, sewage systems, telecommunications, meteorological observation stations, and waterworks. Buildings were constructed of both western-style and traditional Japanese architecture. The farmsteads on the outskirts of the towns and inland resembled those in the Japanese and Okinawan countrysides and had small homes, concrete barns, sheds, cisterns, composting facilities, pigpens, and manure pits.[102]

Garapan and Tinian Town, both located off the Philippine Sea, had nearly all the commodities, conveniences, and luxuries that could be found in large mainland towns. They had bakeries, banks, bathhouses, bicycle shops, cafes, confectionaries, dance halls, furniture stores, geisha and tea houses, gas stations, groceries, herbal medicine shops, ice cream parlors, inns, lumber yards, movie theaters, newspaper printers, pharmacies, pleasure quarters, public parks and gardens, restaurants, bars, tailors, tennis courts, and toy stores.[103] Stores sold books, cameras, china, clocks, dolls, fans, futons, glassware, jewelry, lacquerware, makeup and lip rouge, magazines, purses, radios, record players, sun umbrellas, and more. Street vendors with wooden carts peddled cigarettes, candies, shaved ice, food, and many trinkets. Artist performed traditional Japanese theater (*kabuki, noh,* etc.) and puppet shows (*bunraku* or *ningyo joruri*) in the towns' theaters and on outdoor stages. The Marianas had a vivacious Japanese sociocultural milieu. Garapan was considered the "Tokyo of the South Seas." Saipan schoolgirl Tatsu Sato recalled, "In Garapan, itself, fine two storey buildings were quickly replacing the old one storey wooden affairs. Strings of gay colored lanterns were strung along the street presenting a very lively scene not unlike Tokyo's Ginza of Old."[104]

Smaller towns and villages in the islands, including Chalan Kanoa in southwestern Saipan and Churo (Chulu) in north-central Tinian, also grew. The Saipan District established a branch office on Tinian in 1933 to serve the growing population on the island.[105]

The birth rate in the Marianas was much higher than in mainland Japan; large multichild families were common on Saipan and Tinian.[106] Schools on Saipan that educated the many immigrant and island-born children included the Saipan Public School, Saipan Vocational School, Saipan High School for Girls, and the Matansha, Asurito, Chatcha, Charan Kanoa, and Saipan Advanced Elementary Schools. On Tinian, they included the Kahi, Marupo, Churo, and Tinian Advanced Elementary Schools.[107]

The modernization of Saipan and Tinian brought prosperity to both migrants and Micronesians. Life in the Japanese Marianas was not for all, however. Sugarcane farming was arduous, factory work was tedious and tiring, and the sea was hazardous. The dust from the canefields, roads, and construction sites was overwhelming at times. It made people cough up phlegm and caused respiratory problems. The hot and humid tropical climate was uncomfortable for some migrants from the north. Starry-eyed migrants' dreams of tropical adventure and romance in the palm-fringed South Seas Islands were often not fulfilled, and boredom set in quickly. Infectious tropical diseases destroyed lives. Chamorro man Henry Sablan Pangelinan stated, "tuberculosis was common, so was dysentery. Infant mortality was high. Typhoid ... killed."[108] Conditions off the shore in some areas were dangerous, and people drowned. Minorities faced discrimination from the Japanese and even from other minorities. Many migrants were homesick, and some regretted leaving their ancestral villages and family graves. The South Seas Government recorded a small number of suicides and attempted suicides between 1928 and 1939. The methods of suicide included ingestion of poisons, hanging, drowning, and cutting and slashing.[109] The acts of despair were attributed to melancholy (*yuutsu*), weariness with life (*ensei*), and delirium (*seishin sakuran*).[110] Although some suffered unbearable hardship, many immigrants, with the support of the South Seas Government and private companies, had better qualities of life than they had in their homelands.

3

Cultures and Societies of Saipan and Tinian

The Japanese Marianas was ethnically diverse. There were Chamorros and Carolinians with Micronesian and European customs, as well as several thousands of Koreans and tens of thousands of Okinawans and Japanese from different villages, cities, prefectures, regions, and islands who settled on Saipan and Tinian. The East Asian migrants, who had distinct dialects, folk customs, religious practices, and family and clan traditions, made efforts to preserve their ethnic and cultural identities in tropical Micronesia. The South Seas Government, a colonial government of the Empire of Japan, exclusively supported mainland Japanese culture and religion.

Shinto, the indigenous religion of Japan, was the dominant religion on Saipan and Tinian during the Japanese colonial period. The Japanese built many overseas Shinto shrines (*kaigai jinja*) in the Marianas. There were "government-established shrines" (*seifu setchi jinja*), migrant shrines (*kyoryumin setchi jinja*), and community "settler group shrines" (*kaitakudan jinja*).[1] Small wayside shrines (*hokora*), which enshrined folk kami and deities, were located along dirt paths, farm roads, and jungle trails throughout the islands. The shrines were built in the mainland fashion but had tropical characteristics and decorative plants. In 1914, the IJN built the Katori Shrine, also known as the Saipan Shrine, on a small forested hill just east of Garapan Village.[2] The shrine was named after the Japanese battleship *Katori* (launched in 1905), which was used to capture Saipan and named in honor of the ancient Katori Shrine in Chiba Prefecture. The portable shrine aboard the battleship *Katori* housed a sacred repository object (go*shintai*) where the spirit of *Futsunushi*, a kami of war, resided. A piece of the go*shintai* was taken from the battleship after a "dividing of spirit" rite and was enshrined in the Saipan Shrine.[3]

The Japanese believed or at least liked to think that mysterious kami inhabited natural landscapes and features. They referred to Mt. Tapochau as a "divine body mountain" (*shintai-zan*) or "spirit mountain" (*reizan*). Saipan schoolgirl Akiko Kikuchi stated, "At the mountain's summit on a large flat rock was built a small shrine. The prospect from here was superb, a sea of sugarcane waving their tall green leaves in the breeze."[4] The Hachiman Shrine was built in the jungle-covered limestone ridges at the northwestern edge of Kagman Peninsula on Saipan in the 1930s.[5] The shrine, which housed *Hachiman*, a kami of war, was designed in the mainland fashion and had a torii gate, lion-dog guardian statues (*komainu*), concrete lanterns (*toro*), and a water purification pavilion (*chozuya*).[6] It had an imposing concrete stairwell boarded by high limestone retaining walls that led up to an inner sanctuary (*honden*). A number of other shrines were built

Shinto shrine on Saipan in the 1940s. United States Marine Corps Photograph #83008. National Archives.

on Saipan, including the Nanko Shrine in Chalan Kanoa and Nanyo (Southern Sun) Shrine in Aslito in the south.[7] Shrines on Tinian included the Tinian Shrine and the Sumiyoshi Shrine in Tinian Town, the Izumi Shrine in Marpo Village (south-central Tinian), the Tachibana Shrine in Kahi (central), the Hinode Shrine in Asiga (north), and the Lasso Shrine in Chulu (north-central).[8] Many of the shrines were heavily damaged or destroyed during the battles. The Government-sponsored Great Shrine in the South Seas (*Kampei Taisha Nanyo Jinja*) in Koror, Palau, completed in 1940 to commemorate the mythical 2,600th anniversary of the founding of the Empire of Japan, was the highest ranked shrine in the colony.[9]

Nearly every Japanese family on Saipan and Tinian had a kami shelf (*kamidana*), where they presented offerings of rice, fruit, incense, and ritual sake. Parents had their children participate in Shinto life-cycle rites, such as the newborn's first shrine visit (*Hatsumiyamairi*) and Seven-Five-Three Festival (*Shichi-Go-San*) on November 15, in which girls ages 3 and 7 and boys ages 3 and 5, who were dressed in traditional costume, were taken to shrines to receive the blessings and protection of the kami. Wedding ceremonies (*shinzen kekkon*) were also held at Shinto shrines. Farmers and businessmen partook in special agricultural rites at shrines for bountiful sugarcane harvests. Shinto was intrinsically tied to "Japaneseness" (*Nihon rashisa*), and mainland migrants felt more connected to their homelands by practicing the religion. Genchi Kato, a professor at Tokyo Imperial

University, wrote in 1935, Shinto is "the heart and life of every Japanese subject, male or female, high and low, old and young, educated or illiterate. This is the reason why a Japanese never ceases to be a Shintoist, i.e., an inborn steadfast holder of the national faith or one who embraces the national faith or the Way of the Gods."[10] Many non–Japanese practiced Shinto to enhance their social standing or were pressured to do so.

Buddhism was also a prominent religion in the Japanese Marianas. In 1919, missionaries of the East Honganji Temple True Pure Land Buddhist Sect built a temple on Saipan.[11] In the early 1930s, they built a second temple on Tinian.[12] Migrants, many who experienced homesickness, found comfort in the familiar religion and had Buddhist shrines (*butsudan*) in their homes. Buddhist families attended temple ceremonies and community social activities, held prayer and meditation sessions, and conducted regular ancestor worship rites. They placed Bodhisattva statues along farm paths and mountain trails for protection and good fortune. The Buddhist temples conducted death rituals and funeral services in the islands and had crematories. The cremated remains of deceased migrants were often shipped back north to their ancestral villages.[13] There were also cemeteries on the islands.

Okinawans brought their indigenous religion, which consisted of ancestor worship, animism, and shamanism, to the Marianas. They largely practiced their religion privately in their homes or at sacred groves (*utaki*) and "honorable praying places" (*uganju*) in the islands' caves and jungles because of Japanese cultural suppression policies and prejudice. Okinawan religion was influenced by major South and East Asian religions, including Buddhism, Chinese folk religion, Taoism, Shinto, and Taiwanese aboriginal spiritualism. It centered on annual rites revolving around the lunar calendar and agricultural cycles that served to propitiate the gods, deities, and ancestral spirits. Age-based rites of passage concerning birth, education, and marriage were also observed. Okinawans believed in the concept of *onarigami*, that women possessed spiritual powers. Priestesses (*kaminchu*) and female shamans (*yuta*) performed the rites with amulets, talismans, and other religious devices, while fortune tellers (*sanjinso*) interpreted dreams and gave practitioners guidance concerning health, finances, and other personal affairs.[14] Women were responsible for directing ancestor worship and caring for the household shrines, which held the ancestral memorial tablets (*ihai*), flower vases, incense censers, rice wine cups, and family heirlooms.[15] During ceremonies, food dishes and personal gifts were offered to the shrines with prayer.[16]

The fire god (*hinukan*) was one of the most revered deities in the Okinawan religion.[17] Fire, used for cooking and other daily functions, was always present among Okinawans. They believed the fire god was a messenger from the spiritual realm and a divine intercessor between humans and the higher gods. In ancient and feudal times, Okinawans worshiped the fire god at the hearth, which typically consisted of three large stones. On Saipan and Tinian, most Okinawan families had modern stoves and instead kept a small box filled with three pebbles and ashes in the kitchen to maintain their reverence to the god.[18] Okinawans respected the gods but were wary of evil spirits (*yanamung*) and ghosts (*majimung*).[19] They had statues and objects to guard against malevolent specters. Stone and pottery lions (*karashishi*) were situated on roofs, and *ishigantuu* stone tablets were placed at the entrances of homes and road intersections.[20] Okinawans also sprinkled salt and hearth ashes around their homes and carried protective amulets.[21] They believed misfortune was a form of supernatural retribution inflicted on humans for the defilement of sacred places, improper ritual practice, insufficiency of prayer, or violation of social values.[22]

Koreans on Saipan and Tinian, like those on the peninsula, practiced Buddhism, Christianity, Confucianism, Taoism, Daejonggyo, and Korean Shamanism. Korean Shamanism (*mugyo*), the native religion of Korea, centered on animism and rituals known as the *kut*. The kut, carried out by both male and female shamans (*mudang*), involved ancestor worship, chants, songs, dances, exorcisms, fortune tellings, mythology recitations, ritual purifications, and sacrificial offerings. Shamans performed the kut with amulets, masks, folk costumes, musical instruments, and religious implements. The kut were conducted to appease or expel evil spirits, ghosts, and deities and to communicate with and obtain good fortune from benevolent ones.[23] In the Marianas, shamans often performed kut to interact with spirits associated with agriculture, fishing, and business. Koreans believed, like the Japanese, that the islands' mountains were sacred and that mountain spirits (*sansin*) influenced crop health and yields in the valleys.[24] Families performed rites in their homes, including ancestral worship and sacred observances dedicated to folk and tutelary gods. Koreans largely practiced their religion in secret, as the Okinawans did, because of Japanese oppression and harassment.

Japanese, Okinawan, and Korean migrants continued to celebrate the holidays, agrarian celebrations, and folk festivals of their homelands to the north. Saipan schoolgirl Akiko Kikuchi recalled, "The festivals were celebrated with much enthusiasm. The dedicatory dances, (both Japanese and Okinawan) street stalls, side shows, circus were always thronged with people till late at night."[25] The Japanese celebrated the Gregorian New Year (*Shihohai*), Bean-Throwing Ceremony (*Setsubun*) on February 3, Empire Day (*Kigensetsu*) on February 11, Girls' Day or Doll Festival (*Hinamatsuri*) on March 3, the Vernal (*Shunki Koreisai*) and Autumnal Equinoxes (*Shuki Koreisai*), Boys' Day (*Tango-no-sekku*) on May 5, Star Festival (*Tanabata*) on July 7, and the late summer *Obon* Festival. Emperor Hirohito's birthday (*Tenchosetsu*) and Emperor Meiji's birthday (*Meijisetsu*) were celebrated on April 29 and November 3, respectively. In 1940, during the mythical 2,600th anniversary of the founding of the Empire of Japan, large celebrations with parades, speeches, exhibitions, and artistic performances were held on Saipan and Tinian. Akiko stated, "The celebration of the 2600 year ... was held with flag, lantern and fancy dress processions in which almost everyone took part."[26]

Okinawans and Koreans partook in Japanese holidays and their own holidays, a number which were of Chinese origin. They had special agricultural festivals and observances for the summer and winter solstices and vernal and autumnal equinoxes. Koreans celebrated the Lunar New Year (*Seollal*), Great Full Moon Festival (*Jeongwol Daeboreum*), spring Arrival (*Samjinnal*) on the 3rd day of the 3rd lunar month, Buddha's Birthday (*Chopail*) on the 8th day of the 4th lunar month, and the Autumn Harvest Festival (*Chuseok*) on the 15th day of the 8th lunar month. East Asian and Micronesian Christians celebrated Easter, Christmas, and other holy days. In addition to holidays, migrants to the Marianas also enjoyed both the traditional and modern arts and entertainments of their homelands, including bonsai, calligraphy, crafts, dance, embroidery, flower arrangement, gambling, ink art, kite flying, literature, music, painting, paper cutting and folding, plays, poetry, pottery, sculpture, tea ceremony, theater, weaving, and writing. Children and adults played board games, cards, chess, dice, and tops. Sports were popular, especially baseball, track and field, archery, boxing, sumo, and martial arts. Laborers sang folk songs in the canefields and at sea similar to the *holehole bushi* Japanese immigrants sang in Hawaii.

Migrants continued to eat the staple foods and cuisines of their homelands because of the excellent imperial shipping network, which continually supplied them with imports from the mainland and northern colonies. The Japanese diet, the leading diet in the islands, consisted primarily of rice, miso, seafood, vegetables, noodles, dumplings, eggs and poultry, and soups. The Okinawan diet was heavily influenced by the Japanese and other diets in Asia but varied based on traditional alterations of similar dishes and the incorporation of larger quantities of meats, oils, and vegetables, most notably the sweet potato and legumes. Okinawan and Koreans, unlike most Japanese, ate pork. The Korean diet consisted of rice, kimchi, vegetables, meats, soups, and other foods prepared in the same ways as on the peninsula. All groups enjoyed, tea, medicinal goods, and alcoholic beverages, though the Japanese prohibited Micronesians from purchasing alcohol.[27] Micronesians continued to eat the foods of their ancestors during the Spanish colonial period, which included corn, beef, chicken, lamb, pork, tropical fruits, and vegetables. Gregorio C. Cabrera, a Chamorro young man on Saipan, recalled, "In those days we ate locally grown fruits and vegetables, things like bananas and breadfruit. We also raised pigs and chickens. We didn't eat rice; that was only for the Japanese…. We were still under the Spanish influence. We ate mostly corn meal tortillas."[28]

Clothing, like food, was also shipped to the islands. East Asian migrants, as well as Micronesians, mainly wore imported western-style cotton clothing made by Japanese-owned textile manufacturers. Homespun clothing, created by women for their families and sold at shops, was worn as well. The types and styles of clothing varied based on occupation and class. Businessmen, scientists, and government workers wore suits and women wore dresses. Farmers, fishermen, and manual laborers wore durable apparel suited for the physical demands of their work. Schoolchildren wore standard uniforms. Many East Asians wore the traditional dress of their homelands during holidays, festivals, and shrine visits. The Japanese had kimono and yukata, the Okinawans wore ushinchi or ryuso, and the Koreans had their hanbok. Many upper-class women dressed in kimono daily. Japanese hairstyles and oil-paper umbrellas were also popular. Regarding Micronesians, the Japanese administration reported in 1930, "At present men mostly have their hair cut short and their faces shaved and wear shirts and trousers, some even full suits, while women are generally dressed in a garment resembling the night-gown worn by European ladies."[29] Beginning in late 1941, after Japan went to war with the United States, all wore more austere clothing. Many women put on farmer button downs and loose waist-hugging trousers (*monpe*) every day. They were encouraged to not wear cosmetics and stockings or buy cigarettes and other "luxury" products.[30]

Assimilation and Discrimination

The Japanese implemented forced assimilation (*kyoseiteki doka*) and "Japanization" (*Nihonka*) policies in the Marianas to make Okinawans, Koreans, and Micronesians more compliant and supportive of their colonial rule. The primary vehicles of assimilation were the education system and Shinto religion. Mitsusada Horiguchi, interim-governor of the South Seas Government in late 1931, reported to the League of Nations Permanent Mandates Commission in 1932, "We deliberately selected education and religion as the two methods most likely to ensure in the long run the intellectual development of the inhabitants."[31]

In 1915, the IJN instituted elementary education in the Marianas and continued where the Germans left off.[32] In 1922, Navy-established schools were redesignated as

South Seas Government schools. There were Catholic mission schools attended by islanders and migrants during Japanese rule. In 1935 the Japanese administration mandated that all children attend government schools.[33] The government schools, which were modeled after those in colonial Korea and Taiwan, provided the administration a formal yet intimate environment to indoctrinate the youth of the islands. Before lessons, students in uniforms stood at attention in schoolyards, performed imperial subject calisthenics (*teikoku shimmin taiso*) and drills (*kunren*), and bowed northward toward the imperial palace. They then went into the classroom, bowed to the emperor's portrait (*Tenno no shozo*), shouted out three banzais for him, recited the Imperial Rescript on Education (*Kyoiku ni kansuru chokugo*), and sang the National Anthem of the Empire of Japan (*Kimigayo*). According to one scholar, "School rituals were a means of creating self-governance, conditioning students to voluntarily act upon and autonomously relate to the Japanese national ethos."[34] Chamorro schoolboy Henry Sablan Pangelinan stated, on Saipan, "my teachers were very strict. The Chamorro people at this time were still, you know, under their original customs and these teachers were trying to convert us to the Japanese way of doing things."[35]

Students on Saipan and Tinian learned Japanese language, history, myths, geography, and ethics. They read government textbooks that contained propaganda. According to historian Kenneth J. Ruoff, the "Japanese authorities foisted upon their colonial subjects a fanciful version of the past that sanctified Japan's role in world history."[36] The Japanese Ministry of Education's book *The Cardinal Principles of the National Entity of Japan* (*Kokutai no Hongi*, 1937) was used in government schools to instill patriotism and nationalism in students during the Asia-Pacific War. *Kokutai no Hongi* examined the nature and meaning of Japan's "national essence" (*kokutai*), the mythical history of the Japanese nation, the divinity and sacredness of the emperor, and the duties expected of all imperial subjects. The opening of the book stated, "The unbroken line of Emperors, receiving the Oracle of the Founder of the Nation, reign eternally over the Japanese Empire. This is our eternal and immutable national entity. Thus, founded on this great principle, all the people, united as one great family nation in heart and obeying the Imperial Will, enhance indeed the beautiful virtues of loyalty and filial piety. This is the glory of our national entity. This national entity is the eternal and unchanging basis of our nation and shrines resplendent throughout our history."[37]

During the 1930s and early 1940s, the South Seas Government also used Shinto, and to a lesser extent Buddhism, to assimilate non–Japanese in the islands. They relied particularly on State or National Shinto (*Kokka Shinto*), a form of Shinto that centered on reverence to the emperor. The South Seas Government focused its efforts on the islands' youth and incorporated Shinto rituals into the schools. Children were required to visit, pray at, and clean shrines and attend special Shinto ceremonies throughout the year. Chamorro schoolgirl Escolastica Tudela Cabrera recounted, "Every morning we had to go the Genja [shrine] to bow and pray towards Japan."[38]

The South Seas Government tried to assimilate the older generations as well. It encouraged Okinawan, Korean, and Micronesian adults to learn Japanese and engage in Japanese-led patriotic societies, community volunteer organizations, and sports clubs. The government sponsored annual observation tours to Tokyo and Osaka for Micronesian men and required them, upon their return, to tell their fellow islanders about the modern marvels of the empire's largest industrial centers.[39] Propaganda was the paramount channel for influencing adults. All people in the islands were exposed to Japanese newspapers, magazines, pamphlets, posters, books, motion pictures, music, theater, radio broadcasts, and other forms of communication and entertainment created or censored by the colonial and mainland governments.[40] They did not believe all the propaganda, however. They "listened to some propaganda messages, ignored others."[41] Support for the Japanese administration, or lack thereof, varied among the population.

The Japanese suppressed Okinawan, Korean, and Micronesian cultural identities in order to hasten assimilation and "civilize" them. The South Seas Government reported to the League of Nations in 1937, "The natives ... still adhere to a number of objectionable habits of barbarism, which it will take a long time to eradicate."[42] The Japanese forbade the study and use of non–Japanese languages in schools and censored and banned some ethnic newspapers and publications deemed subversive. The administration reported in 1930, "the sale and distribution of any newspaper containing matter calculated to be injurious to public order or good manners shall be prohibited within the territory."[43] The Japanese regularly disparaged the histories of all three ethnic groups. Taeki Lee, a Korean schoolboy on Saipan, recalled, "the teachers taught Korean history as something inferior."[44] Koreans and Okinawans were pressured to replace their clan and ancestral surnames with Japanese ones.[45] Some of the oppressive policies in the mandate drew international condemnation but continued. For example, the League of Nations Permanent Mandates Commission protested South Seas Government bans on some traditional Micronesian dances, but the proscriptions were not lifted.[46]

Ethnic discrimination and violence accompanied cultural suppression policies on Saipan and Tinian. There was not the "equality of all beneath the emperor's benevolent gaze."[47] Slogans proclaimed by the Japanese such as "impartiality and equal favor" (*isshi dojin*) and "racial harmony" (*minzoku kyowa*) were mere propaganda. Chamorro elder Nicolas Q. Muna stated, "during the Japanese times there was discrimination."[48] Discriminatory practices were carried out not only by high-level administrators, company executives, and the police, but by ordinary, everyday Japanese, including school teachers, shopkeepers, and those in the sugarcane and fishing industries. Of course, not all Japanese people were prejudiced against minorities; every individual had their own views. During all the colonial periods in the Marianas, perspectives on social, cultural, and political matters among colonizers and migrants were never uniform, but there were dominant viewpoints.

Former Okinawan, Korean, and Micronesian students on Saipan and Tinian, interviewed in the postwar period, specified that their time in South Seas Government schools was one of worst facets of Japanese rule save for what they experienced in the battles. Several of their teachers were cruel and abusive. Chamorro schoolgirl Marie Soledad Castro recalled, "Going to school during Japanese times-I was always scared because of the way we were treated.... One time a classmate sitting next to me was caught whispering to me. The teacher punished her by cutting her eyelashes off.... On another occasion when a group of us were late returning to class our fingers were burned with drops of acid."[49] Chamorro schoolgirl Escolastica Tudela Cabrera stated, "If we did something wrong our Japanese teachers hit us ... two students [Soledad Repeki and Alejandro Cabrera] actually died from beatings they received from teachers.... People went to the police to complain about the killings, but they don't listen to Chamorros and Carolinians."[50]

The Japanese administration and later the military were not in favor of Christians and practitioners of the indigenous Korean and Okinawan religions. They disliked the strong influences and authority ethnic religious institutions and leaders held over the people under their rule. They also believed minorities' practice of non–Japanese religions was a form of nationalistic protest of their Shinto-based colonial government.[51] A prominent Japanese scholar of the period wrote, "Christianity is absolutely anti-national…. Since it places emphasis upon the quality of all before God, it does not accept reverence for the Emperor and consequently places no value upon the idea of loyalty. It cares not the least whether the state deteriorates."[52] Although Article 28 of the Constitution of the Empire of Japan granted Japanese subjects the right to "enjoy freedom of religious belief," it came with the provisions that such beliefs could not be "prejudicial to peace and order" or "antagonistic to their duties as subjects."[53]

In the 1920s, the Japanese promoted and subsidized Christian missions in Micronesia.[54] In the late 1930s and early 1940s, however, Japanese ultranationalism was rife and tensions between Japan and the United States, a predominantly Christian nation, escalated. As a result, Japanese enmity against Christians in Micronesia markedly rose. After the attack on Pearl Harbor, intolerance toward practitioners of non–Japanese religions increased.[55] The Japanese police and military, seeking to root out dissidents and spies, raided Christian homes, destroyed religious books and objects, and arrested and detained Christians. The Japanese scheduled compulsory civil defense and paramilitary drills during liturgical service hours to prevent Christians from attending and forced practitioners to regularly visit Shinto shrines and show their reverence to the emperor.[56] Japanese teachers criticized the churches in public schools.[57] Japanese troops murdered a small number of Catholic missionaries and priests in Micronesia during the war.[58]

The Japanese administration, despite its assimilation and uniformization efforts, enforced ethnic segregation in the Marianas. Japanese children attended primary schools (*shogakko*), whereas non–Japanese attended public schools (*kogakko*).[59] Shogakko studies were eight years long and consisted of rigorous writing, science, and mathematics courses. The kogakko studies, on the other hand, only lasted three to five years and taught a rudimentary, practical curriculum (*jissai kyoiku*), which centered on manual skills intended to produce laborers, clerks, drivers, and servants for the Japanese upper-class.[60] According to historian Yumiko Imaizumi, Micronesian students were "seen as less than human and emphasis was placed on teaching them to fulfill their duties as beings ruled by Japan."[61] Teachers taught Japanese language classes in the kogakko, but the lessons were inadequate, and few Micronesians learned to read or write Japanese masterfully. American journalist Willard Price wrote, "teachers admit that the native is not getting enough Japanese at present to give him much in the way of new horizons."[62] Middle and secondary schools, with advanced language classes, were reserved for the Japanese. It was seldom that a non–Japanese progressed beyond the few years at the kogakko. Only Japanese were admitted into the Saipan Business School or the Saipan Vocational School; both were established in the 1930s.[63] The Japanese did not want to disrupt the social hierarchy in the Marianas by creating an educated, non–Japanese elite.[64] Furthermore, an undereducated and poorer ethnic class posed less of a threat to the colonial administration because it was more dependent on the government and less able to express grievances, organize and finance domestic opposition, and communicate with the international community. Few Chamorros and Carolinians could afford to go abroad, and only a small number of European and American foreigners ever visited or were permitted to tour the islands.

There was discrimination and segregation in workplaces on Saipan and Tinian as well. The Japanese regarded Micronesians as less intelligent and industrious than East

Asians and barred them from employment or management in many companies and government departments.[65] Islanders were largely kept out of the sugarcane industry. Approximately 15,000 East Asians were employed in the sugar industry at its height on Saipan and Tinian, whereas less than fifty Micronesian households worked in the canefields and factories.[66] The colonial administration was largely unconcerned with Micronesian workforce services. Hisao Kabayama, an official in the Agriculture and Forestry Section of the South Seas Government, stated, "The promotion of islanders' employment was never a high priority. It was needless to do so because excellent labor was available in Japan."[67] The Japanese told the Mandates Commission in 1932 that they were not training indigenous peoples for administrative positions in the South Seas Government.[68] Minorities also dealt with wage discrimination in the places they were permitted to work in.[69] The Nanyo Kohatsu paid Japanese laborers from the mainland higher daily wages than non–Japanese laborers doing the same jobs.[70] Chamorro Nanyo Kohatsu worker Henry Sablan Pangelinan stated, "My salary was probably thirty to fifty percent lower than that of Japanese employees."[71]

There was some residential segregation, but the colonial administration did not carry out any ghettoizing policies. East Asians and Micronesians lived in some of the same districts in Garapan.[72] There were a few districts in Garapan that were predominantly Japanese and Okinawan because of the expansion of the town beyond were Chamorros and Carolinians had lived for decades prior to the IJN occupation in 1914. Chalan Kanoa and all of Tinian were almost all Japanese, Okinawan, and Korean because they were buildup by the Nanyo Kohatsu and home to its immigrant workers.[73] According to scholar Keiko Ono, "While European colonialism routinely separated the races 'as an object of urban policy,' the local islander population was physically integrated in the Japanese colonial town except in government and company housing precincts."[74]

A number of Japanese from the mainland believed, like European and American colonizers of the period, that they were superior to the peoples of less industrially developed lands and territories they ruled. This belief was amalgamated with ethnocentrism. In 1936, the Tokyo Anthropological Society declared, "The Japanese people were created on the islands of Japan, and are a superior race, supporting an unbroken dynasty for all ages, and having no racial origin outside of the Japanese islands."[75] A passage in *The Cardinal Principles of the National Polity* (*Kokutai no Hongi*, 1937) stated, "Japan is a Land of the gods. Our Imperial Ancestor for the first time set the foundation of the nation, and the Sun Deity forever handeth on the Imperial Throne. This is a thing existing only in our country and without parallel in foreign lands. This is why we call it a Land of the gods."[76] *An Investigation of Global Policy with the Yamato Race as Nucleus* (1943), a report completed by the Population and Race Section of the Ministry of Health and Welfare Research Bureau, stated that the Japanese were the "leading race" (*shido minzoku*) in the world.[77]

The Japanese had different viewpoints concerning Okinawans, Koreans, and Micronesians. Individuals in all three ethnic groups experienced discrimination for being "outside peoples" (*gaichi minzoku*). Marriages between Japanese and non–Japanese were permitted and did happen, but many Japanese disapproved of them. Seitaro Yasutake, an official in the South Seas Government, stated, "it was said that marriage with foreigners would make our blood polluted or make our family record dirty because the Japanese were a so called 'pure race.'"[78] The Japan Hygiene Association (*Nihon Eisei Kyokai*) stated in the early 1940s, "as a nation, mixed blood is a problem that must be avoided in every instance."[79] The Ministry of Health and Welfare also "discouraged intermarriage between the Japanese and people from the neighboring colonized nations."[80] Mixed children were considered inferior. According to scholar Noriko J. Horiguchi, "To maintain the purity of Japanese blood and body, Japanese colonizers were encouraged to take their spouses with them to the colonies so that they would not intermarry with the natives ... mixed-blood children were stigmatized as individual, disease-ridden, and bereft of national spirit, in contrast to the notion of the collective, healthy, and patriotic spirit of the pure Japanese."[81] Ethnic groups, influenced by Japanese discourse and propaganda, discriminated against each other. According to anthropologist Lin Poyer, "Micronesian attitudes toward Korean and Okinawan laborers varied from considering them Japanese to adopting derogatory Japanese attitudes toward them."[82] Some landed Chamorros looked down on poorer Okinawans and Koreans.

A number of Japanese viewed Okinawans as backward second-class subjects, or as one American officer noted, "the Japanese equivalent of 'hillbillies.'"[83] Ota Masahide, a schoolboy on Okinawa during the period, stated, "Because of the past history of Okinawa, various influences from Burma, Thailand, and China entered Okinawan life, and with its different habits, customs, and language, Okinawa was supposed to lack in loyalty and patriotism. Okinawans could not be true members of the pure Japanese."[84] Okinawan migrants, who outnumbered Japanese from the mainland in the Marianas, had strength in numbers but were not part of the wealthy, ruling elite (administrators, company executives, etc.). They were disdained for their cultural differences from Yamato mainlanders (*naichijin*). According to scholar George H. Kerr, mainland Japanese migrants "sought to make sure that they were not mistaken for Okinawans, and the very name 'Okinawan' often carried a derisive or contemptuous overtone. Peculiarities of Okinawan dress, dialect, and diet embarrassed the Japanese.... The strong insularity of Japanese nationalism would not admit the Okinawans easily to full membership in Japanese society."[85]

A number of Japanese regarded Koreans as their unrefined neighbors to the west. As historian Jeffrey Paul Bayliss states, Koreans were described as "filthy, debaucherous, violent, and lacking the will for self-improvement-in other words, the antithesis of the ideal Japanese citizen/subject as conceived by state and majority society."[86] According to historian Takashi Fujitani, the Japanese "constructed an image of Korea as not only backward and uncivilized but also as a land of filth" (*fuketsu*).[87] *Reference Materials for the Education of Soldiers from Korea* (*Chosen shusshinhei no kyoiku sanko shiryo*, 1944), a two-volume manual written by the Inspectorate General of Military Training for Japanese Army officers, stated that Koreans were averse to bathing, weak and effeminate (*bunjaku*), and less able in "complex thought" (*fukuzatsu naru shikoryoku*).[88] Some Japanese possessed animosity toward the people. Japanese human rights violations and crimes against Koreans during their colonial rule were well-documented and included the brutal suppression, torture, and murder of independence activists and purported dissidents with "dangerous thoughts" (*kiken shiso*); the massacre of Koreans in Tokyo, Yokohama, and elsewhere following the 1923 Great Kanto earthquake; the conscription of hundreds of thousands of Koreans as forced laborers; and the sexual slavery of Korean girls and women during the Asia-Pacific War.

Chamorros and Carolinians were seen as a primitive, indolent, and intransigent "savages" with "barbarous customs" at the fringe of the empire.[89] They did not grant Micronesians the "privilege" of being Japanese imperial subjects (*Nihon teikoku shimmin*) as they did for the Okinawans and Koreans.[90] The Japanese regarded South Seas Islanders (*Nanyo tomin or dojin*) as less culturally advanced than the other minorities in part because they were not

Koreans in Japanese Marianas, c. 1930s. Courtesy Don A. Farrell.

East Asians. The colonizers used a number of derogatory epithets to label Micronesians, including darkies (*kuronbo*) and raw savages (*seiban*).[91] They believed the Carolinians were the most inferior people in the islands.[92] The Japanese Government stated in a letter to the Mandates Commission, dated 21 July 1927, "It is a fact that Chamorro tribes are generally more advanced in civilization than Kanaka [Carolinians], but this is only relatively true, even Chamorros being very backward as compared with civilized people."[93]

The Japanese considered Micronesians to be an economic liability to their administration. The government and companies did not rely on Chamorro and Carolinian labor because of the large Japanese, Okinawan, and Korean immigrant populations. The industrial agriculture system and import shipping network also made trade for tropical products and food with islanders unnecessary. The government expressed little concern over the shrinking Chamorro and Carolinian influence in the Marianas.[94] According to Peattie, "Outnumbered, unable to compete economically, their language, customs, and cultural identity submerged beneath those of the Japanese, the Micronesians on many of the islands might not have survived the century as an identifiable ethnic group had not the Pacific War brought a sudden and dramatic end to the Japanese presence."[95] Shigekazu Fujimoto, an official in the Department of Home Affairs, South Seas Government, stated, "The policy of Nanyocho was scarcely concerned with islanders' problems."[96]

Some Burakumin, the largest minority group in the home islands, lived on Saipan and Tinian. The Burakumin experienced discrimination for being the descendants of feudal era workers in "impure" occupations associated with death and defilement (*kegare*), such as butchering, leather tanning, and undertaking. The Burakumin were mainland Japanese but were still looked down on as an inferior people. A Burakumin woman in the mainland recalled, "I cannot forget the discrimination I underwent in school. Often other children would tell me, 'Go away, you stink,' or they would say, 'That girl is from that village,' and would not include me in whatever they were doing." Another Burakumin woman recalled, "Schooling is ordinarily the most important and happiest time in a person's life. But my life was warped by elementary school ... all the children of the class said I was smelly and dirty.... The teacher too began to treat me differently than other children.... I would cry and cower in the corner."[97] A Burakumin man stated, "We were insulted as cow killers ... and called four-legged animals. No one would hire us."[98] The 1871 Edict of Emancipation (*Eta Kaiho Rei*) gave the Burakumin and other ethnic groups in Japan equal legal status, but they continued to face discrimination and exclusion because the family registration system (*koseki seido*) made it nearly impossible for them to hide their supposedly "polluted" heritage.[99] The Burakumin, far from the mainland and living among other ethnic groups, had a slightly more elevated status in the Marianas.

Okinawan, Korean, and Micronesian attitudes concerning Japanese from the mainland varied greatly and ranged from hatred to admiration. Many individuals readily embraced Japanese assimilation policies, and some even took measures to suppress their own cultures. Some Okinawans in the Marianas were actively involved in the Lifestyle Reform Movement (*Seikatsu kaizen undo*), which sought to reduce or eliminate non–Japanese, "inferior cultural traits."[100] Being or acting Japanese was seen as necessary to achieve greater social standings and wealth. Consequently, many accepted the Japanese and their way of life out of self-preservation or for means of advancement.[101] Many liked the progress, new technologies, and consumer goods that came with Japanese rule. Japan, as a modern power, brought the modern world to the Marianas; it greatly improved the economies and infrastructure of Saipan and Tinian. The Japanese administration was more capable of addressing public health concerns than the prior colonial administrations.[102] Living standards rose for nearly all with Japanese ascendancy in the islands. The Chamorro and Carolinian populations steadily grew during Japanese rule.[103] Micronesian families that leased their land to the South Seas Government or private companies prospered.[104] The Japanese administration granted subsidies to some Micronesians who raised cattle and pigs based on the South Seas Government's "Rules for the Encouragement of Stock-farming."[105]

Chamorro woman Lucia Aldan Duenas stated, "the living condition ... was very good during the Japanese administration."[106] Tamayama Kensuke, an Okinawan farmer who immigrated to Tinian, stated, "The difference in life between the homeland and Tinian was that all families had no anxiety regarding life in the islands. Women went to the Nanyo Kohatsu's *shuho* (canteen) at the end of each month by a bull cart and with a passbook. We could shop for vermicelli, miso, *shoyu* [soy sauce], *iriko* [anchovy], sugar, canned beef, and canned sardine, up to 25 yen. There was one *cho* of fallow field. We planted potatoes, taro, peanuts, gourds, and vegetables. There were banana and papaya trees around the house."[107] Victoria Akiyama, whose father was Japanese and mother was Chamorro, recalled, "As a young girl, Saipan was my entire world.... I was happy. My world was defined, safe, and secure."[108] Chamorro girl Escolastica Tudela Cabrera stated, "Before the war during Japanese times things were peaceful."[109] Saipan schoolgirl Tatsu Sato wrote, the Japanese "loved the islands, linked hands with inhabitants and built up islands' prosperity."[110] Some Chamorros reportedly submitted petitions to serve in the Japanese military during the Second Sino-Japanese War (1937–1945), but the requests were denied because they were not imperial subjects.[111]

Despite the positive aspects of their colonial administration, the Japanese were never able to gain the loyalty of most of the people they ruled over because of discrimination, exploitation, and human rights abuses. They were foreign colonizers and ultimately regarded as such. The quality of life for minorities in the Marianas greatly diminished after the attack on Pearl Harbor. There was heightened police brutality against minorities, and the Japanese military used forced labor. Many non-Japanese thoroughly despised their colonial masters by the time the Americans invaded Saipan and Tinian in 1944.

The Japanese police (*keisatsu*), both the local and later military police, were often brutal in their treatment of ethnic minorities. They descended wherever they wished, made arrests based on rumors and suspicion, and tortured and even murdered civilian "dissidents" at times. Chamorro man Benigno Sablan stated, "Japanese policemen were really crazy."[112] Manuel T. Sablan, a Chamorro messenger boy for the police in the early 1940s, remembered the cruel treatment of Koreans. He recalled, "We had a lot of Koreans on Saipan. They were mostly laborers. Working at the police station, I was there when people were arrested and brought in. Many of them were Koreans who were rounded up at night. I don't know why they were arrested, but the police would beat them up."[113] Shintaro Yamamoto, a supervisor in the Police Affairs Section of the South Seas Government, stated that the "special secret police" in the islands were in charge of "regulating thought, anti-military activities, demagogy, rumor, and false report under an internal security law."[114] Carolinian-Chamorro schoolboy David Sablan stated, on Saipan in February 1944, "the Kempeitai came to our ranch early one morning and woke us all up. They took all the books out, tore them all up, slashed them with their bayonets and burned them ... they arrested my father, arrested my sister Maria, my uncle, Mariano Guerrero."[115] The police accused many in the family of being American spies, interrogated them, and imprisoned the father for two months.

Women of Saipan and Tinian

Japanese, Okinawan, Korean, and Micronesian women on Saipan and Tinian experienced sexism and were expected to fulfill the same gender role expectations foisted on women elsewhere in the Empire of Japan. Gender role ideology during the imperial era was based on both East Asian and western-modeled principles and practices of androcentrism and patriarchy, in which masculine interests were given priority, men held a disproportionately large share of power in society, and descent was reckoned in male lines. The ideology subordinated women to men and stressed separate spheres between the sexes; a man's sphere was the public and a woman's was the home.[116] Women were regarded as weak, covetous, indulgent, and in need of men's guidance and directions.[117] A number of women in the empire were victims of domestic violence but could do little to stop it. They were also devalued, excluded, and denied individual initiative, self-fulfillment, and the freedoms men had. No women were in the South Seas Government administration or Nanyo Kohatsu and Nambo management. They could only be secretaries, receptionists, and typists for male directors in these institutions.[118]

Women were expected to be chaste, modest, elegant, quiet, and obedient and had to display feminine virtue through many actions. According to social scientist Susan J. Pharr: "In the prewar period [Japanese] women showed deference to men of their own as well as of higher classes through the use of polite language and honorific forms of address, through bowing more deeply than they, walking behind their husbands in public, and in numerous other ways deferring to men. Ideally, in the extended family arrangement common before the war, a new bride coming into the house was expected to acknowledge her inferior status in a number of ritualized ways: getting up first in the morning, going to bed last at night, taking her bath only after all other family members had bathed, eating after other family members, and taking the least choice servings of food."[119]

Some Japanese men in the empire believed feminine deference was key to national social harmony and progress. Yutaka Hibino wrote in *The National Ideals of the Japanese People (Nippon shindo ron*, 1928): "A happy and orderly mutual relation be-tween husband and wife is of the essence of our national institutions and the foundation of our prosperity. That the husband should command and the wife submit, thus establishing the wholesome home and forming the healthy constituents of the nation, is the true teaching which our people can never afford to neglect.... The vigorous and unimpeded advance of our culture, the constant increment

Chamorro woman in gown on Saipan, c. 1930s. Courtesy Scott Russell, Northern Marianas Humanities Council.

of our wealth and power, our supremacy in the east, our equality with the other great powers, our imposing part upon the stage of human affairs all depend upon the establishment of a healthy home wherein husband determines and wife acquiesces."[120]

A female subject of the empire, including one in the Marianas, was expected to be, above all, a "good wife and wise mother" (*ryosai kenbo*). In accordance with ryosai kenbo, a phrase used by the Japanese Ministry of Education, women were supposed to marry, produce and raise children, complete domestic duties, frugally manage the household finances, and obediently serve their husbands and in-laws.[121] In addition to fulfilling the standards of ryosai kenbo, women on Saipan and Tinian supported their families as wage-earners by working in the islands' canefields, shops, schools, and hospitals. Many also worked as seamstresses, laundresses, and crafters from home. As historian Kathleen S. Uno notes, "neither lower-class urban women nor women in average and poor rural households could afford to specialize solely in reproductive work."[122] It was the wives of Saipan and Tinian's elite who often hired non–Japanese servants to complete domestic and reproductive work (childcare, cooking, washing, housekeeping, etc.). Yet, upper-class women were expected to serve their husbands by bearing children, entertaining house guests, directing servants, and managing home finances.[123]

When some of the men on Saipan and Tinian were conscripted for the war in China and later the Pacific, more responsibility fell on women in the islands to fulfill their duties as ryosai kenbo and income earners. According to scholar David C. Earhart: "During the war, women were expected to shoulder heavier responsibilities while continuing to honor conservative social values. A woman was a chaste wife, nurturing mother, diligent homemaker, and guardian of the family's spiritual well-being. Whenever her husband's work required assistance, she was a loyal helpmate in the fields or in the shop. She prided herself on always maintaining her gracious demeanor, whether at home or in public. She accepted these roles uncomplainingly; she was industrious and frugal as a homemaker, and selfless as a wife and mother."[124]

The imperial government used propaganda during the war years to reinforce women's roles that nurtured its "family-state ideology" (*kazoku kokkakan*) and benefited the empire. According to historian Yoshiko Miyake, it was believed that a "woman's role in preserving the family system was a crucial analogue to the male role of soldier fighting the 'sacred war' for the Japanese family-state ... the Showa version of the family-state ideology, in an attempt to preserve the cohesion of the family system, focused on the imagery of fecundity and warmth of blood relations associated with mothers. The popular image of a soldier fighting well to die calmly, encouraged by his benevolent mother, conveyed a pervasive message to the Showa people: Imperial Japan would exist forever as long as her family system continued."[125] Government publications that promoted this ideology included *The Cardinal Principles of the National Polity* (*Kokutai no hongi*, 1937), *The Truth of the Subject* (*Shinmin no michi*, 1941), and *The Guidelines for Home Education* (*Senji kateikyoiku shido*, 1942).[126]

Not all women in Japan and its colonies were passive victims of the empire. According to scholar Noriko J. Horiguchi, "Japanese women, despite their marginalization in Japanese society, emerged as active

Japanese woman with her child on Saipan, c. 1930s. Courtesy Scott Russell, Northern Marianas Humanities Council.

agents against and for the modern empire of Japan."[127] During the Asia-Pacific War, women on Saipan and Tinian served in government-sponsored patriotic societies and local neighborhood associations (*tonarigumi*). They raised money for the war effort and supported Japanese troops and their families through various morale-raising activities and community events. They made handicrafts and combat protection amulets, such as "companion or safeguarding dolls" (*imon ningyo*) and "thousand stitch belts" (*senninbari*), and arranged farewell ceremonies and parades for departing troops.[128] Greeting parties and events were also held for incoming officers and their men stationed in the islands or visiting. Following Pearl Harbor, the women of Saipan and Tinian organized air raid and firefighting drills, enforced wartime rationing and blackouts, and prayed for victory at shrines. In 1942, all women's patriotic associations in the empire were unified into the Great Japan Women's Association (*Dai Nippon Fujinkai*), which numbered some twenty million members.[129] The Imperial Rule Assistance Association in the South Seas Islands (*Nanyo gunto taisei yokusan-kai*), an organization for both men and women which sought to strengthen "nationalistic consciousness," had 58 branches in Micronesia in the early 1940s.[130] The association promoted frugal living and patriotic activities and events. The war opened up some opportunities for women. According to sociologist Chizuko Ueno, "it is clear that the female masses did not necessarily take a negative view of the war. Women's participation in the public sphere, made possible by war, was both exhilarating and brought with it a new identity for women."[131]

During the 1930s and early 1940s, women in Japan and its colonies were pressured to serve as the empire's "childbearing corps" (*kodakara butai*).[132] Reproduction was viewed as a patriotic duty, as it led to greater numbers of future soldiers and sailors, as well as workers for the wartime economy and colonists for expansion.[133] Population growth was associated with "the power of the state."[134] The imperial government spread propagandic slogans such as "Reproduce and Multiply" (*umeyo fuyaseyo*) and "Motherhood in the interest of the state" (*kokkateki bosei*).[135] Laws were introduced to support Japan's childbearing corps. The Mother-Child Protection Law (*Boshi hogo ho*) of 1937, the first maternal protection law introduced in the empire, provided economic and medical assistance for mothers.[136] The Japanese Ministry of Welfare's "Outline for Establishing Population Growth Policy" (*Jinko seisaku kakuritsu yoko*, 1942) stated that the birth rate in Japan and its overseas territories could be increased through the implementation of greater tax advantages for larger families, the incorporation of women's hygiene training and childbearing education in schools, and the improvement and growth of maternity hospitals.[137]

After producing children (new imperial subjects), women were responsible for nurturing, rearing, and socializing them in the home. They had to teach their children the Japanese language, customs, and manners and instill "Japan's national and imperial values in them."[138] Many women actively and, at times, aggressively supported these ideas. According to Horiguchi, while many women "voiced their opposition to the authoritarian regime, which restricted the space for women's activities by drawing certain boundaries," many others supported it and "associated their reproductive capacity with the power and growth of empire."[139] The government-sponsored Greater Japan Woman's Association for National Defense (*Dai-Nihon Kokubo Fujinkai*) stated in 1943, "It is the mother, not the father, who is the true spiritual center of the household. The mother is the one who experiences the pain of childbirth and raises the children. It is therefore no exaggeration to say that in fact the Japanese spirit is maintained and passed on by splendid mothers."[140]

Despite their importance to the nation, women of the empire had an inferior legal status compared to men. The Japanese Civil Code favored men in divorce, marriage, property rights, and other areas of family law, and the Penal Code punished women more severely for adultery.[141] The Public Peace Police Law (*Chian keisatsuho*) forbade women from membership in political parties and serving in public offices. The Universal Manhood Suffrage Law or General Election Law (*Futsu senkyo ho*) did not extend suffrage to women, and press laws stymied women's rights activists and autonomous women's groups.[142] Consequently, female participation in the policy-making process of the empire was limited.[143] Women had some routes that gave them more autonomy, but they were limited. According to Susan J. Pharr, "Society did offer a range of alternative role options to women. To become part of the demimonde (*mizu shobai*) of geisha, entertainers, and prostitutes ... to eschew normal family arrangements for a solitary life as a nun, a scholar, a writer, or the like—these were also possibilities.... But to elect or even consider these routes was hardly the normal course for the great majority of Japanese women."[144]

Prostitution was a prominent and conspicuous industry on Saipan and Tinian during the Japanese colonial period. Japanese overseas sex workers (*karayuki-san*) resided throughout the Asia-Pacific region during the imperial era. Between the mid-nineteenth century and the First World War, before the Marianas were in Japanese hands, Japanese sex workers were shipped southward to Hong Kong, French Indochina, British Malaya, the Dutch East Indies (Indonesia), the Philippines, the Torres Strait Islands, Australia, and elsewhere.[145] There were many crude labels for these women, including "obscene seller" (*inbai*), "woman in an ugly trade" (*shugyofu*), "woman of a dishonorable calling" (*sengyofu*), and "woman seller of laughter" (*baishofu*).[146]

The South Seas Government permitted prostitution in Micronesia between the 1920s and 1940s because it was already well-established in Japan and abroad and was believed to be beneficial to the islands' economies. It took in migrants' money that may have otherwise been shipped north to their families. Prostitutes were also regarded as necessary to satisfy the sexual desires of Japanese male colonizers expanding and strengthening the empire. There were many brothels on Saipan.[147] "Among the shops" of Garapan, historian Haruko Taya Cook states, "were 47 houses of prostitution, employing as many as 277 women, broken into two classes—31 *geisha*, with presumed artistic abilities, and 246 'sake servers'—divided by ownership and patronage among the different groups, each serving different economic, social, and ethnic clientele."[148] Chamorro man Henry Sablan Pangelinan stated, on Saipan, there was a "whore house using Korean ladies. They entertained Japanese nationals only."[149]

Similar establishments were on Tinian. According to Peattie, "By the 1930s every Japanese town in Micronesia had its *hana machi* 'flower quarters.' In Tinian Town, for example, women from the Japanese mainland graced the rooms of the Nantei (Southern Mansion), the Hassenso (Eight Thousand Grasses), and the Shogetsuro (Shining Moon Mansion); those who felt more at home in the company of Okinawan women could drop in at the Miharashi (Beautiful View), the Komatsu (Small Pine), or the Nangetsu (Southern Moon)."[150] In addition to brothels and geisha restaurants (*ryoriya*), there were "bars and pothouses where, amid fairly dingy surroundings, patrons knocked back glasses of *awamori*, a fierce brandy made from millet, served to them by barmaids (*shakufu*) who derived the greater portion of their income from prostitution."[151]

Some prostitutes were born on the islands in the late 1910s and early 1920s and went into the sex industry at a young age, while others were migrants. Those who chose to become prostitutes often did so to financially assist their impoverished and debt-ridden families, as well as themselves. At times, it was difficult for these women to send their earnings to their families, however, because brothel-keepers and proprietors charged them for food, rent, makeup, clothing, and other necessities. A number had to work off debts deceitfully forced on them. Some women found it liberating to be a prostitute, but many felt trapped in the exploitative and cruel system.

A number of the prostitutes on Saipan and Tinian were sex slaves. They were from poor farming and fishing families in rural Japan, Okinawa, and Korea, as well as the Pacific Islands; they were deceived or kidnapped by procurers in their communities or sold by their parents and shipped off to the Marianas. According to ethnohistorian James Francis Warren, many peasant families in East Asia during the period, influenced by patriarchal traditions, cared little about or even detested "a female child in an over-populated region … in difficult times, the production of every bowl of rice was a struggle. For rural farmers and fishermen survival was a primary, social, and individual goal. Thus for peasant families devoid of natural resources and with a profound, historical sense of vulnerability, the sale of a daughter, who was regarded anyway as an object to be invested in or sold, was the only guarantee of a future."[152] The number of prostitutes and sex slaves in the islands increased annually from 1914 to 1944 because of the continual population growth.

Sex workers experienced physical and psychological injuries. They were often abused by customers and mistreated by brothel-owners and their hired thugs. Proprietors, coveting maximum profits, forced them to serve men nearly every day of the year, even when they were ill and exhausted. Sexually transmitted diseases and other communicable diseases, such as tuberculosis, were rampant among sex workers. The South Seas Government required prostitutes to have annual physical examinations. It reported in 1936 that over 90 percent of prostitutes in the South Seas Islands had venereal diseases.[153] The Mandates Commission questioned why there were so many prostitutes on Saipan and expressed concern about the increasing incidence of sexually transmitted diseases in the islands.[154] The prostitution industry reduced worker productivity in the Marianas due to its role in spreading weakening pathogens. Decreased productivity and increased government and private company expenses on public health and medical services, particularly concerning the import of medicines, was bad for the South Seas Government economy and may have outweighed the profits made from the industry. The diary entry of a young woman sold to a brothel in the Yoshiwara "pleasure district" of Tokyo in the 1920s provides insights about the anguish of some prostitutes in the empire. She wrote:

> Whose fault is it that I am in this despicable state? It is the broker's fault! He took advantage of my naivete and slyly talked me into this situation. But I am also disgusted at my own stupidity. I hate myself! After I came to this place and, as the true state of things became clear to me, I realized that what I had feared was in fact a reality. I then tried to leave, but it was no longer possible.... I can't run away.... I tried to resign myself to the situation by telling myself that this was my fate. But I couldn't resign myself to my plight. I became desperate. I tried to kill myself. But I held back because I had to think about my feeble mother and young sister. All during this past week, I have been in a state of despair. My mind has been so full of desperate thoughts that I nearly collapsed several times. I kept telling myself, "I must kill myself, I must kill myself," and wrote endless numbers of suicide notes.[155]

4

The Asia-Pacific War and Islands' Militarizations

The war in which the mass suicides on Saipan and Tinian occurred had deep roots. Long before the attack on Pearl Harbor, the United States and Empire of Japan contemplated and prepared for a conflict between each other over the mastery of the Pacific. "Few wars in American history," historian Ronald H. Spector states, "had been so long anticipated, so long planned for."[1] As early as the 1890s, American and Japanese military and political circles began discussing and theorizing a war in the Pacific. Tensions first arose between the two nations when the United States expanded and took territories in the Asia-Pacific region. In 1898, the Empire of Japan protested the United States annexation of Hawaii, where Japan had tens of thousands of subjects and commercial interests, as well as the American takeover of the Philippines and Guam.[2] At the time, Japan's main geopolitical interests laid to the west in Korea, however, and grievances faded.

In 1905, Japan defeated the Russian Empire in the Russo-Japanese War (1904–1905) and proved itself as the leading military power in the Asia-Pacific region. After 1905, unofficial discussions and studies in America and Japan concerning a war for primacy in the vast region gave way to formal strategies. War Plan Orange, a collection of United States military contingency plans concerning a war with Japan, began to be formulated in 1906 and was officially adopted by the United States Joint Army and Navy Board in 1924.[3] In 1907, the IJN designated the United States as a theoretical enemy in the Imperial National Defense Policy (*Teikoku kokubo hoshin*) and developed a war plan to destroy the United States Pacific Fleet known as "a general plan for the employment of the empire's forces" (*Teikoku yohei koryo*).[4]

Relations between the two powers were somewhat precarious in the second decade of the twentieth century. In 1907 and again in 1913, there were minor war scares from anti–Japanese sentiment and legislation in the United States, particularly in California.[5] After the IJN's seizure of German Micronesia in 1914, the United States became apprehensive about the defense of its possessions west of the Territory of Hawaii. As one scholar described it, "the Marianas curved menacingly down toward the lone American naval station at Guam; the Carolines and Marshalls lay strewn like caltrops across the path of any American force moving toward the Philippines."[6] Japan, on the other hand, was concerned with the growing American naval presence south of Okinawa Prefecture. Washington was stationing more warships in the Asia-Pacific region and the opening of Panama Canal on August 15, 1914, enabled it to transfer ships from the Atlantic to the Pacific hastily. Tensions also grew from rows concerning the Republic of China's sovereignty and territorial rights. In 1915, Japan forced its "Twenty-One Demands" (*Taika nijuikkajo yokyu*) on China to increase its dominance in continental Asia beyond Korea. The United States, which worried about an expanding Japan, strongly denounced the action. Disputes were not settled until diplomatic concurrences, such as the Lansing-Ishii Agreement of 1917, were made.

In the 1920s, relations between the two countries were amicable. The era of "Taisho Democracy" in Japan and the non-interventionism movement in the United States engendered military arms reduction and the signing of peace treaties during the decade. Some minor tensions arose from America's opposition to the Racial Equality Proposal during the Versailles Peace Conference in 1919 and its enactment of the Asian Exclusion Act in 1924, but strong diplomatic and trade ties eclipsed these. At the Washington Naval Conference (1921–1922), Japan and the United States, among other powers, agreed to limit the production of capital warships, respect the "status quo" in the Asia-Pacific region, and honor the Republic of China's rights as a sovereign nation and its territorial integrity with the signing of the Washington Naval Treaties. On February 4, 1922, Japan signed the Shantung Treaty with the Republic of China, which restored China's sovereignty over the Shantung Peninsula. That same month, the United States, which did not join the League of Nations, officially recognized Japan's South Seas Mandate in return for American "free access" to Yap and its communication stations with the signing of the Yap Treaty on February 11.[7] Immediately after the Great Kanto Earthquake in September 1923, which killed over one hundred thousand people, the United States provided substantial relief aid and supplies to Japan. On August 27, 1928, Japan, the United States, and numerous other countries signed the Kellogg-Briand Pact, in which signatories agreed to the "renunciation of war as an instrument of national policy."

The harmony of the 1920s did not continue into the following decade. Influential Japanese militarists and expansionist led their country into war with the support of many ordinary Japanese.[8] High-level officials and prominent pacifists and moderates who did not were threatened or assassinated. On September 18, 1931, the Imperial Japanese Army (IJA) Kwantung Army group manufactured a bombing on the Japanese-controlled South Manchuria Railway near Mukden, known as the Manchurian Incident (*Manshu jihen*). The Kwantung Army used the ploy as an excuse to invade Chinese Manchuria and rapidly conquered the region. To the south, between January 28 and March 3, 1932, in a small conflict known as the Shanghai Incident, the Imperial Japanese Military (IJM) invaded Shanghai and drove out forces of the Republic of China National Army. On March 1, 1932, the Japanese established the puppet state of Manchukuo in Manchuria.[9] The invasion and occupation of Manchuria violated treaties and pacts the empire signed and ratified in the decades prior. In 1933, Japan withdrew from the League of Nations because of the intergovernmental organization's condemnation of the conquest of Manchuria. The United States did not recognize Manchukuo but also did not do anything to threaten or challenge the empire.

In December 1934, Japan abrogated the Washington Naval Treaty, and in January 1936, it left the Second London Naval Disarmament Conference, thus enabling the empire to initiate unrestrained naval armament.[10] In 1937, the IJA invaded China after the Marco Polo Bridge Incident. The IJA poured into eastern China and conquered one city after another. The Japanese captured Tianjin and Peking (Beijing) in July and Shanghai in November. The Chinese Army retreated to Chungking in southwest China. In December 1937, Nanking, the capital of the Republic of China, fell. Japanese officers and soldiers raped and tortured many Chinese women and girls and killed great numbers of civilians in the Nanking Massacre or "Rape of Nanking." The Americans were outraged by Japanese atrocities and unrestrained territorial aggrandizement in China and did not remain taciturn. In July 1938, the United States government called for an unofficial "moral embargo" on Japan by requesting American manufacturers to halt the sale of aeronautical equipment, raw materials, and technical information that would provide "material encouragement" for the empire's war in China.

In 1940 and 1941, relations between America and Japan rapidly deteriorated. In January 1940, the United States terminated the 1911 Treaty of Commerce and Navigation with the empire, thus opening the way for the imposition of true trade embargoes on the Japanese.[11] In May 1940, the United States Pacific Fleet was relocated from San Diego to Pearl Harbor to act as a deterrent to Japanese aggression in Southeast Asia and the Pacific.[12] In July, the United States passed the Export Control Act, which forbade American manufacturers from selling equipment and materials necessary for war to Japan or other nations. In September, the United States, in opposition to the Japanese occupation of northern French Indochina, placed a steel and scrap metal embargo on Japan. Later that September, the Empire of Japan signed the Tripartite Pact with Nazi Germany and Italy. In July 1941, the Japanese occupied the southern half of French Indochina. Japan was at the doorstep of all of Island Southeast Asia. Japanese-controlled and -militarized territories surrounded the Philippines.

The United States, fearing future Japanese expansion and losing hegemony in the Pacific, retaliated after the occupation of southern French Indochina by freezing Japanese assets in the United States, which effectively ended all trade between the two countries; Japan's oil supply from the United States was cut off. The British and Dutch also restricted the export of oil, tin, and rubber, among other materials, to Japan from their colonial possessions.[13] Australia and New Caledonia reduced sales of metals. America and its allies could afford to be tougher on Japan and more inflexible than in prior years because the empire's ally, Nazi Germany, was locked in a war with Soviet Russia and less of a threat to the British Isles.[14] Japan needed oil and other imports to fuel its war machine and complete the conquest of China. In the fall of 1941, Japan and the United States attempted to ameliorate deteriorating relations through diplomatic meetings but could not reach a peaceful settlement. The Japanese would not accept American demands to end the war in China and withdraw their military. In late 1941, the emperor authorized the attack on Pearl Harbor.

Militarization of the Japanese Marianas

The Empire of Japan, following its conquest of Manchuria in 1932 and withdrawal from the League of Nations in 1933 (effective in 1935), redesignated the Inner South Seas Islands (*Uchi Nanyo* or *Nanyo Gunto*) from a mandate to a Japanese territory and administered it as it pleased. The IJN, with the support of the ministries of Japan and the emperor's approval, desired to use the islands as springboards for "national and economic expansion" into Island Southeast Asia and Melanesia.[15] The IJN believed its increased activities in Micronesia and beyond would elevate its influence and enable it to grow; it was always competing with the IJA for endorsement of its strategies and funding from Tokyo. The IJN wanted larger fleets and highly developed bases to "secure mastery of the Western Pacific" against the growing threat of the United States.[16]

Beginning in 1933, the IJN conducted major military exercises in the Marianas.[17] In 1936, the Ten-year Development Plan of the South Sea Islands (*Nanyo Gunto kaihatsu jukkanen keikaku*), prepared by the Japanese Ministry of Overseas Affairs' investigative committee at the request of the IJN, was initiated. The plan was implemented in order to transform Micronesian islands into advanced military support bases for the eventual takeover of the Outer South Seas (*Omote Nanyo* or *Soto Nanyo*) area, particularly the Dutch East Indies and New Guinea.[18] The Yokosuka Naval Civil Engineering Department (*Kaigun kenchikubu*) and the semi-governmental South Seas Colonization Company (*Nanyo Takushoku Kabushiki Kaisha*) constructed airfields, airway beacons, communication facilities, and weather stations on Saipan and Tinian and improved the islands' harbors and shore facilities.[19] The development plan also promoted the growth of tropical industries (agriculture, fishing, mining, etc.).[20] The South Seas Government Tropical Industries Research Institute (*Nettai Sangyo Kenkyujo*), headquartered in the western Carolines and with branches on Saipan and Ponape, conducted research and prepared reports for the IJN that would aid in the future economic development of conquered islands.[21] In the early 1940s, periphery and insular development initiatives were accelerated because of deteriorating relations with the United States.[22] In 1940, the Greater East Asia Co-Prosperity Sphere (*Daitoa Kyoeiken*), was declared. *Daitoa Kyoeiken* was an expansionist concept that called for the unification of Asian and Oceanic countries and territories, including the South Seas Islands Territory, under Japanese leadership to resist the western powers.

In the late 1930s, the IJN, with Tokyo's authorization, began stationing troops in the South Seas Islands. In 1937, it established seaplane stations in the Marianas and Carolines. In November 1939, the IJN 4th Fleet was deployed to the territory. The fleet was headquartered at Truk Lagoon, in the central Carolines, and had ancillary bases in the Marianas and Marshalls. In December 1940, the 5th Special Base Force of the IJN 4th Fleet, comprised of Naval Land and Guard Forces units, was sent to the Marianas.[23] In late 1941, Saipan was used as a staging area for the Japanese invasion of American Guam. After the attack on Pearl Harbor and capture of Guam, the IJN integrated itself into the South Seas Government administration. In late 1943, it assumed absolute control of Micronesia and began the "Military Administration of the South Sea Islands" (*Uchi-Nanyo gunsei*).[24] Between 1940 and early 1944, the 5th Special Base Force was tasked with maintaining the security of the Marianas from its headquarters on Saipan. The force numbered approximately 919 troops and 220 civilian contractors in 1943 and increased to 1,437 men by early 1944. In September 1943, approximately 1,500 men of the Yokosuka 1st Special Naval Landing Force were also stationed on Saipan, bringing the total number of troops to about 2,717.[25]

The early events of the war greatly affected civilian lives on Saipan and Tinian. Within six months of Pearl Harbor, the Japanese expanded their empire by taking the Philippines, Hong Kong, Singapore, Malaya, the Dutch East Indies, Burma, Borneo, New Britain, Bougainville, and the Gilberts, among other islands and territories in the Asia-Pacific region. However, the rapid conquests and territorial enlargement were not entirely advantageous to Japan; many IJM officers stated after the war that the empire became too large to supply and defend. Furthermore, although the Japanese achieved a strategic victory at Pearl Harbor, major errors were made; namely, that the United States aircraft carriers in the Pacific were out of port when they attacked the base. This mistake led, in part, to the disastrous Japanese naval defeat at the Battle of Midway, over 2,500 miles northeast of the Marianas, in June 1942.

In August 1942, the Americans invaded the southern Solomon Islands in Melanesia. Over the following months, they drove back the IJN and defeated ground forces there. The United States established naval supremacy in the Pacific by 1943. It was wealthier and more industrially and scientifically advanced and was able to build more and typically better ships than Japan. American submarines menaced and sunk Japanese naval and merchant marine vessels throughout the Pacific, including those heading to and leaving the Marianas.[26] Between the summers of 1942 and 1944, food imports to the Marianas and fishing catches drastically decreased because of unrestricted American submarine warfare and problems from overextended supply lines in Japan's massive empire. Kakuichiro Murayama, an agricultural specialist in the Tokyo Liaison Office of the South Seas Government, stated, "Though pigs, cows, chickens and other livestock were constantly sent by ship, many of them were sunk by U.S. attacks."[27] Some of the food supplies that were shipped southward for the people of Saipan and Tinian had to be diverted to Guam, Pagan, Rota, and the smaller islands in the Marianas, as well as other island groups in Micronesia and Melanesia.

The reduction of crucial shipments from the north, which Saipan and Tinian's populations relied on during the entirety of the Japanese colonial period, led to a food crisis in the islands and a rationing system had to be introduced. The presence of the IJN 5th Special Base Force and later other military units exacerbated the crisis. Military personnel were given priority in receiving foodstuffs, and many animals (cows, pigs, chickens, etc.) in the islands were butchered to feed sailors and soldiers.[28] Officers and enlisted men also seized or stole food from civilians. Saipan civilian Dave Sablan, recounted, "There was nothing to eat anymore. That which had grown on the farm, like bananas, sweet potatoes, and other things … was all taken by the Japanese. It was taken because the soldiers themselves were hungry."[29] Additionally, civilians were having difficulty producing subsistence crops. The islands' best farmlands were heavily depleted of minerals and nutrients from the overfarming of sugarcane.[30]

The IJN mobilized Saipan and Tinian's civilian populations for food production. It demanded the large-scale planting of rice crops in the archipelago, but the results were unsatisfactory because of insects and other environmental factors.[31] In late 1943, a number of the islands' canefields were replaced with hardy tropical crops, including corn, bananas, sweet potatoes, cassava, and taro, following the enactment of the "Outline of Food Policies for the South Sea Islands" (*Nanyo Gunto shokuryo taisaku yoko*).[32] That same year, shopkeepers were forced to close their stores and work in military-directed food production and livestock breeding and husbandry programs with the institution of the "Industrial Reorganization Plans" (*Sangyo seibi keikaku*).[33] In February 1944, food production efforts were maximized through all possible means in preparation for a "decisive battle" with the enactment of the "Outline of Urgent Countermeasures for Supplementing Munitions Provisions in the South Sea Islands" (*gunju shokuryo kinkyu taisaku yoko*).[34] Though the reforms had mainly positive results, the military and civilian populations in the Marianas were too large to support on local produce and livestock alone. As a result, malnutrition was a major problem that lasted through the American invasions.

Micronesians and imperial subjects on Saipan and Tinian were required to complete forced labor (*kyosei rodo*) based on the National Mobilization Law (*Kokka sodoin ho*, 1938), the Order for Labor Coordination (*Rodo chosei rei*, 1941), the Order for National Labor Services Cooperation (*Kokumin kinro hokoku kyoryoku rei*, 1941), and the Order for Laborers Notebook (*Romu techo rei*, 1942).[35] Civilian men, women, and children were ordered to take part in the construction of air and naval defense facilities and fortifications. Chamorro schoolgirl Escolastica Tudela Cabrera recalled that the Japanese used children to carry sandbags for the building of an airfield.[36] IJN Sailor Genkichi Ichikawa, who oversaw the construction of defensive positions on Tinian, wrote in his diary in February 1944, "Children and civilians work hard with sweat under the strong sunshine, with pickaxes. The trench for our paratroopers is constructed."[37] Forced labor on military projects and defenses led to crop neglect, which deepened the food crises.[38] Furthermore, new airfields, roads, and military facilities took up good farmland on the islands. In addition to construction projects, girls and women were forced to work for Japanese officers as maids, cooks, and secretaries.[39] These women were vulnerable to sexual assault and rape.

The Japanese also used forced labor for mining activities in the Marianas. According to historian Wakako Higuchi: "The Pacific War required Japan to obtain metals to modernize, expand and mechanize the military, particularly the air force. The Outline for Economic Policies for the Southern Areas [*Nanpo keizai taisaku yoko*] stated, 'Existing mining facilities shall be exploited as rapidly as possible, after which the development of new mines … shall be promoted.' Specialists prospected for minerals, particularly nickel, mica, bauxite, copper, phosphate, and manganese…. The search for mineral resources had boomed in the South Sea Islands since the late 1930s … deposits of phosphate rock and marble (on Saipan, Tinian, and Rota) and manganese and soapstone (on Saipan) were found in the Marianas."[40] Chamorros were also forced to collaborate and work with the secret police and military. Chamorro civilians and constables were required to serve as scouts, interpreters, and officer assistants during the Japanese invasion and occupation of Guam.[41] There were other Saipan Chamorros who covertly aided and protected Guam Chamorros against the Japanese.[42]

A number of Japanese military personnel treated civilian laborers cruelly. "When the fighting started," Escolastica Tudela Cabrera stated, "the Japanese became mean. We became like slaves-forced labor…. They would come to our farm and take whatever they wanted. If we protested they would threaten us."[43] Carolinian schoolboy Felipe Iguel Ruak recalled that the Japanese made his father Jesus Ubet Ruak, a forced laborer on Saipan who ran away from Aslito Airfield when an American airplane was spotted, "put his hands on top of his head, then they hit him with long sticks. My father fell down; his ribs were broken. He stood up and they slapped him around some more…. He died early one morning just before the Americans landed."[44]

While forced labor projects were underway, the battlefront was nearing Saipan and Tinian. The Japanese military incurred several losses in the Pacific in 1943. It was defeated in the Solomons, Aleutians, and Gilberts that year and was suffering military setbacks in and off New Guinea. In late 1943, the Japanese High Command designated an "Absolute Inner Defensive Line" or "Absolute National Defense Sphere" (*Zettai Kokuboken*) and commanded it to be maintained at all costs. The United States Army's official history of the Pacific War states:

> The selection of a new defense line was based on the most careful calculation of Japan's resources and Allied capabilities. Extending from the Kuril Islands southward through the Bonins, Marianas, and Carolines, thence south and west to western New Guinea, the Sunda Islands in the Netherlands Indies, and finally to Burma, this line comprised the minimum area considered essential for the attainment of Japan's war aims. Possession of this area would give Japan the advantage of interior

lines and the raw materials and food needed to meet military and civilian requirements. Since it corresponded also to the Greater East Asia Co-Prosperity Sphere, its security was an essential prerequisite to the political and economic control of the nations included within the Japanese orbit. Any reduction of the area, or the acquisition by the Allies of bases from which to strike important political and industrial targets within it, was bound to affect seriously Japan's political position and capacity to wage war.[45]

In 1944, as part of the empire's new strategy, the Marianas were to be heavily fortified to thwart the American advance in the Pacific and exact heavy casualties. War correspondent Robert Sherrod wrote, "The Tokyo war lords hoped that their bitter-end fighters might make the Pacific war expensive enough to cause Americans to recoil from their casualties, to be willing to settle for something less than unconditional surrender."[46] In the late spring of 1944, the Japanese military and civilian forced laborers built numerous reinforced concrete blockhouses, pillboxes, trenches, and cave defenses and emplaced heavy weapons throughout Saipan and Tinian within a surprisingly small time frame.[47] Tens of thousands of troops were successfully transferred to the two islands to hold them. IJM officers were unable to complete defense preparations in the Marianas before the invasions but made do with what they had and were willing to sacrifice themselves, their men, and even civilians to repel the Americans and protect their nation and empire.

A United States Navy intelligence report, dated 24 May 1944, stated: "It is known that the Japanese have organized certain civilian personnel into 'Home Guard' units on Saipan and Tinian. The training or efficiency of these units is not known but such a move on the part of the enemy clearly indicates that he is preparing to defend his bases in the Southern Marianas in the near future with all available strength at his disposal. Due to the large Japanese civilian population on Saipan and Tinian and the Japanese policy of utilizing the services of all able bodied males, our troops can expect to encounter strong opposition from this source initially as well as from Japanese combat troops."[48]

The IJA and IJN jointly defended the Marianas. IJA Lieutenant General Saito Yoshitsugu and IJN Vice Admiral Chuichi Nagumo commanded approximately 29,660 troops (22,700 IJA soldiers and 6,960 IJN sailors) on Saipan. IJA Colonel Ogata Kiyochi and IJN Captain Goichi Oya commanded approximately 9,162 troops (5,052 IJA and 4,110 IJN) on Tinian.[49] The Japanese Army units on Saipan and Tinian were part of the IJA 31st Army, while Navy units were part of the IJN Central Pacific Area Fleet. Many of the officers and units had combat experience and fought in China or the early naval battles of the Pacific War. In the spring of 1944, in the final months before the American invasions, civilian homes, stores, factories, and other buildings were seized for military purposes.[50] On Saipan, Saito's headquarters was located in the Chalan Kanoa schoolhouse and later the mountains.[51] The Nanyo Kohatsu assisted the military. According to historian Yumiko Imaizumi, "Specifically, NKK offered its farmland, transportation services, buildings, facilities, medical institutions, employees and farmers to the Japanese Army. On the other hand, the Japanese Army exploited NKK's entire personnel/farmland organizations and labor management system, and supervised, managed and gave orders to the members of those organizations while compensating NKK for the loss caused by the discontinuation of business to help them stay afloat."[52] Many Japanese, Okinawan, and Korean civilian men on Saipan and Tinian were conscripted into military support or home guard units.[53]

There were Koreans in the Japanese military in the Marianas.[54] Most were conscripted military laborers, while some were enlisted. Koreans were able to enlist in the

IJA with the promulgation of the Army Special Volunteer System Law (Imperial Ordinance No. 95) in 1938 and the IJN with the Navy Special Volunteer Law (Imperial Ordinance No. 608) in 1943.[55] In 1943, Japan's Military Service Law (*heieki-ho*) was revised, and the conscription of Korean men began in 1944.[56] Korean men were in Naval Guard Force (*Keibitai*) "Establishment Sections" of the 5th Special Base Force, IJN 4th Fleet in the early 1940s.[57] Just before the Battles of Saipan and Tinian, the IJN shipped thousands of Koreans in Naval Civil Engineering and Construction Units (*Kaigun Kenchiku Shisetsu Butai*), Pioneer Units (*Setsueitai*), and tunneling companies (*Suidotai*), all commanded by Japanese officers, to the islands to partake in fortification efforts.[58] The IJA also brought in Korean laborers. According to historian D. Colt Denfeld, "The Japanese Army had six types of labor units: Land Duty Companies (Rikujo Kimmu Chutai) that built roads and bridges; Sea Duty Companies (Kaijo Kimmu Chutai) that loaded and unloaded ships; Construction Duty Companies (Kenchiku Kimmu Chutai) that erected barracks, shops, and hospitals; Labor Units (Sagyo Tai) that assumed the more manual labor tasks and sometimes farmed; Mobile Lumber Squads (Ido Seizan Han) used to clear the jungles; and Airfield Construction Units (Hikojo Settei Tai)."[59] Although most Koreans on the islands were attached to non-combat units, their commanders still ordered them to fight during the battles, and many died.[60] In addition to Korean laborers, there were "contract coolies of the Sankyu Corporation, recruited entirely from Okinawa Prefecture" in the Marianas.[61] A very small number of Taiwanese and Chinese were sent to the islands as laborers as well.[62]

IJM officers also oversaw several civilian paramilitary and volunteer corps (*teishintai*) for adults on Saipan and Tinian. These groups mainly performed construction and combat support assignments. Children and young men and women, referred to as "junior citizens" (*shokokumin*), were organized into patriotic organizations and labor parties. Marine Lieutenant Robert Sheeks, a Language and Intelligence Officer who served on Saipan and Tinian, wrote that in the Marianas,

> the military Air Defense Headquarters had under it two civilian organizations, the *Keibodan* and the *Kanshitai*. The first was not unlike an association of air-raid wardens, trained in fire-fighting and first-aid and responsible for transmission of raid warnings. The second was composed largely of young men who manned observation posts for spotting enemy planes and ships. There were two youth organizations, the Young Men's Corps and Young Women's Corps, enrollment in which was greatly increased by the direct threat of war. These were open to Japanese between the ages of fifteen and twenty-five who were taught some close-order drill, the use of the rifle and lance, and the manning of observation posts. An organization called the *Kinrohoshi*, a patriotic labor group which worked at stevedoring, road-building, airfield construction, and other manual labor "without pay for the Emperor," grew rapidly after the attack, although its original members had been donating a day each week for construction work for some months prior to the first bombing.[63]

Protecting the islands' civilians was not a priority for the IJM, and some Japanese troops raped women and girls on Saipan and Tinian during the militarization of the Marianas. Nanyo Kohatsu businessman Shinozuka Yoshitaro wrote in his memoir *Record of the Last Days on Saipan* (*Saipan saigo no kiroku*, 1951) that a number of Japanese officers and their men treated women in the islands "with the same attitude that had laid waste to occupied China."[64] Civilian men, he explained, had to protect women from "soldiers' unwanted attention."[65] Chamorro schoolgirl Marie Soledad Castro recalled, "In 1943 the Kaigun-Japanese Navy-came to Saipan. The sailors flooded the streets. All we could see in the streets of Garapan were white uniforms. Many of them were drunk and came into houses looking for women. I was in our house with my mother, father, and older sister, Rosalia, when three of them came into our house. They asked my father, 'Are there any ladies here—young ladies?' When my father heard that he had us secretly go out the back door, and told us to go to my cousin's house."[66] Shintaro Yamamoto, a supervisor in the Police Affairs Section of the South Seas Government, stated that IJN sailors "behaved cruelly and harshly" in Micronesia.[67] Japanese occupation troops on Guam, many who were temporarily stationed on Saipan before being sent south, routinely rounded up and raped Chamorro women in the former American possession.[68] Henry Sablan Pangelinan, a Saipan-born Chamorro who served as an interpreter for the Japanese military police on Guam in the early 1940s, recalled when a female prisoner in the jail was repeatedly raped by Japanese officers.[69]

In the late 1930s and 1940s, the Japanese military shipped comfort women to the islands. In the early years of the Asia-Pacific War, the IJM established the military comfort women (*jugun ianfu*) sexual slavery system in occupied areas and imperial territories. The comfort women system somewhat mirrored the existing sex slavery system in Japan. According to historian Keith L. Camacho, "As part of a longer tradition of Japanese sexual slavery at home and abroad, the economic, logistical, and social dimensions of the comfort stations paralleled and imitated the Japanese sex industry."[70] IJA and IJN units had military brothels or "comfort stations" (*ianjo*) where girls and women, held against their will, were raped. Women from Korea, China, Taiwan, Japan, Southeast Asia, and the Pacific Islands were subjected to the terrible system.[71] The women experienced severe pain from the constant rape and were frequently assaulted and tortured. Many took narcotics, including opium and methamphetamine hydrochloride, to lessen their physical and mental suffering.[72] A great number of these enslaved women died during the war, particularly from diseases. Japanese troops sometimes murdered woman too infected or physically damaged to serve them.[73] Some comfort women also committed suicide to escape the anguish. Those who survived the war dealt with diseases, injuries, infertility, post-traumatic stress disorder, and ostracization for the remainder of their lives.[74]

The IJN and later the IJA established comfort stations on Saipan and Tinian.[75] Some of the stations were set up in rudimentary concrete buildings with small rooms that had "beds made from split palms, covered only with thin mattresses and lit by candles, under palm leaf thatch."[76] According to one scholar, "On Tinian Island there were sixty Japanese comfort women, housed in three-mat-sized rooms, in three barrack buildings.... Officers were rostered on Tuesdays, Thursdays, and Saturdays, and men on Mondays, Wednesdays and Fridays. Within each shift it was the custom to draw lots to determine the order of service. The women also attended officers' parties at night."[77] Some comfort women shipped to Micronesia, like sex slaves who arrived in the years and decades prior, were betrayed and sold by their parents. Shiro Okae, a South Seas Government official who oversaw the shipment and entry of comfort women into the territory, stated, "There had been many cases where young women had been sold by their parents for 500 or 600 yen and did not know that they were going to be prostitutes for the military. Each ship transferred 100 or 200 comfort women to Micronesia."[78] Suzuko Shirota was a comfort woman and comfort station bookkeeper in Taiwan and later on Saipan and other islands in Micronesia. When Suzuko was 14, her mother died and, three years later, she was sold by her father. She wrote, "I became, in name and reality, a slave. On Saturdays and Sundays, there would be a line and men would compete to get in. It was a meat market, with no feeling or emotion. Each woman would have to take 10 or 15 men.... If you died you were just thrown into a pit in the jungle. No one would tell your family. I saw this with my own eyes, this hell for women."[79]

Americans encountered comfort women during the Battles of Saipan and Tinian. Marine Lieutenant Dan Williams, a Japanese Language and Intelligence Officer, recalled an incident on Saipan where he came across some 20 comfort women:

> Our patrol had approached the entrance to a concrete bunker of the type the Japanese used for command centers, a possible location of code books, I thought. Soon after my call out, an unarmed Japanese sergeant came out with his hands up and said in perfect English, "My name is George, and I am from Honolulu." He said we could safely enter the bunker, as there were only women inside. To my amazement, the only occupants were dejected and miserable looking Asian "comfort women," about whom I had then never heard, forced to service the Japanese army. George, a Nisei in his early twenties, told us that he had been visiting Japan from his home in Honolulu at the time of Pearl Harbor, was drafted into the Japanese army, and that his current duty was being in charge of those "comfort women."[80]

Fortunately, the women, with Williams's help, were safely transported to Camp Susupe, the American civilian internment camp in southwestern Saipan, and survived the battle.

Marine Jack V. Gilbreath, 23rd Regiment, 4th Division, stated that on Saipan his unit captured "two young ladies.... Samoans apparently ... come to find out they were called comfort women. It's true that the Japanese had them and just denied that it ever existed."[81] Another Marine in the 4th Division who fought on Saipan and Tinian stated:

> I was an ardent souvenir hunter, always looking for swords or flags or other junk and sometimes getting shot at by Japanese. What I did find were hundreds of pictures. The Japanese were always big on photography. Some of these showed Jap soldiers with native girls before the place was destroyed. Found lots of packages of condoms too so there must have been some sexual activity.... One day I was on a truck going back to the beach to pick up cannon ammunition when we passed a prisoner compound. These were Chamorro natives who were being kept out of the combat area.... Anyway, one group of women was beating up on five or six other women. The MPs broke it up, and we asked them what was going on. They said the native women were attacking a group of Korean women who were "Japanese whores." These victims had no one to speak for them.[82]

Marine Sergeant Bill Miller wrote, in Garapan, Americans found "four or five geisha houses for Jap enlisted men.... Each was labeled for the type of personnel it had accommodated—the Jap caste system is thorough if nothing else. Geisha houses for officers were in another part of town."[83] Robert Sherrod wrote that he entered a destroyed "geisha house" in Garapan and saw "thousands of packages of venereal prophylaxis, and much cheap perfume."[84]

Marine Guy L. Gabaldon, 2nd Regiment, 2nd Division, happened upon Korean "comfort women" at Marpi Point on Saipan. He wrote, "The women see us and begin waving. I tell them to continue coming up.... As they reach the edge of the cliffs one of them shouts, 'Chosen saram. Chosen saram!' I immediately commence interrogating them. Her name is Cheuni and her friend is Pokushini.... Cheuni was about twenty-five years old and Pokushini about nineteen ... they were brought to Saipan from Korea by the Japanese military and forced into prostitution. The Japanese thought nothing of making whores out of the 'inferiors.'"[85]

PART 2: 1944

5

Saipan and Tinian Invasions

The American invasions of Saipan and Tinian were rooted in War Plan Orange (1924–1939) and the Rainbow Plans (1939–1941), which were United States military strategic contingency plans concerning a war with the Empire of Japan. The fate of the Philippines, where the largest American military bases and installations west of the Hawaiian Islands were located, was a major matter addressed in Orange and Rainbow. The war plans presumed that the Japanese would capture the Philippines, as well as Guam and smaller American islands in the Pacific, in the early stages of a war. The United States would then have to amass a large battle fleet, defeat the IJN in a decisive naval engagement, and recapture the Southeast Asian archipelago before forcing Japan to surrender.[1] Orange and Rainbow planners recommend a preliminary, step-by-step, Central Pacific drive through Micronesia, in which the United States would conduct amphibious landings and conquer the Marshalls, Carolines, and Marianas and use them as support bases.[2]

On December 8, 1941 (December 7 in the Hawaiian Islands), the Japanese invaded the Philippines and completed the conquest by May 1942. On December 10, they landed on Guam and captured it in less than a day. Guam was renamed the "Island of the Imperial Court" (*Omiyato*). In May 1942, the Japanese began occupying the southern Solomon Islands and constructing air bases there. The bases threatened supply lines and sea communications between the United States and Australia. Consequently, United States military strategists set aside operational plans against the Japanese military in Micronesia and focused on the capture and retention of Guadalcanal and neighboring islands in Melanesia.

In early 1943, following the United States' strategic victory in the Guadalcanal Campaign (August 7, 1942–February 9, 1943), the Americans began to contemplate the "road to Tokyo." There were two routes proposed, the planned Central Pacific drive and the newly envisioned Southwestern Pacific advance. The debate on which one to take was a "long and sometimes bitter conflict of strategic ideas, military interests, and personalities," mainly between upper-level Navy and Army officers.[3] The routes were deliberated in meetings of the Joint Chiefs of Staff (JCS) and Combined Chiefs of Staff (CCS) at the Casablanca Conference (code-named Symbol, January 1943), Third Washington Conference (Trident, May 1943), and Quebec Conference (Quadrant, August 1943).

Army officers, including General Douglas MacArthur, called for the complete bypassing of Micronesia and requested all resources be allocated instead to the invasions of the northern Solomon Islands and eastern New Guinea before the recapture of the Philippines.[4] They contended their route was superior as it would utilize nearby bases in Australia, New Zealand, and southern Melanesia and be supported by land-based aircraft.[5] Navy officers argued that the waters off the Solomons and up to the Philippines were too narrow and treacherous and that their growing fast carrier fleets would fare better in the open waters between Midway and the western Carolines.[6] They declared that within a six month period, dozens of Allied ships were sunk by the Japanese off Guadalcanal.[7] They also noted that the Japanese had achieved a tactical victory in the Battle of the Coral Sea the spring prior in May 1942, in which the carrier *Lexington* was sunk and the *Yorktown* was heavily damaged.

Navy planners believed the Central Pacific drive was necessary in order to (1) eliminate the Japanese garrisons and air forces between Hawaii and the Philippines; (2) force the IJN into a decisive naval engagement; (3) secure east-to-west supply lines and communications; (4) establish forward area refueling, supply, and hospital bases; (5) liberate the former American possession of Guam; (6) most importantly, capture the Marianas.[8] The Marianas sat closer to Tokyo than Allied air bases in southern China. The capture of the islands would enable United States Army Air Forces bombing groups, which had the new Boeing B-29 heavy bombers that could fly over 3,250 miles, to conduct raids on Japanese cities and industrial centers and safely return. American strategists deemed the bombing of the Japanese homeland an essential undertaking to defeat the Empire of Japan. A 1943 JCS Memorandum titled "Strategic Plan for the Defeat of Japan" (JCS 287/1, CCS 220) stated, "It is probable that the reduction of Japan's power and will to resist may only be accomplished by a sustained, systematic, and large-scale air offensive against Japan itself."[9]

Ultimately, President Franklin D. Roosevelt and the JCS, which held "jurisdiction over all matters pertaining to operational strategy" in the war, authorized both the Central Pacific and Southwest Pacific approaches and ordered a two-pronged offensive against Japanese forces in the Pacific.[10] The JCS consisted of Admiral William D. Leahy, Chief of Staff to President Roosevelt; Admiral Ernest J. King, Chief of Naval Operations and Commander in Chief of the United States Fleet; General George C. Marshall, Chief of Staff of the United States Army; and General Henry H. Arnold, Chief of the United States Army Air Forces. The two-direction advance they authorized confused the Japanese High Command and forced the empire to thinly spread its limited forces and resources throughout its vast southern holdings.

In late 1943, the Americans launched the Central Pacific drive with the initiation of the Gilbert and Marshall Islands Campaign (November 1943–February 1944). During the campaign, the United States invaded and captured Tarawa and Makin Atoll in the Gilberts and Kwajalein and Eniwetok (Enewetak) in the Marshalls. Several other islands in the chains, many of which were undefended or lightly guarded, were also taken. In November 1943, at the Cairo Conference (code-named Sextant), President Roosevelt authorized the seizure of the Marianas. The "Overall Plan for the Defeat of Japan" (CCS 417), a report prepared by CCS Planners and approved December 2, 1943, designated the capture of the Marianas as a "specific operation" for the defeat of Japan.[11]

On March 12, 1944, the JCS ordered Admiral Chester W. Nimitz, Commander in Chief of the United States Pacific Fleet (CINCPAC) and the Pacific Ocean Areas (CINCPOA), to commence the capture of Saipan, Tinian, and Guam on June 15, 1944.[12] Rota, Pagan, and the smaller islands of the archipelago were to be bombed and left to "wither on the vine." To the south, Truk and Rabaul, some of the most formidable Japanese military bases in the Pacific, were to be neutralized by air and sea and bypassed along with many other islands in the Carolines and off New Guinea. On May 1, the Navy announced, "Central Pacific Islands now under Japanese sovereignty will, when occupied, be administered under a military government to be established by the occupying forces."[13] The campaign for the seizure and initial occupation of the Marianas was code-named Operation Forager.

Admiral Nimitz had overall command of the Marianas Campaign. Under Nimitz, Admiral Raymond A. Spruance, Commander of the United States Navy Fifth Fleet, oversaw the invasions. Vice Admiral Richmond Kelly Turner, Commander Amphibious Forces Pacific and the Joint Expeditionary Force (Task Force 51), was personally responsible for the execution of the amphibious operations and the capture of the islands.[14] Under Turner, Marine General Holland M. Smith, Commander of Expeditionary Troops Pacific (Task Force 56), directed all ground forces on Saipan and Tinian.

The Northern Troops and Landing Force (NTLF, Task Group 56.1), a task group of Task Force 56 that comprised over 66,700 men in the 2nd and 4th Marine Divisions, the 27th Army Infantry Division, and several smaller combat and combat support units, was ordered to take the two islands.[15] The Southern Troops and Landing Force (STLF, Task Group 56.2) was responsible for recapturing Guam. All three divisions in the NTLF were combat experienced. The 2nd Division fought in the Battles of Tulagi, Guadalcanal, and Tarawa. The 4th Division fought in the Battle of Kwajalein. The 27th Army Division fought in the Battles of Makin and Eniwetok. The three divisions trained for the Marianas Operation and conducted rehearsal invasions in the Hawaiian Islands in the spring of 1944 following the seizure of the Marshalls. The NTLF departed Hawaii in late May and temporarily stopped in the Marshalls for final staging in early June.[16] En route to the Marianas, troops were told about the islands and studied reconnaissance photographs, charts, mosaics, and raised-relief terrain maps.[17] They were informed about Japanese defense structures and installations, booby traps, and the presence of large and potentially hostile civilian populations. They were explicitly warned to stay away from the women of Saipan and Tinian because of venereal diseases.[18] An island guide given to troops stated, "Gonorrhea is widespread among the natives and Japanese in this area. Syphilis also is present. It should be assumed that many women on the island are infected with one or both diseases, and contact with them must be avoided."[19] Tokyo Rose, Japanese female radio broadcasters who played popular American music and disseminated Japanese propaganda in English throughout the Pacific, both entertained and taunted the men as they made their way to the islands.[20]

The Americans conducted only two major bombing raids on Saipan and Tinian before their landing force arrived off the islands in June.[21] They did not want the Japanese to know Saipan was the next planned invasion in the Pacific. On February 22 and 23, 1944, carrier-based aircraft from the Fifth Fleet's Fast Carrier Task Force 58, a force composed of fifteen fast carriers, seven fast battleships, thirteen cruisers, and fifty-two destroyers, bombed and reconnoitered the Marianas.[22] Saipan and Tinian's airfields and harbors were the primary targets. The bombings and fighter sweeps in the two days eliminated most of the Japanese land-based air forces and killed military personnel and civilians.[23] Chamorro young man Gregorio C. Cabrera saw a Japanese child on Saipan killed from one of the bombs.[24] Saipan schoolgirl Victoria Akiyama stated, "One of my older brothers, Shiuichi, was killed during one of these air raids."[25] IJN Sailor Genkichi Ichikawa wrote in his diary, "There was a shower of bombs. Gun-fire attacked us.... The nearby sugarcane fields are burning.... I was disgusted with the damage of Tinian's streets by the enemy's air attacks."[26] In April and May 1944, smaller aerial photograph reconnaissance missions were carried out to obtain better intelligence about the islands.[27]

On June 11, 1944, the United States Navy initiated the pre-invasion bombardment of Saipan.[28] Many high-ranking IJM officers believed the Carolines would be invaded before the Marianas and were somewhat taken aback when the American fleet arrived off Saipan and Tinian in June.[29] For five days, carrier-based planes from Task Force 58 bombed and strafed the island before the landings. On June 13, seven fast battleships and eleven destroyers in Task Force 58 arrived and began shelling Saipan.[30] Tinian, because of its proximity to Saipan, was also bombarded. On the 14th, Admiral Turner's Joint Expeditionary Force, which consisted of seven old battleships, eleven cruisers, and twenty-six destroyers, joined the fast battleships.[31] The Japanese forces in the Marianas had little air cover and no fleet protection; costly naval and air battles in Melanesia and southwestern Micronesia reduced Japan's capability to strike back effectively. The Japanese garrisons defending the island were trapped.

The destruction of the preparatory bombardments was tremendous. Navy Sailor James J. Fahey, aboard the light cruiser USS *Montpelier*, wrote in his diary, "We did enough bombarding to last us a lifetime.... There are an awful lot of sore ears, the cotton and earplugs are no good.... In the daytime we fired low and point blank, but at night we fired higher and further into the shore. Hollywood could get some great pictures, it was like a movie. Big alcohol plants were blown sky high, assembly plants, oil storage plants, ammunition dumps, miles of sugarcane, buildings, railroads, trains, trucks, etc., not to mention the military side of the picture, such as thousands of troops, planes, tanks, airfields etc. Thick smoke miles high was all over the island."[32]

Japanese ammunition dump explosion on Saipan, June 1944. "FLOWERS THAT BOOM ON SAIPAN—Like a giant flower, this huge column of smoke rises skyward, blossoming at the top of this small tree." #83612. National Archives.

IJA Sergeant Yamauchi Takeo, 136th Regiment, 43rd Division, recalled, on Saipan, "Whole sections of the mountains were burned black and the island was dark with smoke."[33] Another Japanese soldier wrote in his diary that the bombardment was "too terrible for words."[34] Chalan Kanoa and Garapan were destroyed. IJA Soldier Taroa Kawaguchi, 43rd Division, wrote in his diary on Saipan, June 11, 1944, "Charan-Kanoa and Tinian area" were "burning terrifically."[35] United States Marines and Army Soldiers, who later entered the towns, noted the destruction. Army Major Kenneth J. Dolan, 105th Regiment, 27th Infantry Division, stated, "what had once been the proud little town of Charan Kanoa was nothing but a shambles with twisted wreckage everywhere. There were plenty of dead Japs all around and the odor of the dead was beyond description."[36] The sugar mill at Chalan Kanoa was in pieces. Correspondent Robert Sherrod wrote, "It was a mass of rubble, pounded by hundreds of tons of high explosives, its vats stinking in the sun and drawing millions of flies. The big smokestack had been pierced a thousand times, but it still stood. A smaller refinery next door was as completely wrecked."[37] Navy Corpsman Chester J. Szech, who was attached to the 6th Regiment, 2nd Marine Division, recalled, Garapan "was gone by the time we occupied it."[38] Marine Albert C. Torgerson, 2nd Division, stated, Garapan was "blasted out of existence.... It was no longer a town."[39]

Many civilians were killed in the pre-invasion bombardments. Taeki Lee, a Korean schoolboy on Saipan, recounted, during the first strikes, "one of my friends was killed while playing near the beach."[40] Chamorro young man Manuel T. Sablan recalled, "Victoria Tudela Borja was killed when an American plane strafed the house she was in ... found her lying there dead. On the way to Talofofo we saw dead people all over the place."[41]

Schoolgirl Victoria Akiyama and her family fled from Garapan to the Aslito Field area during the bombardments and hid under her maternal uncle's home. She recounted:

> I remember ... the house disintegrating and catching fire. My sister Teruko just disappeared. I never found any trace of her after that. I looked over to where my stepmother and baby brother were. His head was cracked open and his brains were hanging out. I am sure he was dead, but his lips were still moving as if sucking on his mother's breast.... I saw my aunt Carmen. She was dead.... Not far from her was my brother, Jose. He had a small hole in his chest, but when I rolled him over his back was shattered.... In the foxhole one of my cousins was praying. She was full of holes and blood kept spurting from her wounds.... I watched so many members of my family die that day. I saw another cousin with her stomach ripped open. She kept trying to push her intestines back in with her dirty hands.[42]

Many civilian contractors in the aviation, logistics, and telecommunication industries were killed in the bombardment. Seiichi Nii, a supervisor in the International Electronic Communication Company (*Kokusai Denki Tsushin Kabushiki*) on Saipan, stated, "the air attack of June 13, 1944 damaged almost all the facilities and almost all of the employees were killed."[43] "Saipan" (1944), a pamphlet written by intelligence officers and distributed to American troops aboard transport ships en route to the Marianas, stated, "We know that much suffering by unoffending people is necessary on military grounds. Many civilians have been killed in London and Berlin, and many will be killed in the bombings before we land on Saipan, in the good-sized towns of Garapan and Charan-Kanoa."[44]

The pre-invasion bombardment of Tinian lasted almost nonstop from June 11 to July 24 and was conducted by carrier aircraft, warships, and later Saipan-based artillery and land aircraft. Napalm, a new incendiary weapon developed in the United States in 1942, was used extensively.[45] Samuel Eliot Morison, who was aboard the light cruiser USS

Saipan aflame, June 1944. #84768. National Archives.

Honolulu, stated, "By nightfall 23 July the island no longer presented its former pleasant appearance of rural opulence. Numerous fires sent up billows of smoke; dust clouds hovered over spots where high caliber shells had exploded; Tinian Town was a shambles."[46]

Battle of Saipan (June 15–July 9, 1944) Overview

The Battle of Saipan lasted 25 days. The Saipan NTLF Operations Report stated, "It was fought over some of the most rugged, mountainous and jungle terrain encountered by U.S. forces in the Pacific."[47] Marine Sergeant Henry C. Michalak, 2nd Regiment, 2nd Division, stated, "That was a big island compared to what Tarawa was. Saipan had mountains on it, big mountains."[48] The canefields were also a problem for the Americans. Marine Lieutenant Frederic A. Stott, 24th Regiment, 4th Division, wrote, "Sugar cane proved a serious hindrance throughout the campaign. The majority of the fields had been fired by the planes and naval gunfire, but the burned stalks remained, and vision in such fields is limited to thirty yards and movement is greatly impeded."[49]

The Americans invaded Saipan on the morning of June 15, 1944.[50] Marines landed at the island's southwestern shore to the north and south of Chalan Kanoa and established a beachhead with air and naval support. The Japanese military resisted the landings with artillery, mortars, tanks, and machine gun, sniper, and small arms fire. They killed many Marines, who landed before Army Soldiers. Japanese artillery also hit some ships providing fire support and killed Sailors aboard.[51] The preinvasion bombardments did not destroy most of the Japanese artillery positioned inland, and the number of Japanese troops on Saipan surpassed American intelligence estimates.[52] Marine Joe E. Ojeda, 24th Regiment, 4th Division, stated, "The landing was disastrous.... There were slain Marines all around us. There were bodies and body parts all over, with everyone yelling for a corpsman."[53] Marine Lieutenant John C. Chapin, 24th Regiment, 4th Division, wrote, "All around us was the chaotic debris of bitter combat: Jap and Marine bodies lying in mangled and grotesque positions; blasted and burnt-out pillboxes; the burning wrecks of LVTs that had been knocked out by Jap high velocity fire; the acrid smell of high explosives; the shattered trees; and the churned-up sand littered with discarded equipment."[54] Marine Sergeant Jerome C. Wachsmuth, 6th Regiment, 2nd Division, stated, "There were guys in our company who said they just couldn't go anymore. If you say you weren't frightened you're lying."[55] Marine Ralph L. Browner, 2nd Regiment, 2nd Division, recalled, everyone was "scared shitless."[56] Marine Michael Gates, 23rd Regiment, 4th Division, stated, "Saipan was a bitch! I thought it was worse than Iwo Jima."[57]

The Marines held the beachhead despite strong enemy resistance. The Japanese conducted a major counterattack before dawn on June 16, but it failed. Marine Sergeant Harold F. Haberman, 2nd Special Weapons Battalion, 2nd Division, stated, "They told everybody to dig in and let the Japs come to us, and that's what we did."[58] The morning sunrise revealed approximately 700 dead Japanese in front of American lines.[59] Marine Richard Meadows, 6th Regiment, 2nd Division, stated, there were "bodies everywhere ... so much blood all over. It was really a gory mess."[60] During the day of June 16, the devastated town of Chalan Kanoa was secured. Soldiers in the 27th Army Infantry Division also began landing on the island, and they immediately witnessed the carnage. Benjamin H. Hazard, a Military Intelligence Service officer attached to the 27th Division, recounted, "The first day I was on Saipan there was the smell of fresh blood. The only time before this when I smelled massive amounts of fresh blood was when I was going to college and I went to slaughterhouses to get the placentas from dead pigs in order to extract hormones.... I never smelled it again after that first day because there was always the odor of dead bodies in the air."[61]

Before dawn on June 17, the Japanese conducted another large counterattack with many tanks. They were repulsed and lost hundreds of men and more than thirty tanks.[62] Marine Roy William Roush, 6th Regiment, 2nd Division, stated, "Japanese tanks were ... plain junk. They were nowhere near the type of tank our Shermans were or even the light tanks we had before that."[63] The Americans planned to seize the southern third of Saipan first. They spent the day fighting in the small hills, sugarcane fields, and coconut groves east of Chalan Kanoa and the "waist deep muck" of the swamp around Lake Susupe.[64] The 27th Division continued to be landed, and most of the Army Soldiers were ashore by the end of the day. On June 18, the Marines and Soldiers advanced inland. They came across pillboxes, blockhouses, zigzag trenches, boobytraps, landmines, spider holes, and tanks and captured Aslito Airfield and reached the eastern shore of the island.[65] The Americans rapidly repaired the airfield and landed planes needed to support assault troops. During June 19 and 20, while the fighting was raging in southern Saipan, the IJN

Smoldering tank and dead Japanese troops after June 16, 1944, nighttime counterattack. #84436. National Archives.

Mobile Fleet attempted to destroy the mightier United States Fifth Fleet west of Saipan in what became known as the Battle of the Philippine Sea or "Great Marianas Turkey Shoot." The Japanese lost three fleet carriers, two tankers, and hundreds of naval aircraft. The Japanese garrisons in the Marianas were on their own afterward. There would be no imperial reinforcements, resupply, or evacuations like the "Tokyo Express" operations in the Solomons and New Guinea.

By June 20, the Americans seized most of the southern third of Saipan, except Nafutan Point which was well defended and had difficult terrain.[66] An Army report stated, it "consisted of steep ridges, deep gulches with cliffs, ground broken with coral pinnacles, and thick jungle type underbrush which impeded progress and made observation impossible."[67] Many civilians were trapped in Nafutan with Japanese troops. Saipan was the first battle in which the Americans encountered large, concentrated civilian populations in the Pacific War. Some Japanese troops used women and children as human shields and decoys during the battle. Many Marines and Soldiers were saddened when they came across noncombatants in the middle of the fighting. The sight of civilians, particularly children, caught in the battle, correspondent Robert Sherrod wrote, "was enough to make a man weep."[68]

Marine Lieutenant Lewis Meyers wrote, "We knew we would find thousands of civilians beyond the beaches. But we did not count on meeting them in the midst of battle, especially the little children…. The most hardened troops react to the sight of a yawning

Civilians taking shelter beneath American amphibious vehicle on the Saipan beach, June 1944. #83978. National Archives.

baby awaking on the back of its dead mother. Or of another big-eyed infant twisting its head around to follow the flight of one of our Grummans down the bench. Marines, many with children at home and pictures in their wallets, find it hard to fit these kids into the battle. Throwing grenades at Japs is what we're there for, but you hate to find babies in the same holes and caves from which the Japs have been firing."[69]

The Marines and Soldiers steadily gained ground on Saipan, but Japanese troops constantly infiltrated their lines or were trying to do so. The Saipan NTLF G-2 (Intelligence) Report stated, on June 23, "One Jap was killed in the regimental CP [Command Post] of the 25th Marines" in the 4th Marine Division's zone of action.[70] The report stated that the following day, on June 24, the 2nd Marine Division killed "95 infiltrating Japs."[71] Hand-to-hand combat occurred throughout the battle. Marine Frank W. Borta, 8th Regiment, 2nd Division, recalled, "One night a Jap jumped into my foxhole. I saw that he had a knife in his hand and I was able to get my knife and stick him in the guts. Then I dumped his body out of the hole."[72]

After seizing most of southern Saipan, the Americans fought for the center of the island. Some of the heaviest fighting of the battle occurred in and around the cave-laced slopes and jungle-covered area immediately southeast of Mt. Tapotchau known as "Death Valley." The Japanese were "dug in" there and slowed, but could not turn back, the American advance. On June 25, the Americans captured Mt. Tapotchau and Kagman Peninsula.[73] In the early hours of June 27, approximately 500 remaining Japanese troops in

Nafutan broke out, attacked Aslito Airfield and the surrounding area, and were killed.[74] On June 28, Nafutan Point was finally secured. The Americans found many dead Japanese troops and civilians when they entered Nafutan.[75] Meanwhile, they continued pushing northward and controlled roughly half of Saipan by June 30.[76] During nights, Japanese bombers raided the island. The United States Strategic Bombing Survey stated that in June and July, "enemy aircraft carried out a series of raids on United States ships in the vicinity of Saipan and on the forces ashore, probably originating initially at Guam, Rota, or Tinian and later from the Carolines.... The number of planes involved totaled perhaps 150 in all raids."[77] Many of the Japanese planes were shot down or crashed, and the raids did not stall the Americans.

The Americans assaulted Garapan after taking the mountainous high ground in the center of the island. There was some street fighting, but most Japanese troops fell back to positions north of Tanapag Harbor. On July 3, Garapan was captured.[78] Dead bodies laid throughout the town. Marine Captain Carl W. Hoffman, 8th Regiment, 2nd Division, wrote, the "choking smell of death hung about like a fog."[79] Items in destroyed buildings were the haunting remnants of more peaceful times. Correspondent Robert Sherrod wrote, "In a neat, wooden house ... there were many photograph albums which apparently had belonged to a well-to-do Jap family. Some pictures showed Japanese women in formal evening gowns and men in full dress. But the wedding pictures were as oriental as the *obis* the women wore. There were pictures of Japanese baseball teams and of groups of expressionless school children. A box full of books also contained maps of various atolls. Scattered around the rooms were wooden shoes and western-style leather shoes."[80]

By July 4, the Tanapag Harbor area was seized and about three-fourths of the island was in American hands.[81] The Japanese military was driven to the northern end of the island and nearing defeat. On July 6, General Saito, issued a message to all officers and men still alive on Saipan, stating, "Whether we attack or whether we stay where we are there is only death.... I will advance with those who remain to deliver still another blow to the American Devils, and leave my bones on Saipan as a bulwark of the Pacific. As it says in the 'Senjinkun' (Battle Ethics) [Field Service Code], 'I will never suffer the disgrace of being taken alive.' Follow Me!"[82] Before midnight, General Saito, fifty-three years old at the time, reportedly had a final meal of sake and canned crab meat and then committed suicide to inspire the remaining defenders. An officer who served on Saito's staff described the general's last moments, "Cleaning off a spot on the rock himself, Saito sat down. Facing the misty East saying 'Tenno Heika! Banzai!' (Hurrah for the Emperor!), he drew his own blood first with his own sword and then his adjutant shot him in the head with a pistol."[83]

Before dawn on the morning of July 7, Japanese forces on Saipan conducted the largest banzai attack of the Pacific War and were annihilated by the Americans. Approximately 3,000 Japanese troops and a number of civilians were killed in the raid.[84] After the major banzai attack, only isolated pockets of organized Japanese resistance remained. The American troops, who were utterly exhausted and filthy by that time, pressed forward. They did not have one solid night of sleep for over three weeks, and a number of them were wearing the same clothes they had on when they landed on the island. Marine Rod Sandburg, 10th Regiment, 2nd Division, recalled, "We ate, slept, and fought in clothes that became so rotten from perspiration and rain that they were very threadbare when the campaigns were over ... our dungarees would rot, from body sweat, right on our bodies."[85] Many were suffering from heat exhaustion, rashes, and diarrhea. Civilians were sick, dehydrated, and malnourished. Many were injured and wounded. International News Service correspondent Howard Handleman wrote on Saipan, "The miserable people from the caves ... [were] sick, tattered, filthy and with so little life left in them."[86] *Chicago Tribune* Correspondent Keith Wheeler wrote about an incident when Marines found a little girl in a farmhouse on Saipan. He stated, "She looked as though she had never been bathed. Flies, heat and filth had cracked the skin of her head."[87]

Between July 7 and 9, the Americans fought for and captured the northern third of Saipan. On July 9, they declared the island "secure." A number of civilians committed suicide and murder-suicide or were murdered by Japanese troops at the end of the battle. However, a far greater number of civilians surrendered or were captured. The Americans put the civilians in the Camp Susupe internment camp, which was initially poorly constructed and unsanitary. A reported 921 Japanese Soldiers and Sailors and 838 Korean laborers of the approximately 29,660 IJM troops on the island survived the battle and were put in a separate POW camp or taken aboard ships. More than 3,400 Americans were killed.[88] Intensive mop-up operations and anti-sniper patrols continued for months after the battle, and more civilians and troops were captured, surrendered, or killed. The Americans obtained valuable intelligence information about Tinian from prisoners and captured documents on Saipan.

Dead Japanese troops on Tinian, August 1944. #92688. National Archives.

Battle of Tinian (July 24–August 1, 1944) Overview

The Battle of Tinian lasted 9 days. The Americans invaded the island on the morning of July 24, 1944. Marine Corps Major General Harry Schmidt commanded NTLF Marines on Tinian under Holland M. Smith's directives. The 27th Army Division was kept on Saipan for mop-up operations and did not fight on Tinian.[89] The Marines landed on Tinian's northwestern shore.[90] They were supported by land-based aircraft and artillery on Saipan, as well as carrier planes and warships. The Japanese military was surprised about the landing location. They thought the Americans would come in at Tinian Harbor or Asiga Bay in the northeast and could only organize light resistance against the first waves and Marine beachhead.[91] On July 25, before dawn, the Japanese conducted a large nighttime banzai attack that was unsuccessful. Many Japanese who survived the raid and attempted to withdraw to the south were killed by American artillery fire, mortars, and warship shelling.[92] The Americans reported over 1,200 enemy dead and many tanks destroyed afterward.[93] The Marines advanced during the next two days and seized the northern third of the island. On July 25, they seized Mt. Maga (390 ft). The next day they took Mt. Lasso (540 ft).[94] After Lasso fell, the Marines advanced southward across the sugarcane island's central valley between July 27 and 29. The canefields were a hindrance for the Marines. Marine Charles Pase, 10th Regiment, 2nd Division, recalled, "The cane was very dense. It was a nightmare trying to work through it."[95] Japanese troops, who hid in the canefields and underground defense positions, frequently infiltrated Marine lines. The Tinian NTLF G-2 Report stated that on July 28, "five (5) Japanese infiltrated into one of the Battalion command posts of the 25th Marines and were killed."[96]

In the last days of July, the Japanese concentrated the remainder of their forces in the southern end of the island at Marpo and Lalo Points, which had cliffs and escarpments. A number of Japanese troops prevented civilians from surrendering and forced noncombatants into the area with them. The Tinian NTLF G-2 Periodic Report no. 44, 29 July 1944, stated, "A Korean civilian stated that 3000 Jap soldiers pulled out ... and all moved to the high ground south of the island, forcing civilians to go with them."[97] On July 30, the Marines assaulted and captured Tinian Town, which was already destroyed.[98] Marine Captain Carl W. Hoffman, 8th Regiment, 2nd Division, wrote, in Tinian Town, the "streets could not be distinguished from its buildings; the entire area was a mass of rubble."[99] The Japanese attempted another counterattack with tanks the night after the town was captured but were repulsed.[100] On the night of July 31–August 1, the last major Japanese counterattack, consisting of over 600 troops, was launched and failed.[101] IJN Colonel Ogata Kiyochi, the garrison commander, reportedly led the raid and was killed.[102] On August 1, the Americans declared Tinian "secure." As on Saipan, a number of civilians committed suicide and murder-suicide or were murdered by Japanese troops during the battle and in the days after the island was secured. According to the Tinian NTLF G-2 Report, after the fall of the island, there were "individual and group suicides by the Japanese military and civilians."[103] Japanese holdouts continued to conduct counterattacks well into August. Of the approximately 9,162 IJM troops, 257 (151 Japanese and 106 Koreans) survived the battle.[104] The Americans lost 389 men on Tinian.[105] Great numbers of sick, dehydrated, and injured civilians surrendered or were captured on Tinian. They were put in the Camp Churo internment camp in north-central Tinian. The Marianas Operation was completed with the capture of Guam to the south on August 10.

6

Mass Civilian Suicides

A number of civilians died from suicides and murder-suicides during the Battles of Saipan and Tinian in the summer of 1944. Areas where this occurred included, but are not limited to, "Banzai Cliff" (coastal cliff, about 100 ft) and "Suicide Cliff" (inland cliff on Mt. Marpi, 600–800 ft) at Marpi Point in northern Saipan and "Suicide Cliff" (coastal cliff, about 120 ft) between Marpo and Lalo Points in southern Tinian. There were many different methods of suicide and murder carried out, which are discussed in detail below. American officers documented the suicides in military reports, which are now held and preserved at the National Archives in College Park, Maryland. Combat correspondents wrote newspaper and magazine articles about them. American combat photographers and cameramen photographed and filmed some of the suicides. A number of troops and civilians discussed the suicides in interviews and writings after the war. Every Marine, Soldier, Sailor, correspondent, and civilian, even those in the same unit or group, saw the suicides or the aftermaths from a different vantage point. The suicides did not occur all at the same time. Rather, there were multiple incidents of suicides over a period of weeks on both islands. Some eyewitnesses were closer than others. Others saw similar, but different suicides on different days. Every testimony is unique and important for understanding what happened on Saipan and Tinian.

Hundreds of civilians and Japanese troops committed suicide by jumping off Saipan and Tinian's coastal and inland cliffs or were thrown, dragged, or pushed off them. Navy Sailor James J. Fahey, aboard the light cruiser USS *Montpelier*, wrote in his diary on July 9, 1944, "I can see smoke coming from the northern tip of Saipan. You can see the Japs jumping off the high cliffs to their death."[1] He recorded the next day, "The Japs were jumping off the high cliffs committing suicide, rather than be captured, hundreds of them landed in the water. Our destroyers tried to pick them up but they refused. Our ships then opened up on them, and they were dying like rats."[2] On July 13, he stated, "Today the water was full of dead Jap bodies, you could see them floating by, men, women, and children. The north section was loaded with floating bodies." On the 16th, he wrote, "It was the first time I ever went to church services and saw dead bodies floating by, the Japs are still floating around, there must be thousands of Japs in the waters near Saipan. The ships just run over them."[3] Sailor Norman Delisle, on the light cruiser USS *Oakland* off Saipan, stated, "At one time we were cruising off the island, and we could see them committing suicide by jumping off the cliffs. The Marines were coming up to them to try to capture them…. The gory details we will spare."[4] Navy Seabee (Construction Battalion Sailor) Karl B. Schroeder, recalled, "On Saipan … the Japs committed suicide by jumping off a cliff. Some natives jumped off too. We tried to stop them, but the Japs had convinced them we would do bad things to them."[5]

Marine Albert C. Torgerson, 18th Engineer Battalion, 2nd Division, recalled, "I guess they believed some of the propaganda that the Japanese gave them because ... they were jumping [off the Marpi Point cliffs] with the Japanese ... and well, we had them cornered."[6] Marine Winton W. Carter, 2nd Armored Amphibian Battalion, stated, "There are corpses floating in the water at the north end of Saipan at the end of the battle. Many Japanese civilians either jump or are pushed off cliffs by Jap military. Hundreds commit suicide rather than be captured by Americans. I remember a young woman holding an infant in her arms and both were nude. I yell 'stop.' My driver [in the amphibious tank] takes it out of gear. Out forward momentum causes us to pass on over the two bodies."[7] Marine Michael Gates, 23rd Regiment, 4th Division, stated, "There were a lot of civilians on Saipan. Toward the end of the battle a lot of them committed suicide by jumping off this cliff. I saw their bodies splattered all over the place at the bottom."[8] Saipan civilian Antonio Benavente recalled, "they continued for hours.... Hundreds of them, leaping from the cliff."[9] Army Soldier Clifford W. Howe, 165th Regiment, 27th Division, recounted, "We saw hundreds of bodies, washing in the surf or lying dead on the rocks below. It made even the most hardened American soldiers sick to see this."[10]

Army Soldier Ran Cochran, a combat photographer, wrote in a letter to his wife, dated July 12, 1944, that a group of Japanese soldiers and civilians standing on a rocky ledge at the coast of Saipan "began to jump from the ledge, the soldiers forcing their families to jump in with them.... Men, women and children thrashing around in the water. They were committing hari-kari."[11] Marine Roy William Roush, 6th Regiment, 2nd Division, remembered, during mop-up operations on Saipan, descending by rope to the "jungle of skeletons" below Suicide Cliff with his unit. He wrote, "There were many large trees growing on the plateau.... They had been greatly damaged by the many bodies that fallen on them.... There were places where dozens of bodies were piled up-lying one on top of another where they fell. Some had been children. But, there wasn't much left of the bodies. They were mostly skeletons dressed in ragged and deteriorated clothing, making them look more like scarecrows.... In many of the damaged trees, were also bodies, or rather skeletons, that had fallen and were caught."[12]

Marine Sergeant William W. Rogal, 2nd Regiment, 2nd Division, wrote, Tinian civilians "were doing as their countrymen had done on Saipan—leaping from the cliffs into the sea."[13] Marine Wilson P. Allmand, 2nd Division, recounted, on Tinian, "the Japanese were jumping off that cliff, throwing little babies off. Women were jumping off."[14] Marine Lieutenant Cliff Graham recalled, on Tinian, "what had seemed to be varicolored rocks at the base of the cliff ... were not rocks, but bodies lying in all sorts of grotesque attitudes, as they had fallen from the cliff above."[15] The Tinian NTLF G-2 Report stated, "The 8th Marines [8th Regiment, 2nd Division] reported they saw many civilians on August 2nd-3rd commit suicide by jumping down from the cliffs in the Marpo Point area into the sea."[16] Marine Lieutenant Dean Ladd, 8th Regiment, 2nd Division, recalled, in southern Tinian, "Many Japanese were killed by our fire, but many also jumped from the ledges, dashing themselves on the rocks below. In front of my unit and to its right Japanese civilians as well as soldiers jumped from a place that we immediately dubbed 'Suicide Cliff.'"[17] Marine Richard R. Stein, 8th Regiment, 2nd Division, stated, at "Suicide Cliff" on Tinian, "they'd jump and about halfway down they'd hit the side of the cliff and their heads would pop off. I saw that happen two or three times. Sometimes they'd take children with them. I remember this one Jap officer, he scooped up a couple of these kids and bailed over the side with them. And this one little girl hung on to him for several seconds and she just looked up at me. And I'm looking over the side of the cliff. This is happening about ten feet below me."[18]

Civilians who jumped or were pushed off the coastal cliffs and did not die from hitting the rocks often drowned. Some, instead of going to the cliffs, went to the beaches or rocky ledges and walked straight into the ocean to end their lives. Marine Lieutenant Lewis Meyers, wrote, off Saipan, "The ocean was dotted with black heads floating in the water, most of them swimming slowly around. For a few minutes the scene resembled a bathing beach on a busy holiday, until the heads began to disappear beneath the surface and did not come up again."[19] Marine John R. Rempke, 23rd Regiment, 4th Division, was watching a group of civilians at the northern coast of Saipan from a distance when "some of them just walked out into the water and disappeared."[20] An August 13, 1944, article in the *Chicago Tribune* titled "Tribune Writer Views Suicide of Jap Civilians: Nightmare Scene on Isle of Saipan Described," written by correspondent Harold Smith on July 10 and sent to the newspaper via air mail, stated, "from a rock cleft south of us [at Marpi Point] there stepped out three dress clad, long haired figures, one apparently an older woman and the others seemingly considerably younger but adult. Keeping close together they walked slowly toward the water.... [The women] toppled into a freshly breaking swell, still clasped together.... We didn't see them anymore."[21] Marine Lieutenant Cliff Graham recalled seeing a girl in a dress on the coast of Tinian who "leisurely combed her long black hair" and then "jumped into the pounding surf."[22]

A dead civilian at the northern coast of Saipan, July 1944. #89718. National Archives.

Suicides and murder-suicides with grenades also happened on Saipan and Tinian. The Saipan NTLF G-2 Report stated, "several instances of finding dead civilians, apparently killed by hand grenades, occurred, but it was never definitively established whether these were murdered by the military or whether these were merely fanatical suicides by the misled civilians."[23] The Saipan NTLF G-2 Periodic Report no. 10, 25 June 1944, stated, "The 27thInfDiv recently reported encountering in the Nafutan Pt. sector 6 pillboxes with 5 bodies in each most of whom were women civilians who had been killed by grenades."[24] Marine Lieutenant Robert E. Wollin, 2nd Armored Amphibian Battalion, stated, "In spite of all efforts to reason with distant civilians over the loudspeakers, many were killing themselves with hand grenades or by jumping off the high cliff or being shot. Also many Japanese military people were committing suicide in plain view of us."[25] Marine Kenneth E. Smith, also in the 2nd Armored Amphibian Battalion, stated, "During the final days of the battle for Saipan we were sent up north beyond Tanapag Harbor where our people had loudspeakers trying to talk civilians from killing themselves with hand grenades or by jumping off the cliff. Jap military were helping the civilians kill themselves, men, women, and children."[26] Marine Sergeant William L. More, 4th Division, recalled, on Saipan, "We could see them a hundred or two hundred yards away. There would be a group of people, women and kids with a guy in the middle. A grenade would go off and the whole family was gone."[27] Marine Joe E. Ojeda, 24th Regiment, 4th Division, recounted, at Marpi Point, "All these women and young children [were] killing themselves. You'd hear an explosion and see body parts flying all over."[28] Marine Albert J. Harris, 24th Regiment, 4th Division, recalled, on Saipan, "The end of the campaign, had the most eerie, bizarre thing I ever saw in my life ... we were there for two or three days just watching people commit suicide. Civilians, basically, jumping into the water, blowing themselves up with grenades ... having their own soldiers shoot them. I've seen whole families standing on a rock right along the ocean then explode a grenade.... I went down with a patrol after about the third or fourth day ... to this big cave ... it was full of bodies. It was piles of Japanese bodies in the middle of it. A stack of them and then millions of flies."[29] The Tinian NTLF G-2 Report stated, "A captured Warrant Officer from the 56th Keibitai [Japanese Naval Guard Force] stated that around 1000 'loyal citizens' among the civilians allowed the military to blow them up in caves."[30]

Suicides and murders with knives, bayonets, swords, and poisons happened on both islands as well. Marine Gabriel J. Vertucci, 25th Regiment, 4th Division, who inspected a large cave on a jungle-covered hill on Saipan, stated, "I looked in. I swear I thought that there was a red carpet on the floor.... I walked right into the goddamned cave ... laying on top of the floor of that cave was I figure roughly about 25 people; kids and women, no men.... And every one of them had their throats cut."[31] Samuel Eliot Morison, aboard the light cruiser USS *Honolulu*, wrote, "men, women and children cut each others' throats" on the northern cliffs of Saipan in view of Americans.[32] Dr. John F. Embree, a Psychological Warfare Supervisor for the Office of War Information, wrote, on Saipan, "One man with whom I talked was a widower because his wife and children died from taking poison. They thought he had been killed and so killed themselves rather than submit to capture by American soldiers. (This man, born in Kanagawa near Tokyo, was formerly an official of the sugar company.)"[33] Tokuichi Kurihara, a Nanyo Kohatsu businessman on Saipan, stated, "many people committed suicide by drinking acid."[34] IJA Sergeant Yamauchi Takeo, 136th Regiment, 43rd Division, stated:

6. Mass Civilian Suicides 89

"Bodies of men, women, and children that died in explosion litter the beach, at Tinian." July 1944. #93619. National Archives.

Those unable to move were told to die by a hand grenade or by taking cyanide. The women and children had cyanide. Those who didn't jumped off cliffs. Ones like me, who from the beginning were thinking about how to become prisoners, were real exceptions.... Late on the thirteenth, deep in the night, I slipped out of the cave and huddled under a tree at the edge of the cliff. I planned to make my way out when the call to surrender began at daybreak. There were several civilians there, too. A young woman of sixteen or seventeen, a middle aged couple, and a man, a little older than me. I couldn't tell if he was a civilian or a soldier. I pleaded with them to let me in their group. The girl spoke with me. All her family members had been killed, she said. Her younger brother by artillery fire. Her parents had killed themselves with cyanide. She, too, took something, but nothing happened to her. That's what her parents must have wanted, she said. I told her, "You must not kill yourself. Your parents tried to spare your life that way." I couldn't actively say, "Let's surrender," because I was worried about what that young man might do.[35]

Some civilians murdered their loved ones, including children, before they committed suicide. Japanese troops and civilians also killed people not related to them. Samuel Eliot Morison, USS *Honolulu*, wrote, "Parents dashed babies' brains out on the cliffs and then jumped over themselves."[36] Marine Carl Pettier, 2nd Division, stated, on Saipan, "we saw mothers bouncing their babies against the rocks to kill them."[37] Correspondent Keith Wheeler wrote, at Marpi Point, "Mothers with babies strapped on piggy-back fashion walked to the shore, stood and contemplated the waiting sea, then walked on into it.... A father with a 2-year-old boy squatted in a coral pothole ... and choked it to death."[38]

A Marine Corps 2nd Armored Amphibian Battalion Special Action Report stated, on July 10, LVTA4s [Landing Vehicles, Tracked (Armored), Mark IV] attached to the 4th Marine Division witnessed a woman "butchering" three children in their zone of action in northern Saipan.[39] Marine Captain Milton Sperling, a combat photographer, stated, "Husbands cut their wives throats, mothers stabbed their own children, men shot, stabbed and bludgeoned to death their mothers and fathers."[40] Marine Lieutenant Jim G. Lucas, who was at Marpi Point, wrote, "I have been eyewitness to one of the most sickening and unbelievable orgies of death any group of men has ever been forced to watch.... Hundreds of Japanese have killed themselves and their families.... I saw today a Japanese woman and girl, their tongues cut out. The girl had been stabbed. Their murderer was the father and husband, who took his own life."[41] Marine Ray T. Harrison, 2nd Division, who was at the northern cliffs on Saipan, stated, "I remember these ladies ... they would comb their hair and fix themselves.... One would get up and throw her baby off the cliff and then she would jump. That was one of the things that sticks with me pretty good."[42] Navy Corpsman H.L. Obermiller, who was attached to the 2nd Marine Division, recalled, "They would throw their kids in and jump in after them."[43]

Navy Corpsman Chester J. Szech, 6th Regiment, 2nd Marine Division, stated, "There was not anything the Americans could do about this terrible situation. We had an LST [Landing Ship Tank] in the water asking them not to jump. We were down below and just sat there and watched them. There were a lot of women and kids.... They would throw the kids, then the wife would jump and then he would jump."[44] Marine Roy William Roush, 6th Regiment, 2nd Division, recalled, on Saipan, "Sometimes a mother would jump off a cliff carrying a baby, or sometimes a family would hold hands and jump off together. It was a terrible thing to witness."[45] Marine Captain Carl W. Hoffman, 8th Regiment, 2nd Division, wrote, "Hundreds of civilians, believing that the end had come, embarked on a ghastly exhibition of self-destruction. Casting their children ahead of them, or embracing them in death, parents flung themselves from the cliffs onto the jagged rocks below. Some waded into the surf to drown or employed other gruesome means of destroying themselves."[46] Marine Olian T. Perry, 18th Regiment, 2nd Division, stated, on Saipan, "It was terrible, a man and woman came out there and threw the kids over the cliff and they jumped in right after them."[47]

Marine combat cameraman John F. Ercole, attached to the 2nd Division, filmed a woman killing her children and then herself. He stated in an interview, "There's a shot on Saipan where I come across a woman. There is a cut in the cliff and she's maybe fifty, sixty yards away me. She's got a child standing here, baby in her hand, and she spots me. Now she sees the camera, which is on the gun stock, but she doesn't notice the camera. So as I raise it up, she kicks this kid off the cliff, throws the baby off the cliff, and she takes a dive. Now that's all on film.... Maybe four seconds."[48] Marine Edwin P. DesRosiers, 14th Regiment, 4th Division, recalled, at Saipan, "The sea was red; red with blood and bodies down there.... The native women were standing there with their babies and the Japs told them you better go over the cliff because you're going to get killed. These women would jump into that ocean with their babies and it was sad. I still shudder when I think of seeing that happen. Lots of them did that."[49] Marine Sergeant Charles B. Rogers, 24th Regiment, 4th Division, told Robert Sherrod at Saipan's northern cliffs, "There are lots of kids with their heads off in pockets on those rocks below. Men from I, K and L Companies who were mopping up here ... said the kids' own parents did it, then jumped off themselves."[50] Marine James W. Jackson, 24th Regiment, 4th Division, recounted, "I remember the kids screaming, and then the mothers screaming!"[51] Marine Samuel T. Holiday, a Navajo Code Talker attached to the 25th Regiment, 4th Division, recalled:

> As we neared the northern part of the island called Marpi Point, the commander ordered the platoon I was moving with to stop a ways from a rocky height. Looking ahead I could see people from a village running to the edge of the cliffs. Some of them shot at us while others remained near the edge. I could hear loudspeakers pleading with them to surrender, trying to get the civilians not to jump. We were told to stop a ways from them in order not to crowd the prisoners with the ocean to their backs. Beneath the point of the cliff were black rocks sticking up like knives in the sea, the waves hitting and splashing against them. Many children and women with babies stood in this group, one woman fixing her hair before running out of the crowd for the cliff. Some civilians grabbed and stopped her before she jumped then dragged her back into the crowd. Another woman threw what looked like a baby wrapped in a blanket into the ocean while others began committing suicide.[52]

Marine Lieutenant Carlton B. Greider, 2nd Division, wrote, on Tinian, "While at the top of this cliff overlooking this plateau I saw sights that were so horrible to be almost unbelievable.... I saw family after family destroy itself—the father and mother throwing their children into the ocean and then jumping in after them, soldiers lining up groups of civilians and shooting them down, large groups blowing themselves to pieces—with the help of the soldiers—with high explosive etc., etc."[53] Navy Sailor Frank

"Baby of one of the Japanese natives of the island of Tinian as it was found in the jungle. Cause of the death is unknown..." July 1944. #93620. National Archives.

Urbanowicz, aboard the destroyer USS *Ralph Talbot* off Tinian, recalled, "there was a cliff and they have another name for it, Suicide Cliff, where people would throw the children, the old ones, off the top and then jump about two hundred feet into the sea ... saw the bodies floating."[54] Navy Sailor Cleatus A. LeBow, aboard the heavy cruiser USS *Indianapolis* off Tinian, stated, "just the last day or two before they secured the island ... the Japanese were backed to the southern end I think and there was a pretty good sized hill with a cliff that went off into the water. They were making all the Japanese civilians that were still on the island [commit suicide].... There was one woman, she looked to be around 20 to 25 years old and had a little boy that would have been about three and she was carrying a baby in her arms. When they got to the end of that cliff she just flung him out and jumped off after him. I wish that I couldn't see that anymore but I still can. It was bad."[55]

Some Americans shot parents trying to kill their children. Marine Sergeant David Dowdakin, 2nd Regiment, 2nd Division, stated, at northern Saipan, "I opened fire and cut down a man who seemed to be struggling with smaller people. I got him and his daughter. He was killing his children with a knife. A figure in a skirt leaped over the double concertina wire and kept running full tilt to the cliffs and leapt over. Another burst of fire from the BAR man next to me and he got a teenaged boy in the head. At dawn we sat eating our C rations calmly in the midst of what could truthfully be described as a slaughterhouse."[56] Americans also shot civilians committing suicide so they would not have a painful death. Marine Michael Witowich, 2nd Division, recalled, on Saipan, "They were throwing the women and children off the cliffs.... As they were throwing the children, I use to shoot the children so they wouldn't suffer when they hit the coral. They jumped and you could hear the screaming of the children on the coral.... A lot of times I use to think about that in my dreams. If it was right for me to do that, but they wouldn't have to suffer when they went down.... It's like shooting the horse that broke its leg, except this a human being."[57]

Civilian Accounts of the Suicides

Ryoko Okuyama

Ryoko Okuyama was born in 1930 and fourteen years old when the Americans invaded Saipan.[58] During the battle, she, along with her parents and three younger siblings, evaded capture. On July 17, a week after the Americans declared the island secure, the family entered a cave on the northeast coast of the island. Inside the cave were an IJA sergeant, a journalist from mainland Japan, and an unattended newborn. Ryoko's 34-year-old mother immediately picked up the baby and took care of it. Soon thereafter, the Americans, who were conducting mop-up operations, entered the area and the baby started crying. The Japanese sergeant demanded that the baby be silenced. Ryoko's mother tried to breastfeed the child, but it continued to cry. She finally stopped the noise by covering the infant's mouth with her clothing; the baby suffocated to death.

When the Americans neared the cave, the men inside decided for everyone to commit suicide rather than be captured. The sergeant and Ryoko's father took out grenades, pulled out the pins, struck them against rocks, and let them go. There were intense blasts.

Ryoko was injured by shrapnel and knocked unconscious. When she woke, she saw the gruesome aftermath. Ryoko's father and all her siblings, as well as the sergeant, were dead. The journalist, severely injured, bashed his head against a rock to end his suffering. Ryoko's mother, in her final moments, tied a small furoshiki cloth pouch filled with money around Ryoko and told her daughter not to die on Saipan. Ryoko held her mother's hand as she bled to death. Ryoko was later saved by the Americans and hospitalized. Two decades after the battle, she published her memoir *Left Alive on Saipan, The Island of Suicide* (*Gyokusai no shima ni ikinokkotte*, 1967) in Japanese.

Sumiko Goeku

Sumiko Goeku was born in 1937 and was seven years old during the Battle of Saipan. Her father, Chose, worked at the Chalan Kanoa sugar factory, and her mother, Tsuru, cared for the family of seven. Sumiko remembered the lushness of the island and the tropical fruit trees. She had just started school when the war came. Her father was drafted into the Imperial Japanese Army and sent abroad after the attack on Pearl Harbor; Sumiko never saw him again. When the Americans invaded Saipan, the Goeku family fled into the island's interior and hid in a cave. Later during the battle, Sumiko's mother was shot when she tried to get food for her children and died shortly afterward. One of Sumiko's sisters died of malnutrition and disease, and her baby brother was stabbed to death with a bayonet by a Japanese soldier. Near the end, an aunt attempted to drown Sumiko in the ocean, but she managed to get away and was later put in Camp Susupe.[59]

Shinsho Kuniyoshi

Shinsho Kuniyoshi was born on Saipan in 1932. His parents migrated to Saipan in 1928 from Okinawa Island and had eight children. The family enjoyed their life in the tropical Marianas. During the battle, they fled to the mountainous interior and later joined a group of approximately 70 civilians and Japanese troops at the north end of Saipan. The leaders of the group decided that it would be better for all of them to commit suicide rather than fall into enemy hands. Kuniyoshi and his family members, who did not want to die, were forced to jump off a cliff into the ocean. He and his father both survived the fall, but his mother and siblings drowned or were killed from the impact. The father and son swam furiously to the shore, surrendered to the Americans, and were transported to Camp Susupe. Two of Kuniyoshi's younger sisters, who had been spared from the suicides by being placed under a tree, were also in the camp but died from malnutrition and disease while in internment. The family of ten was reduced to two. Kuniyoshi was haunted by what happened on Saipan his whole life.

Hiroshi Kikuchi

Hiroshi Kikuchi was born on February 18, 1935, and was nine years old when Saipan was invaded. He was with his parents, two brothers, and sister in Garapan when the city came under bombardment. His third and eldest brother was in the IJA on Saipan. The family took refuge in the caves of Mt. Tapochau and later moved to the northern end of the island to get away from the advancing Americans. Sadly, Hiroshi's mother and brothers were killed before the end of the battle. On July 12, the father took Hiroshi and his sister to the edge of Banzai Cliff to commit suicide. The father was shot and fell into the ocean, however, before he could jump off the cliff. Hiroshi and his sister then leaped into the ocean but survived the fall. There were hundreds of bodies floating around them. Fortunately, nearby Americans saved Hiroshi and his sister before they drowned. The two remained united at Camp Susupe and were later repatriated to Japan. They lost most of their siblings during the war and became orphans, but they had each other.[60]

Koyu Shiroma

Koyu Shiroma was born on Saipan in 1939 and five years old at the time of the battle. His parents Kouye and Yusa were from Yomitan-son Kina, Okinawa Island. The newly married couple moved to Saipan in the 1930s to work as sugarcane farmers and start a family. They had a small farmstead on the island and gave birth to two daughters, in addition to Koyu, with a fourth child on the way in 1944.

When the Americans invaded Saipan, the family of six fled to the northern end of the island. On their way there, the pregnant mother was killed in an American bombardment and Koyu became separated from his father and sisters. Koyu feared being tortured and slaughtered if captured by the Americans and joined a group of civilians that went to the cliffs to commit suicide. He stated in an interview, "My father usually tell me, American people are going to kill you, someday, somehow. It's better off dying than caught by American soldier ... a lot of people jumped from the cliff, so everybody jumping, so I just jumped myself.... I find I was hanging in a tree. Branch caught me, saved me.... I was just hanging there over the cliff. Then a few minutes later, other people jumping. Whole families jumping and some people say 'Tenno Heika Banzai.'" Koyu was rescued from the cliff by the Americans and transported to Camp Susupe. In 1946, he was repatriated to Okinawa. Koyu spent his entire life trying to figure out what happened to his two sisters, Setsuko (born on February 5, 1941) and Shigeko (born on December 16, 1942).[61]

Shizuko Miura

Shizuko Miura was born in Yamagata Prefecture, Japan in 1926 and moved to Tinian with her family in 1927.[62] She relocated to Saipan with her sister in the early 1940s, while her father, mother, and younger sister remained on Tinian.[63] Her older brother served in the IJA on Saipan.

Shizuko was in Garapan when the pre-invasion bombardment began. The city rapidly turned into an inferno. The heat from the fires was intense, and the smoke made it difficult for her to breathe. Rubble, debris, and dead bodies slowed her escape from the conflagration. Shizuko managed to evacuate Garapan and found shelter in a cave east of the city. The suffering and death she saw made her want to serve as a medical aid for the Japanese military and save as many lives as she could.[64] Shizuko left the cave and trekked to a field hospital east of Mt. Tapochau on the slopes of Mt. Donnay. There were hundreds of wounded and dying men at the field hospital, and the smell was overpowering. She located the head IJA surgeon and requested to work under him. He told her to leave and hide in the mountains. She refused to and followed behind him. The surgeon, impressed by Shizuko's tenacity, designated her as a "special volunteer nurse" and gave her a helmet and Red Cross armband to wear.[65] There were only three doctors and seven medics in the camp, and he knew he was going to need her.[66]

Shizuko aided the surgeon in every possible capacity. She was at first nervous but steadily grew more confident. Her duties included everything from changing bandages to performing minor operations and amputations. She was covered in blood, dirt, and sweat and went days without sleep, but the men she treated thought she was an angel. Shizuko reminded them of their wives or sisters, and her presence brought them some warmth before they died. Lieutenant Shinoda, a young officer she attended to, could not see her; he lost his eyes. She applied an antiseptic and bandaged his wounds. She told him that she had an older brother in the army who was killed early in the battle. The young lieutenant took out a picture of his wife in a kimono and showed it to her. He was soothed by Shizuko's gentle care and kind words. The officer later succumbed to his wounds, but Shizuko brought him some peace before he passed.[67]

By the end of June 1944, the Americans were closing in on Mt. Donnay. The surgeons were ordered to move the field hospital to a small village north of Tanapag Harbor. The wounded and dying were told to commit suicide and grenades were dispersed. Shizuko wanted to die with the men under her care, but the surgeons dragged her away. As they proceeded north, Shizuko heard grenade after grenade going off on Donnay's slopes and an overwhelming sorrow came over her.[68]

The withdrawal of the field hospital was unsuccessful. Almost all who accompanied it were sick or injured in some way, and the Americans were advancing too rapidly. The surgeons and others urged Shizuko to surrender and then killed themselves.[69] Shizuko was afraid of being raped and tortured by the enemy and attempted suicide. She picked up a grenade, pulled the pin, hit it against a rock to trigger it, and put her body over it. The grenade went off and severely injured her, but she survived the blast and was later rescued by the Americans.[70] While being transported to the civilian hospital at Chalan Kanoa in a jeep, Shizuko saw the bodies of many civilians along the northwestern coast. She was deeply saddened when she saw the corpse of a young woman with two dead children tightly grasped to it. After seeing the aftermath of the mass suicides, she was glad that she had not died. While recovering from her wounds at the hospital, she did all she could to help other civilian patients. Shizuko was repatriated to Japan in 1946 and published her memoir *Praying on Saipan Island* (*Saipan jima ni inoru*) in 1965 in Japanese.[71]

Torayoshi Nihei

Torayoshi Nihei was born in 1926 and was eighteen years old during the Battle of Tinian. He recounted in an interview how his parents made him kill them because the Americans were nearing their position. "I sit my mom down. She puts her hands together. 'Thank you for all the years,' she's praying. 'Ok let's go.' I aim at her heart and pull the trigger. Bam. My mom, blood just spurting out. Then my dad says, 'there, do it here.' So that's my second shot and he slumps. My kid sister is watching this beside me.... She's nine years old. Acting like it's her turn next, she sits down with our dead mother and puts her own hands together. I take aim. 'Wait big brother.... I want a drink of water.' So I give her a couple of capfuls of water from the canteen. 'Here drink.' She gulps it all down. 'It's delicious; delicious big brother. That's plenty. Now shoot. I'll join mother.'"[72]

American Accounts of the Suicides

Robert Sherrod

Robert Sherrod was born in Thomasville, Georgia, on February 8, 1909, and graduated from the University of Georgia in 1929 with a degree in journalism. He was a reporter for both *Time* and *Life* magazines in the 1940s and one of the most well-known correspondents of the Pacific War. The United States War Department issued him correspondent identification card number 63.[73] He risked his life covering the Battles of Attu, Tarawa, Saipan, Iwo Jima, and Okinawa, among others. Sherrod landed on Saipan while the beaches were under heavy fire in June 1944 and attached himself to Marine Corps regiments. He witnessed the mass suicides, murder-suicides, and atrocities on Saipan and interviewed many Marines and Sailors who also saw them. When not accompanying front line units, he wrote from his desk at press headquarters in Chalan Kanoa.[74]

On July 12, three days after the island was declared secure, Sherrod wrote:

I got into a jeep and drove the twelve miles to Marpi Point. Just beyond the small Marpi Airfield I stood on a 200-foot cliff and watched the sea, 300 yards away. On the edge of the slippery, tide-washed rocks a Japanese boy of perhaps 15, attired in knee-length black trousers, walked back and forth. He would pause in meditation, then he would walk on, swinging his arms. He sat on the edge of the rocks; then he got up. He sat down again, waiting. When a high wave washed the rock, the boy let it sweep him into the sea. At first he lay face down, inert on the surface of the water. Then his arms flailed frantically, as if an instinct stronger than his will power bade him live. Then he was quiet. He was dead. I watched his body rock back and forth on the waves until it was perhaps fifty yards offshore. Then I could see it no more.... Two hundred yards offshore I saw another floating body in what looked like a red print dress. Then another bobbed up nearer the coastline. Almost directly in front of us, from behind the nearest rocks, a five-year old child's body, attired only in a white shirt, floated by. It was followed by that of a woman, then of a man. Around the tip of the cliff, to the right, four more bodies eddied in a slow, gruesome march.[75]

Some of the Jap civilians went through considerable ceremony before snuffing out their lives. In one instance Marines watched in astonishment as three women sat on the rocks leisurely, deliberately combing their long, black hair.... Finally, the women joined hands and walked slowly out into the sea. But the most ceremonious, by all odds, were 100 Japs on the rocks who bowed to the Marines watching from the cliff. Then they stripped off their clothes and bathed in the sea. Thus refreshed, they put on new clothes and spread a huge Jap flag on a smooth rock. Then the leader distributed hand grenades. One by one, as the pins were pulled, the Japs blew their insides out.[76]

Navy Lieutenant Emery Cleaves, an officer on the minesweeper USS *Chief*, told Sherrod, "Part of the area is so congested with floating bodies we simply can't avoid running them down. I remember one woman in khaki

A dead woman floating in the water at the coast of Saipan. Identifier: 77261, Record Group 428. National Archives.

trousers and a white, polka-dot blouse, with her black hair streaming in the water. I'm afraid every time I see that kind of blouse, I'll think of that girl. There was another one, nude, who had drowned herself while giving birth to a baby. The baby's head had entered this world, but that was all of him. A small boy of four or five had drowned with his arm firmly clenched around the neck of a Jap soldier; the two bodies rocked crazily in the waves. I've seen literally hundreds in the water."[77] The mass suicides deeply disturbed Sherrod. He wrote, "Saipan was war at its grimmest, and its scenes were seared into my brain."[78]

Marine General Holland Smith

Marine General Holland Smith was born in Hatchechubbee, Alabama, on April 20, 1882, and graduated from the Alabama Polytechnic Institute in 1901 and University of Alabama Law School in 1903. He was commissioned as a second lieutenant in the Marine Corps in 1905 and served in the Banana Wars and the First World War. Smith worked his way up the ranks before the Pacific War and in 1943 was appointed Commanding General of the Fifth Amphibious Corps of the United States Fifth Fleet. He commanded all ground troops during the Gilberts, Marshalls, Marianas, and Volcano Islands Campaigns. General Smith wrote, on Saipan, "Men, women and children flung themselves over the cliffs or were pushed over by Japanese soldiers, who shot stragglers, and then followed their victims to death, either by jumping after them or destroying themselves with hand grenades."[79]

He stated, on Tinian:

> By August 1, the island was declared secured.... Although we gained a military victory when we drove the few remaining soldiers into the southern caves, it was only then that the battle started for the lives of 13,000 civilians. Terrified men, women and children hid in the hundreds of caves with the soldiers, apparently waiting for death with oriental fatalism. We sent out a jeep, equipped with a load speaker, and broadcast appeals urging the civilians to come down from the 200-foot cliff and we would give them water, food and medical attention. A handful emerged and entered our lines but thousands more did not budge.... While we were calling to them to come down from the cliff, puffs of smoke and sounds of explosions in the caves told us that suicides had started again.... The tragedy that broke the evil spell occurred when a party of Japanese soldiers roped 40 or 50 civilians together and threw a hand grenade among them. Explosives buried in the ground blew the group to pieces. It was a barbaric performance, designed to terrorize the people into joining the death ceremony, but instead, they concluded that even the Americans, represented in Army propaganda as torturers of Japanese prisoners, could not be so cruel as their own people. The civilians ran for their lives, dragging their children and carrying their feeble old people.[80]

Marine Guy L. Gabaldon

Marine Guy L. Gabaldon fought in the Battles of Saipan and Tinian and convinced many civilians on the two islands to surrender with his Japanese language skills. Gabaldon is a controversial figure. Some Marines stated that he assaulted civilians.[81] Others have queried some elements of his testimony. There is no question, however, that he saved civilian lives. Numerous survivors of the battles, on both sides, have confirmed much of his testimony.

Gabaldon was born in Los Angeles, California, on March 22, 1926. During his childhood, he spent many of his days on the streets of East LA. Although he was Mexican

American, the Nakano's, a Japanese American family, took him in under their roof. He worked in the family's floral shop and attended the Rafu Chuo Gakuen Japanese Language School in Los Angeles.[82] In 1943, Gabaldon enlisted in the Marine Corps and completed boot camp in San Diego. Following recruit training, he was assigned to R-2 (Regimental Intelligence), Headquarters and Service Company, 2nd Regiment, 2nd Marine Division.[83] The regiment trained in Hawaii and from there embarked to the Marianas.

On Saipan and Tinian, he stated that he went behind enemy lines at night. He made full use of his Japanese language abilities by capturing civilians and troops despite that he could have been court-martialed, shot by his own troops by accident, or captured and tortured by the Japanese. After many successes, Gabaldon was permitted by his commanding officer to continue his forays into Japanese-held areas and take prisoner as many enemy nationals as possible. He succeeded in capturing and inducing civilians, comfort women, Korean laborers, and Japanese troops to surrender on both islands. Gabaldon witnessed the suicides at Marpi Point. He wrote:

> An old man and woman are trying to hide behind some coral.... I try talking them into coming up the cliff.... I see the old man's hand reach out from behind the rocks. He's about to get a grenade. He's about to commit murder-suicide. "Don't do it. I assure you that you will not be harmed. We will not mistreat you nor your wife. Please do not do anything rash!" He pulls his arm back behind the rock and I hear the "click" peculiar to Japanese grenades, when they hit the detonators against the rock. "Damn, he's done it. Too late to help him now." The grenade goes off right between the old man and his wife and blows their guts all over the coral rocks.... Why do they believe the bullshit propaganda they're fed?... We join a group of Marines firing down at some die-hard soldiers where the cliffs round out and give a view of the entrance to the caves. Suddenly a woman jumps up from the high grass and starts to run for the cliff. I shout at her, begging her not to kill herself and the baby in her arms.... She tosses the baby off, then she looks at me and jumps down to the rocks. The sorry part of all this is that they do not die immediately. They lay there, bodies broken, moaning in the hot tropical sun.[84]

Gabaldon saw many other parents killing their children. He wrote:

> It was sad to see children struggling with their parents pleading not to be thrown off the cliffs.... These parents were dangerous, desperate people who wanted nothing more than to kill the "American Savages" who they thought would roast and eat their children.... I'm begging them to stop killing their children. But I can see that as we approach they jump off in greater numbers.... There were about fifty in that group—it seems that there are about ten left. One who apparently is a leader is yelling at the rest. I can't make out what he's saying but it is obvious that he's telling them not to surrender. The people look down at the rocks below and see their friends moaning down there. Just about then one of them grabs an infant and tosses him off. That seems to have been a signal because they all start jumping off. In a couple of minutes it's all over. The whole bunch lies down below either dead or dying.[85]

Gabaldon rescued civilians and witnessed similar terrible happenings on Tinian. After the battle, he returned to Saipan for mop-up operations and was wounded.[86]

Surrender Leaflets and Broadcasts

The United States military and the Office of War Information (OWI), the government agency responsible for information and propaganda dissemination in America and abroad during the war, jointly produced hundreds of thousands of surrender leaflets for the Saipan and Tinian operations at printing facilities in the Hawaiian Islands.[87] The leaflets, directed to civilians and Japanese troops, were dropped before and during the invasions. The Americans saved the "enemy" because of humanitarianism, laws of war obligations, and military necessity. Civilians, as well as Japanese troops and Korean military laborers, possessed valuable intelligence information. Additionally, any civilian not in the internment camps was considered potentially hostile. Furthermore, taking them off the battlefield made it easier for the Americans to capture the islands. Japanese officers attempted to destroy the leaflets, but too many were dropped.[88] A number of civilians hid the papers under their clothing, so they would not be murdered as traitors by Japanese troops. An Okinawan civilian told Marine Lieutenant Robert Sheeks that "if the Japanese military caught anyone with a surrender leaflet, they would be killed."[89] Marine Lieutenant Jim G. Lucas wrote, on Saipan, "Civilians have reported they were warned by Japanese soldiers that they would be shot and killed merely for possession of surrender pamphlets dropped by our planes."[90]

There were over a dozen different leaflets in Japanese and Korean created for civilians and military personnel. The Tinian NTLF G-2 Report stated, "The native and civilian texts were simple directions to dissociate themselves from the military and come to the American lines. The Korean texts were based on Korean independence aspirations, Japanese oppression, and urged Koreans to dissociate themselves from the Japanese and come to the American lines. All texts guaranteed good treatment once the American lines were reached. Each leaflet carried a 'surrender ticket' called in Japanese and Korean a 'Life-Saving Guarantee'.... This was in the form of a detachable slip, with an English text explaining its nature to the American troops to whom it might be presented."[91] The "Life-Saving Guarantee" instructed civilians and troops how to surrender. It stated: "1. Raise both hands high above your head, and, holding nothing in your hands except this card, advance slowly toward the positions of the American troops. 2. Don't crowd up; advance one by one. 3. Never approach American positions at night unless specifically invited to by radio broadcast. This card can be used by Japanese troops, Japanese civilians, Korean laborers, and islanders. Use this card and save your life."[92] Marine Jack V. Gilbreath, 23rd Regiment, 4th Division, stated, "They would hold up this leaflet, you know, where it could be seen. You weren't supposed to shoot them or kill them. I saw a lot of them saved that way."[93]

Non–Japanese civilians were heavily influenced by the materials. The Saipan NTLF G-2 Report stated:

> Propaganda leaflets apparently found a ready reception by Chamorro natives. Both interrogation of internees and statements of Civil Affairs officers indicated that Chamorros were almost universally contacted by propaganda messages and that they were ready to follow the instructions and surrender. In general Japanese civilians from the main island of Japan (Naichi) had the same reaction to the propaganda leaflets as the Japanese military, many of them feeling that it was a disgrace to surrender and fearing that they would be mistreated by Americans if they did.... With the Okinawans, natives of the Ryukyu (Liu Chiu) Islands, however, it was quite a different story. They are less nationalistic than Naichi Japanese and being downtrodden sharecroppers and to some extent social outcasts, are more amenable to outside persuasion. The Okinawans were almost universally contacted by propaganda and did their best to surrender.[94]

Major General Thomas E. Watson, Commander of the 2nd Marine Division, wrote, "Many Koreans taken, including most of those attached to the military, had seen or heard of our leaflets, which stressed the old cleavages between Japanese and Koreans, the Koreans' long struggle against oppression, and the possibility of a free Korea after the war. All

Koreans who had seen the leaflets felt that they were effective and would always prove so with their nationals."⁹⁵ Many Koreans in the Japanese military were also influenced by the leaflets. Robert Sherrod wrote, "The Korean laborers were usually quite eager to surrender whenever their masters could not prevent it."⁹⁶

A surrender leaflet in Korean dropped on both islands read:

> KOREANS! The Japanese cannot protect you! Even though the Japanese are unable to protect you, you will still die because of them. Have the Japanese bayoneted or shot your people? Kill the Japanese if they threaten to bayonet or shoot you! Even if they haven't bayoneted or shot you it is of course an actual fact that they don't trust you ... look out for yourselves and think of the ways to save your lives. Without hesitation come quickly toward the American lines. Don't worry because the Americans definitely will not kill you. Use this opportunity to save your lives! You are KOREANS! You are not Japanese! Why should you die for the Japanese? Use this opportunity to save yourselves NOW!! Act immediately! Even if you are not able to get ahold of this all-important Life-Saving Guarantee, if you raise your hands over your heads and come toward the American lines, you will be in no danger.⁹⁷

Another Korean leaflet declared, "After Japan is defeated, Korea will become a free country and will be independent.... Korea will expel the Japanese and Korea will be for the Koreans."⁹⁸ A leaflet directed to Micronesians stated, "ISLANDERS! America is not fighting the inhabitants of this island. When the American troops attack this island, take this opportunity to save your life.... The American troops will give you food, clothing and tobacco. If you are wounded, they will give you medicine."⁹⁹

Language and intelligence officers and interpreters, including Japanese Americans, were at the frontlines and implored civilians in Japanese, and sometimes Chamorro or Spanish, to peacefully give themselves up. The language officers used loudspeakers on jeeps and aboard ships to reach civilians on top of the cliffs and deep in the caves and jungles of the islands. Despite the dangers, they also got in front of cave entrances and shouted inside. Sometimes, they even entered them. Korean military laborers and civilian surrenderees aided the language officers.¹⁰⁰ On Tinian, for instance, the superintendent of one of the sugar factories and his wife begged fellow civilians to come to American lines during the daytime.¹⁰¹ Interpreters had maps of the islands and made civilians point out where others were hiding.¹⁰² They were also assisted by combat troops who were given phrase books and taught simple Japanese and Chamorro phrases, such as "Please come out," "Do not be afraid," "We will give you water and food."¹⁰³ Marine Charles Pase, 10th Regiment, 2nd Division, stated, "At that time we had received a little bit of training in Japanese and one of the things that we told them was to come out with your hands up please. We were very polite about it. Please come out with your hands up. We said, 'we will not harm you.'"¹⁰⁴

There were not enough language officers assigned to the Marianas operation. Marine Lieutenant Lewis Meyers wrote, "On the way out on the transports the assault troops were schooled in combat phrases in Japanese. This was the language of all Saipan. A few phrases were stressed for dealing with civilians.... Armed with these and their individual weapons, we thought they could handle civilians trying to surrender. These preparations paid off. But they were inadequate to meet so many non-combatants who were so frightened of Americans. A big part of the answer came in the use of interpreters. The two officer-interpreters attached to our regiment did a tremendous job but they were too few."¹⁰⁵ Regrettably, the Americans did not have many Korean-language interpreters for the operations and occupations. Additionally, there was not enough equipment for language officers. The Tinian NTLF G-2 Report stated, "At least three (3) pack public address

Carolinians on Saipan, June 1944. "Natives of Saipan, ferreted out of the hills by Marines of the 2nd Regiment, await transportation to the rear lines. Frightened at first, due to horror stories told to them by the Japs, they learned soon after being taken into custody that no harm would befall them." #83470. National Archives.

systems and (1) vehicle mount loudspeaker should be allotted to each division for future operations. This equipment proved exceptionally valuable in inducing both military and civilians to surrender during the 'mopping up' phase of the operation but due to the limited number of sets available its use was greatly restricted."[106]

Robert B. Sheeks

Robert B. Sheeks was born in Shanghai, China, on April 8, 1922, to American expats. He obtained foreign language skills there before his family returned to the United States

Interpreter talks with Japanese civilians on Saipan, June 1944. #84050. National Archives.

in 1935. In 1940, he entered Harvard University on scholarship. In January 1942, a month after the attack on Pearl Harbor, Robert was recruited by the Office of Naval Intelligence to become a Japanese language and intelligence officer. He received intensive Japanese language instruction in the United States Navy Japanese Language School (JLS) at the University of California Berkeley from February to June 1942 and then the University of Colorado Boulder between late June 1942 and January 1943. The students were taught primarily by Japanese American instructors and had to pass many difficult tests.

On January 15, 1943, Robert graduated from the Navy JLS and was commissioned as a second lieutenant in the United States Marine Corps.[107] In early 1943, he received advanced combat training at Camp Elliott Marine Corps Base in San Diego, California. Following training, he shipped out to the Pacific and was eventually attached to 2nd Marine Division Intelligence Section (D-2). In his first combat operation, during the Battle of Tarawa in November 1943, he carried out intelligence gathering missions on Betio Atoll in the Gilbert Islands.

On June 15, 1944, Robert, at age 22, landed on Saipan under heavy enemy fire. He carried two small Japanese-English dictionaries he stole from the JLS. His primary orders during the battle were to collect intelligence and convince as many civilians and troops as possible to surrender. Throughout the battle, Robert, at the front lines, used a jeep-mounted loudspeaker system to broadcast surrender appeals. Civilians who surrendered aided Robert. The mission was dangerous; the language officers stood out, and Japanese snipers and artillery and mortar spotters were everywhere. Many Americans were killed while rescuing civilians on Saipan and Tinian. Robert often perilously approached and shouted into the entrance of caves to save those inside. At times, he went in them. Caves with people inside could often be identified by "the aroma of unwashed bodies and human waste" they gave off.[108]

Robert was at the cliffs in northern Saipan in early July 1944. He witnessed the suicides and murder-suicides and saw many dead bodies in the ocean.[109] Robert also served during the Battle of Tinian and saved civilians there. Afterward, he went back to Saipan. There, he got holdouts to surrender and worked with civil affairs for the remainder of the war.

Hoichi Kubo

Army Technical Sergeant Hoichi Kubo, a 23-year-old Japanese American from Hawaii, served as an interpreter in the 27th Army Division Intelligence Section. On July 26, during mop-up operations on Saipan, Hoichi accompanied Company K, 3rd Battalion, 105th Regiment, 27th Army Division along the northern cliffs. In a large cave, a small

Two girls on Saipan receive medical care from Americans, July 1944. #87859. National Archives.

group of Japanese troops was holding more than one hundred civilians hostage. Hoichi got some rope, scaled down to the entrance of the cave, and entered it. After two hours, he managed to convince the troops inside to surrender and let the civilians go.[110] Hoichi and Robert Sheeks were part of a small group of language and intelligence personnel who collectively saved thousands of civilians on the two islands.

A number of Marines and Soldiers, who were not trained for intelligence or civil affairs operations, also risked their lives to save civilians. Marine Lieutenant Lewis Meyers wrote that one Marine jumped into the ocean and "pulled out three women who had changed their minds [from committing suicide] and were struggling against death in the sea."[111] Saipan schoolgirl Akiko Kikuchi stated that she and her younger brother were saved by the Americans after they jumped off a cliff and survived the fall at Marpi Point.[112] Marine Lieutenant Colonel Justice M. Chambers, Commanding Officer of the 3rd Battalion, 25th Regiment, 4th Division, stated, on Saipan, "We ... picked up several civilian prisoners, including some women and children. The thing that really got to me was watching these boys of mine; they'd take all kinds of risks; they'd go into a cave never knowing whether there would be soldiers in there, to bring out these civilians. The minute they got them out, they began to feed them, give them part of their rations, and offer their cigarettes to the men. It made you feel proud of the boys for doing this."[113] Marine Lieutenant Frederic A. Stott, 24th Regiment, 4th Division, wrote:

> In the afternoon we again witnessed the sympathy and pity which is inherent in all of us. While preparing our foxholes, a small patrol scouted out some flimsy shacks to our front. They discovered a couple of soldiers, whom they dispatched, and then retired to our positions. But while on the mission, some had heard the crying of wounded women and children, and the men pleaded for a chance to go out and bring them back. The memory of the ruse which killed Phil Wood and Ervin had not vanished, and permission was refused. Yet the men, fully realizing the possibilities of deception, continued to beg for a chance to go. Finally we relented, and another patrol went out cautiously and retrieved the wounded. They included a mother, badly hurt, with week-old untreated wounds in which gangrene had set heavily, and three less-seriously wounded children. It was clear that the mother's life was ebbing fast, and that she had forced herself to remain alive for the sake of her children. To us, who offered all possible aid, the tragedy of this pain and suffering of innocent mother and child seemed almost as cruel as the loss of our comrades who understood the fight and were at least partially conditioned to it.[114]

7

Causes of the Mass Civilian Suicides

The mass civilian suicides and murder-suicides on Saipan and Tinian resulted primarily from fear and coercion. Civilians, influenced by the portrayal of the enemy in wartime propaganda and by rumors Japanese troops told them, feared the Americans would rape, torture, and kill them. Civilians also feared Japanese officers and enlisted men, a number of whom prevented noncombatants from surrendering and murdered those who tried. Furthermore, a number of Japanese troops forced civilians to commit suicide. Felisa Chargualaf Baza, a Chamorro girl born on February 26, 1930, who survived the Battle of Saipan, recounted that she and other civilians were "scared" of both military forces.[1] Those who were able to get past Japanese troops had to reach American lines without being killed from the fighting. The psychological and physical stressors from being trapped on the battlefields, including dehydration, malnutrition, disease, trauma, and sleep deprivation, also affected the minds of civilians and combatants. Most of the civilians who committed suicide were reportedly Japanese and Okinawans, though Micronesians and Koreans were killed in murder-suicides and atrocities.

Saipan and Tinian civilians were heavily exposed to Japanese propaganda, which portrayed the Americans as a sinister and inhuman people. The Americans were often referred to as demons (*oni*), devils (*kichiku*), monsters (*kaibutsu*), and wild beast (*yaju*). A number of Japanese propaganda graphic renderings and cartoons depicted Americans with claws, fangs, and horns.[2] According to scholar Noriko Tsunoda Reider, "the oni as enemy during wartime in Japan was quickly and artificially created by Japanese leaders and enthusiastic nationalists ... this use of oni was a ploy that exploited fearful associations and thus advanced the Japanese wartime ultra-nationalist agenda."[3] Sasaki Naokata, a student in Miyagi Prefecture during the war, stated, "We were convinced that the Americans and the British were demons. Not human beings."[4] The Japanese government's official newsmagazine the *Photographic Weekly Report* (*Shashin shuho*), in issue 272, 19 May 1943, called the Americans "demon-bastards" and reminded readers that they killed "innocent schoolchildren" during the Doolittle Raid on the mainland on April 18, 1942.[5]

The *Japan Industry and Economics Newspaper* (*Nippon Sangyo Keizai Shimbun*) reported in a 1944 article, "If one considers the atrocities which they have committed against the American Indians, the Negroes and the Chinese, one is amazed at their presumption in wearing the mask of civilization.... The atrocities and inhuman actions perpetrated against the officers and men of the Imperial Forces since the outbreak of the War of Greater East Asia, in utter disregard of international war laws, surpass all former acts of bestiality."[6] The media even stated the Americans desired to exterminate the Japanese people. The weekly *Asahigraph's Great East Asia War Report* (*Asahigurafu Dai To A senso*), issue 112, 1 March 1944, stated, Americans' "animosity and hatred toward Japan is running rampant ... 'wipe the Japanese off the face of the earth' is not merely propaganda, it is the unattainable goal they cherish at the bottom of their hearts."[7]

Japanese troops and civilians on Saipan and Tinian spread rumors about the Americans. Chamorro young man Juan Camacho Diaz, whose family owned a coffee farm in upper Matansa (San Roque) on Saipan, stated that the Japanese told him, "Americans are the very worst enemy. They will cut off your nose and ears and maybe poke out your eyes. Don't be captured by the Americans."[8] Carolinian-Chamorro schoolboy David Sablan recalled, "Because of what the Japanese told us—that the Americans would do terrible things to us if we were captured—we thought of killing ourselves."[9] One rumor circulated was that American men "qualified for the Marine Corps by murdering their parents."[10] Another one was that the Americans were cannibals. Sailor John Barrow, aboard the destroyer USS *Aulick*, stated, "The Japanese Army told these women if the American Marines caught them they would eat their children. It was pretty horrible watching them jump through binoculars."[11] Marine Alvy Ray Pittmann, 20th Regiment, 4th Division, recounted, "When we got down to the end of the island [Saipan], they were jumping off the cliff. They thought we'd kill them and eat them."[12]

Japanese troops also informed civilians about true accounts of Americans in previous campaigns "mutilating Japanese war dead for souvenirs, attacking and sinking hospital ships, shooting sailors who had abandoned ship and pilots who had bailed out, killing wounded soldiers on the battlefield, and torturing and executing prisoners."[13] Some troops and civilians on Saipan and Tinian witnessed war crimes in person during the battles. Additionally, the Americans' collecting and inappropriate use of enemy body parts and bones repulsed them. On Saipan, according to historian Gavin Daws, "Seabees were cruising around in boats decorated with Japanese skulls skewered on stakes like shish kebabs."[14] In another instance on Saipan, the Americans used a dead woman as a mountainside "guidepost" for a number of days before taking care of the body. Marine Lieutenant Edward Bale, 2nd Division, stated, "When they were giving the truck drivers directions to bring supplies up, they'd say, 'Go up to where that dead woman is lying on her back, and then turn left or right.'"[15] Some Americans ripped out gold teeth from dead or sometimes wounded Japanese troops and civilians and even took rings and watches from fellow dead Marines or Soldiers.[16] Marine Michael Gates, 23rd Regiment, 4th Division, stated, on Saipan, "There was one guy in my outfit who carried a pair of pliers with him. Every dead Jap he'd see who had gold teeth he'd pull them out!"[17] Marine Sante DeMarino, 24th Regiment, 4th Division, stated, "As far as the Japs went, some guys would take anything they could get from them. They didn't give a shit about anything. Those guys were animals!"[18]

Civilians were afraid of the Americans because of what they heard or saw. A number of Japanese and Okinawan civilian survivors, including Shinozuka Yoshitaro, Shizuko Miura, Koyu Shiroma, and Miyagi Shinsho, stated in their memoirs and in interviews that they and others around them were convinced the Americans would harm them if they surrendered or were captured. Marine Language and Intelligence Officer Robert Sheeks, who spoke with a great number of civilians on Saipan and Tinian, wrote, "There were many instances of suicide, and nearly every civilian, as well as every soldier, had been issued one or more grenades with instructions to save one for suicide at the end.

Almost to a man, Japanese civilians and a large part of the Koreans and natives held the belief that capture meant hideous torture. For this reason, or due to pressure from Japanese troops, or danger at the front lines, they fell back ... as their troops retreated."[19] Marine Lieutenant Lewis Meyers noted, "It was obvious that the people of Saipan believed the Marines were slack-jawed maniacs ... it was plain that they thought any form of death better than falling into our hands."[20] Marine Lieutenant Colonel Russell Lloyd, Commanding Officer of the 6th Regiment, 2nd Division, wrote, on Saipan, "Some of the things I have seen here are almost unbelievable ... even to the smallest children they have the idea that we are going to kill them to the last soul and that they might just as well die by their own hands as fall into ours."[21] Marine Sergeant Bill Miller stated, a story told among civilians was that "the Americans would make their captives lie down side by side in the road and run over them with heavy trucks."[22] William McGaffin, a war correspondent with *The Saturday Evening Post*, wrote that captured civilians "did not want to get into the trucks which were waiting to take them to the internment camp. They were so certain we were going to kill them they couldn't see why we didn't do it right there, instead of troubling them to get into the trucks first."[23]

A United States military Western Pacific Base Command G-2 survey of five hundred civilian internees at Camp Susupe on Saipan revealed that 72 percent of civilians read or were told that the Americans would torture them and that nearly 70 percent primarily felt fear when they were captured. Only 15.8 percent "stated that they felt shame at being captured."[24] A 27th Army Infantry Division G-2 Interrogation Report stated that Shinozuka Kichitaro, a Nanyo Kohatsu labor supervisor at the Chalan Kanoa sugar factory, murdered his infant son because he believed "that he would be mistreated and tortured if taken into custody. He was asked how this thought had originated in his mind. He could give no definite answer but said it apparently took root in one person's mind and from there spread to others. He thought that this feeling was particularly prevalent on Saipan because this was the first time that Japanese civilians had ever experienced an attack by our forces and had been taken into custody in such large numbers. It was thought that we would kill the men and children by bayoneting them and take the women to 'use for our own pleasures and to satisfy our lusts.'"[25]

Civilians were told that the Americans would rape the women and girls of Saipan and Tinian if they surrendered or were captured. Chamorro schoolgirl Escolastica Tudela Cabrera recalled that a Japanese soldier told her family that "the Americans would kill everybody except the young girls. The girls they would take to the ships to be geishas."[26] Okinawan girl Chiyoko Yokota, stated, on Saipan, "We were told that if the Americans ever got hold of us, we women would become their play things. The men would have one foot tied to one vehicle and one foot tied to another, then they split them up the groin. So we were told to do all we could to avoid capture."[27] The Saipan NTLF G-2 Report stated, "Two (2) Chamorros interrogated said that the Japanese told them that the Americans had landed at Charan-Kanoa and had tortured and killed the men and had delivered the women to Negro troops to be mistreated."[28] Lieutenant Benjamin H. Hazard, a Military Intelligence Service Officer attached to the 27th Army Division, recalled, "While I was still on mop up duty in the Marpi area I met a young Okinawan girl, about eighteen years of age, who had strangled her young brother because the Japanese military had told her that if the Americans captured them they would kill the children and rape the women."[29] Saipan schoolgirl Victoria Akiyama stated that right before the Americans landed, a friend of her father's "shot and killed everyone in his family" out of fear of what the Americans would do to them.³⁰ The Japanese military dispersed propaganda leaflets during the battles to heighten civilian fears of rape. Chamorro schoolgirl Marie Soledad Castro recounted, on Saipan, "While we were in the cave Jose Matsumoto, a Korean, read a Japanese leaflet that said the Americans were going to kill all the men and take the women and children to the ships."³¹

Japanese propaganda and rumors made American rescue efforts more difficult. American intelligence officers found it especially hard to convince frightened civilians to surrender during aggressive advances. Marine Lieutenant Robert Sheeks wrote:

"At times it was necessary to fire at resisting troops and amidst the firing it was difficult to convince frightened civilians that they were not the target. Some civilians and troops crowded at the end of the island, swam out to the high outer edge of the submerged reef, and most drowned themselves when our boats or amphibian tractors approached in an effort to rescue them. Several groups of young men and women of the youth associations banded together at the top of cliffs, sang patriotic songs, and leaped into the sea. Some families threw themselves over cliffs, and in caves there were a number of suicides with grenades or knives."³²

Surrendering was not easy. Lieutenant Sheeks wrote:

The nature of the fighting, especially in the high land, resembled that of jungle warfare, which made it difficult and dangerous to attempt surrender. A civilian wishing to present himself alone or in a group had to face the problem of getting past Japanese troops who would often shoot rather than

Tinian civilians, with their hands up, surrendering to the Americans, July 1944. Many civilians were afraid of the Americans. #93561. National Archives.

permit surrender. Considered an integral part of the defense system, civilians were expected to "Levée en masse" (form a people's army) and, in any case, being Japanese subjects, were supposed, like troops, to commit suicide rather than surrender. Then if the person got through the Japanese lines, he faced artillery barrages, mortar fire, and whatever else was involved in the battle at that point. Surviving this, he had to surrender, usually where visibility was poor, in such a manner that he was not mistaken for a resisting soldier.[33]

The fear of being slaughtered by Japanese troops was another leading reason civilians did not surrender to the Americans. Civilians and troops were often together, especially in the islands' caves and in jungle camps. A number of Japanese officers and enlisted men, armed with guns, swords, and bayonets, threatened to murder anyone who attempted to go to the enemy. Chamorro schoolgirl Escolastica Tudela Cabrera stated, "We were more afraid of the Japanese than the Americans.... Some of the women wanted me to go and tell the Americans that we were in the cave but I was afraid. The Japanese were above our cave firing down at the Americans with machine guns and rifles, and the Americans were firing back. I didn't want to go out. Then some Japanese came by our cave with their big swords and said if anyone went to the Americans they would cut our throats."[34] Marine Lieutenant Edward Bale, 2nd Division, who fought on Saipan and Tinian, stated, "We watched the Japanese soldiers push these women and children off cliffs and watched them throw them off cliffs.... Many of the women who wanted to come through our positions the Japanese Army wouldn't let them.... The Japanese soldiers would not let these civilians come into our lines or anything else."[35] Marine Lieutenant Jim G. Lucas wrote, on Saipan, "There have been instances in which we know the natives have been killed for trying to give themselves up."[36] Marine Richard J. Butler, 2nd Division, who witnessed murders and suicides on Saipan, stated, "Many of the civilians took their lives because the Japanese soldiers refused to let them surrender."[37] The Tinian NTLF G-2 Periodic Report no. 49, 3 August 1944, stated, "Reports indicated Jap soldiers were preventing civilians from surrendering during the day. One report from 2ndMarDiv observers said several hundred civilians with white flags had been turned back by Jap soldiers as they sought to give themselves up."[38]

A number of Japanese troops murdered civilians. Marine Lieutenant Lewis Meyers wrote, an American platoon attacking a jungle hill in enemy hands "found half-crazed drunken Jap soldiers cutting the throats of women and babies as the Marines moved in. Combat is no fun but few things are worse than the sight of a little girl gasping out her life through a slashed windpipe."[39] Marine Sergeant Dan Levin wrote about a woman brought into an American field hospital who had her throat cut by a Japanese soldier on Saipan.[40] The Saipan NTLF G-2 Report stated, on June 26, "A Chamorro woman, who had been holed up in a cave in Kagman Point along with several other native women and children and a Jap soldier belonging to the 'Home Guard,' stated to the 24th Marines who took her to the hospital that the Jap had slashed her throat and those of the other women and children before he killed himself."[41] Chamorro young man Cristino Dela Cruz remembered when a Japanese sniper shot and killed his brother as they were surrendering to the Americans near Fina Sisu (southern Saipan).[42] Chamorro young woman Trinidad Guerrero stated that a Japanese soldier killed her father.[43] Rita Titibau Lieb, a Carolinian woman who lived with her family in northwestern Saipan before the battle, stated that Japanese soldiers shot her mother in the head during the battle.[44]

Marines interviewed by correspondent Robert Sherrod told him that a Japanese sniper at Marpi Point "spotted a Japanese group, apparently father, mother and four children, out on the rocks, preparing to drown themselves, but evidently weakening in their decision. The Jap sniper took aim. He drilled the man from behind, dropping him off the rocks into the sea. The second bullet hit the woman. She dragged herself about thirty feet along the rocks. Then she floated out in a stain of blood. The sniper would have shot the children, but a Japanese woman ran across and carried them out of range."[45] Marine Robert R. Montgomery, 6th Regiment, 2nd Division, stated, on Saipan's Suicide Cliff, "women and children were jumping off the cliff into the sea. And those that did not want to go voluntarily, the Japanese threw them off."[46] Marine Steve Judd, 6th Regiment, 2nd Division, recounted, on Saipan, Japanese troops "threw kids off. Americans with PA systems were right below the cliffs trying to get them to stop."[47] Marine Glenn L. Buzzard, 24th Regiment, 4th Division, stated, on Saipan, "The Japanese soldiers threw the native women and kids over the cliff and jumped over after them.... If they were still alive, a soldier would go right out over the reef, right into the water, and would swim around and drown them."[48] Marine Sante DeMarino, 24th Regiment, 4th Division, stated, "There were these cliffs and the natives were jumping off. If they didn't, the Japs would shoot them."[49] Marine Lewis Jacob Steck, 2nd Regiment, 2nd Division, stated, on Saipan, "Sometimes the Japanese shot the civilians who wouldn't jump."[50]

Sailor Albert Anthony D'Amico, aboard the USS LST [Landing Ship Tank] 278, recalled, on Saipan:

> Instead of surrendering, some would shoot each other or blow each other up, you know. And they would throw these people off this ledge, which was couple hundred feet high in the mountain.... And I was over there. I had this interpreter with the loud speaker yelling in Japanese don't—pleading with the army, the Japanese army ... not to kill the civilians. And they would take them and throw the men, women, and children off the mountain.... And as soon as they hit the bottom, they were dead. You know, men, women, and children. And after, when they're floating in there for about a day.... Then the flies started getting on them. Big, green flies. And they were all over my face and everything, biting me. I had to get out of there.[51]

Marine Lieutenant Frederic A. Stott, 24th Regiment, 4th Division, witnessed many killings by Japanese troops on Saipan. He wrote:

> Gradually a concentration of well over a hundred had collected at the water's edge by early afternoon. Interpreters were summoned, and they pleaded by amplifier for the civilians to come forward in surrender.... Almost imperceptibly a psychological reaction seemed to emerge, and the people drew closer together into a compact mass. It was still predominantly civilian, but several in uniform could be distinguished circling about in the throng using the civilians for protection. As they huddled closer sounds of a weird singing chant carried up to us. Suddenly a waving flag of the Rising Sun was unfurled. Movement grew more agitated, men started leaping into the sea, and the chanting gave way to startled cries, and with them the popping sound of detonating grenades. It was the handful of soldiers, determined to prevent the surrender or escape of their kinfolks, who tossed grenades into the milling throng of men, women, and children, and then dived into the sea from which escape was impossible. The exploding grenades cut up the mob into patches of dead, dying, and wounded, and for the first time we actually saw water that ran red with human blood. Having killed or dispersed this first gathering, the remaining soldiers waited under cover until another similar group had collected. Again our pleas went unheeded, and again came the chanting, flag waving, the bursting grenades, and the dead and dying. These were two of the oft-described Marpi Point mass suicides, and reports from coastal patrol vessels indicated that these were not the only two such killings. The motivation behind these suicides is hard to analyze. Perhaps it was the frozen fear of a cornered helpless animal, terror-ridden and dominated by a handful of fanatical military survivors determined to allow no escape. Surely it was a different reaction from that we had encountered elsewhere on the island. But whatever the reason, the sight was diabolically gruesome, and to some nauseating.[52]

The Tinian NTLF G-2 Periodic Report no. 50, 4 August 1944, stated, "Reports that the Jap military are using force, killing and injuring many civilians to prevent them from surrendering."[53] Marine Charles Pase, 10th Regiment, 2nd Division, stated, on Tinian, "a file of Japanese women and children came out of one of the caves fleeing, trying to get out to surrender, and the women were carrying babies and small children by hand trying to run, and they were cut down by the Japanese. The Japanese soldiers in the caves shot them all."[54]

There were a number of massacres during both battles. Marine Sergeant David Dempsey, detailed an incident on Saipan where Japanese troops were slaughtering civilians in what Marines informally named the "cave of horrors." He wrote, "From inside the cave came a pitiful chorus of wailing babies and the screams of women and old men." When the Marines entered it, they saw "The bodies of men and women and children were blown apart and lay splattered against the walls of the tunnel ... two girls ... throats had been slit." Many people had been shot.[55] The Tinian NTLF G-2 Report stated, "Japanese soldiers, towards the end of the Tinian campaign, massacred a group of forty (40) civilians, most women and children by tying them into a tight group and setting off grenades and a 'satchel charge' in their midst and shooting those who survived."[56] The report also stated, "Language Personnel of the 23rd Marines reported seeing an unidentified Japanese push three (3) men and twelve (12) women and children over a cliff into the sea in the southern part of the island."[57] On August 3, the 23rd Regiment, 4th Marine Division, commanded by Colonel Louis R. Jones, reported during mop-up operations on Tinian, "Several freak incidents occurred during the day (1) Jap children thrown over cliff into ocean; (2) Military grouped civilians in numbers of 15 to 20 and attached explosive charges to them, blowing them to bits; (3) Both military and civilians lined up on the cliff line and hurled themselves into the ocean; (4) Many civilians pushed over cliff by soldiers."[58]

A number of Japanese troops forced parents to murder their children. Nanyo Kohatsu businessman Shinozuka Yoshitaro found several dead infants near Kalabera in northeastern Saipan and believed they were murdered by Japanese troops.[59] IJA Sergeant Takeo Yamauchi recounted his experience in a cave in northern Saipan between July 10 and 14:

> The noncommissioned officer was a little dictator. He ordered the babies to be killed because they were making a noise that could give everyone away to the Americans. At this, one of the mothers got up and walked out of the cave. She said, "I rather die than kill my baby." But the mothers who were left did strangle their babies to death. The cave went quiet. All I could hear was the mothers crying. My only thought was of surrender. I told myself not to get involved in what was happening around me. But, by the third day the cave had started to stink from the rotting bodies of the babies. I couldn't bear it anymore. That night, on the fourteenth of July, I slipped quietly out of the cave. I had made up my mind to surrender.[60]

Marine Lieutenant Colonel Justice M. Chambers, Commanding Officer of the 3rd Battalion, 25th Regiment, 4th Division, stated:

> During this day as we moved along the cliffs and caves, we uncovered civilians all the time. The Jap soldiers would not surrender, and would not permit the civilians to surrender. I saw with my own eyes women, some carrying children, come out of the caves and start toward our lines. They'd be shot down by their own people. I watched any number of women carrying children come down to the cliffs that dropped to the ocean. They were very steep, very precipitous. The women would come down and throw the children into the ocean and jump in and commit suicide. I watched one group at a distance of perhaps 100 yards, about eight or ten civilian men, women and children get into a little huddle and blow themselves up.... It was a sad and terrible thing.[61]

2295-5-25
071/385
Ser.0062-A   G-2 Report ~~~~~~~ Phase III (TINIAN) (cont'd)

SECRET

of the enemy to effect a fairly orderly withdrawal to the south end of the island indicates that some interior communication must have been effected. Intelligence concerning communication with other enemy bases during the operation is not available. Relative to this a Japanese Naval Warrant Officer was captured who had been a supervisor in the coding section of the USHI Point Airfield Radio Station. He was very security conscious and no information could be gained prior to his departure for another base.

For the communications facilities located on TINIAN in March of this year see chart numbers three (3) and four (4) of Appendix C. Although it is believed that changes in this plan were undoubtedly effected by the enemy subsequent to this date, it is thought that their basic communications net closely resembled the charts.

9. Camouflage and camouflage discipline.

During the operational phase of TINIAN the enemy's camouflage and camouflage discipline was excellent. Their infantry troops operated from well concealed positions in caves and heavy growth and restricted the movement of large groups of troops to the hours of darkness. Very few instances were reported where more than twenty (20) or thirty (30) Japanese were observed moving in a group. By proper use of cover and concealment the 1st Battalion 135th Infantry was able to move from TINIAN Town to our beachhead on "J" day with only small groups being observed by our constant air observation. Also, by movement at night the enemy was able to withdraw to the southern end of the island over relatively open terrain without being observed by our troops.

Enemy artillery positions were also well camouflaged in caves and wooded terrain, and positions were picked up principally by observation of gun flashes and sound ranging.

10. Miscellaneous enemy activities.

a. **Atrocities**. Eyewitness accounts by Marine Offic from the 4th Marine Division, two (2) of whose signed statements are set forth below, indicate that Japanese soldiers, towards the end of the TINIAN campaign, massacred a group of forty (40) civilians, mostly women and children by tying them into a tight group and setting off grenades and a "satchel charge" in their midst and shooting those who survived. It cannot be determined if the civilians voluntarily submitted to this procedure but the presence of small children in the group, who must be presumed to have been mentally unable to con-

- 51 -   SECRET

Above and following six documents: Northern Troops and Landing Force reports concerning atrocities (Record Group 38, National Archives).

7. Causes of the Mass Civilian Suicides   113

2295-5-25
071/385
Ser. 0062-A G-2 Report ▮▮▮▮▮ Phase III (TINIAN) (cont'd)

S E C R E T

sent to be massacred, gives the action at least an aspect of an atrocity. The statements are as follows:

"About 1400 on 2 August, I witnessed the massacre of a number of civilians by seven (7) Japanese soldiers. The victims numbered thirty (30) to forty (40) and included a high proportion of women and children, perhaps as high as 75%. The group was formed in a tight circle facing inboard and a rope tied around them by the soldiers. This procedure they accepted with utter hostility. The soldiers then stepped back from the group and almost immediately a hand grenade went off in their midst. This explosion was followed within two (2) or three (3) seconds by a much more violent one that threw bodies as far as thirty (30) feet. The second explosion appeared to be of about an equivalent strength as that produced by a C-2 charge and may have been either a land mine or a mortar shell".

"The incident took place at about T.A.- 505 C,G. Our point of observation was on the high ground to the east at a distance of approximately 800 yards. I watched the entire proceedings through field glasses and was able to distinguish the soldiers by their uniforms and by the rifles that each one carried".

/s/ THOMAS C. SMITH,
2ndLt. USMCR.

# # # # # # # #

"TINIAN,
5th August, 1944.
0900
2ndLt. DAVID L. ANDERSON,
Language Officer, R-2, 23rd Marines.

"On August 2nd while in charge of an Observation Post detail consisting of four (4) scouts and 2ndLt. Thomas Smith, Language Officer from G-2, on the cliff line in T.A.- 505 I witnessed the following incident:

"When the detail arrived at the cliff line I counted sixty-three (63) civilians on the coastal plain and sent one (1) scout back to the radio to warn the advancing troops not to fire on them. Shortly after, following some shouting from the cliff, other civilians started coming out of the thick brush at the cliff base.

- 52 -   S E C R E T

2295-525
071/385
Ser. 0062-A   G-2 Report ▇▇▇▇ Phase III (TINIAN) (cont'd)

SECRET

"At 1330 PFC. Baxter observed two (2) soldiers with rifles among the civilians, and shortly after we observed seven (7) in all armed with rifles. At about 1345 two (2) of the soldiers had gathered together what we estimated to be forty (40) civilians mainly women and children, and were tying them in a tight group with a rope. The other soldiers moved to the right along the cliff line leaving one (1) man to finish the job of roping the civilians.

"At this time we did not know what was planned for the civilians. We though they were to be pushed off the cliff enmasse as some had been jumping off voluntarily. We did not dare fire for the range was approximately eight hundred (800) yards and we could accomplish nothing by firing at that time.

"At 1400 there was a small explosion similar to a hand grenade in the center of the civilian group, this knocked the group to the ground. A few seconds later there was a larger explosion which resembled our composition C-2 charge that blew the civilians' bodies twenty (20) to thirty (30) feet in the air and about fifty (50) feet from the scene of the explosion.

"At this point the soldiers returned and commenc shooting the civilians that remained alive. Again we did not fire for fear of hitting some little children that remained alive and apparently unharmed. For some reason the Japanese soldiers did not kill the children, but began making their way toward another group of civilians east of them.

"Fearing a repetition of the foregoing incident and seeing no civilians for a two hundred (200) yard interval I ordered the scouts to fire. Their fire was observed to hit three soldiers and the entire group of seven (7) were observed to blow themselves up individually. This closed the incident".

/s/ DAVID L. ANDERSON,
2ndLt. USMCR.

Language Personnel of the 23rd Marines reported seeing an unidentified Japanese push three (3) men and twelve (12) women and children over a cliff into the sea in the southern part of the island as our forces advanced in the final stages of the battle of TINIAN.

SECRET

2295-5-25
071/385
Ser.0062-A   G-2 Report ▓▓▓▓ Phase III (TINIAN) (cont'd)
- -

S E C R E T

Reports from the 2nd Marine Division stated that Japanese military were using force, killing and injuring civilians to prevent them from surrendering.

b. <u>Evidence of fanaticism</u>. As the end of the TINIAN campaign approached, the usual Japanese suicidal battle fanaticism appeared. Soldiers committed suicide by using grenades; group suicides with grenades or demolitions were common among the military many of them jumped off cliffs into the sea particularly in the southern part of the island.

The 8th Marines reported they saw many civilians on August 2nd - 3rd commit suicide by jumping down from the cliffs in the MARPO Point area into the sea.

A captured Warrant Officer from the 56th KEIBITAI stated that around 1000 "loyal citizens" among the civilians allowed the military to blow them up in caves.

c. <u>Disposal of dead</u>. The 4th Marine Division reported the discovery of a graveyard located in T.A.- 533 U, with a large crematory nearby. The latter consisted of two (2) kilns constructed of brick, with complete equipment. In the graveyard, freshly buried dead had been buried on top of old graves and in shallow holes. Pits in nearby caves contained an undetermined number of charred and partially burned bodies and one (1) cave was still burning when encountered.

Many enemy dead were hastily buried in canefields as the Japanese retreated.

11. Counter Intelligence.

No difficulty was experienced in denying the enemy information relative to our forces during Phase III, ▓▓▓▓ and all available evidence indicates no breach of security during this operation.

Possible compromise of WHITE Beaches as preferred landing areas resultant from two (2) successive night reconnaissance by our troops, was in part nullified by simultaneous reconnaissance of YELLOW Beaches. It is not believed that our forces were detected on either beach. This is evidenced in part by the weak defense of the landing area and by the statements of POWS and translation of captured documents subsequent to our successful landing, indicating complete surprise over the selection of landing beaches. It is known

- 54 -   S E C R E T

2295-5-25
071/271
Ser.0024A   G-2 Report ▇▇▇▇ Phase I (SAIPAN) (cont'd)

The 27th Division reported that the enemy was still occupying a cliff from TA 285 X to TA 195 U to TA 195 Y where small pockets of enemy were defending with mortar and machine gun fire.

The 4th Marine Division was not in attack during the day.

An enemy tank was destroyed by the 165th in TA 195 K. Both the 106th and 165th reported that Japanese were wearing American helmets.

A captured Jap sergeant major belonging to headquarters troops of the 31st Army said that the Jap Fleet had been expected on the 19th of June. He also related that orders had come down to bury all dead and evacuate all wounded.

A Chamorro woman, who had been holed up in a cave in KAGMAN Point along with several other native women and children and a Jap soldier belonging to the "Home Guard", stated to the 24th Marines who took her to the hospital that the Jap had slashed her throat and those of the other women and children before he killed himself.

At 1800 on D plus 11 (June 26th) the enemy capabilities were as listed in G-2 Periodic Report No. 12 (See: Appendix E).

As of the above date a total of 154 prisoners of war had been taken.

The captured SONAE message for this date from the SONAE Chief of Staff to the AC of S, 29th Division said:

"Situation a.m. 26th. (1) No great change in the battle lines. (2) Naval gunfire--1 cruiser, and 4 DDs, besides coming close ashore, carried out a heavy bombardment of ground installations. (3) As a result of a concentration of mortar fire on the roadway at night, our communications became difficult."

The SONAE Chief of Staff also sent the following order to the CO of the 50th Infantry Regiment on TINIAN (probably the night of the 26th):

"This is a preparatory order. As rapidly as possible you are to carry out an amphibious operation to SAIPAN with 2 large landing craft."

The 2nd Marine Division reported a generally quiet night. The 2nd Marines received more mortar fire than on previous

- 33 -   SECRET

7. Causes of the Mass Civilian Suicides

2295-5-25
071/385
Ser. 0024A   G-2 Report ████ Phase I (SAIPAN) (cont'd)

S E C R E T

prevented from doing so by officers. A Superior Private from an Engineer Company of HOMARE 11935 (136th Infantry) said his unit arrived a SAIPAN on April 12 in a convoy consisting of four (4) transports. Hi unit consisted of 300 men with Captain FUKADA in charge. This POW stated that only about 100 men were left in his unit in the area nort! of KALAPERA PASS. He stated that practically all the soldiers are tired of fighting but are forced to do so by officers who tell them that they will be tortured if captured. Surrender leaflets were seen but taken from the men by the officers. He gave his estimate of troor strength prior to D Day as 30,000 military on SAIPAN

(18) <u>D plus 17 Day (2 July)</u>. Three (3) POWS from the 43rd Division Intendance Unit (HOMARE 11949) said their unit numbered about 2400 men in four (4) companies. They arrived on 7 June with the badly depleted 118th Infantry Regiment. The morale of these POWS was very low, being convinced that their cause was lost. They maintained that the majority of their unit was unarmed. The enemy wa£ using runners for unimportant messages. Six (6) POWS from the 135th Infantry Regiment (SUZUKI Butai) claim their unit was pretty well depleted in strength and food and water were getting critically low, and that the Japanese at this stage were being too sorely pressed to take the time and energy to bury their dead. A POW from the 16th Shipping Engineers said his unit, initially 600 men, had about 200 men left. All engaged in the vicinity of GARAPAN. A POW from the 136th Infantry Regiment stated that the total regimental strength was 1500 - 1600 whe the unit arrived on SAIPAN. The untrained personnel were left in Japa and only trained people brought along. His Battalion had been fightir rear guard action ever since CHARAN-KANOA. A POW stated his unit, the 11th Engineer Regiment was a new construction outfit which arrived SAIPAN early in June. He could not estimate the number of troops in this unit but it was not considered very large. A number of POWS stat that the 43rd Division Intendance unit is composed mostly of farmers, four (4) companies of 600 men each. According to a POW from the 136th Infantry Regiment the SNLF consisted of 3000 - 4000 well equipped men who were hiding in the mountains.

(19) <u>D plus 18 Day (3 July)</u>. Two (2) Chamorros interrogated said that the Japanese told them that the Americans had landed at CHARAN-KANOA and had tortured and killed the men and had delivered the women to Negro troops to be mistreated. They believe that such stories have caused the Chamorros to be afraid to surrender to the American forces. Three (3) completely demoralized POWS from the 135th Infantry Regiment stated that the morale of the soldiers in his unit was extremely low, and that they did not have their hearts in the fighting. A naval warrant officer from the YOSHINO (probably HOSHINO) unit which consisted of 150 men who were being sent to the

S E C R E T

G-2 PERIODIC REPORT

G-2 REPORT

From: 111800K
To : 121800K

SECRET

No. 28

Hq, Northern Troops & Landing Force,
In the Field,
13 July, 1944 - 0800K

Map: Special Air and Gunnery Target Map, SAIPAN, 5 sheets, RF 1:20,000, prepared by 64th Engr. Top. Bn., U. S. Army, April, 1944.

1. ENEMY SITUATION AT END OF PERIOD.

    No change.

2. ENEMY OPERATIONS DURING PERIOD.

    a. *General summary.* All 4th MarDiv line Regiments reported infiltration and sniping during the night. The 24th Marines reported that at 0300 about 20 civilians approached the Regimental CP and when challenged they scattered and Jap soldiers behind them threw hand grenades. Some of the civilians, captured at daybreak, said they were forced by the soldiers to act in this way as shields. The Division continued mopping-up during the day. The 23rd Marines cleaned up the caves along the western beach line, and on the western side of Mt. MARPI. Resistance was reported at 264 C,H,Q, 267 N, 278 H,I, 277 Q,V, 254 L, 269 U, 263 U, 263 A, 262 J, and 275 along the coast. All places were cleaned out.

    The 2ndMarDiv experienced little enemy activity during the night. The 165th reported scattered grenade and rifle fire in the vicinity of the CP which was quickly brought under control around 2100, and some light infiltration during the night. The 6th Marines killed 8 Japs and the 2nd Marines killed 1. The Division continued mopping-up activities during the day. The 2nd Marines killed 2 Japs, 1 being identified as a Private 1st Class of the 135th Infantry. A patrol captured a woman hiding in the woods who claims to have been there the night before with 4 or 5 men armed with grenades. The 6th Marines killed 59 Japs and took 8 POWS. A generator and a small amount of aerial bombs were found in T.A. 229.

    The 27thInfDiv reported a quiet night with some enemy activity on the perimeters of the 105th and 249th FA Bns. One Jap was killed and several Jap civilians, including children, were taken into custody. The Division said anti-sniper patrols for the day were negative. 106th Regiment reported that FLORES Point guards had killed 26 Japs during the past few days.

- 1 -

SECRET

Not all Japanese officers and men committed atrocities. A number left civilians alone and allowed them to flee to American lines. Others were kind to civilians.[62] Saipan schoolboy Miyagi Shinsho, who was shot in the right hand during an American attack, wrote that a Japanese soldier bandaged his hand near the end of the battle before committing suicide.[63] When IJA Captain Sakae Oba's unit found two infants still alive in a destroyed farmhouse, they gave them water, placed them in boxes filled with clothing, and put them under a shade tree marked with a red cloth flag so the Americans could save them.[64] Captain Oba later ordered a large group of civilians camping with his unit to surrender rather than massacring them or forcing them to commit suicide. A number of Japanese troops had families who they loved and cherished, and sympathized with civilians to varying degrees. IJA Soldier Taroa Kawaguchi, 43rd Division, wrote in his final diary entry on Saipan, 7 July 1944, "Dear Krike, Please live with courage. My sincerest regards to mother and brother."[65] IJN Sailor Genkichi Ichikawa, who fought and died on Saipan, wrote in his diary, "Although trying not to think nor write about it today, one year ago was the birth of my daughter. This poor father cannot celebrate her birthday. Supposedly she would be lonely. I am celebrating far away from home at the battlefield, wondering if she can speak a few words or is walking. It fills my heart."[66] Every soldier and sailor, as well as unit, in the Japanese military were different in some way. According to historian Allison B. Gilmore, the IJM "was composed of millions of human beings with diverse personalities, character traits, and temperaments. It was also divided into a multitude of units, each with its own peculiar personality based on the nature of the individuals who belonged to it, the character of its leaders, and its wartime experiences."[67]

A number of Japanese troops did not want to commit suicide or see others commit suicide. However, they were ordered by their superiors to either die fighting or commit suicide. An IJA battalion commander issued a field order in Nafutan Point on June 26 that stated, "Those who cannot participate in combat must commit suicide."[68] IJA Sergeant Yamauchi Takeo, 136th Regiment, 43rd Division, stated, "Now, the Americans began to broadcast surrender advice over loud speakers. From the sea. 'Japanese Forces! Throw down your arms! We will protect the honor of those who have fought hard and who give themselves up. We have water. We have food.' Their Japanese was a little shaky. They said they would resume fighting after a fixed interval. That was the first time I heard an American call to surrender, but I feared that if I surrendered within sight of our own men during daylight, I might be shot in the back."[69] Marine Lieutenant Cliff Graham recalled seeing Japanese officers on Tinian killing their men. In one instance, Graham wrote, "an officer lined up five soldiers, took his pistol and placed a bullet in each of their heads."[70] Tsuruji Akikusa, who fought elsewhere in the Pacific, stated, "There was cruelty between even Japanese soldiers."[71] The Saipan NTLF G-2 Report stated, "Many said that as individuals they would have been willing to surrender but feared social pressure or physical violence from their own officers or NCOs if they tried to give themselves up.... Many POWS came in with propaganda leaflets on their persons and many more bodies were found with leaflets in the pockets.... Another clue was that several Japanese military POWS volunteered to write propaganda texts, to assist in broadcasting, or to assist by doing calligraphy or in any other way."[72]

The Japanese troops who forced civilians and other troops to commit suicide or murdered them did so, in part, because of what they were told and learned in the military. Japanese officers told the men under them to "fight to the bitter end" and resist "desperately

"Victim, Vanquished, and Victors—A Japanese non-commissioned officer captured at Saipan, aids in evacuating native children from front line fighting areas. He volunteered to help move the wounded children after he had been trapped in a cave with a family of native Chamorros." July 1944. #84917. National Archives.

to the last." Surrender was regarded as treason. IJN Sailor Harunori Okoshi, who served in the Pacific, stated, "If you became a prisoner, you were labeled a traitor, and your name struck from your family register in red. That's what we were told."[73] A Japanese medic wrote, to surrender was like "obliterating oneself." Marine Lieutenant Robert Sheeks, who interrogated many Japanese POWs on Saipan and Tinian, stated, "They had been told that no Japanese has been captured and if you were to ever give up you would not be Japanese anymore."[74] IJM troops were regarded as the emperor's troops; their lives "belonged to the emperor."[75] Surrender was an "unthinkable" offense against him, and it was "known informally that any returning Japanese POW would be put to death."[76] The IJA Criminal Code of 1908 stated, "A commander who allows his unit to surrender to the enemy without fighting to the last man or who concedes a strategic area to the enemy shall be punishable by death."[77] Though the code was revised in 1942 to the lesser punishment of imprisonment, Japanese officers on Saipan, Tinian, and elsewhere in the empire still experienced enormous social pressure to die on the battlefield with all of their men.[78]

It was said among troops that when a soldier or sailor surrendered, he brought shame to his entire unit and family back home. According to historian Edward J. Drea, "each infantry regiment had ties with a specific locality, and each had its respective hometown unit. In short, one did not escape one's peers and village by joining the army; they came along, and the consequent motivation not to disgrace one's family or village by delinquent military service was powerful."[79] The Field Service Code of 1941, stated, "Meet the expectations of your family and home community by making effort upon effort, always mindful of the honour of your name. If alive, do not suffer the disgrace of becoming a prisoner; in death, do not leave behind a name soiled by misdeeds."[80] Haruji Mita, who fought in the Pacific, discussed his reluctance to surrender, stating, "I didn't want my parents and siblings to suffer humiliation."[81] Yoshida Osamu, a soldier on Saipan, attempted suicide with a grenade because he was considering "his mother and the rest of his family."[82] The grenade blast only wounded him, however, and he was captured and cared for by the Americans.

An IJA non-commissioned officer who survived Saipan stated, "In those days, Japanese soldiers really accepted the idea that they must eventually die. If you were taken alive as a prisoner you could never face your own family."[83] IJA Soldier Kawamura Kazuo, who fought on Saipan in the Matsumoto 150th Infantry Regiment, remarked about the

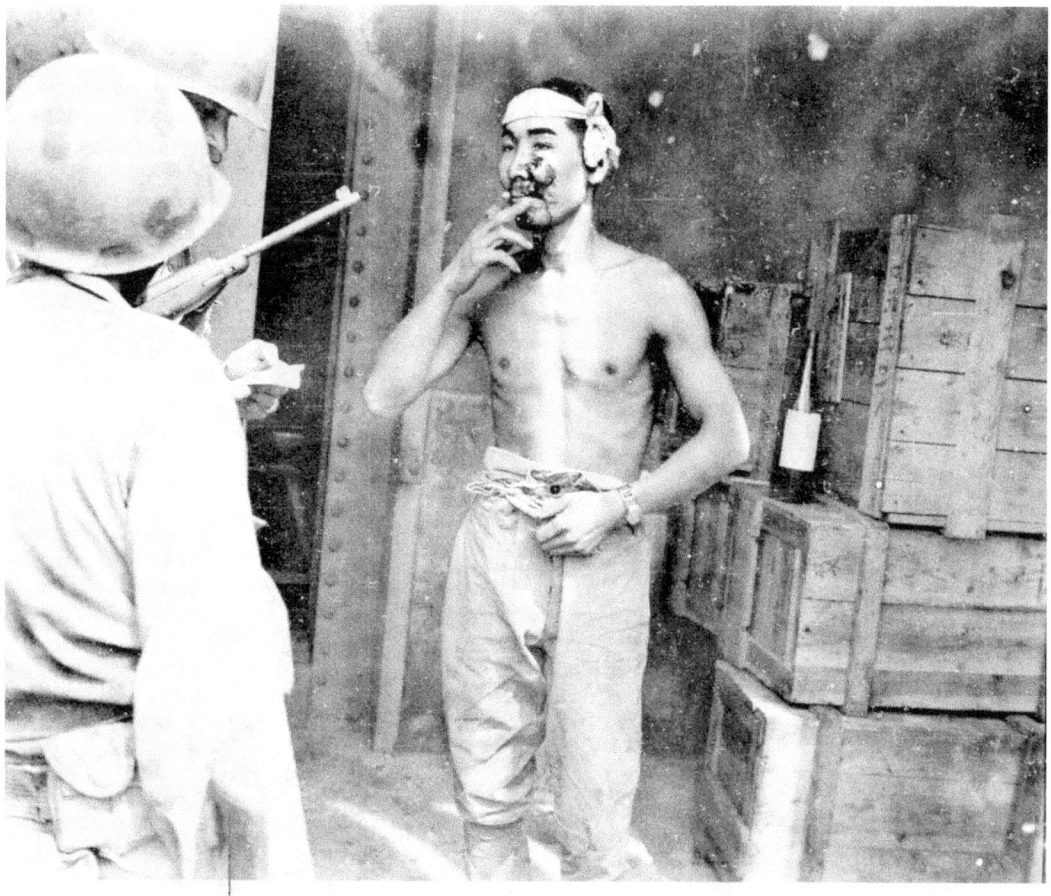

A wounded prisoner of war on Saipan, June 1944. The Japanese garrisons on Saipan and Tinian did not die to the last man. There were a number of Japanese troops who surrendered or were captured. #83121. National Archives.

mentality many Japanese troops had at the time, "'*Ikite ryoushu no hazukashime wo ukezu.*' (A soldier must never suffer the disgrace of being captured alive.) These words, which we soldiers had memorized during our training, haunted me because I was exactly what I knew I should not be—a prisoner. The idea that a prisoner is not human was so deeply engraved on my mind. For a Japanese soldier, becoming a prisoner was the worst thing, and I wanted to kill myself."[84] Kawamura recalled upon returning to the mainland, "In my neighborhood in Azumino, there were many families in which husbands and sons did not return from the war, and because I had been on Saipan, where every soldier had been expected to either win the battle or die for the Emperor, they wondered why I had come back alive. The situation was painful for everyone, and I just realized it was best for me not to talk about it."[85]

Japanese officers on Saipan and Tinian knew if the islands fell that the Americans would use them as bases to attack and invade their homeland. It was their duty to stop the enemy right there and "help improve Japan's rapidly declining military fortunes...with their deaths."[86] A number of Japanese officers on the islands came to think that there were no distinctions between combatant and noncombatant in such a brutal struggle for the safety and existence of the empire/their home. The demarcations between combatants and civilians, including, gender, age, training, and experience, were gone in their eyes. These officers believed all imperial subjects, including their troops and civilian men, women, and children, were to be part of the defending forces on the islands. They felt there were no longer any noncombatants on the battlefield—only defenders and invaders. Nanyo Kohatsu businessman Shinozuka Yoshitaro wrote in his memoir that a soldier

A Japanese sailor killed on Saipan, July 1944. A hand grenade is next to his body. Central Pacific Area, CPA-44-6934. Signal Corps, SC-210539. National Archives.

Marine standing over dead Japanese troops on Saipan, June 1944. #88356. National Archives.

told him "we are no longer soldiers. You are no longer civilians. We are all just Japanese and we all suffer the same."[87] Those who would not or could not fight had to die, because "defenders" were not supposed to surrender. Consequently, some Japanese officers prevented civilians from going to the Americans, forced civilians to commit suicide, and murdered civilians. Again, not all Japanese officers believed civilians had to die. Interactions and relationships between troops and civilians on the islands were varied and were affected by a complex mix of circumstances and individual and unit beliefs. Many civilians on Saipan and Tinian survived because a number of Japanese officers allowed them to surrender. One IJN officer on Saipan told civilians, "You must survive, even if you become prisoners of war."[88]

Many IJM troops believed they were doomed on the islands and some lost or discarded their sense of self-preservation and moral reasoning in the face of imminent death. They assumed or hoped that if they died in combat that their noble spirit (*eirei*) would be able to rest as a kami in the national war-dead shrine of Yasukuni. The highest honor any imperial subject could achieve, it was believed, was to have their spirit enshrined at Yasukuni as a deity or god. Even the emperor and empress worshipped the kami in the shrine.[89] IJA Soldier Taroa Kawaguchi, 43rd Division, wrote in his diary on Saipan, July 7, 1944, "I am carrying out my duty and thus becoming a war god…. It is only regrettable that we have not fought enough and that the American devil is stomping on the Imperial soil."[90] Even if a soldier or sailor raped or murdered civilians, they would still be enshrined as a war god after dying in the field. According to historian Akiko Takenaka, "death on the battlefield made a soldier an *eirei* regardless of his previous actions."[91]

Some Americans' reluctance to take Japanese military prisoners, mostly because of fear of booby traps, revenge for buddies killed, or racial antipathy, aggravated and strengthened Japanese troops' beliefs concerning the need to die on the battlefield and not surrender. There was a "kill-or-be-killed psychology" among troops on both sides.[92] Marine Captain Roy H. Elrod, 8th Regiment, 2nd Division, wrote that in his unit on Saipan, "there was no effort to take prisoners."[93] Marine Frank W. Borta, 8th Regiment, 2nd Division, recalled when they took a "prisoner into the bush and killed him" on Saipan.[94] Marine Sante DeMarino, 24th Regiment, 4th Division, stated, "I remember one crazy bastard who went up to a bunch of sick and wounded Japs on Saipan. He sprayed them with his BAR [Browning Automatic Rifle]."[95] Marine George J. Dorko, 25th Regiment, 4th Division, who fought on Saipan and Tinian, stated, "The word was no prisoners.... No prisoners. No mercy."[96] Understandably, many Japanese troops were afraid to surrender to the Americans. The Saipan NTLF G-2 Report said, an IJA prisoner of war from the 136th Regiment, 43rd Division "stated that practically all the soldiers are tired of fighting but are forced to do so by officers who tell them that they will be tortured if captured. Surrender leaflets were seen but taken from the men by the officers."[97] According to historian Allison B. Gilmore, "Most [Japanese] POWS stated that neither they nor their commanding officers had any knowledge of the Geneva Convention or international laws respecting POWS."[98] According to historian Oleg Benesch, "A US military report on a group of Japanese prisoners of war compiled shortly before the end of the war revealed that 84 per cent of them were convinced that they would be tortured or executed by their Allied captors."[99]

There was also a culture of abuse and violence in the IJM that funneled down the ranks and spilled onto civilians. Japanese officers often beat their men and encouraged brutal hazing and internal squad discipline for even small infractions. IJA recruit Toyoshige Karashima recalled, "Sometimes you'd be hit with fists and sometimes you'd be hit with bamboo sticks. Sometimes in the evening we couldn't even eat our food because our faces were so swollen."[100] Masayo Enomoto stated, "It's called self-punishment. Once the instructor gets tired of beating you up, they have recruits face each other and slap each other."[101] Hajime Kondo recounted, "I was beaten with fists. There is an expression 'seeing stars in your eyes.' Well, when you are beaten like that, you literally do see stars in your eyes. The training was so severe that I felt that I would rather die."[102] Ebato Tsuyoshi stated, "I received absolutely brutal treatment at the hands of seasoned soldiers."[103] Violence was pervasive, normalized, and rationalized in the IJM and subordinates and noncombatants were dehumanized. IJA Sergeant Yamauchi Takeo, with the 136th Regiment, 43rd Division on Saipan, stated, "The soldiers were forced into a slave mentality towards their officers. There was no concept of human rights. The result was, when they were sent abroad, they in turn thought it okay to act brutally against people they saw as inferiors."[104]

Several of the IJA units that fought on Saipan and Tinian came from the war in China, where officers authorized and sometimes forced their men to abuse, torture, rape, and murder civilians in order to "harden" them for combat. IJA non-commissioned officer Masayo Enomoto, who fought in China, stated, "One time, when I was training my students, I brought in a Chinese farmer and I cut him with a big knife from his chest to his stomach.... I wanted to test the courage of the recruits. These soldiers had been in the military for six months and they were going to have to take part in a military operation for the first time in their lives, and I didn't have any other tools to educate them with. And the only thing I could think of was to kill someone in front of them and teach them what it's like to kill someone. And that's the reason I took that strategy."[105]

During the Battles of Saipan and Tinian, Japanese communications were severed, commanders died, and units disintegrated. Cohesion, organization, and order decreased as each day passed.[106] Some IJM officers and enlisted men, who were trained to use violence from the very beginning of their military service, murdered surrendering civilians and their own troops to reinforce military discipline and prevent capitulation within their ranks. Surrendering civilians and troops were also killed so they would not give up Japanese positions or other vital military information to the Americans. Additionally, civilians were using up supplies and crowding caves and good defensive positions; killing them left more for the troops. Immoral commands from officers were sometimes carried out because they were given in the name of the emperor. When asked if he felt any pangs of conscience when raping and slaughtering civilians in China, Masayo Enomoto replied, "I didn't feel any sense of guilt then.... I was fighting for the emperor. He was a god. In the name of the emperor we could do whatever we wanted."[107] Tsuchiya Yoshio, who served in Manchuria, stated, "in that war, we felt free to do anything because of Imperial orders."[108] Enlisted men and young officers also followed immoral orders out of fear, as they would be killed if they did not obey their superiors' commands. Some Japanese troops who had compassion for the people and troops of Saipan and Tinian murdered noncombatants because they believed in the propaganda that the Americans would rape and torture civilians. Troops, at times, also conducted "mercy killings" with the consent of noncombatants.[109] Others murdered because of mental health disorders.

Gyokusai played a role in Japanese atrocities as well. The term *gyokusai* ("shattering jewels") was taken from a line in the sixth-century Chinese classic *Chronicles of Northern Chi*, which stated that a principled man would rather destroy his most treasured possessions than go against his values.[110] Gyokusai was translated as "glorious self-annihilation" or "total annihilation" during the war.[111] "One Hundred Thousand Enemies" (*Tekiwa ikuman*), a popular song in late nineteenth century Japan, had lyrics that read, "Even if enemies are one hundred thousand in number, they are like a group of birds.... We will fight to death even if we shatter like a crystal ball (gyokusai)."[112] The government and media used the term extensively following the Battle of Attu (May 1943) in the Aleutian Islands of America's Alaska Territory. The Japanese garrison on Attu, which was greatly reduced by diseases and the freezing temperatures, conducted a massive banzai charge against American forces. On Attu, according to historian Samuel Eliot Morison, only 28 Japanese troops of a force of over 2,300 were captured or surrendered.[113] Suicidal frontal charges during the Asia Pacific War were extolled and exploited by the state. According to anthropologist Emiko Ohnuki-Tierney, "The state repeatedly aestheticized the gyokusai on Attu as the model for all Japanese."[114] Scholar David C. Earhart states, "The Japanese media's glorified account of the final charge at Attu, disseminated throughout the homeland and the war front, became the template for repeated mass suicides across the Pacific, initially by military men, later by civilians."[115]

The Japanese High Command (the emperor, ministers, and high-level officers) desired that the Saipan garrison perform *gyokusai*, like the Attu garrison. Japan was losing the war. It did not have the weapons and technologies to stop the Americans. The

High Command hoped to intimidate the enemy through mass deaths at the periphery of the empire and make the Americans believe an invasion of mainland Japan would be too costly for both sides. It desired to enter into peace negotiations with the United States and preserve the empire, as opposed to surrendering unconditionally. A June 24, 1944, entry in the Imperial General Headquarters Army Section Confidential War Diary (*Rikugun Daihonei Kimitsu Senso Nisshi*) stated, "The Saipan Defense force should carry out *gyokusai*. It is not possible to conduct the hoped-for direction of the battle. The only thing left is to wait for the enemy to abandon their will to fight because of the '*Gyokusai* of the One Hundred Million.'"[116] The "One Hundred Million" was a reference to the number of imperial subjects in the empire.

It is unknown if the Japanese High Command in the mainland ordered civilians be part of the gyokusai. It is known that the emperor was closely following and concerned about the situation in the Marianas. According to historian Noriko Kawamura, "The loss of Saipan shocked the emperor deeply."[117] A few months later, a "top secret" IJA communication sent to the military command in Okinawa Prefecture, titled "Guidelines for Prefectural Residents" (November 1944), stated that in the event of an American invasion, "Let the army, the government, and the people be as one. A shared life, a shared death."[118] There were some evacuations of civilians in the Marianas to mainland Japan at the end of 1943 and 1944, but the Japanese military took no measures to protect civilian lives during the battles.[119] The Tinian NTLF G-2 Report stated, "There was no organized plan of evacuation or system of shelters set up for civilians on Tinian."[120] The Americans dropped leaflets that urged Japanese troops, as "human beings," to "save the lives of the innocent" and let civilians surrender.[121]

It is also unknown if Japanese garrison commanders on Saipan and Tinian issued a "mass suicide order" (*shudan jiketsu meirei*) at the end of the battles after they realized the IJN would not be coming to save them all. Lieutenant General Saito, before killing himself, reportedly told his staff officer, Major Takashi Hirakushi, "There is no longer any distinction between civilians and troops. It would be better for them to join in the attack with bamboo spears than be captured."[122] A Japanese prisoner of war told American intelligence officers that Vice Admiral Nagumo, before committing suicide, "commanded all civilian and military personnel remaining on the north end of Saipan to commit suicide on 7 July."[123] A number of officers below Saito and Nagumo certainly authorized and ordered the murder of civilians. These officers, who were under much stress from combating a more powerful enemy and pressured by their superiors to not surrender, believed "the military and civilians had a shared purpose and destiny" (*gunmin-ittaika*) to dishearten the enemy's resolve through mass deaths and thereby preserve their nation/empire.[124] According to historian Yuki Tanaka, "the Japanese wartime belief in *gyokusai* ("glorious self-annihilation") contributed to the disregard for basic human rights."[125]

8

Non-Suicide Deaths

Most of the civilian deaths during the Battles of Saipan and Tinian were not from suicides. Marine Lieutenant Robert Sheeks wrote, "While large in total number, civilian deaths by suicide were small in percentage, the greatest number of casualties by far having occurred as a direct result of the continued attack."[1] Civilians and Japanese troops were often hiding together, especially in the caves and jungles, and the Americans conducted aggressive advances supported by artillery, aircraft, and warship fire to take ground and eliminate enemy troops. The Saipan NTLF G-2 Report stated, "The close association between civilian and military undoubtedly was the cause of the death of many of the former from our fire."[2] Many noncombatants also died from dehydration, malnutrition, and diseases, as well as atrocities. Correspondent Keith Wheeler wrote in a letter to his wife on July 16, "This has been a bad place…. It has been bloody, more bloody that I can say in a letter…. I'm sick of seeing the kids of Saipan hurt…. I've seen them cut to ribbons, neglected, eaten with flies in their wounds, starved, thirsty…. They've been picked out of welters of dead flesh-flesh of their fathers and mothers and brothers and sisters."[3] Marine Lieutenant Jim G. Lucas wrote, "For the first time on Saipan, I cried today. It is more than many of us can stand to see horribly maimed boys and girls who look at you with eyes … which are so old and tired as a result of all they've endured…. This afternoon, I saw a husky Marine sitting by the side of a road, brushing flies from the face of a 6-year-old Japanese girl. Tears were streaming down his face. Near by, another group of Marines tried to look after a week-old baby, rescued from a cave beside the dead body of its mother."[4]

There was little to no water in many of the places civilians hid in, and gastrointestinal infections and constant perspiration from the tropical climate accelerated fluid loss. The Saipan NTLF G-2 Report stated that surrenderees were "suffering from lack of water" and "invariably asked for water immediately upon capture."[5] Saipan schoolgirl Komatsu Megumi stated, "The five of us, my parents, my older sister, my younger sister, and I, wandered around the jungle along with other refugees. The greatest hardship was living without water. We were pouring sweat from the hot summer sun."[6] During the Battle of Saipan, there was little rain during almost a month of continuous fighting.[7] Lieutenant Robert Sheeks stated, "it was very hot and dry … people were dying of thirst."[8] "Thirst," Maria Angelica Salaberria explained, "was one of the greatest hardships we faced during the month we crisscrossed the hills and jungles from south to north. There was no rain, and we could not move about during the daytime."[9] The Tinian NTLF G-2 Report stated, "water was very scarce after the third day of the operation."[10] Marine combat correspondent Irving Schlossenberg wrote that surrendering civilians on Tinian "had only one word on their parched lips, 'Mizu, mizu.' 'Water, water.'"[11]

Many civilians survived by drinking the liquid from cut vines and roots. Sugarcane juice was a lifesaver. Maria Angelica Salaberria recounted, on Saipan, "When we were forced to walk at night, Remedios would go into the sugar cane fields and bring each of us a piece of sugar cane to chew as we walked, and it helped. At the end of a month of insufficient liquid, our throats were so parched that there were days when we could not swallow our food."[12] Even American troops, who received supplies from ships, lacked water at times and drank cane juice. Marine Lieutenant John C. Chapin, 24th Regiment, 4th Division, wrote, "With water so scarce, one of our chief sources of liquid sustenance was sugar cane juice. We'd whack off a segment of the cane with our combat knives, then chew and suck on it till only the dry fibers were left. In these burnt-out fields we weren't even able to do this, as the cane was spoiled and tasted lousy."[13] Many civilians also survived by "licking the moist cave walls where the dew formed every morning."[14] Others, unfortunately, tried to drink sea water. Chamorro schoolgirl Marie Soledad Castro, who hid

Wounded and dehydrated child on Saipan receiving water from the Americans, June 1944. #83544. National Archives.

A woman on Saipan preparing a meal for her family while in internment, June 1944. Many civilians were malnourished during the battle. #84642. National Archives.

in a cave with her family on Saipan, recalled, "We had run out of water and everyone was very thirsty. We prayed for rain but it never came, so my father went down to the ocean to fetch some sea water. When he came back everybody surrounded that bucket.... It was too salty.... Nobody could swallow it."[15] Civilians drank dirty and contaminated water as well. Chamorro young man Maximo Tudela Arriola recalled that on Saipan his family drank from a water tank with two dead Japanese soldiers inside.[16]

Malnutrition was another major problem. Civilians were malnourished even before the battles because of the reduction of food imports from the north beginning in the summer of 1942. During the battles, many civilians were holed up and had little provisions. Saipan civilian Dave Sablan, who hid in a cave with his family for three weeks, stated, "we had nothing but sugar cane to eat."[17] Some civilians ate grass, tree bark, leaves, bugs, giant snails, rats, and uncooked livestock meat. Chamorro schoolboy Gregorio Muna Quitugua recounted how he and members of his group feasted on the raw meat of dead cattle and goats to survive on Saipan.[18] Carolinian-Chamorro young man Jesus Taisakan Wabol, whose family hid in Kannat Tabla Cave on Saipan, stated, "I saw everything during the war and I am not sorry to say that it was ugly.... Whenever we found dead animals, the meat was eaten raw."[19] Civilians also had to deal with Japanese troops and other civilians who stole food from them or hoarded supplies for themselves. Some civilian groups were fortunate to find abandoned IJM rations, which included rice, dried fish, canned beef and crab, senbei crackers, rock candy, beer, and lemon pop.[20]

Dehydration and malnutrition weakened immune systems, and many civilians died from diseases. Saipan schoolgirl Kimiko Nishikawa stated that her little brother fell ill and died in a cave near Banzai Cliff.[21] Chamorro schoolgirl Primitiva Reyes Lizama recounted that her three-month-old sister Margarita Pia Tudela Reyes died because her mother was unable to produce any breast milk. Gregorio C. Cabrera, a young man who worked at the Oshima Soap Factory on Saipan and hid in the Tanapag area during the battle, remembered when a woman in their group died shortly after giving birth.[22] International News Service correspondent Howard Handleman wrote about a girl he came across in the mountains on Saipan who was suffering from jungle rot and dying. She had "a high fever and was in a coma, a writhing, pain-wracked coma."[23] Marine Lieutenant Frederic A. Stott wrote, civilians on Saipan "had suffered, were filthy, diseased, and wounded."[24] Some Japanese officers did not allow IJM doctors to treat civilians because there were too many wounded troops to attend to.[25]

Marine Robert F. Graf, 23rd Regiment, 4th Division, recalled the poor state of the civilians of Saipan:

One sad incident I recall was when a captured civilian Japanese woman came up to me. She was crying and when she got close to me she started hitting me on the arm and pointing to my pack. I did not

Wounded and sick children on Saipan being taken away from the front lines, June 1944. Wounds from being caught in the fighting and diseases, not suicides, were the leading causes of death among civilians in the battles. #83541. National Archives.

know what she wanted until an interpreter came over and explained that she wanted some food and water for her dead child. She pointed to a wicker basket that contained her dead infant. I gave her what she requested, and she placed the food and water in the basket so that the child could have nourishment on the way to meet the baby's ancestors. Physical conditions of many were pitiful. Every illness that we had been briefed on was observed: leprosy, dengue fever, yaws and many cases of elephantiasis. Most of them were skeleton thin, as they had no nourishment for many days. Many were suffering from shock caused by the shelling and bombing, and frightened because they did not have the vaguest idea as to what we would do to them. Civilians caught in a war that was not of their making.[26]

Corpses were all over Saipan and Tinian during the fighting. Marine Lieutenant Lawrence F. Snowden, 23rd Regiment, 4th Division, stated that he found a pile of 20 dead civilian bodies in Chalan Kanoa early in the Battle of Saipan.[27] Navy Corpsman Tony Julian, who was attached to the 25th Regiment, 4th Marine Division, saw "entire families" dead inside "huts" on Saipan.[28] On June 28, the 2nd Battalion, 105th Regiment, 27th Army Infantry Division reported that they found "about 200 dead soldiers and civilians" after securing Nafutan Point."[29] American units reported finding several abandoned enemy field hospitals with hundreds of "dead Japs."[30] H.C. Randolph, who fought on Saipan, wrote in a letter his parents in 1944, "Every way you turned about all you could see was dead Japs and it took a man with no nose and a steel-plated stomach to take it..."[31] IJA Sergeant Yamauchi Takeo, 136th Regiment, 43rd Division, stated, "Below us beneath the caves of Tapotchau, was a valley about six hundred meters long, filled with corpses. Corpses burned black. Hanging from the branches of trees, tumbled onto the ground. Corpses crawling with maggots. Without passing through that valley there was no escape."[32] Schoolgirl Marie Soledad Castro remembered seeing "burned bodies and burned trees everywhere" on Saipan.[33] Schoolgirl Komatsu Megumi, whose family survived by hiding in the jungles of Saipan, recalled, "Our senses had become numb to the mountains of dead bodies of Japanese and island natives, and we felt nothing."[34]

Flies, which covered the corpses on the islands, flew onto civilians and troops' wounds and food supplies and spread diseases. Marine Sergeant William W. Rogal, 2nd Regiment, 2nd Division, wrote, "The flies of Saipan were somewhat larger than the common housefly and were somewhat greenish in hue. And they were present in the trillions.... We guessed the presence of thousands of dead bodies provided them with places to lay their eggs."[35] Marine William D. Smith, 2nd Regiment, 2nd Division, stated that flies "feasted on the mutilated bodies" and then the rations they ate.[36] Marine Rod Sandburg, 10th Regiment, 2nd Division, recalled, "There were more flies than any of us had ever seen. It was impossible to keep them off our food. Our shit skillets [mess kits] would be covered with blow flies so deep one couldn't see the food.... We had to cover our faces with hankies to keep from breathing the insects."[37] Marine Arwin J. Bowden, 2nd Regiment, 2nd Division, stated, "when we were moving up on Topatchau there was a native Chamorro lady came in carrying a baby, she had just given birth and the baby wasn't an hour old. We put her on a stretcher and sent her and the baby back to the division hospital. The thing I remember most about that incident is that you never saw so many flies in all your life. The baby and the mother both just covered with flies."[38] The use of human feces or "night soil" in farming on Saipan and Tinian and the lack of latrines and toilets also caused the spread of diseases. The Saipan NTLF Operations Report stated, "Tetanus and gas bacillus infections in the civilian and enemy military personnel and gas bacillus infections in our own troops will continue to be a real menace in future operations over the 'night soil' contaminated terrain of this theater."[39]

Dead Japanese troops in a building on Saipan, June 1944. #85368. National Archives.

Japanese War Crimes

Many civilians on Saipan and Tinian died from Japanese war crimes. Some Japanese officers and enlisted men used noncombatants as human shields. Marine George E. Gray, 10th Amphibian Tractor Battalion, stated, Japanese troops "would put a bunch of civilians ahead of them. Of course you couldn't keep from killing the civilians, because they were in the line of fire."[40] Marine Paul E. Cooper, 14th Regiment, 4th Division, remembered when Japanese troops set off a tripwire in front of their position on the night of July 2 and they opened up on them. At dawn, they found dead children among the bodies.[41] Marine George J. Dorko, 25th Regiment, 4th Division, recalled, "…the only thing I didn't like on Saipan was, they would send out the gooks—we called them gooks, Koreans, or whatever they were—upfront with the kids, and they try to come up as backups.... The women, the kids, and guys ... not fight, just push them out there ... covers. Shields, that's what it was."[42] The Saipan NTLF G-2 Periodic Report no. 28, 13 July 1944, stated, "The 24th Marines reported that at 0300 about 20 civilians approached the Regimental CP and when challenged they scattered and Jap soldiers behind them threw hand grenades. Some of the civilians, captured at daybreak, said they were forced by soldiers to act in this way as shields."[43] Marine Lieutenant Jim G. Lucas wrote that children on Saipan were "forced to run through cane fields to draw our fire."[44] The Japanese also used civilians to locate American positions. Marine Jack V. Gilbreath, 23rd Regiment, 4th Division, recounted, on Saipan "one night the Japanese had some civilian people out in front of them, trying to find our location. And they drove the women and children right into the front lines. Naturally, the Marines didn't know but that it was the Japanese themselves and they started firing and they killed all the women and children."[45]

Japanese troops with grenades disguised themselves as civilians and tried to infiltrate American lines. Marine Burnes R. Whitehead, 2nd Regiment, 2nd Division, recalled, a group of Japanese troops "dressed as civilians" and pretending to surrender attacked his unit near Garapan.[46] The ploys endangered civilians who were trying to surrender safely. Marine Sergeant William W. Rogal, 2nd Regiment, 2nd Division, wrote, on Saipan, "As we continued the advance on Saipan we began taking more and more Jap civilians prisoner; almost all were women and children. There were expectations. Among one group I spotted a nervous male in army pants with a civilian shirt. He was, like many of the refugees, carrying a woven straw bag which contained personal effects. We always searched these bags but this guy at first refused to hand it to me. The reason soon became obvious. Beneath his clothing in the bag were four grenades! I resisted the urge to kill him; butt stroked him with my rifle and sent him to the rear."[47] The Tinian NTLF G-2 Periodic Report no. 50, 4 August 1944, stated, "The 6th Marines reported that the Jap military are throwing away their uniforms, changing into civilian clothes, and mixing with the civilians."[48] Not all Japanese troops disguised as civilians were trying to kill Americans.[49] Some mixed with or dressed as noncombatants so that the Americans, who Japanese combatants feared did not take military prisoners, would not murder them.

Some Japanese troops on Saipan and Tinian booby-trapped civilians. Marine Rod Sandburg, 10th Regiment, 2nd Division, recalled, Japanese officers would order their men, as well as women and children, to place grenades "under their arm pits with the pin pulled and pretend to give themselves up; when they lifted their arms the hand grenade would fall on the ground and explode killing them and those around them."[50] Marine Glenn L. Buzzard, 24th Regiment, 4th Division, recounted, "We were out in the open in a cane field, and about twenty people came out of those trees. They were women and children and the men were holding up babies, just little babies. That was a distraction, and the interpreter was trying to talk to them.... 'Take it off,' that's one of the Japanese phrases they taught us. You had to get them undressed because the men would have grenades stuck under their clothes, and as soon as they got a chance they would throw it at you."[51]

Some Japanese troops also used civilians as decoys to lure Americans into ambushes. A United Press article, dated June 28, 1944, stated, "Japanese civilians on Saipan island in the Marianas waved white flags to American assault troops and while the U.S. fighting men held their fire, Jap soldiers hidden in sugar-cane fields, turned machine guns on the Americans."[52] Marine Lieutenant Frederic A. Stott, 24th Regiment, 4th Division, wrote,

"Saipan. Retreating Jap Forces carried civilians with them. This Japanese mother and child were killed during the fighting." July 1944. CPA-44–6939. SC-210542. National Archives.

on Saipan, in early July, "Using civilian men, women, and children as decoys, the Jap soldiers managed to entice a volunteer patrol forward into the open to collect additional civilian prisoners. A dozen men from 'A' Company were riddled as the ruse succeeded."[53] The Second Armored Amphibian Battalion Special Actions Report stated, in northern Saipan, on July 10, "two groups of civilians were observed on the shore; permission was obtained from Lt. Colonel Dillon, and two LVTA4's approached the beach waving white flags and calling to the civilians to surrender. As they moved to do so Japanese soldiers hidden in the undergrowth to their rear threw hand grenades at them."[54]

A number of Japanese troops refused to let civilians looking for shelter enter their caves or took over civilians' hiding places and forced them out into the open while the fighting was going on. Others Japanese troops kept noncombatants in the caves with them as hostages. On the other hand, a number of civilians chose to stay close to Japanese troops because they feared the Americans. Unbeknown to these people, however, was that some Japanese officers and enlisted men decided to murder civilians before killing themselves. Marine Officer Warren S. Adams stated, "at the very tip of Saipan … there was a big cliff going down, and caves ... a lot of the Jap soldiers were killing themselves and killing civilians that they had taken hostage down there."[55]

Marine Guy L. Gabaldon, 2nd Regiment, 2nd Division, recalled:

> During the Saipan-Tinian Campaign the suicides of whole families is widely known, but the inadvertent killing of civilians who were used as hostages by the Japs is little known. One case in particular which has always remained in my mind took place in the push for Garapan. As we advanced towards the city I noticed three Marines throwing grenades into a bunker-dugout. Not seeing anyone firing back from the dugout I yelled at them to stop firing.... "Hold your fire," I shouted, as I ran towards the dugout.... I said, "Let me try to talk to them, if they are not already dead." I continue calling them out, hoping that someone was still alive ... [eventually] two brothers drag out the mother, who is dead, and the sister is who is in very bad shape. They go after the father and the soldiers. The tally is: two dead soldiers, the mother is dead, and the sister is bleeding to death; the father has one eye and both of his eardrums blown out. The little girl's leg is hanging by a shred and blood is pouring out. The father sits alongside his daughter with his hand on her thigh just above the wound.... We are completely helpless. I shoot both of my morphine vials in her leg.... One of the Marines ties a tourniquet on her thigh, but she continues to bleed. Her face is white as a sheet.... The eight year old girl dies. We had all just stood there and watched her die.[56]

Japanese troops murdered civilians suspected of being spies or aiding the Americans. Chamorro schoolboy Gregorio Muna Quitugua stated that Japanese soldiers killed a woman accused of spying for the enemy in a cave he was hiding in.[57] Some Japanese troops also murdered Micronesian ammunition carriers and combat support assistants to prevent them from revealing the location of stockpiles and military positions.[58] On Tinian, according to historian Gavan Daws, the IJM slaughtered a great number of Korean laborers before the Americans invaded the island "so as not to have hostiles at their back."[59] It must be stated that a number of captured and surrendered civilians and even IJM Pows did provide American intelligence officers with crucial information regarding Japanese military defenses and locations.[60] Micronesians also served as scouts and translators for the Americans during the battles and mop-up operations.[61]

A small percentage of the civilians on the islands took up arms against the Americans. A G-2 document titled "Project 1055, Behavior of Japanese Population on Saipan," 10 November 1944, stated, "the civilian population of Saipan (Japanese) were probably instructed and/or compelled to resist with the Japanese armed forces the invading Allied forces."[62] The document also stated, "A prisoner from Saipan is reported as saying that during the last days, each civilian worker, was given a sharpened bamboo stick to use as a spear against the enemy, should an opportunity arise."

A small number of Saipan and Tinian women fought against the Americans. Some freely did so, while others were coerced. NTLF G-2 Periodic Reports noted the presence of female combatants in the battles. The Saipan G-2 Periodic Report no. 13, 28 June 1944, stated, "The 106th [Infantry Regiment, 27th Army Division] reported the discovery of a Jap woman who appeared, according to the regiment, to have been killed fighting."[63] Report no. 16, 1 July 1944: "K Co. [3rd Battalion, 6th Regiment, 2nd Marine Division] killed a party of 2 Jap officers, 6 men and a woman" during a night raid.[64] Report no. 30, 15 July 1944: "During the day mopping up continued and in the morning the 2nd Marines killed 4 women dressed in Jap uniforms.... The women were carrying hand grenades."[65] Report no. 31, 16 July 1944: "The 27thInfDiv reported that the 106th Regt. killed 3 Japs ... one of whom was a woman dressed in Army uniform."[66] Report no. 38, 23 July 1944: "Army Garrison Force units continued their mopping up operations and anti-sniper patrols during the period ... 65 Jap soldiers were killed together with 10 civilians, 3 of whom were women armed with grenades."[67] The Tinian G-3 (Military Operations) Periodic Report no. 38, 22 July 1944, stated, during mopping-up operations on Saipan, "The 105th Infantry reported killing … nine armed civilians, three of which were women armed with hand grenades."[68] Marine Lieutenant George C. Hill stated, on Saipan, "There were about nine Japs behind the revetment right in front of our lines. This little girl came out from behind it...The Japs had filled her bloomers with grenades. She'd take out the pin of a grenade, tap it on a rock and then throw it at us." The girl, who looked no older than nine years old, went back behind the wall and sadly, the Americans killed her, along with all the Japanese troops, in a bazooka attack. [69]

The Marine Corps Dispatch Summary for Tinian, 8 August 1944, stated, "The 20th Marines reported a skirmish at 1330 today in which 7 Japanese and 1 woman were killed…. The woman was carrying a grenade."[70] The Tinian G-2 Periodic Report no. 55, 9 August 1944, stated, "At 1400 near the CP of the 20th Marines a group of 8 Japs were soon running across the road…. They were surrounded and fired on. All of them were killed or committed suicide. 7 were army personnel; the eighth was a woman who died with a grenade clutched in her hand."[71] Not all of the women mentioned in the field reports were trying to kill Americans. Some women were forced to be shields or decoys. Others purposely

Most civilians did not take up arms against the Americans or carry out murder-suicides. They cared first and foremost about their loved ones and did all they could to protect them. Notice the children on the parents' backs and the daughter in the dress holding her mother's arm, June 1944. #82411. National Archives.

stayed with troops for protection or were nurses given hand grenades to defend or kill themselves.

Nonetheless, Americans recounted in interviews and writings about some incidents were women voluntarily took American lives or attempted to do so. Marine Sergeant Keith A. Renstrom, 25th Regiment, 4th Division, stated, in northern Saipan, "a marine moved down a hill to save a baby in front of a cave, only to be shot and killed by a woman hiding behind the rocks. The marines then opened fire, killing the woman and her child."[72] Renstrom also recalled, "We had a Marine officer named Billen. One of their women came over to surrender to him and when she got close enough, she threw a grenade at the poor guy. They could be nasty!"[73] Army Lieutenant Joseph J. Meighan, 105th Regiment, 27th Division, remembered when a woman pretending to surrender on Saipan took out a grenade hidden under her skirt and killed some of his friends.[74] Marine Lieutenant Colonel Russell Lloyd, Commanding Officer of the 6th Regiment, 2nd Division, wrote, women on Saipan "come down at night with the men and some are armed with either bayonets tied on sticks or carry hand grenades."[75] Marine Lewis J. Steck, 2nd Regiment, 2nd Division, stated, on Saipan, "One time an old woman threw a hand-grenade at a buddy of mine, and it went off. He got wounded."[76] Marine Sante DeMarino, 24th Regiment, 4th Division, stated, "We couldn't trust anybody. Some Japs would come over to surrender, but they would have grenades in their hands. They'd jump into a bunch of our guys. Even women from the island [Saipan] would do that. Anybody that came near us, we shot."[77] Marine Gabriel J. Vertucci, 25th Regiment, 4th Division, recounted how he killed a woman hiding under a jeep whom he believed was waiting to ambush his squad on Saipan. He stated, "And that is one bad thing.... I lived with it all my life."[78] Some nurses also fought against the Americans. Marine Roy William Roush, 6th Regiment, 2nd Division, recalled, on Tinian, "I saw a large shellhole containing about a dozen bodies and some of them were nurses in uniform. They all had rifles and had fought and died with the soldiers."[79]

Correspondent Robert Sherrod wrote, "On Saipan and, nine months later, on Okinawa, we found some evidence of women and children attempting to fight. One soldier on Saipan said his squad had encountered a woman wildly firing a rifle; the squad's sharpshooter took careful aim, shot the woman through the leg, then took her to the hospital."[80] Sherrod also stated, on Mt. Tapochau, among a group of dead Japanese troops, there was "a woman in blue and white slacks. Her face was calm in death. I thought she was prettier than any live Jap woman I had seen in the civilian compounds. She and her companions apparently had been killed by artillery."[81] Marine Robert L. Williams, 24th Regiment, 4th Division, recounted, on Saipan, "We stopped in this one area, and the next thing you know, maybe 10–15 feet away, one of our fellows is hollering 'Halt! Who goes there?' Somebody answers, 'Me Maline, me Maline.' The Japanese had trouble saying the letter R. Couldn't say Marine, it comes out as 'Maline.' I could hear this one fellow from our company cussing like mad, shouting 'You are not!' and a couple guys start shooting. It was two people trying to get through the lines. One was a Japanese soldier, dead as a doornail. The other didn't have a scratch and was undressed from the waist up, so somebody rolled him over. It was a civilian lady."[82]

Some Japanese troops used women to lure and ambush advancing Americans. Marine Stan Ellis, 25th Regiment, 4th Division, stated: "You couldn't always trust those civilians though.... I had just lit up a cigarette when I spotted three beautiful nude Japanese women. Hell, I thought it was a mirage, but they were for real. They were bent over with their tushies pointed toward us. They had twisted their heads so we could see they were smiling. Jeez, we're taking this all in. I can remember one of my buddies nodding his head. 'Not bad, not bad,' he says. 'We should definitely liberate these beauties.' Then Jap fire opened up on us from both sides.... Personally, I've always felt that was the cheapest trick the Japs pulled, tempting a man like that—those dirty bastards!"[83]

The "Saipan" (1944) pamphlet warned Marines and soldiers about some civilians fighting against them. It stated:

> We think of ourselves, and most other people think of us, as being fair to anyone who is helpless. We also think of the German and Japanese military as being ruthless in their treatment of civilians. It has come as a surprise to us, though, to learn that the enemy thinks we, too, are brutal and ruthless. Many of the Japanese prisoners we have taken thought that we were going to torture them to death. They have a number of gruesome stories about us, that they believe in, such as the one that we slowly cut off various parts of a prisoner's anatomy until he is reduced to hopeless pain, then run over his still-living body with a steam-roller. Ridiculous as these sound to us, if Japanese soldiers and sailors believe them, the chances are that some Japanese civilians will also believe them. And if they believe them, they are going to do what most of the soldiers do, and continue to fight, taking some of us down with them.[84]

Marine Guy L. Gabaldon, 2nd Regiment, 2nd Division, wrote, "Most Americans do not understand the nature of the Japanese civilians who faced the 'American Devils' in battle. These civilians were as dangerous as any Jap soldier and at times more so. I witnessed many 'civilians' tossing their whole families off the high cliffs of Saipan. When a person is fanatical enough to kill his family, he is fanatical enough to kill an enemy that he believes is causing the deaths of his children."[85] One day, after clearing a cave and killing everyone inside, Gabaldon recalled finding "five soldiers and two women ... the women each had rifles in their hands and grenades alongside."[86]

Some civilians were involved, either voluntarily or by force, in the numerous counterattacks during the battles, including the largest banzai attack of the Pacific War on Saipan. Before dawn on July 7, 1944, approximately 3,000 Japanese troops and a number of civilians, carrying bayonet-fitted rifles, grenades, knives, swords, machetes, pikes, farm tools, and even tree limbs and broomsticks, attacked the Americans north of Garapan.[87] A Japanese soldier noted in his diary that the attack occurred on the seventh day of the seventh month of the year and on the seventh anniversary of the start of the Second Sino-Japanese War (1937–1945).[88] The Japanese assembled near the small seaside village of Makunsha in northwestern Saipan and charged southward down the coast.[89] Army Major Edward McCarthy, Commander of the 2nd Battalion, 105th Regiment, 27th Division, recounted, "It reminded me of one of those old cattle stampede scenes of the movies ... the Japs just kept coming and coming. I didn't think they'd ever stop."[90] Japanese officers sometimes had women and children put in the front of the counterattacks. Army Lieutenant Joseph J. Meighan, 105th Regiment, 27th Division, recalled, "I heard all this yippin.' I look down to my right and holy Jesus they're coming. A bunch of women ahead of them.... They sent their women."[91] Army Soldier Samuel R. Dinova, 105th Regiment, 27th Division, stated, "You could see these kids, women ... they had bamboo poles with bayonets on them, shovels, picks, pitchforks, they had everything. These are civilians in with soldiers too.... I don't know what they hell was going on. I can't explain it to you. Kids hollering, women screaming, machine gun firing..."[92]

The early morning sunrise of July 7 revealed the carnage that took place as a result of the banzai attack. Thousands of corpses were along the western coast of Saipan north of Mutcho Point. Marine Sergeant Jerome C. Wachsmuth, 6th Regiment, 2nd Division,

Koreans digging graves on Saipan, June 1944. #82426. National Archives.

recalled, "you couldn't take a step without stepping on bodies or body parts."[93] Army Lieutenant Colonel M. Oakley Bidwell, Commander of the G-1 Personnel Section of the 27th Division, stated, "I don't think I can draw a picture more horrible than my memory of Tanapag Plain. It appeared to be virtually solid dead soldiers. A creek ran through a shallow ravine, emptying into a beautiful turquoise-blue lagoon. The creek and its banks seemed filled with bodies. And while I watched, a huge crimson flower grew out of the mouth of the creek."[94] The Americans "requisitioned" captured Korean laborers, who were designated as "non-enemy Asiatics," to drag and carry the rotting corpses into mass graves.[95] The NTLF Administrative Order Number 3–44, issued before the battles, stated, "In the event of acute labor shortages, labor requisitioning of native inhabitants and other non-enemy Asiatics may be resorted to."[96] Marine Captain Roy H. Elrod, 8th Regiment, 2nd Division, wrote that the Americans and Koreans also attempted to burn bodies in piles with gasoline, but it "just sort of cooked them."[97] Instead, they disposed of a number of bodies by pulling them into buildings and houses which were set aflame. The Koreans had or were given white clothing, kerchiefs, and headbands so that they would not be mistaken for the enemy and be killed.

Chieko Aono

Chieko Aono moved to Saipan with her family in 1929. Her father Yoshi Aono was a chemical engineer at the Chalan Kanoa sugar factory and she worked as a nurse at the hospital in Garapan before the battle. When the Americans invaded the island in 1944, she and her family took refuge in a cave in the hills east of Garapan. They had no food and little water.[98] Yoshi believed the Americans would rape and torture his wife and two daughters if they were captured and he would not let them surrender.[99]

A group of IJA soldiers later took over the family's hiding place. They set up a defensive position and fired on the advancing Americans from the mouth of the cave. The Americans counterattacked, and Chieko's younger sister, Mitsuko, was killed. A grenade then went off in the cave and killed her father, mother, and the soldiers. Chieko, concussed and wounded by the blast, was the only one left alive. She attempted to kill the approaching Americans with a heavy machine gun at the cave's entrance but collapsed before she could do so.[100] The Americans believed everyone inside was dead and moved on from the position.

Chieko later joined a large group of civilians hiding in the mountains. She cared for two orphaned children, Emiko and Akira, whose father was the headmaster of the elementary school in Garapan.[101] Like many civilians, she was dressed in military clothing because of their durability and the lack of alternatives. Her group later joined IJA Captain Sakae Oba's camp, which was in the jungles near Takoyama Hill. At the camp, Chieko spent nearly all her time treating wounded men and civilians. To prevent infections and save supplies, she removed the bandages of the injured, boiled them, cleaned the wounds, and reapplied the bandages.

The camp continued to hold out out after the islands fell in early July. After months of privation, however, the health and mental states of those in Oba's camp declined.[102] Water and food were scarce, and medical supplies were depleted. The Americans were desperate to get the holdouts, the last major resistance on Saipan, to surrender. They sent a captured Pow and former soldier of Oba's, Corporal Kumihara, to the area to convince them to turn themselves in. When Kumihara met with the camp and told them that Japan was going to be defeated, Chieko stabbed him to death.[103] She hated the Americans for killing her family and hated "traitors" as well. She refused to surrender and was killed during a raid on an American pharmacy one week before the end of the war.[104] Oba's unit surrendered three months later on December 1, 1945.

American War Crimes

A small number of Americans, like some of their Japanese counterparts, murdered civilians during the battles. Racial animosity and hatred for the enemy were major contributing factors. For some Americans there was no distinction between killing civilians and troops; in their eyes, they were all enemy "Japs" or "Nips." Marine Orvel E. Johnson, 23rd Regiment, 4th Division, recalled that he was ordered to fire "several bursts into the crowded masses on the street of Charan-Kanoa" early in the Battle of Saipan.[105] The Saipan G-2 Periodic Report no. 18, 3 July 1944, stated, "At 0835 the 2ndMarDiv reported about 15 civilians waving flags and trying to surrender at RJ 625 (TA 213) being fired on by 27thInfDiv troops."[106] Army Lieutenant Joseph J. Meighan, 105th Regiment, 27th Division, discussed in an interview how his unit captured a large group of sixty to seventy civilians, mostly women and young men, near a creek in northern Saipan. Lt. Meighan and his men brought the group to headquarters near dusk so they could be transported to the internment camp. A high ranking officer stopped him from getting the civilians to Camp Susupe, however, and ordered him to "go out and kill them all." Lt. Meighan hesitated, and his superior said, "I told you, go over there in the cliff and shoot every goddamn one." Lt. Meighan was unable to do it, and a noncommissioned officer and other men carried out the order. Joseph told the interviewer, "You talk about atrocities, there's one for you."[107] Carolinian-Chamorro schoolboy Francisco Igwer Babauta stated, "Even though the Japanese at that time were very cruel to some of us, I saw a lot of cruelty during the invasion by soldiers on both sides."[108]

Some Americans, fearing ambushes and booby traps, murdered noncombatants because of the danger associated with taking prisoners.[109] Marine Captain Carl W. Hoffman, 8th Regiment, 2nd Division, wrote, "After several Marines were killed in sincere efforts to extricate civilians, patience became somewhat worn."[110] There were incidents when some Americans even killed their own men. Marine Edwin P. DesRosiers, 14th Regiment, 4th Division, recalled that one night on Saipan the men in his unit killed a fellow sergeant, who was drunk on captured Japanese saki and hollering, because he was giving away their position. "This happened other times," DesRosiers stated.[111]

The "Saipan" (1944) pamphlet warned troops not to murder noncombatants. It stated:

> We must, however, be absolutely sure in our own minds that a civilian is fighting us or harming our installations before we shoot him. International law clearly demands that civilians who do not fight back at us—whether they are Japanese or Korean civilians working as laborers or specialist for the military, or noncombatants in the armed forces, like doctors and nurses, or ordinary civilians with no connection with the military—must, whenever possible, be taken alive, and must not be injured or have their possessions taken from them except after a due trial by competent authority. Neither such a person nor his property are the property of any one of us who captures him. It is one thing to kill a Japanese soldier in battle; it is an entirely different thing to kill civilians who have not fought against us, whether they are Japanese or not. The latter is murder, nothing more nor less.[112]

Some Americans assaulted civilians. On Saipan, Marine Lieutenant Robert Sheeks had to draw his pistol on an officer who was hitting surrenderees.[113] In another instance, he saw a fellow Marine break the jaw of an elderly civilian being questioned.[114] There were also a small number of American medical personnel who refused to treat civilians. Lieutenant Benjamin H. Hazard, a Military Intelligence Service officer who accompanied the 165th Regiment, 27th Army Division during mop-up operations in the Marpi area, recalled, "there was a boy about 12 years old, and he was the only one alive. The rest had killed themselves with grenades. I was looking at him and he seemed all right, but he was moaning. Then I raised his sweater and his abdomen looked like a hamburger. He told me his father had placed a grenade against him. I called for a medic.... The medic then asked the medical officer for some plasma. The medical officer said, 'We don't give plasma to Japs.'" Benjamin had medics take the boy to a surgical hospital, but he died on the operating table.[115]

It is known that some American and Japanese troops murdered civilians on Saipan and Tinian. The rape of Saipan and Tinian women and girls by some troops on both sides and some civilian men unquestionably occurred during the battles and occupations, as well. Sex crimes, like many other war crimes in the Pacific, were not recorded by the military for obvious reasons. Rapes were carried out in secret at the most opportune times. They were done in secluded locations, including the dark caves and jungles, and thus never discovered. If discovered, few men were willing to implicate their "buddies." Officers did not report rapes as it was considered a disgrace to their unit and the service and often handled such vile acts discretely, if at all. War correspondents, if they saw or

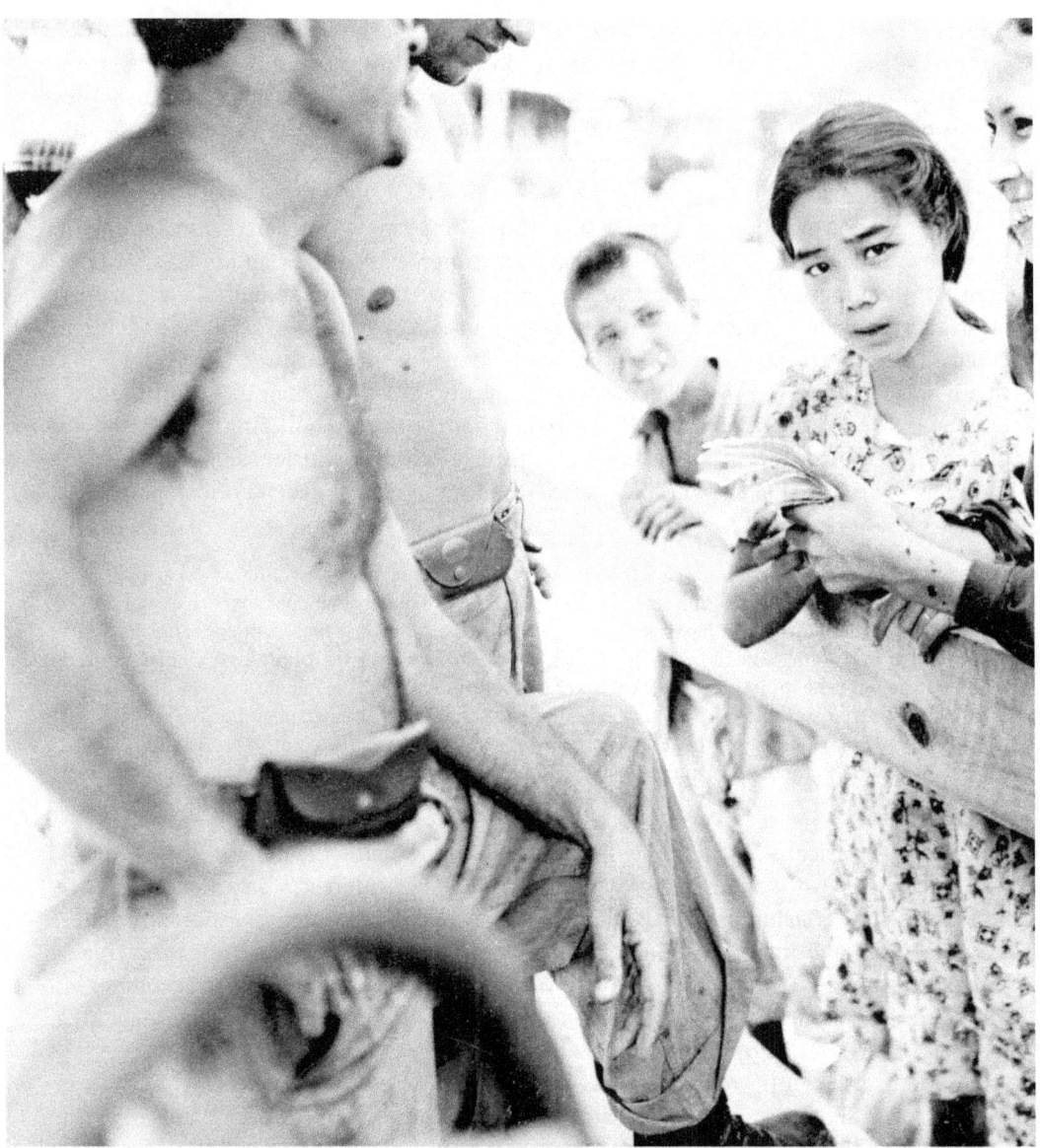

Army guards talking with civilian women in internment camp on Saipan. CPA-44-7644. Courtesy New York State Military Museum.

were told anything, could not disclose American war crimes because they wrote under censorship. William McGaffin, a war correspondent with *The Saturday Evening Post* who was on Saipan, explained, "It is not permitted to write of atrocity stories."[116] Civilian women, fearing reprisal and facing a language barrier, often did not and could not report rapes committed by the Americans and Japanese to the new occupiers. They also worried about stigmatization. There were few resulting pregnancies from the rapes as the women were often sick and malnourished and thus did not conceive or had early miscarriages. Women were also murdered immediately after being raped.

The NTLF command did take some precautions to limit rape. Marine Corps Major

General Harry Schmidt issued an order to troops that stated: "Civilians and Prisoners of War will be treated with humanity, and their persons and honor will be respected. Rape and other mistreatments will be severely and quickly punished. The clothing of captured civilians will not be removed except in cases of emergency, and then only for the purpose of searching, after which the person will be allowed to reclothe. Women and children will not be required to undress except under the most extraordinary conditions, and then only upon the order and in the presence of an officer."[117]

The rape of civilian women and purchase of sexual services in the civilian internment camps by American troops was an issue. An American military government report, dated 27 April 1945, stated that a "chief problem on Saipan was not to keep the civilians in the camp but to keep the [American] military out. Sex, souvenir hunting, and sheer curiosity were the impelling motives for the forays."[118] Dr. John F. Embree, a Psychological Warfare Supervisor for the Office of War Information, noted that "protective measures" had to be taken in the camps "against American Soldiers and Sailors in search of women."[119] A December 8, 1944, *Chicago Tribune* article written by correspondent Harold Smith titled "Tribune Writer Tells Lessons of Pacific War" stated, "Sex is sex, even in war, and it was noticeable that the prettiest girls in the civilian detention areas [on Saipan] got special treatment from our marines and soldiers."[120] Marine Halley Young, 24th Regiment, 4th Division, stated, "I know one of the guys in our outfit got gonorrhea and he was on the outside of the fence on Saipan."[121] Sexual violence occurred during the Battle of Okinawa in 1945 as well.[122] There are testimonies that some Americans, in the same units that were on Saipan, raped women on Okinawa.[123] Unfortunately, the rape and murder of women by a small number of American military personnel on Okinawa continued after 1945 into the twenty-first century.

Brutal Tactics

The Americans used brutal tactics during the Battles of Saipan and Tinian. Many Marine and Army units destroyed caves without checking for civilians or attempting to get them out because of the pandemonium of the battles, shortage of interpreters, orders from commanders to move rapidly and achieve objectives, and the danger associated with taking prisoners. Marine Steve Judd, 6th Regiment, 2nd Division, recounted, "We just blew it all up. We don't know if there was women and children [inside the caves] or whatever, we just blew them up. We just didn't have time to waste. Some people will tell you today—cruel and inhuman.... You weren't there. We were."[124] Marine Sergeant Jerome C. Wachsmuth, 6th Regiment, 2nd Division, stated that many Marines were "not concerned with who might be hiding in there."[125] Marine Captain Roy H. Elrod, 8th Regiment, 2nd Division, wrote, "we'd find a cave, shoot into it ... then a marine tossed a charge into the opening, and this would cave it in, trapping any survivors inside.... Some of these caves went back very deep."[126] Taeki Lee, a Korean schoolboy on Saipan, recalled, "When the Americans arrived where we were hiding they came in firing their guns. Four Korean adults were killed before we could raise our hands and surrender."[127] Marine Guy L. Gabaldon, 2nd Regiment, 2nd Division, wrote, "The caves were safe places during a bombing but they were tombs when hit with flame throwers or grenades. Thousands of Japs died in the caves of Saipan.... Many were roasted alive with flame throwers. I met a Korean in Seoul three years ago who fought as a Japanese soldier on Saipan. He had

"Marines searching for Japs." Saipan, July 1944. #90357. National Archives.

all the hair on his head burned off in a Saipan cave. Many Koreans were forced to fight alongside their hated captors."[128]

Marine Robert F. Graf, 23rd Regiment, 4th Division, discussed a common method used to clear caves:

> … our specialist would advance to near the mouth of the cave. A satchel charge would then be heaved into the mouth of the cave, followed by a loud blast as the dynamite exploded. Other times it might be grenades thrown inside the cave, both fragment type which exploded sending bits of metal all throughout the cave, and other times phosphorous grenades that burned the enemy. Also the flamethrower was used, sending a sheet of flame into the cave, burning anyone that was in its path. Screams could be heard and on occasions the enemy would emerge from the caves, near the entrance, we would call upon the tanks, and these monsters would get in real close and pump shells into the opening.[129]

Many caves were "made into time capsules by bulldozers that piled tons of rock and dirt over the entrances, leaving their terrified human inhabitants to suffocate or die of thirst and hunger."[130] Navy Seabee Karl B. Schroeder, who served on Saipan and Tinian, stated, "I had to bulldoze over caves where there were people who wouldn't come out."[131] One officer on Saipan stated, "It's a sick job."[132] On Tinian, after Mt. Lasso was taken, a number of Japanese officers in a cave hospital in the mountain reportedly prevented the wounded from surrendering. The Americans sealed the entrance, thus burying alive everyone inside.[133] Landing craft infantry gunboats LCI(G)s and other vessels were used to fire into and destroy caves along the coast.[134]

It was very dangerous for civilians to hide in caves with or near Japanese troops during the battles. Marine Roy William Roush, 6th Regiment, 2nd Division, recalled, on Saipan, "Sometimes, Japanese soldiers in uniform would be with a group of civilians. If so, they usually would fight back and also prevent the civilians from surrendering. In such cases, we would have to blow up the entire cave."[135] Carolinian schoolboy Felipe Iguel Ruak stated his sister Rosiana and her son were killed by a grenade tossed in a cave they were all hiding in on Saipan near an area being defended by Japanese troops and under American attack.[136]

Marine William B. Hoover, 2nd Armored Amphibian Battalion, stated in an interview:

> My wife is the only person I have ever told about what happened one afternoon in combat during the closing days of the battle for Saipan. On July 11th, 1944, my platoon was ordered to move down the beach about twenty yards off shore. Our orders were to strafe and shell any caves that opened into the ocean, where we knew Japanese soldiers had taken positions. A Marine infantryman on shore pointed to a cave a few yards ahead, and said he saw about 20 or 30 soldiers wade into the cave.... My Tank Commander, Sgt Wallace Johnson, said it would do little good to use machine guns, so as gunner I was told to open fire with our 75mm canon. I fired off 4 or 5 rounds and we could hear people screaming inside the cave. We ceased fire and asked and yelled for anyone inside to please come out and surrender. Instead, we received machine gun and rifle fire, as well as a couple of hand grenades. I fired in another 10 or 15 rounds of 75mm HE; then we were told a team of Marines were going to go

Marine flametank fires into cave at the edge of jungle on Saipan, July 1944. "Leatherneck riflemen stand by to account for any of the Japs who make a run for it." #85822. National Archives.

in and make sure it was secure. At this time, the water flowing out of the cave was red with blood. When the infantry team came back out they reported there were at least 50 Japanese soldiers as well as a dozen or so civilians, all dead. Some of the civilians were women, who were not allowed to surrender to us, under threat of being killed by the Jap soldiers. I regret to this day we had to take the action we did, but we could not leave an enemy force at our backs. Nor would I now.[137]

Life photographer W. Eugene Smith wrote about two civilians fleeing a cave the Americans were attacking on Saipan. He stated, "A terrified mother and child wheel in bewilderment behind a shell-broken tree-tattered, filthy, starving, their bodies scratched and insect-bitten. Trapped in a cave, they were flushed from it by threats, by promises, by grenades and smoke bombs. They burst out, stumbling, dazed, choking and nearly blind from fumes, pass the still-warm corpses of a man and a boy. Trying to escape when there was no escape."[138] Smith also wrote, a "baby was found with its head under a rock. Its head was lopsided and its eyes were masses of pus. Unfortunately, it was alive. We hoped that it would die."[139]

Marine Charles Pase, 10th Regiment, 2nd Division, stated:

> There were a number of small canyons in Tinian with caves … the Japs had retreated into these caves and a lot of the civilians, some of them Chamorros perhaps, natives, some of them Japanese men, women and children, not combatants…. They had been told we cut the throats of everybody, raped all the women, butchered the children…. These civilians, many of them retreated back into the caves with the Jap soldiers. We had to burn them out, blow them out, explode them out. Whatever we had to do to get them out. None of them would surrender. We had big loudspeakers up on the cliffs overlooking these caves and Japanese interpreters telling them to come out with their hands up and unarmed and they would be treated as Prisoners of War and civilians would not be harmed. They were told all of this in Japanese. Nobody came out. Our 75 guns, we man-handled them, pulled them up onto the edge of the cliffs and pointed the snouts down toward the caves and fired explosive shells with delayed fuses into the caves to explode them and kill everybody. Our infantrymen and our special demolition teams would get above the caves 37 51 and swing on ropes charges of TNT into the cave entrances. They called them satchel charges. We would set up there with our machine gun and any time any soldiers showed up we tried shoot them. We fired AP shells and tracer ammunition into these caves…. We came to one place that there was a miniature cave. Almost like a little dugout down in the ground…. We could hear the noises down there, snuffling, somebody coughing and this sort of thing. We yelled at them and hollered at them and nobody came out…. [A fellow Marine] fired a clip into this cave, into this little dugout … out came a woman and three little children. She was carrying a baby and one of those carbine bullets had gone through the baby and through her breast and out her shoulder. I don't think that the baby was alive.[140]

The Americans fired at or destroyed any structure that could potentially shelter Japanese troops, including homes, barns, sheds, and vegetation. Like the caves, they often did so before determining if civilians were present in them. Marine Carl W. Matthews, 23rd Regiment, 4th Division, stated that every potential hiding place "became the recipient of hundreds of rounds of small arms fire."[141] Chamorro young man Gregorio C. Cabrera recalled, "There was the remains of a house near us [in the Tanapag Area] and hiding under the house were five Japanese, four adults and one baby. The Americans killed everybody under there except the baby. A Chamorro who was hiding under a dried cow hide was run over by a tank. His head was crushed…. Joaquin 'Oma' Sablan was killed by a machine gun about the same time."[142] Marine Frank W. Borta, 8th Regiment, 2nd Division, remembered when he entered a farmhouse on Saipan to capture the occupants but another Marine "rushed in and sprayed the room with bullets. The walls were riddled with holes, and on the floor, drenched in blood, lay an old man, a woman, and a young child."[143] Army Lieutenant Arthur G. Hansen, 105th Regiment, 27th Division, recalled, during mop-ups operations on Saipan, "We came across a barn-like structure, which we could detect contained some Japs. We set it afire and none of the occupants chose to come out and perished in the fire."[144] Some civilians and troops hid in water cisterns on farms but died in them.[145] Some civilians also hid in abandoned military fortifications and were killed by the advancing Americans.

The Americans relied heavily on portable M1A1 and M2 flamethrowers and M3A1 light and M4A2 medium flame tanks to "flush out" the enemy and clear caves, fortifications, buildings, and canefields on Saipan and Tinian.[146] Civilians were inevitably wounded or killed by the flame weapons. Saipan schoolgirl Victoria Akiyama, recalled that she "screamed hysterically" when she was burned by a flamethrower.[147] Chamorro-Carolinian Mariana Wabol recounted how she lost both of her baby nieces that she was carrying and suffered severe burns on her chest during a flamethrower attack on Saipan.[148] Marine Carl W. Matthews, 23rd Regiment, 4th Division, stated, "always felt bad when the Japanese would run out of their hole, almost naked, but with fuel and fire from the flamethrowers covering their bodies, screaming and dying."[149] After Saipan was declared secure, Lieutenant Robert Sheeks came across a woman along the road who was severely burned by a flame weapon and wounded with shrapnel. "Her skin, what was left of it, was crusted bright red with sickening black splotches." Her face was "burned away ... she was still breathing, her chest twitching, spasms of breathe rasping in and out of an opening that had once been her mouth."[150] White phosphorous and other incendiaries

An American brings out a little girl from a cave on Saipan. CPA-44-6854. Courtesy New York State Military Museum.

were also used during the battles.[151] A Navy Corpsman who served in the Pacific stated, "The thing about a phosphorous grenade is that you can't get it off the skin, so it just keeps burning into a person.... Mostly I remember the women burning."[152] Many survivors discussed after the war that they never forgot the "very strange" and sickening smell of human beings burning and decomposing on Saipan and Tinian.[153]

Although the Americans relied on brutal tactics, there were many Marines and Soldiers who cared deeply about not killing civilians. Marine Captain Roy H. Elrod, 8th Regiment, 2nd Division, wrote, that civilians on Saipan were "confused, frightened, actually terrified, because here they were right between both forces. We didn't want to harm them."[154] Marine Joseph P. Fiore, a flamethrower in the 18th Regiment, 2nd Division, stated, just before he was about to burn a hut down on Saipan, "this little old lady came out of there and she had three or four kids with her and I just shook my head.... If I'd ever burned that place, at that point in time, I think I would have blown my brains out."[155] Marine Jack V. Gilbreath, 23rd Regiment, 4th Division, stated that after a buddy in his unit accidentally shot and killed a group of women and children on Saipan one night, "he ... committed suicide."[156] Marine Samuel T. Holiday, a Navajo Code Talker attached to the 25th Regiment, 4th Division, recalled, "Looking at them really made me feel sad. I wondered how many people we were killing because of the code talkers' work. I had not realized how much damage we were doing with the Navajo language or how many people were dying. I remembered what my mother had said about not killing anything without purpose. This meant not even killing a lizard or plant and here we were killing human beings. It was sickening, but it was war so we moved on."[157]

Marine Sergeant William W. Rogal, 2nd Regiment, 2nd Division, wrote about an incident on Saipan that deeply disturbed him his whole life:

> As we proceeded across the battlefield we came upon a number of deep, partially covered emplacements dug to serve as bomb shelters. The first one we hit contained what appeared to be a dead Jap soldier. One of our four men from the Third Platoon jumped into the hole to investigate and was shot dead by the Jap, who had been playing possum. After that we threw grenades in the holes to make sure they contained no live Japs. But that procedure resulted in tragedy. The Second Platoon, operating to my left, heard a noise of some sort in a large, almost completely covered emplacement and dropped in a grenade. To our horror the explosion produced screams and crying of children. Six or seven little Chamorro girls in school uniforms had taken shelter in the hole. Our corpsmen did what they could for their wounds but some of them looked pretty far gone. This was the only time I saw combat Marines with tears in their eyes.[158]

Civilians and Japanese soldiers who surrendered or were captured were surprised by the kindness exhibited by many Americans. IJA Sergeant Takeo Yamauchi, 136th Regiment, 43rd Division, recounted, "The minutes and hours after I surrendered were really a time of a culture shock to me. I was marveled to find American soldiers who had been the very object of fear for us being all around me acting carefree and cheerful and yelling and joking to each other. How they looked humane! And how I felt grateful that I was a fortunate survivor of the Saipan battle, more, of the Second World War itself!"[159] IJA Soldier Kawamura Kazuo, with the Matsumoto 150th Infantry Regiment on Saipan, stated, "I had been taught to expect the worst from the Americans, but it didn't happen. Instead, they treated me kindly, and in my turbulent frame of mind, this was almost a letdown."[160] Schoolgirl Victoria Akiyama recalled, "Sometimes American soldiers would call us over to the barbed wire fence [at Camp Susupe] and give us chocolate."[161] *Life* magazine photographer W. Eugene Smith wrote, "The soldiers who had lost so many comrades ... now

"Japanese mother and children after their rescue from a cave…" Civilians struggled for their lives and cared for others during the battles. One brave little girl on Saipan continues to smile despite what she and her family experienced. CPA-44–6850. SC-392668. National Archives.

showered them (especially the kids) with candy or anything else they had. It was a magnificent example of fair play and lack of a blinding hatred such as can overcome decency and reason. This was real Americanism."[162] After Navy Corpsman Floyd R. Cox treated two boys severely wounded by shrapnel on Tinian, their mother offered him a fine white comb, her sole possession, but he smiled and refused.[163] Chamorro schoolgirl Marie Soledad Castro stated, "I have always wanted to express my thankfulness to the Marines, because I felt we were so oppressed during Japanese times. When the Marines came, life came to us. I feel they saved our lives."[164]

Accidental Killings

Many civilians, who were looking for water, food, shelter, or their family members at nighttime, were mistaken for Japanese infiltrators and accidentally killed by the Americans. Marine Lieutenant Dean Ladd, 8th Regiment, 2nd Division, stated, during the first night of the Battle of Saipan, along the western edge of the Lake Susupe swamp, "we spotted two shadowy figures moving toward us from the direction of the air-raid shelter. We assumed they were Japanese and shot them a few yards from our hole. They lay groaning and crying out and sometimes screaming, and there wasn't a damn thing anyone could or would do about it. The next morning several men went out to inspect the bodies and discovered they were women. They must have come to us seeking refuge from the fighting and we had killed them instead.... Mistakes like that happened all the time."[165] During the night of June 19, on Saipan's southern coast, "a group of twenty to thirty civilians stumbled into the perimeter of Company L, 105th Infantry, [27th Division] and were all killed."[166] Marine Lieutenant Frederick A. Stott, who fought on Saipan and Tinian, wrote, "Nights ... are terrifying mainly because of the unknown."[167] Navy Corpsman Mate H.L. Obermiller, attached to the 2nd Marine Division, remembered finding a wounded little girl one night on Tinian. She was mistakenly shot in the abdomen near American lines and her left kidney was protruding out of her body. Her father, whose back she was clinging to, was dead. Obermiller stated, "I sent her down to the aid station in the morning when the sun came up. I frankly don't know how she could have lived. It's an incident that has haunted me for a long time."[168] An American surrender leaflet dropped on Tinian warned civilians, "Avoid moving at night when Americans are nearby. It is impossible to distinguish you from Japanese snipers at night."[169]

Japanese troops also mistook civilians and their own troops for probing Americans at night and shot at them. Saipan schoolgirl Kimiko Nishikawa recounted, "One night my father [Tsunetaro] and oldest brother went out from the cave to find water and food. They were passing by a sugar cane field when a machine gun opened fire on them. My father was hit in the legs. Both he and my brother laid face down on the ground until the firing stopped. Then my brother carried my father back to the cave where he died later that night."[170] The family attempted to move to a safer location after the father's death. "We left at night but had gone only a short distance when once again a machine gun started to fire in our direction. My mother [Nami] was hit."[171] The mother later died of her wounds. By the end of the battle, the family of eight had been reduced to Kimiko and her older brother. Four of her siblings, Mitsuko (age 23), Nagako (15), Hiroji (13), and Noboru (7), died on Saipan along with her parents.[172]

Many civilians were inadvertently killed by American and Japanese weapons during

There are few photographs and little footage of what happened at night during the Battles of Saipan and Tinian. In this photograph, Garapan is burning in the distance while star shells are flaring overhead, Saipan, June 1944. #85171. National Archives.

the battles. Chamorro Juan Blanco, a worker for Nanyo Kohatsu prior to the Battle of Saipan, recalled, "There is a large cave not far from Calabara cave. There were maybe 1,000 Japanese in the cave. I stayed there for about two weeks. There was a large boulder in front of the mouth to that cave, and one day while I was in there with my NKK co-workers a bomb landed between that boulder and the mouth of the cave, killing many people."[173] Chamorro Cristino S. Dela Cruz stated, "Before we were captured two of my sisters were killed by a bomb."[174] Correspondent Robert Sherrod wrote that he entered a farmhouse on Saipan and found the owner of the home "dead on the floor of his lower sleeping shelf. Beside him, on a red cassock, lay a year-old baby, neatly covered. Both had been killed apparently by the bullets of a strafing plane which had punctured the tin roof in many places."[175] The Saipan NTLF G-2 Periodic Report no. 39, 24 July 1944, noted that Army Soldiers killed "46 Jap soldiers" and "numerous civilians" during mop-up operations for the day.[176] Japanese schoolgirl Tatsu Sato stated in her memoir *Living in the Battle Flames of Saipan* (*Saipan no senka ni ikite*, 1996) that American mop-up units killed her mother and father after the island fell.[177]

The Americans often had difficulty telling apart combatants and noncombatants because many civilians had only military and paramilitary clothing to wear. Correspondent Robert Sherrod wrote, "Some men who might have been classed as civilians wore a sort of homeguard uniform."[178] Marine Lieutenant Robert Sheeks wrote, "The members of many of the civilian organizations and of the sugar company were issued uniforms of olive drab or khaki, not unlike a military uniform, and many men wore wrapped cloth leggings. Caps similar to those worn by troops were issued to the Young Men's Association but, due to the strict clothing rationing in effect for the past two years, the only clothing available to civilians consisted primarily of discarded military uniforms or work uniforms of the same color. This clothing created a serious problem for United States troops who found it very difficult during the campaign to distinguish Japanese civilians from military personnel."[179] An American surrender leaflet dropped on Tinian urged, "Wear civilian clothing easily distinguishable from Japanese uniforms (red, yellow, white cloth). Don't wear cast-off Japanese uniforms!"[180]

Miyagi Shinsho

Okinawan schoolboy Miyagi Shinsho was born in 1934 and lived and worked on his family's farm near Mt. Tapochau. When Saipan was invaded, Miyagi and his parents and older brother fled to the northern end of the island.[181] While the family was on the move, Miyagi's father was killed by a shell blast or bomb, and his mother was shot in the chest and stomach and died.[182] Miyagi was shot in the right hand. By the time he and his brother surrendered to the Americans, Miyagi's wound had turned gangrenous and his hand had to be amputated. In 2002, he published his memoir *A Boy and the Battle of Saipan* (*Saipan no tatakai to shonen*) in Japanese.

Benjamin Quinzon Abadilla

Filipino-Chamorro boy Benjamin Quinzon Abadilla was home with his mother and aunt in southwestern Saipan when the pre-invasion bombardment began. The three fled to the interior of the island. One day, while on the move, Benjamin's mother, who was in her third trimester of pregnancy, fell and hit her head on a rock and bled to death. Benjamin and his aunt could not stay in the area to care for the body. Later, a Japanese soldier shot Benjamin's aunt in the neck and killed her while they were hiding in the thick swamp near Susupe. Benjamin hid in safety until he found his father helping the Americans burying dead bodies. He and his father later learned that a family friend cut open his dead mother's stomach and saved his baby sister, Elaine.[183]

Rosa Reyes Agulto

When the Americans invaded Saipan, Chamorro young woman Rosa Reyes Agulto fled with her family of six to a concealed underground tunnel which her father Jose dug before the invasion. The family rationed the small amount of supplies and water they had. They decided to leave the tunnel and flee to the north when the Americans came near their position. While heading northward, Rosa's pregnant mother Nicholasa and younger brother were shot. Her brother died instantly. Nicholasa and the baby died in the American field hospital. Later, Rosa's father was shot and killed by Japanese soldiers. Rosa and her two sisters, Stephania and Juliana, survived the war.[184]

9

Civilian Internment Camps

The United States Navy directed the military governments and civilian internment camps on Saipan and Tinian and the Army garrisoned the islands.[1] The Americans did not adequately prepare for the internment and care of civilians. High-level planners were fixated on combat operations and not the United States' responsibility, as the new occupier, to the welfare of the civilians of the islands. The Saipan Naval Military Government record of operations between June 1944 and December 1945, stated, "To the men responsible for the successful prosecution of the war against Japan, military government bulks smallest in their strategical considerations."[2] The Saipan NTLF Civil Affairs Report, 13 August 1944, stated, "There was little of the civil affairs operation on Saipan, which the Americans could be proud.... Civil affairs must be more than an advisory staff, it must have sufficient hand picked personnel and supplies or gear to meet the requirements of the operation."[3]

The naval military governments on Saipan and Tinian were set up immediately following the amphibious landings and establishment of beachheads in the summer of 1944.[4] Admiral Nimitz, CINCPAC/POA, was appointed by President Roosevelt and the Joint Chiefs of Staff as the military governor of all conquered Japanese islands in Micronesia.[5] Under Nimitz, Admiral Raymond Spruance, Commander of the Fifth Fleet, directed military government operations during the assault phases of the battles.[6] While the fighting was raging, Naval Military Government officers and Marine Corps Civil Affairs officers removed civilians from combat zones, established and maintained civilian stockades, and distributed relief supplies.[7]

During the occupation phases, which began after the islands were declared secure, military government command in the Marianas passed from Admiral Spruance to Vice Admiral John H. Hoover, Commander Forward Area Central Pacific and Commander Marianas Area. Hoover was responsible for the administration of the military governments based on CINCPOA's directives.[8] Island Commanders, subordinate to Hoover, directly oversaw military government operations, the garrison forces, and base development on their respective islands. Army Major General Sanderford Jarman was designated the Island Commander of Saipan.[9] Marine Corps Major General James L. Underhill served as Island Commander of Tinian from early August to late November 1944. Army Brigadier General Frederick V.H. Kimble succeeded Underhill.[10] The military governments they oversaw were responsible for supply distribution, public health, construction and engineering projects, and the operation of the civilian internment camps on the islands.

The two military governments were entirely unprepared to care for the tens of thousands of civilians that survived the battles. The Navy did not assign enough officers and enlisted men to the military governments during both the assault and occupation phases. Norman Meller, a Naval Military Government Officer on Saipan, wrote, the administration was beset by "inadequate preplanning and a military government staff insufficient in numbers and unprepared by training for the magnitude of the task they would have to undertake."[11] Moreover, the command was weakened by poor leadership and petty quarrels. One officer noted, during military government staff meetings, "most of the time is devoted to personal tirades, views and philosophies, with little time spent toward mapping out the ensuing days' or weeks' work."[12]

The military governments were also debilitated by supply problems. The Saipan NTLF Operations Report, 12 August 1944, stated, "The personnel, transportation, supplies, and medical assistance available was not adequate for the civil affairs agency to properly perform its functions. Corrective measures must be arranged for in future operations."[13] The Navy did not furnish the military governments with the provisions and equipment needed for civilian relief.[14] Strangely, military government resupply was not included in the logistics plans for the Marianas Operation.[15] Furthermore, unnecessary supplies were unloaded for the military governments in the early weeks of the invasions. For example, on both islands, large crates of questionnaires, registration forms, and armbands for civilian labor came ashore before basic lifesaving items.[16] Military government officers were forced to beg, borrow, and even steal food, medicine, and other supplies for civilians from other commands.[17] The Navy was slow to fulfill officers' emergency supply requests and outright rejected them at times. In one case, when an officer requested fishing supplies to reduce malnutrition and disease, CINCPOA "sat on them [the requi-

Civilians in an American stockade on Saipan, June 1944. There is little shelter from the elements. #88450. National Archives.

9. Civilian Internment Camps

Koreans in a stockade on Tinian, August 1944. Some people had little clothing and no shoes. #92262. National Archives.

sitions], sent a survey party to the area, awaited their reports, planned a long range plan, cancelled Saipan's requisitions and had their 'experts' order what they thought Saipan and other islands needed."[18] The American Red Cross provided crucial relief items, including soap and baby bottles, that the Navy could not seem to manage.[19]

The Americans set up makeshift civilian stockades surrounded by barbed wire fencing early in the battles. On Saipan, in mid–June 1944, the 4th Marine Division built three stockades for Japanese, Okinawan, and Korean civilian prisoners on the island's southwestern shore near Chalan Kanoa. The 2nd Marine Division built a stockade for Chamorro and Carolinian civilians nearby, and the 27th Army Division later built one on the beach in their zone of action. On Tinian, in late July, the 4th Marine Division set up a stockade at the destroyed village of Churo in north-central Tinian, and the 2nd Marine Division built a stockade near the southern end of Ushi Point Airfield.[20] The civilians in the stockades, many of whom were ill and injured, had little access to fresh water, and food was limited to American field rations. They had no shelter and were unprotected from the elements. The Saipan NTLF Civil Affairs Report stated, the "stockades were without shade from the tropical sun, had insufficient canvas or shelter and were exposed to constant clouds of dust from the road."[21] Japanese artillery, gunfire, and mortars, as well as American "friendly fire," came into the stockades at times and killed civilians.

In late June 1944, the military government established Camp Susupe, a rear-line civilian internment camp between Chalan Kanoa's beaches and Lake Susupe on Saipan.[22] Camp Susupe consisted of three compounds segregated based on ethnicity. There was a camp for Chamorros and Carolinians (Area I), one for Koreans (Area II), and the largest for both Japanese from the mainland and Okinawans (Area III).[23] There was a separate compound for Japanese and Korean prisoners of war.[24] Comfort women were put in the civilian camps. The Americans interned Micronesians, not only for their safety but because they believed the Chamorros and Carolinians were "Japanized" and could not be entirely trusted.[25] A number of Americans believed they were racially superior to the Chamorros and Carolinians, as well as the East Asians. Marine Charles Pase, 10th Regiment, 2nd Division, stated, "Of course these weren't Japanese.... We called them 'gooks' and thought that they were some subhuman sort of thing."[26] In August 1944, Camp Churo was established on Tinian and replaced the 4th Marine Division's stockade at the village. Churo was divided into a Japanese camp and Korean camp.[27] All captured Japanese soldiers and Korean laborers on Tinian, as well as the small number of Micronesians on the island, were transferred to Saipan. Many Japanese military POWs were later transferred to Hawaii and the United States. All civilians remained interned on the islands past the end of the war.

Upon entering the internment camps, civilians were interrogated for intelligence and sent to a reception area where they were fed, allowed to bathe, and registered.[28] The registration process included "a complete personal record for each internee, replete with photograph and thumbprint. From these were later issued identification papers, which the internees were to carry at all times under pain of punishment.... Questioning during registration permitted recordation of each internee's education, prior work experience, and potentially useful skills, all of which facilitated the assignment of everyone of employable age to an appropriate job, whether inside or beyond the boundary fences of Camp Susupe."[29] There were many children and orphans in the camps. Robert Sherrod wrote, on Saipan, "Nearly all the women of child-bearing age had babies strapped to their backs. Many of the babies were asleep, their heads rocking loosely in the hot morning sun."[30] Marine Combat Correspondent Irving Schlossenberg wrote, "Most of the women [on Tinian] had babies strapped to their backs."[31] Chamorro schoolgirl Marie Soledad Castro recalled, before entering Camp Susupe, "On the way we came to two little Japanese girls standing in the road. One was four years old and the other was eight. They were dressed in nice kimonos. One of the Marines told us that their mother had dressed them in their best clothes, given them some money, and told them to keep walking until somebody found them. I think their parents committed suicide. They were crying and saying, 'Please take care of us.'"[32]

Military police escorted civilians to the internment camps, guarded them, enforced curfews, and organized civilian labor.[33] Micronesian security guards, assigned by the Americans, aided the MPs.[34] Some civilians tried to escape the camps but were shot.[35] Civilians were sometimes killed in the camps by stray gunfire during the battles and mop-up operations or died in weapons accidents. A February 1945 Saipan military government report stated, "Nine Children killed, 27 wounded by anti-tank grenade accidentally exploded by Japanese children in school garden on 8 February."[36]

The building and operation of civilian internment camps were given little attention in the pre-invasion plans. The Navy unwisely arranged to shelter civilians in the buildings of Chalan Kanoa, Garapan, and Tinian Town, which were all inevitably and purposely

Women and children in Camp Susupe nursery. CPA-44-6955. Courtesy New York State Military Museum.

destroyed during the battles.[37] As a result, the military government did not have the construction materials needed to build satisfactory facilities for noncombatants in the late summer of 1944. A Civil Affairs Report, dated 28 August 1944, stated, "It is impossible to set up and maintain a creditable civilian internment camp without adequate equipment and material…. It should be clearly understood that without adequate materials, an adequate job cannot be done."[38] Saipan schoolgirl Victoria Akiyama stated, "We were provided no shelter. We had to make our own with whatever materials we could salvage. Pieces of rice sacking might be all we had for a door. We were all covered with lice. We must have looked like monkeys at times, all sitting in a line picking bugs out of the hair of the person in front of us."[39] Chamorro young man Manuel T. Sablan recalled, "It was hard in Camp Susupe. There really wasn't much of a place to sleep. Some of us men had to sleep on the ground with just a blanket, but under a tent. We hadn't eaten anything in two weeks except for some sugar cane."[40] Schoolgirl Kimiko Nishikawa explained, "Camp Susupe was awful; just tents with sand for floors."[41]

Eventually, Naval Construction Battalions (Seabees) salvaged and transported metal and wood debris from the demolished cities, villages, and farmsteads to Camp Susupe and Camp Churo and built barrack-like structures. The overcrowded structures had corrugated tin and tarpaulin canvas roofs; palm frond, reed, and rice sack siding; and no floors.[42] A United States Naval Military Government record stated, there were "as many as 200 persons occupying 800 square feet…"[43] Dr. John F. Embree, a Psychological Warfare Supervisor for the Office of War Information, wrote, "Housing was one of the most depressing aspects of life in Camp Susupe. One visiting Military Government officer commented that he never expected to find the American Military Government responsible for such a slum."[44]

The camps initially had no waste management systems or sewage infrastructure. Internees had to use overfilled latrines and open pits and trenches in the ground and sometimes had nowhere to go, which increased the spread of infectious diseases among the cramped populations and gave the camps foul odors.[45] Dr. Embree wrote, "At first there were no housing and sanitation facilities whatsoever, the people sleeping on the ground, performing natural functions almost everywhere and in general living at a very low level."[46] There were flies and rats everywhere. One Japanese civilian in Susupe commented, "We are living like pigs."[47] Correspondent Richard W. Johnston wrote, "Camp Susupe is full of evil smells and tragic sights…"[48] Correspondent William L. Worden wrote, "The first inevitable impression of the camp is one of concentrated human misery."[49] The navy did not have personal hygiene supplies for civilians shipped to the islands. A military government report stated, "Soap, a most important item from the medical and sanitary point of view, was almost entirely lacking until about Dplus 30 when a small supply of Japanese salt-water soap was found."[50] Period photographs show that most civilians were also barefooted. The lack of medical supplies and facilities was an even greater problem.

The United States military planners were negligent in preparing for and providing medical treatment and establishing hospitals for civilians during the battles and early months of the occupations. The Saipan NTLF Operations Report stated, "Future prior planning must include adequate provision for civilian medical care."[51] The Saipan NTLF Medical Report, 5 August 1944, stated, "Hospitalization for civilian casualties proved to be a serious problem."[52] The report urged, "Prior planning must include definite provisions for hospitalization of civilian sick and wounded."[53] The Tinian NTLF Medical Report, 10 August 1944, stated, "At Tinian, as at Saipan, inadequate prior planning for civilian hospitalization was manifest. Some of this hospitalization, at least, must be landed with the assault shipping during the first week if it is to adequately care for the influx of civilian casualties which begin building up in appreciable numbers by the end of the first week."[54]

American planners did not establish or designate medical units for civilian care and treatment before the invasions. Assault force medical units, strained by heavy American casualties, were required to treat noncombatants.[55] Civilians also had to be taken aboard ships for medical attention. Navy Lieutenant Lawrence A. Marsden, on the attack transport USS *Doyen* off Saipan, wrote, "a Chamorro mother and her baby boy were brought aboard. Both had been wounded. The woman's arm was badly shattered, and the boy had been hit in the stomach."[56] On Saipan, a full week passed before commanders tasked Unit B of the 31st Field Hospital, an Army unit, with treating civilians.[57] Unit B lacked the staff and resources to treat the thousands of civilians in need of medical attention. The same problem occurred on Tinian, where assault units and Company E of the 2nd Medical Battalion (Army), were swamped with wounded and ill civilians.[58] The small and overtaxed American medical units worked tirelessly to save as many as possible and relied on the assistance of civilian nurses, midwives, and stretcher-bearers.[59]

9. Civilian Internment Camps

The Americans did not ship sufficient quantities of medicine and supplies for civilians and had to use captured IJM stocks.[60] A Navy report, dated 25 August 1944, stated:

> Medical supplies were reported inadequate during the assault phase on Tinian and Saipan and only the early salvage of large quantities of Japanese medical supplies saved the day ... large numbers of severe wounds and fractures were encountered and plaster of paris, had it been available in large quantities, would have saved the medical officers many hours of labor. They were forced to use bandage to a large degree and consequently the redressing of wounds created a big problem due the lack of personnel and the shortage of bandage. The care of children has proven to be a tremendous problem. They are often brought in to camps in an extremely emaciated condition, very dirty, often severely injured and with severe dysentery or parasitic worm infections. Since many are orphans, their care is a big problem.... Feeding these children was and is very difficult because of the shortage of milk, bottles and nipples.... The mortality was high and all medical officers agree a pediatrician would have been a great asset. Everywhere sanitation, medical personnel, food, medical and water supplies, care of children and construction materials were and to a degree still are critical problems.[61]

Naval Military Government Officer Norman Meller wrote, on Saipan, "The civilian mortality rate was gruesome, with some two thousand known deaths tallied in the first three

American medical personnel treating civilians on Saipan, June 1944. A number of people, including the children in this photograph, required amputations. #83538. National Archives.

months after D day, almost nineteen hundred of them Japanese. Diarrhea, dysentery, and malnutrition are listed as the principal causes of death, but wounds and their attendant infections must also have been major contributors. For October, the fourth month, infants and children accounted for over half of the total deaths reported."[62] On Tinian, large numbers of civilians also died in internment from diseases and wounds. Reported causes and contributors of deaths among civilian internees on Saipan and Tinian included malnutrition, diarrhea, dysentery, wounds, exposure, pulmonary edema, tetanus, gangrene, intestinal parasites, pneumonia, tuberculosis, peritonitis, premature birth, toxemia pregnancy, beri-beri, epilepsy, cerebral hemorrhage, burns, measles, asthma, cardiac failure, dengue, undetermined fever, convulsions, jaundice, kidney disease, cerebral contusion, hepatitis, and other causes.[63] The Americans may have inadvertently spread some diseases to the peoples' of the island. The "Saipan" pamphlet issued to troops stated, "The natives are very susceptible to our common respiratory diseases. It is possible for germs that our troops carry, and to which they have become immune, to infect natives."[64]

Malnutrition, which weakened immunities and increased susceptibility to disease, was a leading contributor to civilian deaths. Assistant Civil Affairs Officer P. Druiding wrote: "Apart from actual casualties, malnutrition is the big medical problem. The people become so weak and their resistance becomes so low that diarrhea and dysentery and other diseases are easily contracted and in many instances are fatal. Deficiency diseases

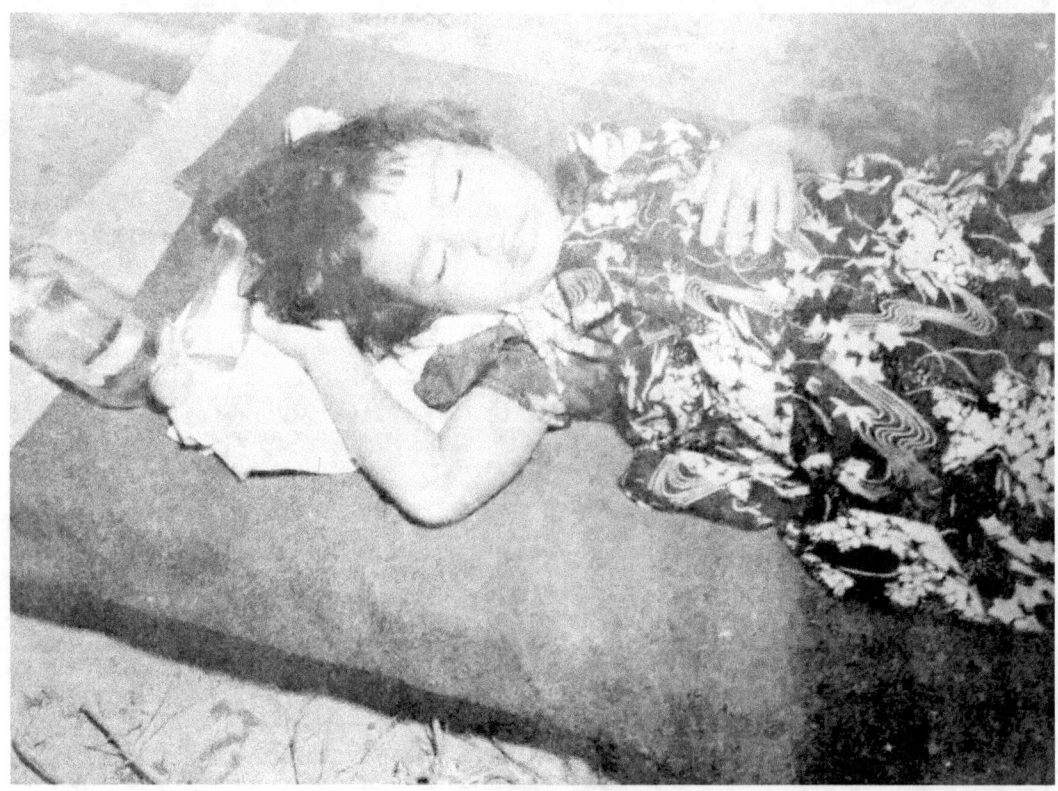

Sick girl in Camp Susupe, Saipan. United States Navy #3245. Military Government Photographic Record.

such as beri-beri and scurvy are common. Conditions are not likely to improve so long as they are on their present diet. Hence, the early development of agriculture and fishing becomes important to public health."[65] Dr. N.B. Kurnick, a physician serving at the 369th Station Hospital laboratory on Saipan, wrote:

> About three months after the invasion of Saipan, the hospital admissions to the civilian hospital began to include a large number of patients with peripheral edema, some of whom also had ascites and hydrothorax. Most of these patients complained of muscular weakness, characterized particularly by difficulty in arising from the customary squatting position ... these cases probably represented nutrition edema due to protein deficiency.... The subjects had been living in the hills or in an internment camp on a diet consisting of rice, a few greens, onions, and about an ounce of fish daily.... The death rate was very high. One hundred of those who died were examined post mortem by Drs. Klosterman, Hirsch, and the author. Malnutrition was constant and advanced pulmonary tuberculosis was very common.[66]

Saipan schoolgirl Victoria Akiyama recalled, "In Camp Susupe we were always hungry."[67] Unfortunately, there were instances when American troops purposely destroyed large stockpiles of captured food and medicine on Saipan and Tinian simply because they were enemy property.[68] Marine Sergeant Bill Miller wrote, "Much civilian property was destroyed in the Marianas.... For every can of food and pound of rice wasted by combat or other troops, more will have to be shipped all the way across the Pacific to feed the alien population coming under U.S. Jurisdiction."[69] Americans, who had "K," "C," and sometimes "10-in-1" rations, also killed and ate enemy livestock that could have gone to civilians.[70] Marine Lieutenant Frederic A. Stott, wrote, along with rations, "impromptu additions to the menu soon appeared in the form of captured chickens, ducks, and even two or three pigs which failed to evade tackling Marines."[71] Marine Michael Gates, 23rd Regiment, 4th Division, stated, on Saipan, "We caught a pig and a chicken and started roasting them."[72]

Civilians brought their complaints concerning the lack of food to the Saipan military government, but the administration at first ignored their pleas.[73] When one medical officer told a chief civil affairs officer that the civilians were too ill and malnourished to work as laborers, the civil affairs officer replied, "What difference does it make if they die? Put them to work at once."[74] Norman Meller wrote about the apathy of the head military government officers:

> I, of course, had no contact with the admiral who was theater commander in charge of all military operations on Saipan, and in addition to his other duties, was responsible for military government on the island. The same pretty much held true for his deputy, an army colonel charged with administering the affairs of Camp Susupe. I have no memory of having been introduced to the colonel when joining the Susupe staff. Rather my recollection of him is of a far different nature, centering around the frame house, with walls of *cariso* matting (a woven island material) located on the swimming beach outside the camp's civilian area, which the colonel had ordered built for his personal use. It was pointed out to me during my orientation to Camp Susupe as the first "permanent" structure erected by the military government—at a time when providing minimum shelter for civilians still remained critical. Although separated by some distance from the rest of the "officers territory" on the beach, I could occasionally see, and hear, the colonel and his guests from Island Headquarters enjoying the amenities of his quarters. Given the fact that Island Headquarters had been constructed at considerable cost high on the side of Mt Tapotchau, well above the heat of the island's littoral plain, and Navy Headquarters were similarly sited on heights closer to Saipan's harbor, I early concluded that the military "brass" were not averse to assigning high priority to their own personal comfort.[75]

The high-level military planners and government officers' negligence concerning civilian care was partly a manifestation of the racial enmity harbored by a number of Americans. Embree stated that they "looked down" on civilians because of "a general American race prejudice in regard to Orientals, heightened by the fact that the Japanese were our enemies in the war. In addition, the extremely degrading conditions of Susupe in the early days, and in some extent later, where the people had been reduced to a very low level of sanitation and social life."[76] Meller wrote:

> The appalling conditions under which civilians at first lived when gathered in protective custody served to reinforce the attitudes of military government personnel. Hungry, thirsty, sick, some with untended wounds, and others traumatized by shock, they entered camp demoralized. In the early period as many as thousand civilians a month died from malnutrition, wounds, and disease.... Little

Chamorro children in Camp Susupe school, July 1945. Conditions in Susupe and Churo greatly improved following the fall of 1944. #129091. National Archives.

wonder that seeing this squalor and human degradation, the mind-set of some of the military government personnel was to regard whatever was done by way of housing, sanitation, and care for the internees as being far better than what they were accustomed to—and for which they should be eternally grateful. As enemy aliens, the Japanese were considered to be in the poorest position from which to complain about the care received. In the parlance of the time, while all the internees were "gooks," they were at the bottom of the civilian heap, and to be treated accordingly.[77]

In late 1944 and early 1945, the Americans improved the conditions at the internment camps and the civilian death rate substantially declined.[78] The military governments carried out sanitary engineering projects and implemented stricter hygiene and waste management procedures, which reduced the spread of infectious diseases. They also built new wells, water purification plants, and wooden barrack houses.[79] The Americans established good hospitals and dental clinics and imported medical and food supplies in sufficient quantities. Children began attending school, while a voluntary paid labor system was set up. Civilians were paid with United States "Hawaiian Series" emergency issue currency.[80] Trade stores were created so that civilians could purchase additional foodstuffs and goods, such as cloth, sewing equipment, and soap. Through the wages they obtained from their labor, the Korean communities on both Saipan and Tinian even managed to donate thousands of dollars to the Korean National Association in Honolulu to support Korean independence from the Japanese.[81] Unfortunately, the Saipan and Tinian Koreans experienced another war after returning to their home.

Not all civilians on Saipan and Tinian were interned in the summer of 1944. Hundreds of noncombatants and troops refused to surrender following the end of the battles and continued to hide in the islands' caves and jungles. These holdouts surrendered or were captured in small numbers until the end of the war and even afterward. Lieutenant Robert Sheeks wrote, "Except for some time spent during the Tinian campaign and a diversionary operation at Okinawa, I was on Saipan for fourteen months. Believe it or not, while we were at Saipan and getting ready for the invasion of Japan, we were still getting people out of caves."[82] The caves were a disgusting environment to survive in. Oftentimes, blood, excrement, and body fluids were all over the place. Chamorro schoolboy Henry Taimanao Indalecio recalled, they were "hot, smelly, and pitch black."[83] Some caves were so small that civilians had to lay on top of one another or crunch up. The cave holdouts were a filthy, sickly, and miserable group. Meller wrote, "Having long become night people who emerged to search for food only after the sun had set, their skins had turned a pasty white, giving them the appearance of walking ghosts."[84] Marine Combat Correspondent Irving Schlossenberg wrote, "Some were clothed in rags ... some were almost nude. All were haggard, all were dirty, all were weary, all were confused, and all were resigned to a sad fate."[85]

10

Number of Civilian Deaths and Suicides

Correspondent Robert Sherrod estimated that somewhere between 7,000 to 17,000 civilians died on Saipan.[1] The *War History Series* (*Senshi Shosho*), Vol. 6, the official history of the Japanese military in the Marianas during the Pacific War published in 1967, estimated that 8,000 to 10,000 civilians died on Saipan.[2] John Toland stated in his Pulitzer Prize-winning book *The Rising Sun: The Decline and Fall of the Japanese Empire 1936–1945* (1970) that almost "22,000 Japanese civilians—two out of three—perished needlessly" on the island.[3] The United States Marine Corps History and Museums Division's narrative of the Battle of Tinian stated that an estimated 4,000 civilians died on Tinian.[4] Analysis of Japanese and American primary sources created in the 1940s reveal that less than 11,000 civilians died from all causes during the Battle of Saipan and in Camp Susupe. On Tinian, the civilian death toll was less than 3,000.

The 1942 General Survey of the South Seas Islands (*Nanyo Gunto yoran: Showa junana-nenban*), produced by the South Seas Government, stated that the total population of Saipan, Tinian, and Rota in December 1941 was 53,753 people (48,923 Japanese, including Okinawans and Koreans; 4,808 Chamorros and Carolinians; 22 foreigners).[5] The civilian population of the three islands remained relatively unchanged between late 1941 and early 1944 as immigration to them mostly ceased and few civilians were permitted to leave the islands after the attack on Pearl Harbor. According to historian Wakako Higuchi, "The navy had been refusing repatriation of Japanese nationals to the homeland in order to maintain a labor force, but finally agreed in February 1944. The navy needed to reduce food consumption by elderly and female laborers because they were considered inferior to male workers."[6] The Japanese government was also concerned that evacuated civilians would "leak news" about the empire's military defeats in the Pacific.[7] A number of male imperial subjects, who were scheduled for the conscription exam for military service and would have been sent away to train and fight, were granted a moratorium and remained on the islands.[8]

The Saipan NTLF Civil Affairs Report stated that an estimated 3,000 to 5,000 civilians from Saipan and Tinian were evacuated from the islands.[9] According to historian Yumiko Imaizumi, 4,238 Japanese residents (2,580 from Saipan and 1,658 from Tinian) were evacuated.[10] Many were Japanese from the mainland, including the family members and friends of government officials and sugar company executives. No Chamorros or Carolinians were evacuated.[11] Unlike on Iwo Jima, where the entire civilian population of over 1,000 people was removed, Saipan and Tinian's civilians were too many in number and too far away from the home islands to be saved before the battles. Moreover, the American invasion of the Marianas came earlier than the Japanese High Command had anticipated. Many Japanese officers believed the Carolines were to be invaded before the Marianas and that they had more time to get civilians out.[12]

A number of Saipan and Tinian evacuees were killed at sea before the battles when the ships carrying them were torpedoed and sunk by American submarines. On March 4, 1944, the *America Maru* departed Saipan for Yokosuka, Japan with civilian evacuees. Two days later, on March 6, about 420 miles north-northwest of Saipan, torpedoes from the *USS Nautilus* hit the *America Maru*'s port side. The ship sunk in less than two minutes and only 43 of the 642 passengers aboard survived. On May 31, the *Chiyo Maru* departed Saipan for Yokosuka. On June 2, 250 miles west of Farallon de Pajaros, two torpedoes from the USS *Shark* struck the *Chiyo Maru*'s port side under the rear of her bridge. The ship sunk in about ten minutes and 97 of the 143 passengers aboard were killed. Two days later, on June 4, the *Hakusan Maru*, which was also heading for Yokosuka, was sunk 317 miles west-southwest of Iwo-Jima by the USS *Flier*. Approximately 277 of 375 passengers, mostly women and children, went down with the ship.[13] The United States Strategic Bombing Survey stated, during the preinvasion bombardment in June 1944, "a convoy of the main bulk of shipping trying to escape from Saipan, some 21 ships altogether ... was caught about 220 miles to the northwest and effectively disposed of."[14] Civilians who survived the sea voyage were not entirely safe once they arrived in Japan because the Americans began bombing the mainland in November 1944.

Japanese ships seeking to enter the islands' harbors met the same fate as those departing them. American submarines were positioned off the island. Carolinian-Chamorro schoolboy David Sablan recalled, "During the war there were American submarines a few miles off Saipan and they were sinking Japanese ships as they came into the harbor.... There were also natives who were going to school in Japan and were returning on those ships."[15] Chamorro schoolgirl Escolastica Tudela Cabrera recounted, "One day before the actual fighting started on Saipan I was down by the lagoon buying fish.... A Japanese ship was coming into harbor when it suddenly blew up. Many people were killed on that ship."[16]

On Rota, which was not invaded, the civilian population was 5,562 people (1,019 Japanese, 3,572 Okinawans, 181 Koreans, 790 Chamorros) at the surrender.[17] Subtracting the Rota civilian population, 919 IJM troops in the islands,[18] and estimated 4,238 evacuees from the 1941 population of Saipan, Tinian, and Rota, the combined Japanese, Okinawan, Korean, and Micronesian civilian population of Saipan and Tinian on June 15, 1944, was approximately 43,034 people. The Tinian NTLF G-2 Periodic Report no. 48, 2 August 1944, stated, "Translation of captured census records by the D-2, 4th MarDiv, reveals that there were 16,029 civilians on Tinian, 15 April."[19] If 1,658 people were evacuated from Tinian after April 15, 1944, the civilian population of Tinian would have been 14,371 people. The population of Saipan, therefore, would have been approximately 28,663 people. This figure corresponds with oral testimonies. The Saipan NTLF Civil Affairs Report, 13 August 1944, stated, "There is no way of knowing the population of Saipan on 15 June. Estimates secured from several Japanese, Koreans, and Chamorros, range from 24,800 to 30,000."[20]

The "Report of Surrender and Occupation of Japan and Korea," prepared by CINC-PAC/POA, 11 February 1946, stated that there were 27,030 East Asian civilian survivor internees on Saipan and Tinian. The approximate number of East Asian civilian internees on Saipan at the time of repatriation was 14,999 (11,156 Okinawans, 2,392 Japanese, and 1,451 Koreans) and on Tinian 12,031 (7,589 Okinawans, 1,863 Japanese, 2,575 Koreans, and 4 Chinese).[21] Korean IJM laborers were not classified as civilians and were not included in these numbers, but comfort women were. Most Korean laborers were repatriated by the end of 1945.[22] Of the 27,030 East Asian civilian internees, 300 came from Aguiguan (172 Japanese and 128 Koreans) to Camp Churo, Tinian in the fall of 1945, making the original number of internees on Saipan and Tinian 26,730 East Asians.[23] A total of 3,236 Micronesians (2,426 Chamorros and 810 Carolinians) were interned on Saipan in April 1945.[24] This included the small number of Micronesians on Tinian, less than 30, who were transferred to Saipan.[25] There were also approximately 22 civilian foreigners on Saipan. With these numbers in mind, the interned population for all ethnicities on Saipan and Tinian in 1945 was 29,988.

Subtracting the 29,988 internees from the spring 1944 civilian population of 43,034, the total number of civilian deaths on Saipan and Tinian was approximately 13,046.[26] This number excludes the Saipan and Tinian civilian evacuees killed in submarine attacks in spring 1944 or later in Japan from firebombings. From the data about survivors in the internment camps, it can be estimated that around 10,436 East Asian and Micronesian civilians died on Saipan and 2,610 died on Tinian in the battles and internment camps. According to the Marianas Memorial in American Memorial Park on Saipan, 929 Chamorros and Carolinians "lost their lives as a result of war-related causes from the beginning of American aerial bombardment in Saipan on June 11, 1944, to the closure of

Saipan civilians being moved to a place of safety by Marines, June 1944. Over 29,000 civilians surrendered or were captured on Saipan and Tinian combined. #83015. National Archives.

Tinian civilians who surrendered or allowed themselves to be captured, July 1944. Mass surrenders occurred far more than mass suicides among civilians in the Marianas. #93621. National Archives.

civilian camps on July 4, 1946."[27] Approximately 18,227 civilians survived the Battle of Saipan and 11,761 survived the Battle of Tinian.

The number of civilian suicides on Saipan and Tinian in 1944 will never be known. The fact that many civilians were murdered or forced to commit suicide makes it impossible to even provide approximate figures. Furthermore, hundreds of civilians committed suicide or were murdered, out of the view of the Americans, with grenades, blades, and other weapons in the caves and jungles on the islands. There were little to no survivors from these groups who could provide testimonies of what happened. A *New York Times* article, dated February 16, 1945, stated, American officers "believe that stories of civilian suicides on Saipan were greatly exaggerated; it doubtful if the suicides exceeded 200, or 1 per cent of the population."[28] Marine Lieutenant Robert B. Sheeks stated that the number of suicides from people "jumping off the cliffs" alone was probably in the "few hundreds."[29] Robert Sherrod wrote, "From what I saw and from what other observers saw, I believe at least 1,000 Saipan civilians killed themselves. The number may have been much larger."[30] An intelligence officer on Saipan gave the same figure of 1,000 people.[31] Major Paul C. Bosse, Assistant Chief of Staff, G-2, of the Western Pacific Base Command, who spoke with civilians in Camp Susupe, stated, "stories of mass suicide that appeared in the press were, on the whole, greatly exaggerated. It is extremely unlikely that as many as 1,000 of the Saipan Japanese took the way of Seppuku."[32] Even if there were one thousand civilian suicides on Saipan, they would account for less than 4 percent of the total population and less than 10 percent of the estimated 10,436 deaths on Saipan. There are fewer oral testimonies and records concerning the number of people who committed suicide on Tinian, but the numbers were likely comparable to or lower than Saipan.

Aftermath

Saipan and Tinian were devastated during the preinvasion bombardments, battles, and mop-up operations. Homes, factories, farms, shrines, and latte stones were damaged or destroyed. Garapan, Chalan Kanoa, and Tinian Town, along with numerous villages, were obliterated. What remained of them, mostly rubble, debris, and gutted buildings, was bulldozed and the land was used for military purposes. Unexploded artillery shells, bombs, and booby traps remained scattered throughout the two islands. Human remains laid unburied in the caves and jungles, and mass graves were not marked. Many families were torn apart during the fighting and bloodlines were wiped out. Saipan schoolgirl Victoria Akiyama stated, "Even though I watched most of my family get killed, I still had hope that my father was still alive, and that he would take care of me, and would be well again.... All that next day, and for some days afterward I sat outside my shelter [at Camp Susupe] and waited and watched, but my father never came."[1] Tatsu Sato, who was also a schoolgirl on Saipan, wrote in the 1980s, narrowly "escaping from death under the severe battle, even now forty years from the war, I am squeezed my chest thinking of [my] parents dead in vain..."[2] Nanyo Kohatsu businessman Shinozuka Yoshitaro wrote in his memoir that he felt much guilt for not being able to keep alive his eight-year-old daughter Kumiko. The two were separated during the battle and he never found out how she died.[3]

According to historian Haruko Taya Cook in her article "The Myth of the Saipan Suicides" (1995) and later publications, the mass civilian suicides on Saipan were sensationalized and mythologized immediately after the fall of the island. Although almost two-thirds of Saipan's civilian population survived the battle, the Japanese government made it seem, by not reporting the capture or surrender of any noncombatants like the American media had, that all of the civilians on the island died. This was done in order to galvanize the population of mainland Japan to repulse the imminent invasion of the home islands and to threaten the Americans with the possibility of large-scale mass deaths. According to Cook, "The strategy in Japan that exploited the image of Saipan and the Marianas amounted to a threat of national self-destruction and suicide embraced by Japan's leadership to stave off abject surrender and acceptance of American demands at any cost."[4]

On July 18, 1944, Imperial General Headquarters (IGH) announced to the Japanese public that civilians fought and died with the IJM on Saipan.[5] Tamura Tsunejiro, an elderly man and small business owner in Kyoto, wrote in his diary on July 19, 1944, "The American enemy has occupied Saipan, and I hear that Japanese civilians on the island, together with the military, committed *gyokusai*."[6] IGH did not mention anything about civilian suicides. The Japanese government and media did not learn about the mass civilian suicides through military communications. Rather, they were apprised of them, nearly a month after the battle, through correspondent Robert Sherrod's August 7, 1944, *Time Magazine* article "The Battle of Saipan: The Nature of the Enemy" and subsequent American magazine and newspaper articles, such as the *Chicago Tribune*'s August 13, 1944, article "Tribune Writer Views Suicide of Jap Civilians."[7] Sherrod and several other prominent American correspondents did not cover the Battle of Tinian and, consequently, the mass suicides and murders there received little attention.

In mid–August 1944, the Japanese media began publishing articles about the mass suicides on Saipan. Japanese writers and journalists omitted the coerced suicides, murders, and capture, surrender, and internment of civilians that Sherrod discussed. Instead, they wrote about and embellished the suicides of women and children. The *Asahi Shimbun*, a major newspaper in the empire, was the first Japanese paper to announce the suicides. An August 17, 1944, Asahi article, stated: "The facts that all of our loyal and courageous officers and soldiers defending Saipan Island died in action and that even the Japanese civilians who were able to fight participated in combat and shared the fate of the officers and soldiers, were reported worldwide through the announcement of the Imperial General Headquarters July 18, and their loyal, courageous and noble acts have impressed the world. [Now] it has been reported that noncombatants, women, and children have chosen death rather than to be captured alive and be shamed by the demon-like American forces. The world has been astounded by the strength of the fighting spirit and patriotism of the entire people of Japan."[8]

Two days later, on August 19, 1944, the *Asahi Shimbun* ran a similar article with a headline that stated: "THE HEROIC LAST MOMENTS OF OUR FELLOW COUNTRYMEN ON SAIPAN SUBLIMELY WOMEN TOO COMMIT SUICIDE ON ROCKS IN FRONT OF THE GREAT SUN FLAG PATRIOTIC ESSENCE ASTOUNDS THE WORLD."[9] On August 20, 1944, the *Mainichi Shimbun*, another major newspaper, stated that Saipan women: "CHANGED INTO THEIR BEST APPAREL, PRAYED TO THE IMPERIAL PALACE, SUBLIMELY COMMIT SUICIDE IN FRONT OF THE AMERICAN DEVILS SACRIFICE THEMSELVES FOR THE NATIONAL EXIGENCY TOGETHER WITH THE BRAVE MEN."[10] The *Yomiuri Hochi*, which had a massive circulation, stated on August 20: "WOMEN COMBED THEIR HAIR AND PUT ON MAKE-UP IN DEPARTURE FOR DEATH PURIFIED THEIR BODIES, PRAYED TO THE SUN FLAG, AND COMMITTED GROUP SELF-EXPLOSION BY HAND GRENADE."[11]

Intellectuals and propagandists, influenced by the articles, glorified those who committed suicide on Saipan. Dr. Hiraizumi Kiyoshi, a history professor at Tokyo Imperial University in 1944, wrote, "The women and children of Saipan taught us how splendid the power of blood and tradition was, and they gave us courage which will grow one hundred, no, one thousand times, and will live in the minds of the one hundred million."[12] In the August 20, 1944, issue of the *Yomiuri*, Poet Saito Ryu described the suicides of Saipan women as "beautiful" and likened their deaths to well-known mythical and historical suicides in Japan. He stated, the women achieved a "grand last moment, by coloring red the rocks of the South Ocean," with "sublime Japanese blood."[13] Poet Saito Fumi wrote, "I swear to the sisters of Saipan that we will fight to the end with the pride of the women who fought to the last in a sea of blood, and with the encouragement of death, and together with the spirits of the women who have fallen beside the soldiers."[14]

In a Japanese propaganda film produced after the battle, an officer proclaimed to a crowd of school children, "We have heard that all our soldiers on Saipan died bravely.

All the Japanese civilians on the island cooperated with the Army and shared their fate."[15] Reiko Akata, a young girl who worked at the Okunoshima Island chemical weapons factory in Hiroshima Prefecture, still remembered many decades after the war the lyrics of a song, "The Island where the Bright Berries Grow," which was about mass suicides on Saipan.[16] Artist Fujita Tsuguharu's canvas "Our Compatriots on Saipan Remain Loyal to the End," which appeared in issue no. 367 of the Japanese government's weekly newsmagazine the *Photographic Weekly Report* (*Shashin shuho*) on April 18, 1945, romantically depicted the suicides. According to scholar David C. Earhart: "In the center of the painting, a group of women and girls huddle together, surrounded by soldiers, many of them wounded and inert. Mothers comforted their children … they are preparing to hurl themselves and their children over the cliffs to their deaths. The central figure is a woman holding a child in one arm, a pike in the other. Behind her are the cliffs, with one body in mid-fall. She looks in the direction of the enemy, her posture communicating the anguish of being torn between her duty to save her children from the shame of capture and her duty to fight and protect the nation."[17]

The Marianas mass suicides became so well-known that the Japanese government offered compensation for the civilians who died with the troops. According to historian Yumiko Imaizumi, "On 30 September 1944, shortly after the fall of Saipan and Tinian, the Japanese government announced an 'agreement' that it would compensate the bereaved families and the Japanese living in the South Sea Islands by … designating 'general Japanese people' (excluding preschool children) who sacrificed their lives for the Japanese Army/Navy as 'Gunzoku [civilian employees for the military].' This was intended to calm public unrest and boost morale for the war."[18] Jiro Nakano, a telegraph operator in the 753rd Naval Aviation Force who was on Saipan before transferring to the Dutch East Indies with his unit in the spring 1944, stated many decades after the war that the civilians on Saipan, particularly the children, protected "the honor of their families, their emperor, and their country" and "died hero's deaths."[19]

Mass suicides happened elsewhere in the Pacific following the fall of Saipan and Tinian. There were coerced suicides and murders on Tokashiki, Zamami, Iejima, Geruma, Okinawa Island, and other islands in Okinawa Prefecture in 1945.[20] Unfortunately, there have been efforts to "whitewash" Japanese troops' war crimes in the islands.[21] According to historian Janice Matsumura, "Since the 1980s Ministry of Education officials have attempted to downplay the coerced deaths of Okinawans in school textbooks, calling for the deletion of references to soldiers forcing individuals to take their lives or simply killing them in order to defend the honor of wartime troops."[22] Many Japanese and Okinawan people and organizations have condemned these attempts to cover up what happened.[23]

In the months before and during the Battle of Okinawa, Saipan and Tinian were transformed into major United States Army Air Forces airdromes.[24] From November 1944 to August 1945, Marianas-based B-29 heavy bombers, loaded with incendiary cluster bombs, raided over a hundred Japanese cities.[25] The March 9–10, 1945, nighttime firebombing raid on Tokyo alone killed an estimated 83,793 people, the majority who were civilians.[26] According to the United States Strategic Bombing Survey (USSBS), 15.8 square miles of the heart of Tokyo were set ablaze, and "Persons attempting to flee from the attacked area were burned in the streets by the intense heat.… Many fled to the canals and were literally scalded to death or died from the effects of hot gases."[27] The loss of Saipan, which the Japanese High Command declared an "impregnable shield," has been called the "beginning of the end" of the Empire of Japan. Writer Kaneko Mitsuharu's poem "Song of the Tart," which was about women and the defeat and occupation of Japan, read, "You rewrote your eyebrows and lips; On the model of the false mask of the Saipan shield."

Tinian-based B-29s delivered the Hiroshima and Nagasaki bombs. A 1945 study conducted by the USSBS estimated that 330,000 people were killed and 473,000 were injured from all United States air raids on Japan during the Second World War.[28] Other studies place the numbers much higher. Hundreds of thousands of people perished from bomb blasts, burns, carbon monoxide poisoning, crushing, suffocation, radiation exposure, and other injuries. Burns were the leading cause of death in the firebombing raids. A USSBS report stated, "It is natural to expect that burns would stand foremost as a cause of injuries and deaths resulting from bombing of Japanese urban areas with incendiary bombs. The cities were thickly populated; the light wooden buildings were easily ignited and burned rapidly; and the streets were narrow making escape difficult and this difficulty was increased by the development of large conflagrations from which escape to the perimeter was impeded by distance, the crowding of the streets, and also by the force of the 'fire storm' winds rushing toward the center of the conflagrations."[29] Admiral Osami Nagano, Supreme Naval Advisor to the Emperor, remarked after the fall of Saipan, "Hell is on us."[30] The Japanese military committed numerous atrocities throughout Asia and the Pacific and needed to be stopped, but did the Japanese civilians in the homeland need to die? According to historian Asada Sadao, the war "dehumanized both victor and vanquished alike."[31]

The American bombings and the emperor's lack of confidence that the IJM and his subjects could stop the conquest of the home islands by the United States, Soviet Union, and other Allies led the Empire of Japan to surrender on August 15, 1945. The instrument of surrender was formally signed on September 2, 1945. The Japanese destroyed many documents, including communications sent to Saipan and Tinian commanders, before the American occupation forces arrived. With the war over, the Americans ordered the repatriation of Japanese, Okinawans, and Koreans in the islands.

In late 1945, Admiral Raymond A. Spruance, the newly appointed Commander in Chief of the United States Pacific Fleet and Pacific Ocean Areas, directed Navy Task Force 94 (TF 94) to repatriate all "enemy nationals" in the Marianas.[32] Vice Admiral George D. Murray, Commander of the Marianas Area and TF 94, directed the Marianas Evacuation and Occupation Command (TG 94.3). Under Murray, Rear Admiral Francis Eliot Maynard Whiting, Island Commander of Saipan, personally oversaw the Saipan and Tinian Evacuation Task Unit (TU 94.3.6).[33] American ships and Japanese merchant marine vessels were used.[34] Between late 1945 and mid–1946, the unit evacuated most of the tens of thousands of East Asian civilian internees on Saipan and Tinian to the designated ports of debarkation, including Yokohama and Uraga in Japan, Busan in Korea, and Naha in Okinawa.[35] The repatriation of civilians was completed by late 1946.[36] Camp Churo and Camp Susupe were shut down. Some East Asians who married into Micronesian families and had half-Chamorro or Carolinian children evaded the repatriations. The "disappearance" of Japanese, Okinawan, and Korean civilians from Saipan and Tinian after the war, because of the reparations, partly influenced American myths that all the East Asians on the islands died during the battles. Of course, poor historical research was the main cause of the myths.

Repatriates (*hikiagesha*), upon arriving at the ports of their ancestral homelands, were processed, disinfected, immunized, and quarantined at regional repatriation centers.[37]

A woman with her child on Saipan after surrendering, June 1944. *Love* played a major role in what happened and what did not happen on Saipan and Tinian. A small number of parents killed their children or made them commit suicide because they loved them and did not want to them to be tortured by the enemy or slaughtered by Japanese troops. Most parents did everything they could to keep their children alive; their families/bloodlines continue today because of love.

Following quarantine, they were issued repatriate identification papers (*hikiage shomeisho*) and provided transportation to their registered domiciles.[38] The repatriates faced many difficulties once they were processed out of the centers. Many had only the clothes on their backs and no photographs of their family members they lost during the battles. Some repatriates' parents and siblings in East Asia, who they left behind to migrate to

Micronesia, died while they were away or were killed in the war. A number found their family homes, particularly those on Okinawa Island and in mainland Japan cities, destroyed. Although there were relief organizations and some social services existed, most repatriates had to rely on the black markets, relatives, political organizations, and other resources to survive.

Saipan and Tinian repatriates faced stigmatization in their homelands. They were looked down on as "outsiders" tainted by Japan's "failed colonial project."[39] Children, the majority who were born and raised in the South Seas, felt especially alienated. According to historian Lori Watt:

> People who had returned from the colonies as children or teenagers were particularly affected, by having their childhood experiences in the colonies invalidated and their authenticity as Japanese called into question by their peers.... Colonial Japanese children were old enough to have internalized passionate feelings of patriotism during the war years, only to experience a profound sense of betrayal of those ideals, compounded by a sense that their government had abandoned them at the end of the war. Some had believed the rhetoric that Japan was working to free Asia from the grip of white colonialism, but when they returned to Japan, its occupation by the United States military exposed the contradictions in the colonial project. They survived the violent end of empire, but, rejected in some cases by their classmates as insufficiently Japanese, chafed within its borders in a kind of reverse exile.[40]

Okinawans in the Marianas returned to an island group that was in American hands until 1972, when it went back to Japan. However, Okinawa Island continues to be garrisoned by American troops in the twenty-first century. Understandably, Okinawan experiences on Saipan and Tinian before and during the war were and continue to be overshadowed by narratives of the Battle of Okinawa, the American militarization and exploitation of Okinawa, and the unauthorized crimes, rapes, and murders committed by a small number of United States military personnel. According to historian Manako Ogawa, Okinawans have endured "a long, bitter struggle against the land acquisition and construction of military bases, crimes committed by US servicemen and perfunctory penalties imposed on offenders, contamination of the soil by the leakage of toxic chemicals, constant noise caused by takeoffs and landings of airplanes at bases built in the middle of residential areas, and other negative consequences of the military presence."[41]

The 4,026 Korean civilian internees and comfort women and hundreds of military laborers on Saipan and Tinian returned to a divided and dangerous homeland. A number of Saipan and Tinian Korean repatriates died from violence and diseases in their peninsula in the late 1940s and early 1950s. More than a handful of American officers and enlisted men who fought on or offshore the Marianas and witnessed the suicides and murders fought again in the Korean War (1950–1953). Some even served in Vietnam. War correspondent Robert Sherrod, in his long career, covered the Pacific, Korean, and Vietnam Wars. In the twenty-first century, there are still bitter memories and views among some Koreans and Okinawans about the Japanese. Matters concerning Japan's war memory, responsibility, and accountability for atrocities, sexual slavery, colonial exploitation, and other issues are unresolved and highly contentious in East Asia. In the Marianas, Chamorro and Carolinian memories of the war are poignant and intense as well, but not as acrimonious as they are to the north.

The Americans released the Chamorro and Carolinians from Camp Susupe almost two years after the battles on July 4, 1946.[42] Many Americans stationed on the islands were demobilized and sent home. Chamorros and some Carolinians on other islands in the

Pacific, whose families left the Marianas during the prior three colonial rules, returned to Saipan and Tinian.[43] The United States did not give back sovereignty of the islands to the islanders. The Americans were unwilling to let go of an archipelago captured with their blood and money, and that was strategically located between the United States and Communist Asia.[44] They were determined to maintain hegemony in the Pacific. Nevertheless, they did not want to outright annex the islands and be regarded as another empire or "set a precedent" for the Soviet Union to start grabbing up faraway lands where ever it pleased.[45]

The Americans "remedied" their postwar, takeover problem by cleverly seeking permission from the United Nations to administer the island. The United Nations was established in 1945 immediately after the war "to maintain international peace and stability," among other purposes. The United States, as an architect and founding member of the United Nations, held immense influence in shaping the intergovernmental organization's decisions. It was one of the five permanent member nations of the United Nations Security Council, a principal organ of the United Nations that held the "primary responsibility" for maintaining peace and determining the adoption of resolutions. On February 1, 1947, the United States submitted a draft to the Security Council to administer Micronesia. The Soviet Union, another permanent member, did not protest because they were allowed to keep Sakhalin (Karafuto) and the Japanese Kuril Islands, which they invaded and occupied at the end of the war.[46] On April 2, 1947, the United Nations Security Council, at its 124th meeting in Lake Success, New York, unanimously adopted Resolution 21, which designated the United States as the "administering authority" of Japan's former South Seas Mandate. The United States was given "full powers of administration, legislation, and jurisdiction over the Territory." It was entitled to "establish naval, military and air bases and to erect fortifications" and "station and employ armed forces."[47] The naval military government on Saipan and Tinian officially ended and was replaced by a naval civil administration.[48] Saipan and Tinian were incorporated into the newly established Trust Territory of the Pacific Islands (TTPI). On July 18, 1947, the United States government ratified the Trusteeship Agreement and officially became the fourth colonizer of Saipan and Tinian. To the south, Guam became an unincorporated territory of the United States in 1950.

Saipan and Tinian were part of the Trust Territory of the Pacific Islands between 1947 and 1986. The Navy held interim administrative control of the Trust Territory from 1947 to 1951. In 1951, the United States Department of the Interior assumed authority of the islands. In 1952, the last holdouts on Saipan, two Japanese soldiers, were captured.[49] They were listed as dead for over seven years. Between 1953 and 1962, the Navy once again controlled Saipan and Tinian. It used the islands as military supply and training areas and kept them under security closure.[50] In mid-1962, the Department of the Interior was given back authority of the islands. Saipan, Tinian, and all other islands in the Marianas north of Guam became part of the TTPI Mariana Islands District (Northern Marianas). Saipan was the site of the TTPI headquarters from 1962 to 1986. The United States made a number of mistakes in its administration of the two islands, particularly concerning economic policies, and the islands were held and used for military purposes. However, it did not continue the flagrant discriminatory practices and human rights violations that the prior colonial administrations carried out. Furthermore, the United States did not turn the Marianas into a nuclear testing and proving ground or make it part of its ballistic missile defense program as it did in the Marshalls.

During the trusteeship period, islanders renamed or reverted in name many of Saipan and Tinian's cities, villages, mountains, points, and other geographical features. Tinian Town, for example, was renamed San Jose. English became the lingua franca of the islands, though Chamorro and Carolinian were still actively spoken and taught. Following the 1960s, the islands, particularly Saipan, were redeveloped and transformed by foreign investment. Japanese and Korean tourists, whose countries experienced "economic miracles," traveled to the islands for romantic and relaxing tropical vacations. The Chamorros and Carolinians, despite their strong memories of colonization and war, largely welcomed the tourists.[51] They distinguished the postwar Japanese from the old imperial Japanese. Currently, relations between the Japanese and the people of Saipan and Tinian are very amicable. Nevertheless, there are some people, particularly those whose family members were murdered by Japanese troops in 1944, who have mixed feelings or residual antipathy for the Japanese.

There are lingering issues concerning war reparations. While in internment, Chamorros and Carolinians filed claims with the United States military for losses incurred during the battles. Shortly after the war, they began seeking compensation for war damages from both Japan and the United States. In the 1960s, the Department of the Interior started looking into Micronesian war claims. According to historian Wakako Higuchi, in 1971, the United States "negotiated Japanese contributions to a Micronesian claims fund, established a Micronesian Claims Commission, and appropriated money for claims for wartime and postwar damages."[52] Some Chamorros and Carolinians believe the compensation was inadequate and desire new and larger reparations from both countries. Higuchi wrote, "Concerning Micronesia, there is no expiration date for Japan's responsibility for reparations." Japan, she asserted, needs to "assume both moral and financial responsibility for the war damages it inflicted."[53]

During and following the disastrous Vietnam War, the Americans became more relaxed in their administration and control of the islands. In the 1970s, the United States allowed Micronesians the right to self-determination. Most Chamorros and Carolinians, by that time, did not want an independent nation, but to remain and be more fully part of the United States. Islanders elected local legislators and organizations spearheaded initiatives for political union with the United States. In 1972, territorial status negotiations began, and in 1978, a new government and constitution in the Marianas went into effect.

On November 4, 1986, the trusteeship officially ended and the Mariana Islands north of Guam were made into a full commonwealth and unincorporated territory of the United States of America. The Commonwealth of the Northern Mariana Islands (CNMI) is headed by a governor and has a two-house legislature and independent judiciary.[54] The official languages of the CNMI are Chamorro, Carolinian, and English. The official seal of the CNMI consists of "a circular field of blue having in its center a white star superimposed on a gray latte stone, surrounded by the traditional Carolinian mwaar [head wreath] consisting of the following flowers: langilang, flores mayo (seyur) angagha, and teibwo, on the outer border, and the words encircling the mwaar, 'Commonwealth of the Northern Mariana Islands' and 'Official Seal.'" The official flag of the CNMI has "a rectangular field of blue, a white star in the center, superimposed on a gray latte stone, surrounded by the traditional Carolinian mwaar."[55] The star represents the Commonwealth and "symbolizes protection from intruders." The blue exemplifies the "cleanliness of the islands, its people, the sky, the water and agriculture."[56]

The Chamorros and Carolinians of Saipan and Tinian became United States citizens in 1986, though they cannot vote in presidential elections and have limited representation in Congress because the Northern Marianas are not a state.[57] Many Chamorros and Carolinians have served in the United States military and fought in America's foreign wars. Islanders celebrate their Liberation Day on July 4, which commemorates their release from the American internment camps that same day in 1946 and coincides with Independence Day celebrations.[58] American Memorial Park on Saipan, established in 1978 and operated by the United States National Park Service, honors the American and Micronesian people who died in the islands in 1944.

In the three decades following the establishment of the Commonwealth in the 1980s, the Northern Marianas economy experienced highs and lows with fluctuations in East Asian tourism and the rise and fall of the controversial garment industry.[59] The garment industry was supported by cheap East Asian labor, mostly Chinese women. There were questionable working conditions and practices and a number of abuses. It ended in the 2000s. Foreign investment and tourism drive the economy today, and the Commonwealth receives significant financial assistance and grants from the United States government. There is a small agricultural industry in the islands, but the sugarcane industry was never revived. International airports and modern resorts, casinos, and golf courses sit below the islands' dominating mountains were the canefields, homesteads, and Japanese factories once were. The population of the two islands combined is over 50,000. It is diverse and multi-ethnic with Chamorros, Carolinians, Chinese, Filipinos, Japanese, Koreans, Americans, and other peoples and communities. The United States has been conducting a military buildup in the Marianas because of the geopolitical tensions in the Asia-Pacific region and strong Okinawan objection to its military bases in Okinawa. The military's "leasing" and use of land in the Marianas, however, is a highly contentious issue and will continue to be well into the future.

Memorialization and Commemoration

The northern cliffs of Saipan and southern cliffs of Tinian are sites of memorialization and commemoration concerning the mass suicides. Banzai Cliff and Suicide Cliff on Saipan are listed on the United States National Register of Historic Places and are part of a National Historic Landmark District. They are protected and maintained by the United States Department of the Interior's National Park Service. Suicide Cliff on Tinian is included in the CNMI Historic Preservation Office's historic site inventory.

There are many Japanese, Okinawan, Korean, and Micronesian memorials and monuments on top or near the cliffs dedicated to the civilians and troops who died on the islands. Shortly after the end of the Pacific War, the Micronesian Repatriation Association (MRA), made up of Okinawan survivors of the Battles of Saipan and Tinian and others who lived in Micronesia during the Japanese colonial period, was founded. East Asians were not allowed to travel to Saipan and Tinian in the late 1940s and the 1950s because of the naval security closure. In the 1960s, however, the restrictions were lifted, and survivors and their families began making annual pilgrimages to the Marianas. They conducted "spirit-consoling services" (*ireisai*) and prayed for the departed souls (*rei*) of lost family members and all those who died during the battles.[60] The East Asian returnees (*Nanyo gaeri*) were able to mourn, reminisce, and discuss their experiences with others and heal. With the support of their governments, private organizations, shrines, temples, and veterans, they built memorials in the Marianas. In 1968, the Ryukyu Islands government, at the request of the MRA, built the Okinawa Tower monument on Saipan. In 1981, the Korean Tower was erected.[61] A great number of memorials were built in the subsequent years and decades.

In the twenty-first century, annual services continue to be held for the civilians who died in the islands and peace cranes, flowers, sake, fruit, and other items are left at the memorials. Efforts have been made to get the younger generations involved to keep the services and activities alive in the future. People of all ethnicities and nationalities living on or visiting Saipan and Tinian have expressed an interest in the islands' history and visit the sites.[62] There have also been many "bone collecting" missions on Saipan and Tinian by different organizations.[63] The Korean Memorial Service Association for the Deceased Compatriots Overseas, for example, recovered and sent back home the remains of Koreans who died in the battles and internment camps.[64] The collection of remains (*ikotsu shushu*) are carried out for religious, cultural, and historical purposes.

American veterans have also returned to Saipan and Tinian. Like the repatriates and islanders, many Americans suffered from mental health disorders for a long time after the war because of what they saw during the battles. Marine Lieutenant Jim G. Lucas, who was on Saipan, wrote, "At Marpi Point this morning, I met another Marine, so sickened by all that he had seen that he was actually begging to be taken back to the rear. He had gone through twenty-four days of bitter fighting without flinching, but he was made almost hysterical by what he had seen … all of us pray we will never have to witness this sort of thing again."[65] Marine Michael Witowich, 2nd Division, who saw women and children being murdered at the Marpi Point cliffs, recalled, "I had a lot of years of post-traumatic stress from the war."[66] Marine Lewis J. Steck, 2nd Regiment, 2nd Division, stated, "That was rough watching those families kill themselves … it bothered the hell out of me later on."[67] Marine Jim Blane, 4th Division, who visited the memorials, stated, of "all the horrors of war," it was the mass suicides on Saipan that "keep me awake many nights."[68] Blane suffered from alcoholism for many years after the war.[69]

The last civilian survivors are in their twilight years and many are passing on. They remember and think about their family members and friends whose lives were cut short in the battles and internment camps and who they have outlived by many decades. A number of them continue to visit Saipan and Tinian or live on the islands. They read about human remains from the battles still being found today and wonder if they are their loved ones' bones. They have seen or been informed about many wars and conflicts with great numbers of civilian deaths since the Asia-Pacific War. Many of them abhor war. Shinsho Kuniyoshi, who lost his mother and seven siblings on Saipan, stated, "War is a monster that tears up happy lives."[70] Akiko Kikuchi stated, "War is nothing more than futile carnage and destruction. The grief felt by those left behind is deep. Each passing year makes the importances of peace seem that much more great."[71]

Chapter Notes

Preface

1. South Sea Islands Album Publication Committee, *A Record of the Japanese Pioneers' Achievements Obliterated by the War: Photographic Collections of Saipan, Tinian, Rota* (Tokyo: South Sea Islands Album Publication Committee, 1985), 22.

Introduction

1. *The Cambridge History of the Second World War. Volume 1: Fighting the War.* Edited by John Ferris and Evan Mawdsley (Cambridge, United Kingdom: Cambridge University Press, 2015), 448.
2. John Toland, *The Rising Sun: The Decline and Fall of the Japanese Empire, 1936–1945* (New York: Random House, 1970), 519.
3. Robin Cross, *History of the United States Fighting Forces* (London: Chevprime Limited, 1989), 238–239; Deryck Scarr, *The History of the Pacific Islands: Kingdoms of the Reefs* (South Melbourne, Australia: The Macmillan Company of Australia, 1990), 284; Jim B. Smith, *The Last Mission* (Mt. Pleasant, Iowa: J.B. Smith Enterprises, 1995), 223; H.P. Willmott, *The Second World War in the Far East* (London: Cassell, 1999), 142; John Keegan, *Who's Who in World War II*. Reprint (New York: Routledge, 2002), 134; John A. Glusman, *Conduct Under Fire: Four American Doctors and Their Fight for Life as Prisoners of the Japanese, 1941–1945* (New York: Viking Penguin Books, 2005), 370; Raymond W. Clanton, *Fire, Fear and Guts: The B-29 and Her Gallant Crewmen* (Camp Verde, Arizona: Ray/Jan Publisher, 2005), 213; Jerome Beser and Jack Spangler, *The Rising Sun Sets: The Complete Story of the Bombing of Nagasaki* (Bloomington, Indiana, Authorhouse, 2012), 54; James A. Stone, "Interrogation of Japanese POWs in World War II: U.S. Response to a Formidable Challenge" in *Interrogation: World War II, Vietnam, and Iraq* (Washington, D.C., National Defense Intelligence College, 2008), 31. Steve Bergsman, *Passport to Exotic Real Estate: Buying U.S. And Foreign Property in Breathtaking, Beautiful, Faraway Lands* (John Wiley & Sons, 2008), 106; Kathleen Broome Williams, *The Measure of a Man: My Father, the Marine Corps, and Saipan* (Annapolis, Maryland: Naval Institute Press, 2013): 134; James Webb, *I Heard My Country Calling: A Memoir* (New York: Simon & Schuster, 2014), 333; Jennifer F. McKinnon, "Difficult Heritage: Interpreting Underwater Battlefield Sites," in *Between the Devil and the Deep: Meeting Challenges in the Public Interpretation of Maritime Cultural Heritage*, ed. Della A. Scott-Ireton (New York: Springer, 2014), 177; Howard D. Kibel, "Rashomon Revisited: A Re-analysis of the Film and Implications for Mass Psychology," *International Journal of Group Psychotherapy* 66, no. 1 (2016): 80. Michael Dudley, *Great Battles of World War II: How the Allies defeated the Axis Powers* (London: Arcturus Publishing Limited, 2017), 222.
4. Eric Hammel, *Pacific Warriors: The U.S. Marines in World War II: A Pictorial Tribute* (St. Paul, Minnesota: Zenith Press, 2005), 189.
5. David M. Kennedy, Margaret E. Wagner, Linda Barrett Osborne, Susan Reyburn, and Staff of the Library of Congress. *The Library of Congress World War II Companion* (New York: Simon & Schuster, 2007), 589.
6. Haruko Taya, Cook. "The Myth of the Saipan Suicides," *MHQ: The Quarterly Journal of Military History* 7, no. 3 (1995): 12–19.
7. Shunsuke Tsurumi, *An Intellectual History of Wartime Japan 1931–1945*, Reprint (New York: Routledge, 2011), 80–81. First published in Japanese in 1982 by Iwanami Shoten, Tokyo.
8. David R. Beisel, 'The German Suicide, 1945," *The Journal of Psychohistory* 34, no.4 (2007): 308.
9. Matthew C. Price, *The Wilsonian Persuasion in American Foreign Policy* (Youngstown, New York: Cambria Press, 2007), 207.
10. Albert Marrin, *Uprooted: The Japanese American Experience During World War II* (New York: Alfred A. Knopf, 2016), 160.
11. Richard Carl Bright, *Pain and Purpose in the Pacific: True Reports of War* (Victoria, British Columbia, Canada: Trafford Publishing, 2010), 122.
12. Cook, "Myth of the Saipan Suicides," 583, 595.
13. Michael Dudley, *Great Battles of World War II: How the Allies defeated the Axis Powers* (London: Arcturus Publishing Limited, 2017), 222; Samuel Hynes, Anne Matthews, Nancy Caldwell Sorel, and Roger J. Spiller. *Reporting World War II: American Journalism 1938–1946* (New York: The Library of America, 2001), 786; Michael Dudley, *Great Battles of World War II: How the Allies defeated the Axis Powers* (London: Arcturus Publishing Limited, 2017), 222.
14. David Bergamini, *Japan's Imperial Conspiracy* (New York: William Morrow and Company, 1971), 1301; Russell Braddon, *Japan Against the World, 1941–2041: The 100-year War for Supremacy* (New York: Stein and Day Publishers, 1983), 82; Margaret S. Buse, "WWII Ordnance Still Haunts Europe and the Asia-Pacific Rim," *Journal of Conventional Weapons Destruction* 4, no. 2 (2000): 84–85; Mary L. Hanneman, *Japan Faces the World, 1925–1952*. Reprint. (New York: Routledge, 2013), 75.

15. Lou Dubose and Jan Reid, *The Hammer Comes Down: The Nasty, Brutish, and Shortened Political Life of Tom Delay* (New York: Public Affairs, 2004), 182.
16. David Rees, *The Defeat of Japan* (Westport, Connecticut: Praeger Publishers, 1997), 36; Dorothy Cave Aldrich, *Four Trails to Valor*, Revised Edition (Santa Fe, New Mexico: Sunstone Press, 2007), 275; Bill Sloan, *Their Backs Against the Sea: The Battle of Saipan and the Largest Banzai Attack of World War II* (New York: Da Capo Press, 2017), 202.
17. Joanna Bourke, *The Second World War: A People's History* (Oxford: Oxford University Press, 2001), 94.
18. Joseph R. Conlin, *The American Past: A survey of American History*, Tenth Edition (Boston, Massachusetts: Wadsworth, 2014), 727.
19. Atcom, "Undercurrent: The Private, Exclusive Guide for Serious Divers," (New York: Atcom, 1977), 4.
20. Alan L. Rein, *Two Minutes to Die: A Lifetime to Live* (Mustang, Oklahoma: Tate Publishing & Enterprises, 2011), 65.
21. Yumiko Imaizumi, "Mobilization and Perspectives by the Japanese Army on Japanese Civilians and Local People during the Pacific War in Saipan and Tinian," 3rd Marianas History Conference (Mangilao, Guam: Guampedia, 2017), 7.
22. Norman Meller, *Saipan's Camp Susupe* (Honolulu: Center for Pacific Island Studies, University of Hawaii, 1999), 34, 84.
23. Samuel Eliot Morison, *New Guinea and the Marianas, March 1944-August 1944*. Volume VIII of "History of United States Naval Operations in World War II" (Boston: Little, Brown and Company, 1953), 339; Northern Troops and Landing Force, Headquarters, In the Fied, "Northern Troops and Landing Force Operations Report, Phase III (Tinian)," G-2 Periodic Report no. 56, 10 August 1944, 1
24. Beatrice Trefalt, "The Battle of Saipan in Japanese Civilian Memoirs: Non-combatants, Soldiers and the Complexities of Surrender," *The Journal of Pacific History* 53, no. 3 (2018): 263.
25. Trefalt, 259.
26. Merriam-Webster. https://www.merriam-webster.com/dictionary/suicide
27. Janice Matsumura and Diana Wright, "Japanese Military Suicides During the Asia-Pacific War: Studies of the Unauthorized Self-killings of Soldiers," *The Asia-Pacific Journal: Japan Focus* 13, Issue 25, Number 2 (June 2015): 3.
28. Edward E. Bollinger, *The Cross and the Floating Dragon: The Gospel in Ryukyu* (Pasadena, California: William Carey Library, 1983), 267; Norma Field, *In the Realm of a Dying Emperor* (New York: Vintage Books, 1993), 61; Mariko Asano Tamanoi, *Memory Maps: The State and Manchuria in Postwar Japan* (Honolulu: University of Hawaii Press, 2009), 68; Gavan McCormack and Satoko Oka Norimatsu, *Resistant Islands: Okinawa Confronts Japan and the United States* (New York: Rowman & Littlefield Publishers, 2012), 19; Ishihara Masaie, "Memories of War and Okinawa," translated by Douglas Driestadt, in *Perilous Memories: The Asia-Pacific War(s)* (Durham, North Carolina: Duke University Press, 2001), 91–94.
29. Wakako Higuchi, email to author, April 14, 2018.
30. Jessica Jordan, "Surviving War on Pagan," 1st Marianas History Conference, Late Colonial History (Mangilao, Guam: Guampedia Foundation, 2012): 82.
31. Emiko Ohnuki-Tierney, *Kamikaze, Cherry Blossoms, and Nationalisms: The Militarization of Aesthetics in Japanese History* (Chicago: The University of Chicago Press, 2002), 114–115; David C. Earhart, *Certain Victory: Images of World War II in the Japanese Media* (Armonk, New York: M.E. Sharpe, 2008), 393.
32. I.C.B. Dear and M.R.D. Foot, *The Oxford Companion to World War II* (Oxford: Oxford University Press, 1995), 975.
33. Toshio Iritani, *Group Psychology of the Japanese in Wartime* (New York: Kegan Paul International, 1991), 153.
34. Barak Kushner, *The Thought War: Japanese Imperial Propaganda* (Honolulu: University of Hawaii, 2006), 10.
35. Louise Young, *Japan's Total Empire: Manchuria and the Culture of Wartime Imperialism* (Berkeley: University of California Press, 1998), 408–411; Mariko Asano Tamanoi, *Memory Maps: The State and Manchuria in Postwar Japan* (Honolulu: University of Hawaii Press, 2009), 58, 67–70, 124; Mayumi Itoh, *Japanese War Orphans in Manchuria: Forgotten Victims of World War II* (New York: Palgrave Macmillan, 2010), 20–23, 30, 46–47, 65–66, 207; Andrew E. Barshaw, *The Gods Left First: The Captivity and Repatriation of Japanese POWs in Northeast Asia, 1945–1956* (Berkeley: University of California Pres, 2013), 217.
36. Ichikawa Miako, "Child survivor of forced mass suicide in Manchuria still loves hero who saved her," *The Asia-Pacific Journal: Japan Focus* 3, Issue 8; Mayumi Itoh, *Japanese War Orphans in Manchuria: Forgotten Victims of World War II* (New York: Palgrave Macmillan, 2010), 23; Tamanoi, *Memory Maps*, 69.
37. Tamanoi, *Memory Maps*, 70.
38. Tamanoi, 68.

Chapter 1

1. Don A. Farrell, *History of the Mariana Islands to Partition* (Saipan: CNMI Public School System, 2011), 2.
2. Alexander Spoehr, *Marianas Prehistory: Archaeological Survey and Excavations on Saipan, Tinian, and Rota* (Chicago: Chicago Natural History Museum, 1957), 28.
3. Robert Sherrod, *On to Westward: War in the Central Pacific* (New York: Duell, Sloan, and Pearce, 1945), 45.
4. Michael F. Wong and Barry R. Hill, *Reconnaissance of Hydrology and Water Quality of Lake Susupe, Saipan, Commonwealth of the Northern Mariana Islands, 1990*, United States Geological Survey, Water-Resources Investigations Report 00–4054 (Honolulu: United States Geological Survey, 2000), 2.
5. David Stanley, *South Pacific Handbook* (Chico, California: Moon Publications, 1985), 496.
6. Wong and Hill, *Lake Susupe*, 3.
7. Scott Russell, *Tinian, the Final Chapter* (Saipan: CNMI Division of Historic Preservation, 1995), 1.
8. Mike T. Carson, *First Settlement of Remote Oceania: Earliest Sites in the Mariana Islands* (New York: Springer, 2014), 113–114; Mike T. Carson and Hsiao-chun Hung, *Substantive Evidence of Initial Habitation in the Remote Pacific: Archaeological Discoveries at Unai Bapot in Saipan, Mariana Islands* (Oxford, United Kingdom: Archaeopress Publishing Ltd, 2017), 1.
9. Andrew Pawley and Roger Green, "Dating the Dispersal of the Oceanic Languages," *Oceanic Linguistics* 12, no. 1/2 (1973): 1, 4; Rosalind Hunter-Anderson, "An Anthropological Perspective on Marianas Prehistory, Including Guam," in *Guam History: Perspectives Volume Two*, edited by Carter, L.D., Wuerch, W.L. and Carter,

R.R. (Mangilao, Guam: Micronesian Area Research Center Educational Series, 2005), 27, 31; Mike T. Carson, *Archaeological Landscape Evolution: The Mariana Islands in the Asia-Pacific Region* (Switzerland: Springer, 2016), 72.

10. Rosalind L. Hunter-Anderson and Joanne E. Eakin, "Chamorro Origins and the Importance of Archaeological Context," 3rd Marianas History Conference (Mangilao, Guam: Guampedia, 2016), 74.

11. Alexander Spoehr, *Saipan: The Ethnology of a War-devastated Island* (Chicago: Chicago Natural History Museum. 1954), 34.

12. Farrell, *History of the Mariana Islands*, 69.

13. Lawrence J. Cunningham, *Ancient Chamorro Society* (Honolulu, HI: The Bess Press, 1992), 26; Darlene R. Moore, "Archaeological Evidence of a Prehistoric Farming Technique on Guam," *Micronesica* 38, no. 1 (2005): 101.

14. Spoehr, *Saipan*, 35; Hunter-Anderson, Rosalind L., Gillian B. Thompson, and Darlene R. Moore, "Rice as a prehistoric valuable in the Mariana Islands, Micronesia," *Asian Perspectives* (1995): 69–89.

15. Cherie K. Walth, "Naton Beach Site, Guam: A Look Back in Time," 3rd Marianas History Conference (Mangilao, Guam: Guampedia, 2017), 44–45.

16. Francis X. Hezel, *Before We Began Counting Years*, Documentary, Northern Marianas Humanities Council and Best Sunshine Enterprise, 2018.

17. Moore, "Farming Technique on Guam," 111.

18. Carson, *Archaeological Landscape Evolution*, 57–58.

19. Carson, *Archaeological Landscape Evolution*, 58.

20. Paul Rainbird, *The Archaeology of Micronesia* (Cambridge, United Kingdom: Cambridge University Press, 2004), 125; Farrell, *History of the Mariana Islands*, 47, 70.

21. Cunningham, *Ancient Chamorro Society*, 39.

22. Farrell, *History of the Mariana Islands*, 74–75.

23. Rainbird, *Archaeology of Micronesia*, 110; Spoehr, *Saipan*, 35–36.

24. Carson, *First Settlement*, 45–48.

25. Walth, "Naton Beach Site," 50.

26. Scott Russell, *Tiempon I Manmofo'na: Ancient Chamorro Culture and History of the Northern Mariana Islands* (Saipan: CNMI Division of Historic Preservation, 1998), 153.

27. Russell, 155–156.

28. Cunningham, *Ancient Chamorro Society*, 152.

29. Spoehr, *Saipan*, 36.

30. Donald Denoon, *The Cambridge History of the Pacific Islands* (Cambridge, United Kingdom: Cambridge University Press, 1997), 91–93.

31. Cunningham, *Ancient Chamorro Society*, 86; Robert F. Rogers, *Destiny's Landfall: A History of Guam* (Honolulu: University of Hawaii Press, 1995), 29.

32. Cunningham, *Ancient Chamorro Society*, 196.

33. Frank Quimby, "The Hierro Commerce: Culture Contact, Appropriation and Colonial Entanglement in the Marianas, 1521–1668," *The Journal of Pacific History* 46, no. 1 (June 2011): 3–4.

34. Alice Joseph and Veronica F. Murray, *Chamorros and Carolinians of Saipan: Personality Studies* (Cambridge, Massachusetts: Harvard University Press, 1951), 5–6; Augusto Viana, *In the Far Islands: The Role of Natives from the Philippines in the Conquest, Colonization and Repopulation of the Mariana Islands, 1668-1903* (Manila, University of Santo Tomas Publishing House, 2004), 13.

35. Alexandre Coello de la Rosa, *Jesuits at the Margins: Missions and Missionaries in the Marianas (1668-1769)* (New York: Routledge, 2016), 23; Francis X. Hezel, "When Cultures Clash: Revisiting the 'Spanish-Chamorro Wars'" (Saipan, CNMI: Northern Marianas Humanities Council, 2015), 3; Viana, *In the Far Islands*, 4; Quimby, "The Hierro Commerce," 5.

36. Quimby, 1.

37. Hezel, "When Cultures Clash," 3–4; Quimby, "The Hierro Commerce," 8–9.

38. Francis X. Hezel, "From Conversion to Conquest: The Early Spanish Mission in the Marianas," *Journal of Pacific History* 17, no. 3 (1982): 117; Coello, *Jesuits at the Margins*, 25; David Atienza, "A Mariana Islands History Story: The Influence of the Spanish Black Legend in Mariana Islands Historiography," *Pacific Asia Inquiry* 4, no. 1 (2013): 14.

39. Coello, *Jesuits at the Margins*, 342–343.

40. Coello, 269, 342.

41. Rogers, *Destiny's Landfall*, 16.

42. Paul Carano and Pedro C. Sanchez, *A Complete History of Guam,* Fifth Printing (Rutland, Vermont: Charles & Tuttle Company, 1969), 52.

43. Marjorie G. Driver and Francis X. Hezel, *El Palacio: The Spanish Palace in Agana, 1668-1898* (Mangilao, Guam: Micronesian Area Research Center, 2004), 13.

44. Quimby, "The Hierro Commerce," 22.

45. David Atienza, "Indigenous Adaptive Resistance in the Mariana Islands: Rethinking Historical Eras," 3rd Marianas History Conference (Mangilao, Guam: Guampedia, 2017), 113.

46. Coello, *Jesuits at the Margins*, 32.

47. Augusto Viana, "Belgian Missionaries in 17th Century Marianas: The Role of Fr. Peter Coomans and Fr. Gerard Bouwens," *Philippiniana Sacra* 46, no. 136 (2011): 387–388; Hezel, "When Cultures Clash," 24; Coello, *Jesuits at the Margins*, 35, 37, 48.

48. Coello, *Jesuits at the Margins*, 38.

49. Augusto Viana, "The Pampangos in the Mariana Mission 1668-1684," *Micronesian Journal of the Humanities and Social Sciences* 4, no. 1 (2005): 2.

50. Viana, "Belgian Missionaries," 373, 388–389.

51. Hezel, "When Cultures Clash," 19, 23.

52. Coello, *Jesuits at the Margins*, 42; Viana, *In the Far Islands*, 27; Francis X. Hezel, "The Early Spanish Period in the Marianas, 1668-1698: Eight Theses," *San Vitores Theological Review*, Volume 1 (2014): 5.

53. Coello, *Jesuits at the Margins*, 38.

54. Hezel, "When Cultures Clash," 22; David Atienza, "Priests, Mayors and Indigenous Offices: Indigenous Agency and Adaptive Resistance in the Mariana Islands (1681 -1758)," *Pacific Asia Inquiry* 5, no. 1 (2014): 36.

55. Coello, *Jesuits at the Margins*, 36; David Atienza, "The Mariana Islands Militia and the Establishment of the 'Pueblos de Indios': Indigenous Agency in Guam from 1668 to 1758," 2nd Marianas History Conference (Mangilao, Guam: Guampedia, 2013), 3–4.

56. Quimby, "The Hierro Commerce," 26.

57. Coello, *Jesuits at the Margins*, 45, 84, 96, 98, 111; Hezel, "When Cultures Clash," 35, 42, 44, 46, 65; Viana, "The Pampangos," 4; Viana, *In the Far Islands*, 30.

58. Hezel, "When Cultures Clash," 61.

59. Coello, *Jesuits at the Margins*, 122.

60. Viana, "Belgian Missionaries," 376; Coello, *Jesuits at the Margins*, 251; Viana, *In the Far Islands*, 57, 98.

61. "Letter from Fr. Solorzano to Fr. Francisco Garcia, dated Guam 20 May 1681," Translated by Rodrigue Levesque, in *History of Micronesia: A Collection of Source Documents. Volume 7-More Turmoil in the Marianas, 1679-1683* (Gatineau, Canada: Levesque Publications,

1996), 440.

62. Stephanie Mawson, "Rebellion and Mutiny in the Mariana Islands, 1680-1690," *The Journal of Pacific History* 50, no. 2 (2015): 130-131; Hezel, "When Cultures Clash," 55-56; Viana, *In the Far Islands*, 78.

63. Spoehr, *Saipan*, 56; Coello, *Jesuits at the Margins*, 338.

64. Hezel, "When Cultures Clash," 80.

65. Atienza, "Indigenous Adaptive Resistance," 67.

66. Spoehr, Saipan, 54; Coello, *Jesuits at the Margins*, 86.

67. Coello, *Jesuits at the Margins*, 142.

68. Driver and Hezel, *El Palacio*, 9.

69. Viana, *In the Far Islands*, 67; Rogers, *Destiny's Landfall*, 76; Spennemann, *Edge of Empire*, 264.

70. Viana, "Belgian Missionaries," 385; Coello, *Jesuits at the Margins*, 159; Viana, *In the Far Islands*, 71; Driver and Hezel, *El Palacio*, 12; Atienza, "Indigenous Adaptive Resistance," 114.

71. Farrell, *History of the Mariana Islands*, 112; Ulrike Strasser, "Copies with Souls: The Late Seventeenth-century Marianas Martyrs, Francis Xavier, and the Question of Clerical Reproduction," *Journal of Jesuit Studies* 2 (2015): 569-570.

72. Rogers, *Destiny's Landfall*, 12.

73. Jose S. Arcilla, *An Introduction to Philippine History*, Third Edition (Quezon City: Ateneo de Manila University Press, 1984), 24.

74. Carano and Sanchez, *History of Guam*, 54; Arcilla, *Philippine History*, Third Edition (Quezon City: Ateneo de Manila University Press. 1984), 24.

75. Rogers, *Destiny's Landfall*, 74; Laura Thompson, *Guam and its People*, Reprint (New York: Greenwood Press, 1969), 59.

76. Coello, *Jesuits at the Margins*, 140, 156.

77. Rogers, *Destiny's Landfall*, 347.

78. Carano and Sanchez, *History of Guam*, 53; Rogers, *Destiny's Landfall*, 74.

79. Atienza, "'Pueblos de Indios,'" 2.

80. Peter B. Villella, *Indigenous Elites and Creole Identity in Colonial Mexico, 1500-1800* (New York: Cambridge University Press, 2016), 9.

81. Atienza, "Indigenous Agency," 31.

82. Coello, *Jesuits at the Margins*, 85; Rogers, *Destiny's Landfall*, 74-75.

83. Moore, "Farming Technique on Guam," 104-105; Coello, *Jesuits at the Margins*, 117, 151; Viana, *In the Far Islands*, 75-76.

84. Coello, *Jesuits at the Margins*, 152.

85. Coello, 156.

86. Coello, 269.

87. Spennemann, *Edge of Empire*, 101.

88. Hezel, "The Early Spanish Period," 13; Coello, *Jesuits at the Margins*, 85-86, 106, 131, 143, 151.

89. Coello, *Jesuits at the Margins*, 150-151; Alexandre Coello de la Rosa, "Lights and Shadows: The Inquisitorial Process Against the Jesuit Congregation of Nuestra Señora de la Luz on the Mariana Islands (1758-1776)," *Journal of Religious History* 37, no. 2 (2013): 219, 223; Francis X. Hezel, "From Conquest to Colonization: Spain in the Mariana Islands 1690 to 1740" (Saipan: Division of Historic Preservation, 1989), 33-34, 36.

90. Coello, *Jesuits at the Margins*, 35, 38; Hezel, "When Cultures Clash," 24, 46.

91. Coello, *Jesuits at the Margins*, 105.

92. David Atienza De Frutos and Alexandre Coello De La Rosa, "Death Rituals and Identity in Contemporary Guam (Mariana Islands)," *The Journal of Pacific History* 47, no. 4 (2012): 463.

93. Scott Russell, *Tiempon Aleman: A Look Back at German Rule of the Northern Mariana Islands, 1899-1914* (Saipan: CNMI Division of Historic Preservation, 1999), 28-30.

94. Cunningham, *Ancient Chamorro Society*, 29; Carson, *Archaeological Landscape Evolution*, 58.

95. Spoehr, *Saipan*, 25.

96. Rainbird, *Archaeology of Micronesia*, 129; Nicholas J. Goetzfridt, *Guahan: A Bibliographic History* (Honolulu: University of Hawaii Press, 2011), 35.

97. Viana, *In the Far Islands*, 79.

98. Goetzfridt, *Guahan*, 477.

99. Rogers, *Destiny's Landfall*, 102-103.

100. Atienza and Coello, "Death Rituals," 460.

101. Atienza and Coello, 469.

102. Atienza and Coello, 463.

103. Atienza and Coello, 472.

104. Goetzfridt, *Guahan*, 305.

105. Atienza, "'Pueblos de Indios,'" 2.

106. Coello, *Jesuits at the Margins*, 3.

107. Koichi Hagimoto, *Trans-Pacific Encounters: Asia and the Hispanic World* (Newcastle, United Kingdom: Cambridge Scholars Publishing, 2016), 46-47.

108. Driver and Hezel, *El Palacio*, 25; Rainbird, *Archaeology of Micronesia*, 128.

109. Scott Russell, *From Arabwal to Ashes: A Brief History of Garapan Village, 1818 to 1945* (Saipan, CNMI: Isssi Program for Social Studies, Department of Education, Commonwealth of the Northern Marianas. 1984), 18.

110. Farrell, *History of the Mariana Islands*, 305-306; Francis X. Hezel, *Strangers in Their Own Land: A Century of Colonial Rule in the Caroline and Marshall Islands* (Honolulu: University of Hawai'i Press, 1995), 277; Goetzfridt, *Guahan*, 328-329.

111. Thompson, *Guam and its People*, 205.

112. Farrell, *History of the Mariana Islands*, 273.

113. Viana, *In the Far Islands*, 92, 113.

114. Spoehr, *Saipan*, 326; William H. Alkire, "The Carolinians of Saipan and the Commonwealth of the Northern Mariana Islands," *Pacific Affairs* 57, no. 2 (1984): 272.

115. Viana, *In the Far Islands*, 85.

116. Russell, *From Arabwal to Ashes*, 13, 27.

117. Dave Tuggle, "The Archaeological Landscape of Japanese-Era Tinian, Mariana Islands," *Pan-Japan* 11, no. 1 & 2 (2015): 82; Don A. Farrell and Carmen Dela Cruz Farrell, *Tinian* (Saipan: Micronesian Productions, 1989), 11.

118. Scott Russell and Genevieve S. Cabrera, "An Archaeological Survey of the *Hachiman Jinja* Site, Kannat Taddong Papago, Saipan" (Saipan: CNMI Division of Historic Preservation, 2003), 5.

119. William H. Alkire, *Lamotrek Atoll and Interisland Socioeconomic Ties* (Urbana, Illinois: University of Illinois Press, 1965), 28.

120. Alkire, 74.

121. Russell, *From Arabwal to Ashes*, 13-15.

122. Alkire, *Lamotrek Atoll*, 77-80.

123. Russell, *Tiempon Aleman*, 39; Neal M. Bowers, "Problems of Resettlement on Saipan, Tinian and Rota, Mariana Islands" (Ph.D. Dissertation, University of Michigan, 1950), 199.

124. Russell, *From Arabwal to Ashes*, 9.

125. Alkire, *Lamotrek Atoll*, 114.

126. Viana, "The Pampangos," 6; Spennemann, *Edge of Empire*, 13-14.

127. W. O. Henderson, *The German Colonial Empire, 1884-1919* (London: Frank Cass & CO., 1993), 22-23.

128. Hezel, *Strangers in Their Own Land*, 46; Kees

van Dijk, *Pacific Strife: The Great Powers and Their Political and Economic Rivalries in Asia and the Western Pacific, 1870-1914* (Amsterdam: Amsterdam University Press, 2015), 55.

129. Mary Evelyn Townsend, *Origins of Modern German Colonialism, 1871-1885* (New York: Columbia University Press, 1921), 41; Spennemann, *Edge of Empire*, 8.

130. Gerd Hardach, "Defining Separate Spheres: German Rule and Colonial Law in Micronesia," in *European Impact and Pacific Influence: British and German Colonial Policy in the Pacific Islands and the Indigenous Response 1997*, ed. Hermann Hiery and John M MacKenzie (London: I.B. Tauris Publishers, 1997), 233; Sebastian Conrad, *German Colonialism: A Short History* (Cambridge, United Kingdom: Cambridge University Press, 2012), 54.

131. Dijk, *Pacific Strife*, 55.

132. W. O. Henderson, *Studies in German Colonial History* (Chicago: Quadrangle Books, 1962), 48; Henderson, *German Colonial Empire*, 68.

133. Richard V. Pierard, "The German Colonial Society," in *Germans in the Tropics, Essays in German Colonial History* 1987, ed. Arthur J. Knoll and Lewis H. Gann (New York: Greenwood Press, 1987), 19.

134. Townsend, *German Colonialism*, 13.

135. Townsend, 13-17, 195.

136. Townsend, 195; Conrad, *German Colonialism*, 22.

137. Dijk, *Pacific Strife*, 26.

138. Winfried Baumgart, "German Imperialism in Historical Perspective," in *Germans in the Tropics, Essays in German Colonial History* 1987, ed. Arthur J. Knoll and Lewis H. Gann (New York: Greenwood Press, 1987), 155-156; Hardach, "Defining Separate Spheres," 232.

139. Spennemann, *Edge of Empire*, 9.

140. Spennemann, 7-8, 14.

141. Spennemann, 20-21.

142. Hardach, "Defining Separate Spheres," 233.

143. Spennemann, *Edge of Empire*, 22-23.

144. Hermann Hiery and John M MacKenzie, *European Impact and Pacific Influence: British and German Colonial Policy in the Pacific Islands and the Indigenous Response* (London: I.B. Tauris Publishers, 1997), x.

145. Spennemann, *Edge of Empire*, 14, 23-24.

146. David Campbell Purcell, Jr., "Japanese Expansion in the South Pacific, 1890-1935," (Ph.D. History Dissertation, University of Pennsylvania, 1967), 57; Spennemann, *Edge of Empire*, 86.

147. Purcell, Jr., 62-64.

148. Spennemann, *Edge of Empire*, 39.

149. Spennemann, 39.

150. Hezel, *Strangers in Their Own Land*, 100.

151. Spennemann, *Edge of Empire*, 183.

152. Hardach, "Defining Separate Spheres," 234.

153. Dijk, *Pacific Strife*, 397; Hezel, *Strangers in Their Own Land*, 104.

154. Hardach, "Defining Separate Spheres," 233.

155. Arthur J. Knoll and Lewis H. Gann, *Germans in the Tropics: Essays in German Colonial History* (New York: Greenwood Press, 1987), 6-7.

156. Conrad, *German Colonialism*, 58.

157. Hardach, "Defining Separate Spheres," 249-250.

158. Hezel, *Strangers in Their Own Land*, 101-102, 109; Spennemann, *Edge of Empire*, 198-202.

159. Spennemann, *Edge of Empire*, 192.

160. Spennemann, 36, 206.

161. Don A. Farrell, *History of the Northern Mariana Islands* (Saipan: CNMI Public School System, 1991), 273; Spennemann, *Edge of Empire*, 81.

162. Spennemann, *Edge of Empire*, 83.

163. Conrad, *German Colonialism*, 112.

164. Hardach, "Defining Separate Spheres," 236-237.

165. Hardach, 237-238; Spennemann, *Edge of Empire*, 39.

166. Purcell, Jr., "Japanese Expansion," 46.

167. Purcell, Jr., 60.

168. Purcell, Jr., 58; Spennemann, *Edge of Empire*, 101.

169. Hardach, "Defining Separate Spheres," 238.

170. Daniel Joseph Walther, *Sex and Control: Venereal Disease, Colonial Physicians, and Indigenous Agency in German Colonialism, 1884-1914* (New York: Berghahn. 2015), 41.

171. Walther, 66.

172. Spennemann, *Edge of Empire*, 174-175, 267-269.

173. Spennemann, 271.

Chapter 2

1. Mark R. Peattie, introduction to *The Japanese Colonial Empire, 1895-1945*, ed. Ramon Hawley Myers, Mark R. Peattie, and Jingzhi Zhen (Princeton, New Jersey: Princeton University Press, 1984), 17.

2. Jun Uchida, *Brokers of Empire: Japanese Settler Colonialism in Korea, 1876-1945* (Cambridge, Massachusetts: Harvard University Asia Center, 2011), 9.

3. Roy Hidemichi Akagi, *Japan's Foreign Relations, 1542-1936, A Short History* (Tokyo: Hokuseido Press, 1936), 265.

4. Akitoshi Hiraoka, *Japanese Advance into the Pacific Ocean: The Albatross and the Great Bird Rush* (Singapore: Springer, 2018), 3.

5. Peattie, *Nanyo*, 8, 13-15.

6. Tomiyama Ichiro, "The 'Japanese' of Micronesia: Okinawans in the Nanyo Islands," in *Okinawan Diaspora 2002*, ed. Ronald Y. Nakasone (Honolulu: University of Hawaii Press, 2002), 63.

7. Hiraoka, *Japanese Advance*, 19.

8. Peattie, *Nanyo*, 24.

9. Peattie, 23.

10. Hermann Joseph Hiery, *The Neglected War: The German South Pacific and the Influence of World War I* (Honolulu: University of Hawaii Press, 1995), 28.

11. Japanese Government, *Report to the League of Nations on the Administration of the South Sea Islands under Japanese Mandate for the Year 1937*, 1.

12. Wakako Higuchi, *Micronesia Under the Japanese Administration: Interviews with Former South Sea Bureau and Military Officials* (Mangilao, Guam: Micronesian Area Research Center, The University of Guam, 1987), 38.

13. Peattie, *Nanyo*, 45; Japanese Government, *Annual Report to the League of Nations on the Administration of the South Sea Islands under Japanese Mandate for the Year 1925* (Tokyo, Japan: 1925), 25.

14. Peattie, *Nanyo*, 64; Paul H. Clyde, *Japan's Pacific Mandate* (New York: The Macmillan Company, 1935), 66.

15. Clyde, *Japan's Pacific Mandate*, 109.

16. Yumiko Imaizumi, "Northern Marianas Under Japanese Navy Administration (1914-1922)," 2nd Marianas History Conference (Mangilao, Guam: Guampedia, 2013), 296-297.

17. Scott Russell, "From Company Town to Capital Village: A Brief History of Chalan Kanoa, Saipan, CNMI" (Saipan: CNMI Division of Historic Preservation, 2018), 17.

18. Peattie, *Nanyo*, 67.

19. Imaizumi, "Japanese Navy Administration," 293.

20. Imaizumi, 297.
21. Imaizumi, 290.
22. Higuchi, *Micronesia*, 28.
23. Japanese Government, *Year 1925*, 18.
24. Higuchi, *Micronesia*, 60–61.
25. Peattie, *Nanyo*, 73.
26. Higuchi, *Micronesia*, 39.
27. Higuchi, 54.
28. Higuchi, 38.
29. Clyde, *Japan's Pacific Mandate*, 68; Peattie, *Nanyo*, 70.
30. Spennemann, *Edge of Empire*, 164, 236.
31. Japanese Government, *Year 1937*, 6; Higuchi, *Micronesia*, 54.
32. Peattie, *Nanyo*, 75–76.
33. Lin Poyer, Suzanne Falgout, and Laurence Marshall Carucci, *The Typhoon of War: Micronesian Experiences of the Pacific War* (Honolulu: University of Hawai'i, 2001), 18; Peattie, *Nanyo*, 74.
34. Japanese Government, *Year 1937*, 4; Peattie, *Nanyo*, 76.
35. Japanese Government, *Year 1925*, 34–35.
36. Keith L. Camacho, *Cultures of Commemoration: The Politics of War, Memory, and History in the Mariana Islands* (Honolulu: University of Hawaii Press, 2011), 138.
37. Keith L. Camacho, "The Politics of Indigenous Collaboration: The Role of Chamorro Interpreters in Japan's Pacific Empire, 1914–45," *The Journal of Pacific History* 43, no. 2 (2008): 213.
38. Purcell, Jr., "Japanese Expansion," 171; David C. Purcell, Jr., "The Economics of Exploitation: The Japanese in the Mariana, Caroline and Marshall Islands, 1915–1940," *The Journal of Pacific History* 11, no. 3 (1976): 197.
39. Peattie, *Nanyo*, 96.
40. Purcell, Jr., "Japanese Expansion," 174.
41. Purcell, Jr., "Japanese Expansion," 176–177; Purcell, Jr., "Economics of Exploitation," 197.
42. Higuchi, *Micronesia*, 70.
43. Peattie, *Nanyo*, 124.
44. Peattie, *Nanyo*, 155.
45. Purcell, Jr., "Japanese Expansion," 27.
46. Imaizumi, "Japanese Navy Administration," 295.
47. Peattie, *Nanyo*, 124.
48. Purcell, Jr., "Japanese Expansion," 26–29.
49. Ti Ngo, "Mapping Economic Development: The South Seas Government and Sugar Production in Japan's South Pacific Mandate, 1919–1941," *Cross-Currents: East Asian History and Culture Review*, University of California Berkeley, 2 (March 2012): 20.
50. Purcell, Jr., "Japanese Expansion," 29.
51. Peattie, *Nanyo*, 126.
52. Japanese Government, *Year 1925*, 61.
53. James Stanlaw, "Japanese emigration and immigration: From the Meiji to the modern," in *Japanese Diasporas: Unsung pasts, conflicting presents, and uncertain futures* 2006, ed. Nobuko Adachi (New York: Routledge, 2006), 40–43.
54. Ronald Y. Nakasone, "An Impossible Possibility," in *Okinawan Diaspora 2002*, ed. Ronald Y. Nakasone (Honolulu: University of Hawaii Press, 2002), 17.
55. Ichiro, "Okinawans in the Nanyo Islands," 58.
56. Clarence J. Glacken, *The Great Loochoo: A Study of Okinawan Village Life* (Berkeley: University of California Press, 1955), 36.
57. Lori Watt, *When Empire Comes Home: Repatriation and Reintegration in Postwar Japan* (Cambridge, Massachusetts: Harvard University Press, 2009), 26.

58. John Alvin Decker, *Labor Problems in the Pacific Mandates* (London: Oxford University Press, 1940), 37; Peattie, *Nanyo*, 156.
59. Purcell, Jr., "Japanese Expansion," 182.
60. Boyd Dixon, "The Archaeology of Rural Settlement and Class in a Pre-WWII Japanese Plantation on Tinian, Commonwealth of the Northern Mariana Islands," *International Journal of Historical Archaeology* 8, no. 4 (December 2004): 286; Boyd Dixon, "Okinawa as Transported Landscape: Understanding Japanese Archaeological Remains on Tinian Using Ryukyu Ethnohistory and Ethnography," *Asian Perspectives: The Journal of Archaeology for Asia and the Pacific* 54, no. 2 (Fall 2015): 289; Japanese Government, *Annual Report to the League of Nations on the Administration of the South Sea Islands under Japanese Mandate for the Year 1930* (Tokyo, Japan: 1930), 85.
61. Akiko Iida, Yoji Kurata, Satoshi Osawa, and Mikiko Ishikawa, "Industrial Development and its Impacts on the Environment of Micronesian Islands under the Japanese Administration: A Case Study of Babeldaob Island, Palau," *Pan-Japan: The International Journal of the Japanese Diaspora* 10, no. 1 & 2 (2014): 34.
62. Peattie, *Nanyo*, 128.
63. Peattie, 129.
64. Spoehr, *Saipan*, 84; Peattie, *Nanyo*, 129; Russell, "Chalan Kanoa," 17–18.
65. Bowers, "Problems of Resettlement," 24.
66. Russell, "Chalan Kanoa," 21.
67. Tuggle, "Japanese-Era Tinian," 81; Purcell, Jr., "Economics of Exploitation," 201.
68. Tuggle, 82–84.
69. Clyde, *Japan's Pacific Mandate*, 10.
70. Japanese Government, *Year 1925*, 83.
71. Scott Russell, *Rising Sun over the Northern Marianas: Life and Culture Under the Japanese Administration (1914–1944)* (Saipan: CNMI Department of Education, 1983), 10.
72. Wakako Higuchi, *The Japanese Administration of Guam, 1941–1944: A Study of Occupation and Integration Policies, with Japanese Oral Histories* (Jefferson, North Carolina: McFarland & Company, 2013), 112.
73. Department of the Navy, Office of the Military Governor for the Pacific Islands, Commander, Marianas Area; "Memorandum, Comments and Recommendations on Civil Affairs Based on Experience on Saipan and Tinian, August 30 1944"; Box 38, Record Group 313: Records of Naval Operating Forces; National Archives at College Park, Maryland.
74. Higuchi, *Japanese Administration of Guam*, 91.
75. Japanese Government, *Year 1937*, 18.
76. Purcell, Jr., "Japanese Expansion," 189.
77. Higuchi, *Micronesia*, 93.
78. Willard Price, *The South Sea Adventure: Through Japan's Equatorial Empire* (Tokyo: The Hokuseido Press, 1936), 234.
79. United States Department of Commerce, Bureau of Foreign and Domestic Commerce, *The Cane Sugar Industry: Agricultural, Manufacturing, and Marketing Costs in Hawaii, Porto Rico, Louisiana, and Cuba*, Miscellaneous Series no. 53 (Washington, D.C.: Government Printing Office, 1917), 12–13.
80. Department of Commerce, 114–116.
81. William C. Stubbs and D. G. Purse, *Cultivation of Sugar Cane* (Savannah, Georgia: The Morning News Print, 1900), 82.
82. Department of Commerce, *Cane Sugar Industry*, 41.

83. Stubbs and Purse, *Cultivation of Sugar Cane*, 144–145.
84. Department of Commerce, *Cane Sugar Industry*, 163.
85. Department of Commerce, 164–165.
86. Department of Commerce, 165–166.
87. Department of Commerce, 167.
88. Price, *The South Sea Adventure*, 234.
89. Peattie, *Nanyo*, 120.
90. Peattie, 123.
91. Peattie, 121–122.
92. Peattie, 121–122.
93. Higuchi, *Micronesia*, 88; Wakako Higuchi, "Pre-war Japanese Fisheries in Micronesia-Focusing on Bonito and Tuna Fishing in the Northern Mariana Islands," *Immigration Studies* 3 (2007): 56–58.
94. Higuchi, 50, 61.
95. Higuchi, 57.
96. Peattie, *Nanyo*, 142.
97. Bowers, "Problems of Resettlement," 173.
98. Wakako Higuchi, "Pre-war Japanese Fisheries," 60–61.
99. Higuchi, 51, 57.
100. Peattie, *Nanyo*, 130, 150; Higuchi, *Micronesia*, 91; Higuchi, *Japanese Administration of Guam*, 87.
101. Spennemann, *Edge of Empire*, 92.
102. Dave Tuggle and Wakako Higuchi, "Concrete Terraces and Japanese Agricultural Production on Tinian, Mariana Islands," 1st Marianas History Conference. Late Colonial History (Mangilao, Guam: Guampedia Foundation, 2012): 69–70; Dixon, "Okinawa as Transported Landscape," 275.
103. Keiko Ono, John P. Lea, and Tetsuya Ando, "A Study of Urban Morphology of Japanese Colonial Towns in Nanyo Gunto: Part 1 Garapan, Tinian and Chalan Kanoa in Northern Marianas," *Journal of Architecture, Planning, and Environmental Engineering*, Architectural Institute of Japan, no. 556 (2002): 335.
104. South Sea Islands Album Publication Committee, *Japanese Pioneers' Achievements*, 2.
105. Don A. Farrell, *Tinian: A Brief History* (Honolulu: Pacific Historic Parks, 2012), 27.
106. Donald R. Shuster, *Major Patterns of Social Change Instituted in Micronesia during Japanese Colonial Rule, 1914–1940* (Honolulu: Department of Educational Foundations, University of Hawaii, 1978), 12.
107. Department of the Navy, Office of the Chief of Naval Operations, *Civil Affairs Handbook. Administrative Organization and Personnel of the Japanese Mandated Islands*, OPNAV 50E-4, Washington, D.C., 1 January 1944, 17–19.
108. Petty, *Oral Histories*, 80.
109. David C. Purcell, "Suicide in Micronesia: The 1920s and 1930s," *Pacific Studies* 14, no. 2 (1991): 79.
110. Purcell, 77.

Chapter 3

1. Michio Nakajima, "Shinto Deities that Crossed the Sea: Japan's 'Overseas Shrines,' 1868 to 1945," *Japanese Journal of Religious Studies* 37, no. 1 (2010): 24, 39.
2. Nakajima, 35.
3. Alexie Villegas Zotomayor, "Japanese Shrine in Chinatown to Mark Centennial," *Marianas Variety* (Saipan, CNMI), July 23, 2014.
4. South Sea Islands Album Publication Committee, *Japanese Pioneers' Achievements*, 22.
5. United States Department of the Interior, National Park Service, "National Register of Historic Places Registration Form for the Hachiman Jinja, Saipan, CNMI," NRIS Reference Number: 03000549, NPS Form 10-900, OMB No. 1024-0018, 2003.
6. Russell and Cabrera, "*Hachiman Jinja* Site," 20–22.
7. Russell, "Chalan Kanoa," 29; Scott Russell, e-mail message to author, February 8, 2018.
8. Tuggle, "Japanese-Era Tinian," 103.
9. Donald R. Shuster, "State Shinto in Micronesia during Japanese Rule, 1914–1945," *Pacific Studies* 5, no. 2 (1982): 27.
10. Otto D. Tolischus, *Through Japanese Eyes* (New York: Reynal & Hitchcock, 1945), 15–16.
11. Peattie, *Nanyo*, 84.
12. Dixon, "Okinawa as Transported Landscape," 293.
13. Dixon, 293.
14. Okinawa Prefectural Government, *Keys to Okinawan Culture* (Okinawa, Japan: Okinawa Prefectural Government, 1992), 29–30.
15. James C. Robinson, *Okinawa: A People and Their Gods* (Rutland, Vermont: Charles E. Tuttle Company Publishers, 1969), 64.
16. Okinawa Prefectural Government, *Keys to Okinawan Culture*, 33.
17. William P. Lebra, *Okinawan Religion: Belief, Ritual, and Social Structure* (Honolulu: University of Hawaii Press, Second Printing, 1985), 23.
18. Okinawa Prefectural Government, *Keys to Okinawan Culture*, 30–31.
19. Lebra, *Okinawan Religion*, 29–30.
20. Robinson, *Okinawa*, 54.
21. Lebra, *Okinawan Religion*, 54–56.
22. Lebra, 32–37.
23. Donald Dean Owens, "Korean Shamanism: Its Components, Context, and Functions" (Doctoral Dissertation, University of Oklahoma Graduate College, 1975), 61.
24. Owens, "Korean Shamanism," 79.
25. South Sea Islands Album Publication Committee, *Japanese Pioneers' Achievements*, 21.
26. South Sea Islands Album Publication Committee, 21.
27. Japanese Government, *Year 1937*, 43.
28. Petty, *Oral Histories*, 31.
29. Japanese Government, *Year 1930*, 6.
30. Earhart, *Certain Victory*, 59, 153.
31. Clyde, *Japan's Pacific Mandate*, 107.
32. Japanese Government, *Year 1925*, 22.
33. Peattie, *Nanyo*, 91.
34. M. J. Rhee, *The Doomed Empire: Japan in Colonial Korea* (Brookfield, Vermont: Ashgate Publishing, 1997), 72.
35. Petty, *Oral Histories*, 79.
36. Kenneth J. Ruoff, *Imperial Japan at Its Zenith: The Wartime Celebration of the Empire's 2,600th Anniversary* (Ithaca: Cornell University Press, 2010), 30.
37. Japanese Ministry of Education, *Kokutai No Hongi: Cardinal Principles of the National Entity of Japan*, trans. John Owen Gauntlett (Cambridge, Massachusetts: Harvard University Press, 1949), 51.
38. Petty, *Oral Histories*, 25.
39. Japanese Government, *Year 1937*, 101; Peattie, *Nanyo*, 109.
40. Delmer M. Brown, *Nationalism in Japan: An Introductory Historical Analysis* (Berkeley, University of California Press, 1955), 213–215.
41. Kushner, *The Thought War*, 32.
42. Japanese Government, *Year 1937*, 41.

43. Japanese Government, *Year 1930*, 19.
44. Petty, *Oral Histories*, 51.
45. Utsumi Aiko, "Japan's Korean Soldiers in the Pacific War," in *Asian Labor in the Wartime Japanese Empire, Unknown Histories*, ed. by Paul H. Kratoska (New York: M.E. Sharpe, 2005), 83.
46. Clyde, *Japan's Pacific Mandate*, 111.
47. Takashi Fujitani, *Race for Empire: Koreans as Japanese and Japanese as Americans during World War II* (Berkeley: University of California Press, 2011), 54.
48. Camacho, *Cultures of Commemoration*, 33.
49. Petty, *Oral Histories*, 48.
50. Petty, 25.
51. Sebastian C. H. Kim and Kirsteen Kim, *A History of Korean Christianity* (New York: Cambridge University Press, 2015), 109–110.
52. Brown, *Nationalism in Japan*, 120.
53. Helen Hardacre, *Shinto and the State, 1868–1988* (Princeton, New Jersey: Princeton University Press, 1989), 119.
54. Shuster, *Major Patterns of Social Change*, 55–57; Imaizumi, "Japanese Navy Administration," 292–293.
55. Poyer, Falgout, and Carucci, *Typhoon of War*, 52.
56. Joseph and Murray, *Chamorros and Carolinians*, 47; Peattie, *Nanyo*, 301–302.
57. Spoehr, *Saipan*, 88.
58. Higuchi, *Micronesia*, 153, 156; Higuchi, *Japanese Administration of Guam*, 58.
59. Japanese Government, *Year 1925*, 22.
60. Peattie, *Nanyo*, 92–93.
61. Imaizumi, "Japanese Navy Administration," 292.
62. Price, *The South Sea Adventure*, 288.
63. Shuster, *Major Patterns of Social Change*, 36.
64. Shuster, 4.
65. Shingo Iitaka, "Remembering Nanyo from Okinawa: Deconstructing the Former Empire of Japan through Memorial Practices," *History & Memory* 27, no. 2 (2015): 128.
66. Purcell, Jr., "Japanese Expansion," 182–184.
67. Higuchi, *Micronesia*, 92.
68. Shuster, *Major Patterns of Social Change*, 5.
69. Japanese Government, *Year 1937*, 48; Camacho, "Chamorro Interpreters," 211; Joseph and Murray, *Chamorros and Carolinians*, 45, 48; Purcell, Jr., "Economics of Exploitation," 195–196.
70. Wakako Higuchi, *Japanese Administration of Guam*, 113.
71. Petty, *Oral Histories*, 80.
72. Ono, Lea, and Ando, "Garapan, Tinian and Chalan Kanoa," 335.
73. Ono, Lea, and Ando, 336.
74. Ono, Lea, and Ando, 339.
75. Tolischus, *Through Japanese Eyes*, 16
76. Japanese Ministry of Education, *Kokutai No Hongi*, 105.
77. John W. Dower, *War Without Mercy: Race and Power in the Pacific War* (New York: Pantheon Books, 1993), 263–264.
78. Higuchi, *Micronesia*, 62.
79. Noriko J. Horiguchi, *Women Adrift: The Literature of Japan's Imperial Body* (Minneapolis: University of Minnesota Press, 2012), 25.
80. Horiguchi, 15.
81. Horiguchi, 15–16.
82. Poyer, Falgout, and Carucci, *Typhoon of War*, 60.
83. Paul C. Bosse, "Polling Civilian Japanese on Saipan," *The Public Opinion Quarterly* 9, no. 2 (1945): 178.
84. Cook, *Japan at War*, 461.

85. George H. Kerr, *Okinawa: The History of an Island People*, Revised Edition (Rutland, Vermont: Tuttle Publishing, 2000), 448–449.
86. Jeffrey Paul Bayliss, *On the Margins of Empire: Buraku and Korean Identity in Prewar and Wartime Japan* (Cambridge, Massachusetts: Harvard University Asia Center, 2013), 383.
87. Fujitani, *Race for Empire*, 58.
88. Fujitani, 54, 57–58.
89. Japanese Government, *Year 1937*, 43; Imaizumi, "Japanese Navy Administration," 291.
90. Higuchi, *Micronesia*, 32; Mark R. Peattie, "The Nanyo: Japan in the South Pacific, 1885–1945," in *The Japanese Colonial Empire, 1895–1945*, ed. Ramon Hawley Myers, Mark R. Peattie, and Jingzhi Zhen (Princeton, New Jersey: Princeton University Press, 1984), 189; Imaizumi, "Mobilization and Perspectives," 7.
91. Ichiro, "Okinawans in the Nanyo Islands," 64; Robert Thomas Tierney, *Tropics of Savagery: The Culture of Japanese Empire in Comparative Frame* (Berkeley: University of California Press, 2010), 133, 139, 145.
92. Camacho, "Chamorro Interpreters," 212.
93. Shuster, *Major Patterns of Social Change*, 6.
94. Price, *The South Sea Adventure*, 161.
95. Peattie, *Nanyo*, 115.
96. Higuchi, *Micronesia*, 128.
97. Marjorie Wall Bingham and Susan Hill Gross, *Women in Japan: From Ancient Times to the Present* (St. Louis Park, Minnesota: Glenhurst Publications, 1987), 188.
98. Bingham and Gross, 188.
99. George De Vos and Hiroshi Wagatsuma, *Japan's Invisible Race: Caste in Culture and Personality* (Berkeley, California: University of California Press, 1967), 34.
100. Ichiro, "Okinawans in the Nanyo Islands," 65.
101. Ichiro, 66.
102. Japanese Government, *Year 1937*, 70–74; While public health standards were improved on Saipan during Japanese rule, some have argued that Micronesians on the island received lower quality medical care. Dr. Benusto Kaipat, a Carolinian physician on Saipan in the postwar period, stated, "Health care during the Japanese occupation was considered good for the Japanese, Okinawans and well-to-do native families who could afford expensive treatment. The majority of the natives, both the Chamorros and the Carolinians, were left in the hands of witch doctors…According to Dr. Torres and Felipe Seman, who were here the longest during that time, during the 30 years of Japanese occupation, they could only remember about two or three Caesarian cases among the natives. Most of the complications among the Japanese or the Okinawans here were sent to Japan for Cesarean sections" (Shuster, *Major Patterns of Social Change*, 18).
103. Shuster, *Major Patterns of Social Change*, 11.
104. Shuster, 48.
105. Japanese Government, *Year 1930*, 86–87.
106. Camacho, *Cultures of Commemoration*, 33.
107. Dixon, "Okinawa as Transported Landscape," 289.
108. Petty, *Oral Histories*, 17.
109. Petty, 27.
110. South Sea Islands Album Publication Committee, *Japanese Pioneers' Achievements*, 2.
111. Imaizumi, "Mobilization and Perspectives," 10.
112. Camacho, *Cultures of Commemoration*, 140.
113. Petty, *Oral Histories*, 35.
114. Higuchi, *Micronesia*, 109.
115. Petty, *Oral Histories*, 42.
116. Horiguchi, *Women Adrift*, 33.

117. Earhart, *Certain Victory*, 167.
118. Department of the Navy, *Civil Affairs Handbook*, OPNAV 50E-4, 17–19.
119. Susan J. Pharr, *Political Women in Japan: The Search for a Place in Political Life* (Berkeley: University of California Press, 1981), 49.
120. Hibino, *Nippon Shindo Ron*, 93–94.
121. Horiguchi, *Women Adrift*, ix.
122. Kathleen S. Uno, "Women and Changes in the Household Division of Labor," in *Recreating Japanese Women, 1600–1945*, ed. Gail Lee Bernstein (Berkeley: University of California, 1991), 38.
123. Uno, "Women and Changes in the Household Division of Labor," 27.
124. Earhart, *Certain Victory*, 148.
125. Yoshiko Miyake, "Doubling Expectations: Motherhood and Women's Factory Work Under State Management in Japan in the 1930s and 1940s," in *Recreating Japanese Women, 1600–1945*, ed. Gail Lee Bernstein (Berkeley: University of California, 1991), 271.
126. Miyake, "Doubling Expectations," 270–271.
127. Horiguchi, *Women Adrift*, viii.
128. Ellen Schattschneider, "The Bloodstained Doll: Violence and the Gift in Wartime Japan," *The Journal of Japanese Studies* 31, no. 2 (2003): 330.
129. Cook, *Japan at War*, 172.
130. Wakako Higuchi, *Micronesians and the Pacific War: The Palauans* (Mangilao, Guam: Micronesian Area Research Center, The University of Guam, 1986), 18.
131. Chizuko Ueno, *Nationalism and Gender*, trans. by Beverley Yamamoto (Melbourne, Trans Pacific Press, 2004), 38.
132. Earhart, *Certain Victory*, 158.
133. Horiguchi, *Women Adrift*, 23.
134. Horiguchi, 23.
135. Ohnuki-Tierney, *Kamikaze, Cherry Blossoms*, 151; Miyake, "Doubling Expectations," 271.
136. Miyake, "Doubling Expectations," 272.
137. Miyake, 278–279.
138. Horiguchi, *Women Adrift*, 21–22.
139. Horiguchi, 43, 46.
140. Horiguchi, 26.
141. Pharr, *Political Women in Japan*, 50.
142. Horiguchi, *Women Adrift*, 32–33; Earhart, *Certain Victory*, 152.
143. Horiguchi, *Women Adrift*, 181.
144. Pharr, *Political Women in Japan*, 48.
145. Yuriko Nagata, "The Japanese in Torres Strait," in *Navigating Boundaries: The Asian Diaspora in Torres Strait* (Canberra, Australia: Pandanus Books, 2004): 138–159.
146. Shimizu Hiroshi and Hirakawa Hitoshi, *Japan and Singapore in the World Economy: Japan's Economic Advance into Singapore, 1870–1965* (New York: Routledge, 1999), 19.
147. Ono, Lea, and Ando, "Garapan, Tinian and Chalan Kanoa," 334.
148. Haruko Taya Cook, "Turning Women into Weapons: Japan's Women, the Battle of Saipan, and the 'Nature of the Pacific War,'" in *Women and War in the Twentieth Century: Enlisted with or Without Consent*, ed. Nicole Ann Dombrowski (New York: Garland Publishing, 1999), 251.
149. Petty, *Oral Histories*, 80.
150. Peattie, *Nanyo*, 209.
151. Peattie, 208.
152. James Francis Warren, *Ah Ku and Karayuki-san: Prostitution in Singapore, 1870–1940* (Singapore: Oxford University Press, 1993), 29.
153. Purcell, Jr., "Japanese Expansion," 225.
154. Shuster, *Major Patterns of Social Change*, 25.
155. Mikiso Hane, *Peasants, Rebels, and Outcastes: The Underside of Modern Japan* (New York: Pantheon Books, 1982), 216–217.

Chapter 4

1. Ronald H. Spector, *Eagle Against the Sun: The American War with Japan* (New York: Random House, 1985), 9.
2. Thomas A. Bailey, "Japan's Protest Against the Annexation of Hawaii," *The Journal of Modern History* 3, no. 1 (1931): 52.
3. Edward S. Miller, *War Plan Orange: The U.S. Strategy to Defeat Japan, 1897–1945* (Annapolis, Maryland: Naval Institute Press, 1991), 2, 25.
4. Sadao Asada, *From Mahan to Pearl Harbor: The Imperial Japanese Navy and the United States* (Annapolis, Maryland: Naval Institute Press, 2006), 47; David C. Evans and Mark R. Peattie, *Kaigun: Strategy, Tactics, and Technology in the Imperial Japanese Navy, 1887–1941* (Annapolis Maryland: Naval Institute Press, 1997), 149.
5. Roger Daniels, *The Politics of Prejudice: The Anti-Japanese Movement in California and the Struggle for Japanese Exclusion* (Berkeley: University of California Press, 1977), 142.
6. Mark R. Peattie, *Nanyo: The Rise and Fall of the Japanese in Micronesia, 1885–1945* (Honolulu: University of Hawaii Press, 1988), 48.
7. Charles Noble Gregory, "The Treaty as to Yap and the Mandated North Pacific Islands," *The American Journal of International Law* 16, no. 2 (1922): 250.
8. Cook, *Japan at War*, 50.
9. Akagi, *Japan's Foreign Relations*, 495.
10. Akagi, 543, 546–547.
11. Chicago Tribune. "America's Step Opens Way for Embargo Order," *Chicago Tribune*, July 27, 1939.
12. Miller, *War Plan Orange*, 51.
13. Higuchi, *Japanese Administration of Guam*, 36.
14. Sidney Pash, *The Currents of War: A New History of American-Japanese Relations, 1899–1941* (Lexington, Kentucky: The University Press of Kentucky, 2014), XV.
15. Higuchi, *Japanese Administration of Guam*, 10.
16. Higuchi, 35.
17. Higuchi, *Micronesia*, 117.
18. Higuchi, *Japanese Administration of Guam*, 31.
19. Higuchi, 28.
20. Higuchi, 33.
21. Higuchi, 32.
22. Higuchi, 36.
23. Crowl, *Campaign in the Marianas*, 55.
24. Higuchi, *Japanese Administration of Guam*, 42–43.
25. Crowl, *Campaign in the Marianas*, 55–56; Department of the Navy; CINCPAC-CINCPOA Translations, Item # 11,601; "5th Special Base Force (Saipan) Situation Report," 12 February 1944; Record Group 38: Records of the Office of the Chief of Naval Operations; National Archives at College Park, Maryland.
26. Department of the Navy, CINCPAC-CINCPOA Translations, "5th Special Base Force (Saipan) Situation Report."
27. Higuchi, *Micronesia*, 71.
28. Higuchi, *Japanese Administration of Guam*, 107–109.
29. Richard Carl Bright, *Pain and Purpose in the Pacific: True Reports of War* (Victoria, British Columbia, Canada: Trafford Publishing, 2010), 104.

30. Tuggle, "Japanese-Era Tinian," 92.
31. Higuchi, *Japanese Administration of Guam*, 100.
32. Higuchi, 101, 117.
33. Higuchi, 117.
34. Higuchi, 118.
35. Higuchi, 114.
36. Petty, *Oral Histories*, 25.
37. Douglas Westfall and Ryozo Kimihira, *The Taking of Saipan: Two Sides to Every Battle in WWII*, The Memoirs of Cpl. Richard Meadows & Cpl. Genkichi Ichikawa (Orange, California: The Paragon Agency Publishers, 2014), 33.
38. Bowers, "Problems of Resettlement," 47.
39. Poyer, Falgout, and Carucci, *Typhoon of War*, 56.
40. Higuchi, *Japanese Administration of Guam*, 104.
41. Petty, *Oral Histories*, 80; Camacho, "Chamorro Interpreters," 216–217.
42. Camacho, 219.
43. Petty, *Oral Histories*, 27.
44. Petty, 46.
45. Louis Morton, *Strategy and Command: The First Two Years*, The War in the Pacific, United States Army in World War II Series (Washington, D.C.: Office of the Chief of Military History, Department of the Army, 1962), 546–547.
46. Sherrod, *On to Westward*, 16.
47. Department of the Navy, Engineer, Expeditionary Troops (Task Force 56); "Report on Japanese Defensive Plan for the Island of Saipan Southern Marianas," July 1944; Box 322, RG 127: Records of the United States Marine Corps; National Archives at College Park, Maryland; Harold J. Goldberg, *D-Day in the Pacific: The Battle of Saipan* (Bloomington: Indiana University Press, 2007), 35–36.
48. Department of the Navy, NTLF, "Operations Report Phase I (Saipan)," G-2 Summary no. 20, 24 May 1944, 6.
49. Department of the Navy, Office of the Chief of Naval Operations, Office of Naval Records and Library, Northern Troops and Landing Force, Headquarters, In the Field, "Northern Troops and Landing Force Operations Report, Phase I (Saipan)," 12 August 1944, Record Group 38: Records of the Office of the Chief of Naval Operations, National Archives at College Park, Maryland, G-2 Report, 69; Carl W. Hoffman, *The Seizure of Tinian*, United States Marine Corps Historical Division Monograph (Washington, D.C.: Government Printing Office, 1951), 156.
50. Imaizumi, "Mobilization and Perspectives," 10.
51. Department of the Navy, NTLF, "Northern Troops and Landing Force Operations Report, Phase I (Saipan)," G-2 Report, 10.
52. Imaizumi, "Mobilization and Perspectives," 11.
53. Poyer, Falgout, and Carucci, *Typhoon of War*, 67.
54. Department of the Navy, NTLF, "Operations Report, Phase III (Tinian)," 12 August 1944, G-2 Report, 47; Iitaka, "Remembering Nanyo from Okinawa," 147
55. Fujitani, *Race for Empire*, 44.
56. Fujitani, 45.
57. Department of the Navy, NTLF, "Operations Report, Phase I (Saipan)," G-2, V Amphibious Corps, Special Study of Troop Strength in the Southern Marianas, Discussion of Naval Land Forces in the Central Pacific by a JICPOA representative, 9 May 1944. 5.
58. Department of War, "War Department Technical Manual TM-E 30-480, Handbook on Japanese Military Forces, 15 September 1944" (Washington, D.C.: Government Printing Office, 1944), 80; D. Colt Denfeld, "Korean Laborers in Micronesia during World War II," *Korea Observer* 15, no. 1 (Spring, 1984), 9.
59. Denfeld, 8.
60. Denfeld, 9–10.
61. Department of the Navy, NTLF, "Operations Report, Phase I (Saipan)," G-2, V Amphibious Corps, Special Study of Troop Strength in the Southern Marianas. Discussion of Naval Land Forces in the Central Pacific by a JICPOA representative, 9 May 1944. 3.
62. Denfeld, "Korean Laborers in Micronesia," 4, 8.
63. Robert B. Sheeks, "Civilians on Saipan," *Far Eastern Survey* 14, no. 9 (1945): 109.
64. Beatrice Trefalt, "After the Battle for Saipan: The Internment of Japanese Civilians at Camp Susupe, 1944–1946," *Japanese Studies* 29, no. 3 (2009): 340.
65. Petty, *Oral Histories*, 48.
66. Beatrice Trefalt, "The Battle of Saipan in Japanese Civilian Memoirs: Non-combatants, Soldiers and the Complexities of Surrender," *The Journal of Pacific History* 53, no. 3 (2018): 257.
67. Higuchi, *Micronesia*, 109.
68. Higuchi, *Japanese Administration of Guam*, 187; Goetzfridt, *Guahan*, 57.
69. Petty, *Oral Histories*, 81.
70. Camacho, *Cultures of Commemoration*, 145–146.
71. David Andrew Schmidt, *Ianfu: The Comfort Women of The Japanese Imperial Army of The Pacific War* (New York: The Edwin Mellen Press, 2000), 2.
72. Yuki Tanaka, *Japan's Comfort Women: Sexual Slavery and Prostitution during World War II and the U.S. Occupation* (New York: Routledge, 2002), 58.
73. Schmidt, *Ianfu*, 128.
74. Yoshimi Yoshiaki, *Comfort Women: Sexual Slavery in the Japanese Military During World War II* (New York: Columbia University Press, 2000), 193–197.
75. Goldberg, *D-Day in the Pacific*, 110; Petty, Saipan, 27.
76. George Hicks, *The Comfort Women: Japan's Brutal Regime of Enforced Prostitution in the Second World War* (New York: W.W. Norton & Company, 1995), 117.
77. Hicks, *The Comfort Women*, 117.
78. Higuchi, *Micronesia*, 131.
79. China Daily, "Memoir of comfort woman tells of 'hell for women,'" *China Daily*, July 6, 2007.
80. Meehl, *One Marine's War*, 169–170.
81. National Museum of the Pacific War, Interview with Jack Gilbreath, August 19, 2005.
82. Schmidt, *Ianfu*, 158–159.
83. Bill Miller, "Beachhead Government," *Marine Corps Gazette* (November 1944): 42.
84. Sherrod, *On to Westward*, 98.
85. Guy Gabaldon, *Saipan: Suicide Island* (Saipan: Guy Gabaldon, 1990), 107–111.

Chapter 5

1. Morton, *Strategy and Command*, 27.
2. Morton, 33.
3. Crowl, *Campaign in the Marianas*, 2.
4. Spector, *Eagle Against the Sun*, 255–256.
5. Crowl, *Campaign in the Marianas*, 10.
6. Spector, *Eagle Against the Sun*, 252.
7. James D. Hornfischer, *Neptune's Inferno: The U.S. Navy At Guadalcanal* (New York: Bantam Books, 2011), Appendix.
8. Morison, *New Guinea and the Marianas*, 5–6, 157.
9. Morton, *Strategy and Command*, 645.
10. Morton, 618.
11. Morton, 669.
12. Crowl, *Campaign in the Marianas*, 1–2, 19.

13. Department of the Navy, NTLF, "Operations Report Phase I (Saipan)," Enclosure (A), Appendix #1 to Annex Dog to Northern Troops and Landing Force Administrative Order Number 3–44, 1 May 1944, 4.
14. Crowl, *Campaign in the Marianas*, 33.
15. Department of the Navy, NTLF, "Operations Report, Phase I (Saipan)," 12 August 1944, G-1 Report, 5.
16. Department of the Navy, NTLF, "Operations Report, Phase I (Saipan)," 10 August 1944, G-3 Report, 11.
17. Department of the Navy, NTLF, "Operations Report, Phase I (Saipan)," 12 August 1944, G-2 Report, 4.
18. Goldberg, *D-Day in the Pacific*, 51.
19. Second Marine Division, "Saipan" (HM9–16) (Pearl Harbor, Hawaii, Division Headquarters, 1944), 14.
20. James Campbell, *The Color of War: How One Battle Broke Japan and Another Changed America* (New York: Crown Publishers, 2012), 168.
21. Department of the Navy, NTLF, "Operations Report, Phase I (Saipan)," G-2 Report, 2.
22. Goldberg, *D-Day in the Pacific*, 21, 94.
23. Petty, *Oral Histories*, 53.
24. Petty, 32.
25. Petty, 18.
26. Westfall and Kimihira, *The Taking of Saipan*, 35.
27. Department of the Navy, NTLF, "Operations Report, Phase I (Saipan)," G-2 Report, 2.
28. Crowl, *Campaign in the Marianas*, 72.
29. Crowl, 120.
30. Crowl, 74.
31. Crowl, 76; Goldberg, *D-Day in the Pacific*, 54.
32. James J. Fahey, *Pacific War Diary, 1942–1945* (Boston: Houghton Mifflin Company, 1991), 166.
33. Cook, *Japan at War*, 283.
34. Crowl, *Campaign in the Marianas*, 75.
35. Department of the Army, The Adjutant General's Office; "Translation of the Diary of Japanese Serviceman Taroa Kawaguchi Detailing Combat Activity on Saipan," 1944; Identifier: 6922040, Record Group 407: Records of the Adjutant General's Office; National Archives at College Park, Maryland.
36. Goldberg, *D-Day in the Pacific*, 146.
37. Sherrod, *On to Westward*, 68.
38. Goldberg, *D-Day in the Pacific*, 109.
39. Steven Doughton interview with Albert Conrad Torgerson.
40. Petty, *Oral Histories*, 53.
41. Petty, 37.
42. Petty, 19–20.
43. Higuchi, *Micronesia*, 133, 138.
44. Second Marine Division, "Saipan" (HM9–16), 2.
45. Morison, *New Guinea and the Marianas*, 359.
46. Morison, 360.
47. Department of the Navy, NTLF, "Operations Report, Phase I (Saipan)," G-2 Report, 64.
48. Sloan, *Their Backs Against the Sea*, 63.
49. Frederic A. Stott, *Saipan Under Fire* (Andover, Massachusetts: Frederic A. Stott, 1945), 7.
50. Department of the Navy, NTLF, "Operations Report, Phase I (Saipan)," G-3 Report, 14.
51. Carl W. Hoffman, *Saipan: The Beginning of the End*, United States Marine Corps Historical Division Monograph (Washington, D.C.: Government Printing Office, 1950), 69.
52. Department of the Navy, NTLF, "Operations Report, Phase I (Saipan)," 26.
53. Goldberg, *D-Day in the Pacific*, 79.
54. John C. Chapin, *Breaching the Marianas: The Battle for Saipan*, "Marines in World War II Commemorative Series" (Washington, D.C.: History and Museums Division, U.S. Marine Corps Headquarters, 1994), 2.
55. Goldberg, *D-Day in the Pacific*, 116.
56. Goldberg, 70.
57. Richard David Wissolik et al., *They Say There Was a War* (Latrobe, Pennsylvania: Center for Northern Appalachian Studies, Saint Vincent College, 2005), 121.
58. Sloan, *Their Backs Against the Sea*, 47.
59. Hoffman, *Saipan*, 27.
60. Westfall and Kimihira, *The Taking of Saipan*, 65.
61. Petty, *Oral Histories*, 136.
62. Department of the Navy, NTLF, "Operations Report, Phase I (Saipan)," G-3 Report, 15.
63. Sloan, *Their Backs Against the Sea*, 57.
64. Hoffman, *Saipan*, 92–93.
65. Department of the Navy, NTLF, "Operations Report, Phase I (Saipan)." G-2 Report, 14.
66. Department of the Navy, 18.
67. Crowl, *Campaign in the Marianas*, 160.
68. Sherrod, *On to Westward*, 77.
69. Lewis Meyers, "Japanese Civilians in Combat Zones," *Marine Corps Gazette* 29 (February 1945): 11, 15.
70. Department of the Navy, NTLF, "Operations Report, Phase I (Saipan)," G-2 Report, 27.
71. Department of the Navy, 29.
72. Petty, *Oral Histories*, 102.
73. Department of the Navy, NTLF, "Operations Report, Phase I (Saipan)," G-2 Report, 30.
74. Department of the Navy, 34.
75. Department of the Navy, 37.
76. Department of the Navy, NTLF, "Operations Report, Phase I (Saipan)," G-3 Report, 19.
77. United States Strategic Bombing Survey (Pacific), Naval Analysis Division, *The Campaigns of the Pacific War* (Washington, D.C.: Government Printing Office, 1946), 212.
78. Department of the Navy, NTLF, "Operations Report, Phase I (Saipan)," G-3 Report, 20.
79. Hoffman, *Saipan*, 196.
80. Sherrod, *On to Westward*, 126.
81. Department of the Navy, NTLF, "Operations Report, Phase I (Saipan)," G-2 Report, 37.
82. Department of the Navy, 58.
83. Department of the Navy, NTLF, "Operations Report, Phase I (Saipan)," Captured Japanese officer's personal account of 'The Last Days of Lieutenant General SAITO,' 14 July 1944, 1.
84. Department of the Navy, NTLF, "Operations Report, Phase I (Saipan)," G-2 Report, 58; Department of the Navy, NTLF, "Operations Report, Phase I (Saipan)," G-3 Report, 22; Crowl, *Campaign in the Marianas*, 258.
85. Goldberg, *D-Day in the Pacific*, 131.
86. Moline Daily Dispatch,"Dying Jap Girl is Rushed to Hospital," *Moline Daily Dispatch* (Moline, Illinois), July 15, 1944.
87. Honolulu Star-Bulletin, "The War is Hard on Children of Saipan; U.S. Marines Smooth Way," *Honolulu Star-Bulletin*, July 18, 1944.
88. Morison, *New Guinea and the Marianas*, 339.
89. Crowl, *Campaign in the Marianas*, 276.
90. Department of the Navy, NTLF, "Operations Report, Phase III (Tinian)," G-3 Report, 8.
91. Department of the Navy, NTLF, "Operations Report, Phase III (Tinian)," G-2 Report, 9.
92. Department of the Navy, NTLF, "Operations Report, Phase III (Tinian)," G-2 Periodic Report no. 44, 29 July 1944, 2.
93. Department of the Navy, NTLF, "Operations

Report, Phase III (Tinian)," Narrative of the assault on Tinian, 12.
94. Hoffman, *Seizure of Tinian*, 79.
95. National Museum of the Pacific War, Interview with Charles Pase, April 12, 2001.
96. Department of the Navy, NTLF, "Operations Report, Phase III (Tinian)," G-2 Report, 15.
97. Department of the Navy, NTLF, "Operations Report, Phase III (Tinian)," G-2 Periodic Report no. 44, 29 July 1944.
98. Hoffman, *Seizure of Tinian*, 97.
99. Hoffman, 97.
100. Department of the Navy, NTLF, "Operations Report, Phase III (Tinian)," G-2 Report, 16.
101. Department of the Navy, 18.
102. Department of the Navy, 21–22.
103. Department of the Navy, 19.
104. Department of the Navy, NTLF, "Operations Report, Phase III (Tinian)," G-2 Periodic Report no. 56, 10 August 1944, 1.
105. Hoffman, *Seizure of Tinian*, 122.

Chapter 6

1. Fahey, *Pacific War Diary*, 187.
2. Fahey, 189.
3. Fahey, 191.
4. National Museum of the Pacific War, Interview with Norman Delisle.
5. Lynn L. Sims, *"They Have Seen The Elephant," Veterans Remembrances From World War II for the 40th Anniversary of V-E Day* (Fort Lee, Virginia: United States Army Logistics Center, 1985).
6. Steven Doughton interview with Albert Conrad Torgerson.
7. Second Armored Amphibian Battalion Association, *2nd Armored Amphibian Battalion USMC WWII, Saipan, Tinian, Iwo Jima* (Washington, D.C., Second Armored Amphibian Battalion Association, 1991), 117.
8. Wissolik et al., *There Was a War*, 122.
9. Frank Rosario and Floyd Takeuchi, "Saipanese Recall a Day in June when Thousands Leapt to Death," *Pacific Islands Monthly* 45, no. 9 (September, 1974): 58.
10. Goldberg, *D-Day in the Pacific*, 202.
11. Raymond A. Cochran, "Enquirer Man Photographs Mass Hara-Kiri of Japanese Soldiers, Families On Saipan," *The Cincinnati Enquirer, Kentucky Edition*, August 8, 1944.
12. Roy William Roush, Open Fire! (Marceline, Missouri: Walsworth Publishing Company, 2003), 557.
13. William P. Rogal, *Guadalcanal, Tarawa, and Beyond: A Mud Marine's Memoir of the Pacific Island War* (Jefferson, North Carolina: McFarland & Company, 2010), 173.
14. National Museum of the Pacific War, Interview with Wilson Allmand.
15. Cliff Graham, "48 Hours at Tinian," *Coronet Magazine* (June 1945): 550.
16. Department of the Navy, NTLF, "Operations Report, Phase III (Tinian)," G-2 Report, 54.
17. Dean Ladd and Steven Weingartner, *Faithful Warriors: A Combat Marine Remembers the Pacific War* (Annapolis, Maryland: Naval Institute Press, 2009), 205.
18. Ladd and Weingartner, 205.
19. Meyers, "Japanese Civilians," 14–15.
20. Goldberg, *D-Day in the Pacific*, 202.
21. Harold Smith, "Tribune Writer Views Suicide of Jap Civilians," *Chicago Tribune*, August 13, 1944.
22. Graham, "48 Hours at Tinian," 127.
23. Department of the Navy, NTLF, "Operations Report, Phase I (Saipan)," G-2 Report, 112.
24. Department of the Navy, NTLF, "Operations Report, Phase I (Saipan)," G-2 Periodic Report no. 10, 25 June 1944, 4.
25. Second Armored Amphibian Battalion Association, *2nd Armored Amphibian Battalion*, 125.
26. Second Armored Amphibian Battalion Association, 126.
27. Goldberg, *D-Day in the Pacific*, 200.
28. Goldberg, 202.
29. New York State Military Museum, Interview with Albert J. Harris.
30. Department of the Navy, NTLF, "Operations Report, Phase III (Tinian)," G-2 Report, 54.
31. New York State Military Museum, Interview with Gabriel J. Vertucci.
32. Morison, *New Guinea and the Marianas*, 338.
33. John F. Embree, "Military Government in Saipan and Tinian: A Report on the Organization of Susupe and Churo," *Applied Anthropology* 5, no. 1 (1946): 5.
34. John M. Lee, "Japanese Search Pacific Isles for Bones of War Dead," *The New York Times*, March 15, 1972.
35. Cook, *Japan at War*, 289–290.
36. Morison, *New Guinea and the Marianas*, 338.
37. National Museum of the Pacific War, Interview with Carl Pettier.
38. Keith Wheeler, "Jap Soldiers and Civilians Facing Capture, Chose Death," *The Arizona Daily Star*, November 11, 1944.
39. Second Armored Amphibian Battalion Association, *2nd Armored Amphibian Battalion*, 161.
40. Maryville Daily Forum, "Japanese Commit Mass Suicide on Saipan Isle," *The Maryville Daily Forum* (Maryville, Missouri), September 13, 1944.
41. Marine Corps Combat Correspondents, *Semper Fidelis: The U.S. Marines in the Pacific, 1942–1945* (New York: William Sloane Associates, 1947), 224.
42. National Museum of the Pacific War, Interview with Ray Harrison.
43. National Museum of the Pacific War, Interview with H.L. Obermiller.
44. Goldberg, *D-Day in the Pacific*, 202.
45. Roush, *Open Fire!*, 454.
46. Hoffman, *Seizure of Tinian*, 245.
47. National Museum of the Pacific War, Interview with Olian T. Perry.
48. Richard Schickel, *Shooting War: World War II Combat Cameramen*, Documentary, DreamWorks L.L.C., 2000.
49. Veterans History Project, Central Connecticut State University, Interview with Edwin P. DesRosiers.
50. Sherrod, *On to Westward*, 145.
51. Bright, *Pain and Purpose*, 91.
52. Samuel Holiday and Robert S. McPherson, *Under the Eagle: Samuel Holiday, Navajo Code Talker* (Norman: University of Oklahoma, 2013), 140.
53. Bright, *Pain and Purpose*, 164.
54. Wisconsin Veterans Museum Research Center, Interview with Frank Urbanowicz.
55. National Museum of the Pacific War, Interview with Cleatus A. LeBow.
56. Goldberg, *D-Day in the Pacific*, 199.
57. Laurence Rees, *Horror in the East*, Documentary, United Kingdom, British Broadcasting Corporation, 2001.
58. Toland, *The Rising Sun*, 517–519.

59. Steve Metzer, "Relatives Tried To Drown Child Before Killing Selves," *The Lawton Constitution*, December 10, 2017.
60. Bright, *Pain and Purpose*, 99–102.
61. Austin Hoyt, *Victory in the Pacific*, "American Experience," Documentary, WGBH Educational Foundation, PBS Distribution, 2005
62. Trefalt, "After the Battle," 340.
63. Toland, *The Rising Sun*, 487.
64. Toland, 492.
65. Trefalt, "After the Battle," 340.
66. Toland, *The Rising Sun*, 493.
67. Toland, 496, 508.
68. Toland, 510.
69. John Toland, 515.
70. John Toland, 516.
71. Trefalt, "The Battle of Saipan in Japanese Civilian Memoirs: Non-combatants, Soldiers and the Complexities of Surrender," *The Journal of Pacific History* 53, no. 3 (2018): 256.
72. Japan Broadcasting Corporation, Nippon Hoso Kyokai, NHK, directed by Yasuhiro Miyamoto and Naoki Yonemoto, *The Pacific War: Despair on the Battlefield*, Documentary, Japan, NHK, 2013.
73. Ray E. Boomhower, *Dispatches from the Pacific: The World War II Reporting of Robert L. Sherrod* (Bloomington, Indiana: Indiana University Press, 2017), 14.
74. Sherrod, *On to Westward*, 145.
75. Sherrod, 145–147.
76. Sherrod, 147.
77. Sherrod, 147.
78. Sherrod, 150.
79. Holland M. Smith and Percy Finch, *Coral and Brass* (New York: Charles Scribner's Sons, 1949), 200.
80. Smith and Finch, *Coral and Brass*, 210–211.
81. Meehl, *One Marine's War*, 188; Goldberg, *D-Day in the Pacific*, 199.
82. Gabaldon, *Saipan*, 31.
83. Gabaldon, 64.
84. Gabaldon, 108.
85. Gabaldon, 109.
86. Gabaldon, 127.
87. National Park Service, Interview with Robert B. Sheeks.
88. Department of the Navy, NTLF, "Operations Report, Phase III (Tinian)," G-2 Report, 62.
89. Meehl, *One Marine's War*, 161.
90. Marine Corps Combat Correspondents, *Semper Fidelis: The U.S. Marines in the Pacific, 1942–1945* (New York: William Sloane Associates, 1947), 224.
91. Department of the Navy, NTLF, "Operations Report, Phase III (Tinian)," G-2 Report, 55.
92. Department of the Navy, NTLF, "Operations Report, Phase III (Tinian)," Translations of Propaganda used on Marianas Operation (Tinian), 2.
93. National Museum of the Pacific War, Interview with Jack Gilbreath.
94. Department of the Navy, NTLF, "Operations Report, Phase I (Saipan)," G-2 Report, 122.
95. Benjamin P. Hegi, "Extermination Warfare?," 110.
96. Sherrod, *On to Westward*, 15.
97. Department of the Navy, NTLF, "Operations Report, Phase III (Tinian)," Translations of Propaganda used on Marianas Operation (Tinian), 6.
98. Department of the Navy, Translations, 9.
99. Department of the Navy, Translations, 4.
100. Meehl, *One Marine's War*, 6–7, 167.
101. Department of the Navy, NTLF, "Operations Report Phase III (Tinian)," Mailbrief serial no. 00305-3, 3 August 1944.
102. National Park Service, Interview with Robert B. Sheeks.
103. Sheeks, "Civilians on Saipan," 111; United States Pacific Fleet and Pacific Ocean Areas, "Psychological Warfare, Part 1" (Pearl Harbor, Hawaii. United States Pacific Fleet and Pacific Ocean Areas, 1944), 6.
104. National Museum of the Pacific War, Interview with Charles Pase.
105. Meyers, "Japanese Civilians," 15.
106. Department of the Navy, NTLF, "Operations Report, Phase III (Tinian)," G-2 Report, 66.
107. Meehl, *One Marine's War*, 62.
108. Meehl, 167.
109. Meehl, 177.
110. Francis A. O'Brien, *Battling for Saipan* (New York: Ballantine Books, 2003), 316–317.
111. Meyers, "Japanese Civilians," 15.
112. South Sea Islands Album Publication Committee, *Japanese Pioneers' Achievements*, 22.
113. Chapin, *Breaching the Marianas*, 29.
114. Stott, *Saipan Under Fire*, 18.

Chapter 7

1. Alexie Villegas Zotomayor, "Tan Felisa's Story," *Marianas Variety*, Saipan, CNMI. March, 21, 2011.
2. Dower, *War Without Mercy*, 194–195, 238, 244.
3. Noriko T. Reider, *Japanese Demon Lore: Oni from Ancient Times to the Present* (Logan, Utah: Utah State University Press, 2010), 110.
4. Cook, *Japan at War*, 468.
5. Earhart, *Certain Victory*, 364.
6. Brown, *Nationalism in Japan*, 233.
7. Earhart, *Certain Victory*, 366.
8. Tuten-Puckett, "We Drank Our Tears," 86.
9. Petty, *Oral Histories*, 43.
10. Dower, *War Without Mercy*, 61.
11. Don Moore, "John Barrow saw Japanese women at Saipan throw babies off cliff then jump themselves," *Charlotte Sun*, December. 21, 2015.
12. Geoffrey C. Ward and Ken Burns, *The War: An Intimate History, 1941–1945* (New York: Alfred A. Knopf, 2007), 232–233.
13. Dower, *War Without Mercy*, 61–62.
14. Gavan Daws, *Prisoners of the Japanese: POWS of World War II in the Pacific* (New York: William Morrow and Company, 1994), 278.
15. Sloan, *Their Backs Against the Sea*, 143.
16. Petty, *Oral Histories*, 33.
17. Wissolik et al., *There Was a War*, 122.
18. Wissolik et al., 66.
19. Sheeks, "Civilians on Saipan," 111.
20. Meyers, "Japanese Civilians," 15.
21. Hegi, "Extermination Warfare?," 108 (Brigadier General Russell Lloyd, Letters, July 1944, Box 3, Personal Paper Collection, Marine Corps University Research Center).
22. Miller, "Beachhead Government," 44.
23. William McGaffin, "What the Japanese Civilian Fears Most," *Saturday Evening Post* 217, no. 16 (October 14, 1944): 35.
24. Bosse, "Polling Civilian Japanese," 179.
25. Department of the Navy, Office of the Military Governor for the Pacific Islands, Commander, Marianas Area; "Shinozuka Kichitaro, Civilian Internee Interrogation Report, Interrogation by G-2 Section, 5 Septem-

ber 1944, Headquarters 27th Infantry Division, A.P.P. 27"; Box 38: A1—A2 1944—A17—A19 1944, Record Group 313: Records of Naval Operating Forces; National Archives at College Park, Maryland.

26. Petty, *Oral Histories*, 26.

27. Jonathan Lewis, *Hell in the Pacific*, Documentary, United Kingdom, ITV Studios Global Entertainment, 2001.

28. Department of the Navy, NTLF, "Operations Report, Phase I (Saipan)," G-2 Report, 90.

29. Petty, *Oral Histories*, 140.

30. Petty, 18.

31. Petty, 50.

32. Sheeks, "Civilians on Saipan," 112.

33. Sheeks, 110–111.

34. Petty, *Oral Histories*, 26.

35. National Museum of the Pacific War, Interview with Edward Bale.

36. Marine Corps Combat Correspondents, *Semper Fidelis: The U.S. Marines in the Pacific, 1942–1945* (New York: William Sloane Associates, 1947), 224.

37. Mary Johann, "A Jap Jump Into Foxhole With Butler." *Des Moines Tribune*, November 7, 1944.

38. Department of the Navy, NTLF, "Operations Report, Phase III (Tinian)," G-2 Periodic Report no. 49, 3 August 1944, 1.

39. Meyers, "Japanese Civilians," 15.

40. Marine Corps Combat Correspondents, *Semper Fidelis: The U.S. Marines in the Pacific, 1942–1945* (New York: William Sloane Associates, 1947), 251.

41. Department of the Navy, NTLF, "Operations Report, Phase I (Saipan)," G-2 Report, 33.

42. Petty, *Oral Histories*, 39.

43. Tuten-Puckett, "We Drank Our Tears," 74.

44. Tuten-Puckett, 114.

45. Sherrod, *On to Westward*, 146.

46. National Museum of the Pacific War, Interview with Robert Montgomery.

47. Goldberg, *D-Day in the Pacific*, 202.

48. Gail Chatfield, *By Dammit, We're Marines!: Veterans' Stories of The Heroism, Horror, and Humor in World War II on The Pacific Front* (Paragould, Arkansas: Wyndham House, 2008), 63.

49. Wissolik et al., *There Was a War*, 66.

50. Wissolik et al., 415.

51. Veterans History Project, Central Connecticut State University, Interview with Albert A. D'Amico.

52. Stott, *Saipan Under Fire*, 20–21.

53. Department of the Navy, NTLF, "Operations Report, Phase III (Tinian)," G-2 Periodic Report no. 50, 4 August 1944, 1

54. National Museum of the Pacific War, Interview with Charles Pase.

55. David Dempsey, "Saipan Civilians Wailed As Japs Murdered Them in 'Cave of Horrors,'" *Des Moines Tribune*, July 17, 1944.

56. Department of the Navy, NTLF, "Operations Report, Phase III (Tinian)," G-2 Report, 51.

57. Department of the Navy, NTLF, "Operations Report, Phase III (Tinian)," G-2 Report, 53.

58. Hoffman, *Seizure of Tinian*, 119.

59. Beatrice Trefalt, "The Battle of Saipan in Japanese Civilian Memoirs: Non-combatants, Soldiers and the Complexities of Surrender," *The Journal of Pacific History* 53, no. 3 (2018): 263.

60. Jonathan Lewis, *Hell in the Pacific*, Documentary.

61. Chapin, *Breaching the Marianas*, 35.

62. Beatrice Trefalt, "Civilian Memoirs," 260.

63. Trefalt, "After the Battle," 341.

64. Don Jones, *Oba, The Last Samurai: Saipan 1944–45* (Novato, California: Presidio Press, 1986), 82–83.

65. Department of the Army, "Translation of the Diary of Japanese Serviceman Taroa Kawaguchi."

66. Westfall and Kimihira, *The Taking of Saipan*, 26.

67. Allison B. Gilmore, *You Can't Fight Tanks with Bayonets: Psychological Warfare against the Japanese Army in the Southwest Pacific* (Lincoln, Nebraska: University of Nebraska Press, 1998), 71.

68. Department of the Navy, NTLF, "Operations Report, Phase I (Saipan)," G-2 Report, 34.

69. Cook, *Japan at War*, 290–291

70. Graham, "48 Hours at Tinian," 127.

71. Japan Broadcasting Corporation, Nippon Hoso Kyokai, NHK, Directed by Seijo Naito, Hideki Yamagishi, and Izuru Yamamoto, *The Island of Death*, Iwo Jima Documentary, Japan, NHK, 2006.

72. Department of the Navy, NTLF, "Operations Report, Phase I (Saipan)," G-2 Report, 121.

73. Japan Broadcasting Corporation, *The Island of Death*, Documentary.

74. National Park Service, Interview with Robert B. Sheeks.

75. Matsumura and Wright, "Japanese Military Suicides," 1.

76. Ulrich Straus, *The Anguish of Surrender: Japanese POWs of World War II* (Seattle: University of Washington Press, 2003), 3.

77. Saburo Ienaga, *The Pacific War, 1931–1945* (New York: Pantheon Books, 1978), 49.

78. Gilmore, *Psychological Warfare*, 44–45.

79. Edward J. Drea, *In the Service of the Emperor: Essays on the Imperial Japanese Army* (University of Nebraska Press: Lincoln, Nebraska, 1998), 80.

80. Beatrice Trefalt, "Fanaticism, Japanese soldiers and the Pacific War, 1937–45," in *Fanaticism and Conflict in the Modern Age* (New York: Frank Cass, 2005), 40.

81. Shizuoka Broadcasting System, SBS, Directed by Tatsuya Kishimoto, *Message from a Japanese Soldier*, Iwo Jima Documentary, Japan, SBS, 2009.

82. Straus, *The Anguish of Surrender*, 83–84.

83. Cook, *Japan at War*, 289.

84. Karen Ann Takizawa, "War Stories (1): The Battle of Saipan (June 15-July+α, 1944)," *Honsei Journal of Sociology and Social Sciences* 59.1, 211 (2012): 7.

85. Takizawa, 15.

86. John Orbell and Tomonori Morikawa, "An Evolutionary Account of Suicide Attacks: The Kamikaze Case," *Political Psychology* 32, no. 2 (2011): 297–322.

87. Beatrice Trefalt, "The Battle of Saipan in Japanese Civilian Memoirs: Non-combatants, Soldiers and the Complexities of Surrender," *The Journal of Pacific History* 53, no. 3 (2018): 261.

88. Trefalt, 261.

89. Earhart, *Certain Victory*, 156.

90. Department of the Army, "Translation of the Diary of Japanese Serviceman Taroa Kawaguchi."

91. Akiko Takenaka, *Yasukuni Shrine: History, Memory, and Japan's Unending Postwar* (Honolulu: University of Hawaii Press, 2015), 11–12.

92. Gilmore, *Psychological Warfare*, 3, 62.

93. Elrod, *Guadalcanal, Tarawa, and Saipan*, 230.

94. Petty, *Oral Histories*, 104.

95. Wissolik et al., *There Was a War*, 63.

96. Veterans History Project, Interview with George John Dorko.

97. Department of the Navy, NTLF, "Operations Report, Phase I (Saipan)," G-2 Report, 90.

98. Gilmore, *Psychological Warfare*, 137.

99. Oleg Benesch, *Inventing the Way of the Samurai: Nationalism, Internationalism, and Bushido in Modern Japan* (Oxford, United Kingdom: Oxford University Press, 2014), 208.
100. Rees, *Horror in the East*, Documentary.
101. Rees, Documentary.
102. Rees, Documentary.
103. Directors System Co., directed by Minoru Matsui, *Riben Guizi*, Documentary, Directors System Co., Japan, 2001.
104. Jonathan Lewis, *Hell in the Pacific*, Documentary.
105. Beatrice Trefalt, "The Battle of Saipan in Japanese Civilian Memoirs: Non-combatants, Soldiers and the Complexities of Surrender," *The Journal of Pacific History* 53, no. 3 (2018): 258.
106. Laurence Rees, *Horror in the East*, Book (London: BBC Worldwide, 2001), 29.
107. Rees, *Horror in the East*, Book, 38.
108. Beatrice Trefalt, "The Battle of Saipan in Japanese Civilian Memoirs: Non-combatants, Soldiers and the Complexities of Surrender," The Journal of Pacific History 53, no. 3 (2018): 256, 263.
109. Directors System Co, *Riben Guizi*, Documentary.
110. Dower, *War Without Mercy*, 231
111. Samuel Hideo Yamashita, *Leaves from an Autumn of Emergencies: Selections from the Wartime Diaries of Ordinary Japanese* (Honolulu: University of Hawaii Press, 2005), 28.
112. Ohnuki-Tierney, *Kamikaze, Cherry Blossoms*, 133.
113. Samuel Eliot Morison, *Aleutians, Gilberts and Marshalls, June 1942-April 1944*, Volume VII of "History of United States Naval Operations in World War II," (Boston: Little, Brown and Company, 1951), 50.
114. Ohnuki-Tierney, *Kamikaze, Cherry Blossoms*, 114–115.
115. Earhart, *Certain Victory*, 393.
116. Cook, "Turning Women into Weapons," 250.
117. Noriko Kawamura, *Emperor Hirohito and The Pacific War* (Seattle: University of Washington Press, 2015), 128.
118. Japan Broadcasting Corporation, *Despair on the Battlefield*, Documentary.
119. Imaizumi, "Mobilization and Perspectives," 6.
120. Department of the Navy, NTLF, "Operations Report, Phase III (Tinian)," G-2 Report, 43.
121. Department of the Navy, NTLF, "Operations Report Phase III (Tinian)," G-2 Report, Leaflet no. 4.
122. Toland, *The Rising Sun*, 511.
123. George Carroll Dyer, *The Amphibians Came to Conquer: The Story of Admiral Richmond Kelly Turner* (Washington, D.C.: Government Printing Office, 1972), 922–923.
124. Ota Masahide, "Ryukyu Shimpo, Ota Masahide, Mark Ealey and Alastair McLauchlan, Descent into Hell: The Battle of Okinawa," *The Asia-Pacific Journal* 12, Issue 48, no. 4 (2014): 7.
125. Tanaka, Yuki, *Hidden Horrors: Japanese War Crimes in World War II* (Boulder, Colorado: Westview Press, 1996), 9.

Chapter 8

1. Sheeks, "Civilians on Saipan," 112.
2. Department of the Navy, NTLF, "Operations Report, Phase I (Saipan)," G-2 Report, 112.
3. Tampa Morning Tribune, "A Message on War," *Tampa Morning Tribune*, August 7, 1944.
4. Marine Corps Combat Correspondents, *Semper Fidelis: The U.S. Marines in the Pacific, 1942–1945* (New York: William Sloane Associates, 1947), 224–225.
5. Department of the Navy, NTLF, "Operations Report, Phase I (Saipan)," G-2 Report, 17.
6. Asahi Shimbun, *Senso: The Japanese Remember the Pacific War; Letters to the Editor of Asahi Shimbun*, Expanded Edition, ed. Frank Gibney, trans. by Beth Cary (New York: Routledge, 2015), 101.
7. Sheeks, "Civilians on Saipan," 112.
8. National Park Service, Interview with Robert B. Sheeks.
9. Maria Angelica Salaberria, *A Time of Agony: The War in the Pacific in Saipan, The Personal Account of Sister Maria Angelica Salaberria*, 1944, Reprint, trans. by Marjorie G. Driver and Omaira Brunal-Perry (Saipan: Committee on the Commemoration of the 50th Anniversary of World War II, 1994), 22.
10. Department of the Navy, NTLF, "Operations Report, Phase III (Tinian)," G-2 Report, 44.
11. Irving Schlossenberg, "Jap Civilians on Tinian Surrender After Promised Water by Marines," *Harrisburg Telegraph*, Dec 23, 1944.
12. Salaberria, *A Time of Agony*, 22.
13. Chapin, *Breaching the Marianas*, 15.
14. Campbell, *The Color of War*, 227.
15. Petty, *Oral Histories*, 50.
16. Tuten-Puckett, "We Drank Our Tears," 26.
17. Bright, *Pain and Purpose*, 104.
18. Tuten-Puckett, "We Drank Our Tears," 140.
19. Tuten-Puckett, 192.
20. Sherrod, *On to Westward*, 71; Gabaldon, *Saipan*, 92.
21. Petty, *Oral Histories*, 23.
22. Petty, 32.
23. Howard Handleman, "Dying Jap Girl is Rushed to Hospital," *Moline Daily Dispatch* (Moline, Illinois), July 15, 1944.
24. Stott, *Saipan Under Fire*, 4.
25. Department of the Navy, NTLF, "Operations Report, Phase III (Tinian)," G-2 Report, 43–44; Hoffman, *Seizure of Tinian*, 138.
26. Chapin, *Breaching the Marianas*, 19.
27. Bright, *Pain and Purpose*, 64.
28. Josh McAuliffe, "South Scranton man saw horrors of World War II treating wounded Marines in Pacific Theater," *The Times-Tribune* (Scranton, Pennsylvania), May 26, 2013.
29. Department of the Navy, NTLF, "Operations Report, Phase I (Saipan)," G-2 Report, 37.
30. Department of the Navy, NTLF, "Operations Report, Phase I (Saipan)," G-2 Report, 39.
31. Gaffney Ledger Staff, "Randolph Sees Many Dead Japs on Saipan Isle," *The Gaffney Ledger* (Gaffney, South Carolina), August 1, 1944.
32. Cook, *Japan at War*, 288.
33. Petty, *Oral Histories*, 51.
34. Asahi Shimbun, *Senso*, 101.
35. Rogal, *A Mud Marine's Memoir*, 168.
36. Goldberg, *D-Day in the Pacific*, 134.
37. Goldberg, 134.
38. National Museum of the Pacific War, Interview with Arwin J. Bowden.
39. Department of the Navy, NTLF, "Operations Report, Phase I (Saipan)," G-2 Report, 34.
40. National Museum of the Pacific War, Interview with George Gray.
41. Petty, *Oral Histories*, 107.
42. Veterans History Project, Interview with George John Dorko.

43. Department of the Navy, NTLF, "Operations Report, Phase I (Saipan)," G-2 Periodic Report no. 28, 13 July 1944, 1.
44. Marine Corps Combat Correspondents, *Semper Fidelis: The U.S. Marines in the Pacific, 1942–1945* (New York: William Sloane Associates, 1947), 224.
45. National Museum of the Pacific War, Interview with Jack Gilbreath.
46. National Museum of the Pacific War, Interview with Burnes R. "B.R."
47. Rogal, *A Mud Marine's Memoir*, 172–173.
48. Department of the Navy, NTLF, "Operations Report, Phase III (Tinian)," G-2 Periodic Report no. 50, 4 August 1944, 1.
49. Meehl, *One Marine's War*, 127.
50. Goldberg, *D-Day in the Pacific*, 137.
51. Chatfield, *By Dammit, We're Marines!*, 63.
52. Roush, *Open Fire!*, 492.
53. Stott, *Saipan Under Fire*, 16.
54. Second Armored Amphibian Battalion Association, *2nd Armored Amphibian Battalion*, 161.
55. National Museum of the Pacific War, Interview with Warren S. Adams.
56. Gabaldon, *Saipan*, 94–95.
57. Tuten-Puckett, "We Drank Our Tears," 141.
58. Goetzfridt, *Guahan*, 56.
59. Daws, *Prisoners of the Japanese*, 278, 429.
60. National Park Service, Interview with Robert B. Sheeks.
61. Rosario and Takeuchi, "Saipanese Recall a Day," 57–58.
62. Department of War, Office of the Director of Intelligence (G-2); "Project 1055, Behavior of Japanese Civilian Population on Saipan"; 10 November 1944; Record Group 165: Records of the War Department General and Special Staffs; National Archives at College Park, Maryland; 2.
63. Department of the Navy, NTLF, "Operations Report, Phase I (Saipan)," G-2 Periodic Report no. 13, Phase (I) Saipan, 28 June 1944. 2.
64. G-2 Periodic Report no. 16, 1 July 1944, 2.
65. G-2 Periodic Report no. 30, 15 July 1944, 1.
66. G-2 Periodic Report no. 31, 16 July 1944, 1.
67. G-2 Periodic Report no. 38, 23 July 1944, 1.
68. Associated Press Article, "Japanese Girl Had Grenades in Bloomers," *Amarillo Daily News*, August 9, 1944.
69. Department of the Navy, NTLF, "Operations Report, Phase III (Tinian)," G-3 Periodic Report no. 38, 22 July 1944, 2.
70. Department of the Navy, NTLF, "Operations Report, Phase III (Tinian)," Daily Dispatch Summary Mailbrief for Tinian, 8 August 1944.
71. Department of the Navy, NTLF, "Operations Report, Phase III (Tinian)," G-2 Periodic Report no. 55, 9 August 1944, 1.
72. Goldberg, *D-Day in the Pacific*, 195.
73. Henry Berry, *Semper Fi, Mac: Living Memories of the U.S. Marines in World War II* (New York: Arbor House, 1982), 210.
74. New York State Military Museum, Interview with Joseph J. Meighan.
75. Benjamin P. Hegi, "Extermination Warfare?," 101 (Brigadier General Russell Lloyd, Letters, July 1944, Box 3, Personal Paper Collection, Marine Corps University Research Center).
76. Wissolik et al., *There Was a War*, 415.
77. Wissolik et al., 66.
78. New York State Military Museum, Interview with Gabriel J. Vertucci.
79. Roush, *Open Fire!*, 524.
80. Sherrod, *On to Westward*, 149.
81. Sherrod, 113.
82. The Veteran Voices of Pittsburgh Oral History Initiative, Interview with Bob Williams.
83. Berry, *Semper Fi, Mac*, 210.
84. Second Marine Division, "Saipan" (HM9-16), 2.
85. Gabaldon, *Saipan*, 85.
86. Gabaldon, 86.
87. Department of the Navy, NTLF, "Operations Report, Phase I (Saipan)," G-2 Report, 58; Department of the Navy, NTLF, "Operations Report, Phase I (Saipan)," G-3 Report, 22; Crowl, *Campaign in the Marianas*, 257.
88. Hoffman, *Seizure of Tinian*, 12.
89. Crowl, *Campaign in the Marianas*, 258.
90. Hoffman, *Saipan*, 223.
91. New York State Military Museum, Interview with Joseph J. Meighan.
92. New York State Military Museum, Interview with Samuel Rocco Dinovk.
93. Goldberg, *D-Day in the Pacific*, 190.
94. O'Brien, *Battling for Saipan*, 310–311.
95. Meehl, *One Marine's War*, 5–6, 163.
96. Department of the Navy, NTLF, "Operations Report Phase I (Saipan)," Administrative Orders 3-44 through 4-44, Enclosure (A), Appendix #1 to Annex Dog to Northern Troops and Landing Force Administrative Order Number 3-44, 1 May 1944, 2-4.
97. Elrod, *Guadalcanal, Tarawa, and Saipan*, 231.
98. Jones, *Oba*, 32.
99. Jones, 33.
100. Jones, 35.
101. Jones, 127.
102. Jones, 131.
103. Jones, 191.
104. Jones, 215.
105. Goldberg, *D-Day in the Pacific*, 81.
106. Department of the Navy, NTLF, "Operations Report, Phase I (Saipan)," G-2 Periodic Report no. 18, 3 July 1944, 2.
107. New York State Military Museum, Interview with Joseph J. Meighan.
108. Tuten-Puckett, "We Drank Our Tears," 32.
109. Dower, *War Without Mercy*, 67.
110. Hoffman, *Seizure of Tinian*, 220.
111. Veterans History Project, Central Connecticut State University, Interview with Edwin P. DesRosiers.
112. Second Marine Division, "Saipan" (HM9-16), 2.
113. Meehl, *One Marine's War*, 174.
114. Meehl, 188.
115. Petty, *Oral Histories*, 140.
116. McGaffin, "What the Japanese Civilian Fears Most," 35.
117. Department of the Navy, Office of the Military Governor for the Pacific Islands, Commander, Marianas Area, Headquarters Camp Susupe; "Camp Susupe Duty Assignments, 15 November 1944"; Box 1: Administration 1944; Enclosure No. 2, CINCPAC Civil Affairs Section, Record Group 313: Records of Naval Operating Forces; National Archives at College Park, Maryland.
118. Dorothy E. Richard, *United States Naval Administration of the Trust Territory of the Pacific Islands*, Volume I: *The Wartime Military Government Period, 1942–1945* (Washington, D.C.: Office of the Chief of Naval Operations, 1957), 472.
119. Embree, "Military Government," 13.
120. Chicago Tribune, "Tribune Writer Tells Lessons of Pacific War," *Chicago Tribune*, December 8, 1944.

121. Wisconsin Veterans Museum Research Center, Interview with Halley Young.
122. Alastair A. McLauchlan, "War Crimes and Crimes Against Humanity on Okinawa: Guilt on Both Sides," *Journal of Military Ethics* 13, no. 4 (2014): 364–365.
123. Tanaka, *Japan's Comfort Women*, 110–112; George Feifer, *Tennozan: The Battle of Okinawa and the Atomic Bomb* (New York: Ticknor & Fields, 1992), 178; Gavan McCormack and Satoko Oka Norimatsu, *Resistant Islands: Okinawa Confronts Japan and the United States* (New York: Rowman & Littlefield Publishers, 2012), 24, 28–29.
124. Jonathan Lewis, *Hell in the Pacific*, Documentary.
125. Goldberg, *D-Day in the Pacific*, 125.
126. Elrod, *Guadalcanal, Tarawa, and Saipan*, 220.
127. Petty, *Oral Histories*, 53.
128. Gabaldon, *Saipan*, 86.
129. Chapin, *Breaching the Marianas*, 17–18.
130. Petty, *Oral Histories*, 1.
131. Sims, *Veterans Remembrances*, 1985.
132. Sloan, *Their Backs Against the Sea*, 141.
133. Ladd and Weingartner, *Faithful Warriors*, 226.
134. Department of the Navy, NTLF, "Operations Report Phase I (Saipan)," Narrative of Assault on Saipan, 26.
135. Roush, *Open Fire!*, 454.
136. Petty, *Oral Histories*, 47.
137. Veterans History Project, Interview with William B. Hoover.
138. W. Eugene Smith, *W. Eugene Smith: His Photographs and Notes* (New York: Aperture Foundation, 1993), 11.
139. W. Eugene Smith, 12.
140. National Museum of the Pacific War, Interview with Charles Pase.
141. Petty, *Oral Histories*, 129.
142. Petty, 32.
143. Campbell, *The Color of War*, 237.
144. O'Brien, *Battling for Saipan*, 315.
145. Patrick O'Day and Nicole Vernon, "The Archaeology of Landscape Transformation in Colonization and Conflict: Historic Japanese Cultural Resources of the Carolinas Heights Region of Tinian Island, Commonwealth of the Northern Marianas Islands," *Pan-Japan* 11, no. 1 & 2 (2015): 16.
146. Brooks E. Kleber and Dale Birdsell, *The Chemical Warfare Service: Chemicals in Combat*, The Technical Services, "United States Army in World War II" Series (Washington, D.C.: Office of the Chief of Military History, Department of the Army, 1966), 560–562.
147. Petty, *Oral Histories*, 20.
148. Tuten-Puckett, "We Drank Our Tears," 190.
149. Goldberg, *D-Day in the Pacific*, 125.
150. Meehl, *One Marine's War*, 173.
151. Crowl, *Campaign in the Marianas*, 288.
152. Feifer, *Tennozan*, 446.
153. Petty, *Oral Histories*, 51; Campbell, *The Color of War*, 266.
154. Elrod, *Guadalcanal, Tarawa, and Saipan*, 229.
155. New York State Military Museum, Interview with Joseph P. Fiore.
156. National Museum of the Pacific War, Interview with Jack Gilbreath.
157. Holiday and McPherson, *Under the Eagle*, 138.
158. Rogal, *A Mud Marine's Memoir*, 155–156.
159. American Memorial Park, U.S. National Park Service, Visitor Center Exhibit, Garapan, Saipan, CNMI.
160. Takizawa, "Battle of Saipan," 8.
161. Petty, *Oral Histories*, 21.
162. Lily Rothman and Liz Ronk, "What One Photographer Saw at the Battle of Saipan," *Time*, June 15, 2016.
163. Daily Herald Staff, "First Aid Men on Tinian Take Care of Natives too," *Daily Herald* (Provo, Utah), September 11, 1944.
164. Petty, *Oral Histories*, 51.
165. Ladd and Weingartner, *Faithful Warriors*, 149.
166. Crowl, *Campaign in the Marianas*, 141.
167. Stott, *Saipan Under Fire*, 4.
168. Sloan, *Their Backs Against the Sea*, 220.
169. Department of the Navy, NTLF, "Operations Report Phase III (Tinian)," G-2 Report, Leaflet no. 3.
170. Petty, *Oral Histories*, 23.
171. Petty, 23.
172. Tuten-Puckett, "We Drank Our Tears," 8–11.
173. Petty, *Oral Histories*, 30.
174. Petty, 38.
175. Sherrod, *On to Westward*, 72.
176. Department of the Navy, NTLF, "Operations Report, Phase I (Saipan)," G-2 Periodic Report no. 39, 24 July 1944, 1.
177. Beatrice Trefalt, "The Battle of Saipan in Japanese Civilian Memoirs: Non-combatants, Soldiers and the Complexities of Surrender," *The Journal of Pacific History* 53, no. 3 (2018): 258.
178. Sherrod, *On to Westward*, 25.
179. Robert B Sheeks, "Civilians on Saipan," *Far Eastern Survey* 14, no. 9 (1945): 110.
180. Department of the Navy, NTLF, "Operations Report Phase III (Tinian)," G-2 Report, Leaflet no. 3.
181. Trefalt, "After the Battle," 340.
182. Trefalt, 341.
183. Tuten-Puckett, "We Drank Our Tears," 2–4.
184. Tuten-Puckett, 14–21.

Chapter 9

1. Richard, *United States Naval Administration*, Volume I, 429.
2. Military Government Section, United States Navy, *Camp Susupe: A Photographic Record of The Operation of Military Government on Saipan*, June 1944 to December 1945, United States Naval Military Government on Saipan, Navy Number 3245 (Saipan Island, Marianas Islands), FPO San Francisco, 1945, 1.
3. Department of the Navy, NTLF, "Operations Report, Phase I (Saipan)," Civil Affairs Report, 6.
4. Richard, *United States Naval Administration*, Volume I, 170.
5. Richard, 169.
6. Richard, 170.
7. Richard, 432–433.
8. Richard, 173, 431.
9. Embree, "Military Government," 4.
10. Richard, *United States Naval Administration*, Volume I, 539.
11. Meller, *Saipan's Camp Susupe*, 15.
12. Richard, *United States Naval Administration*, Volume I, 453.
13. Department of the Navy, NTLF, "Operations Report, Phase I (Saipan)," Narrative of Assault on Saipan, 35.
14. Richard, *United States Naval Administration*, Volume I, 181–182.
15. Richard, 435.
16. Richard, 177, 435.

17. Richard, 308.
18. Richard, 308.
19. Richard, 258, 565.
20. Richard, 537.
21. Department of the Navy, NTLF, "Operations Report, Phase I (Saipan)," Civil Affairs Report, 2.
22. Department of the Navy, NTLF, "Operations Report, Phase I (Saipan)," Narrative of Assault on Saipan, 34.
23. Embree, "Military Government," 5.
24. Department of the Navy, NTLF, "Operations Report, Phase I (Saipan)," G-1 Report, 9.
25. Camacho, *Cultures of Commemoration*, 71.
26. National Museum of the Pacific War, Interview with Charles Pase.
27. Richard, *United States Naval Administration*, Volume I, 556.
28. Department of the Navy, NTLF, "Operations Report, Phase I (Saipan)," Civil Affairs Report, 3.
29. Meller, *Saipan's Camp Susupe*, 37.
30. Sherrod, *On to Westward*, 70.
31. Schlossenberg, "Jap Civilians on Tinian."
32. Petty, *Oral Histories*, 50–51.
33. Department of the Navy, Office of the Military Governor for the Pacific Islands, Commander, Marianas Area; "Standard Operating Procedure for Civilian Control, November 1944"; Box 38, Record Group 313: Records of Naval Operating Forces; National Archives at College Park, Maryland; 5.
34. Embree, "Military Government," 6; Department of the Navy, Office of the Military Governor for the Pacific Islands, Commander, Marianas Area; "Saipan-Military Government (Civil Administration)-Report for month of May 1945, 1 June 1945"; Box 40, Group 313: Records of Naval Operating Forces; National Archives at College Park, Maryland.
35. Department of the Navy, NTLF, "Operations Report, Phase I (Saipan)," Civil Affairs Report, 4.
36. Department of the Navy, Office of the Military Governor for the Pacific Islands, Commander, Marianas Area; "Summary of Military Government Matters, Marianas, Period: 4–17, February 1945"; Box 40, Record Group 313: Records of Naval Operating Forces; National Archives at College Park, Maryland.
37. Meller, *Saipan's Camp Susupe*, 32.
38. Department of the Navy, Office of the Military Governor for the Pacific Islands, Commander, Marianas Area; "Marianas Operation, Subject Report of Civil Affairs, 28 August 1944"; Box 1: Administration 1944, Record Group 313: Records of Naval Operating Forces; National Archives at College Park, Maryland.
39. Petty, *Oral Histories*, 20.
40. Petty, 38.
41. Petty, 24.
42. Military Government Section, United States Navy, *Camp* Susupe, 21–22.; Richard, *United States Naval Administration*, Volume I, 438–439.
43. Military Government Section, 19.
44. Embree, "Military Government," 9.
45. Tuten-Puckett, "We Drank Our Tears," 149.
46. Embree, "Military Government," 9.
47. Embree, 31.
48. Richard W. Johnston, United Press, "Numbed Natives Glad to Get Out of Saipan Caves," *Medford Mail Tribune*, August 18, 1944.
49. Associated Press, William Worden, "Youngsters Play but Internment Camp is a Tragic Scene of Human Misery." *The Abilene Reporter News* (Abilene, Texas), August 10, 1944.

50. Department of the Navy, Office of the Military Governor for the Pacific Islands, "Marianas Operation, Subject Report of Civil Affairs, 28 August 1944."
51. Department of the Navy, NTLF, "Operations Report, Phase I (Saipan)," 34.
52. Department of the Navy, NTLF, "Operations Report, Phase I (Saipan)," Medical Report, 11.
53. Department of the Navy, 19.
54. Department of the Navy, NTLF, "Operations Report, Phase III (Tinian)," Medical Report, 6.
55. Department of the Navy, NTLF, "Operations Report, Phase I (Saipan)," Narrative of Assault on Saipan, 34; Department of the Navy, NTLF, "Operations Report, Phase I (Saipan)," Medical Report, 2.
56. Lawrence A. Marsden, *Attack Transport: The Story of the U.S.S Doyen* (Minneapolis, Minnesota: University of Minnesota Press, 1946), 100.
57. Department of the Navy, NTLF, "Operations Report, Phase I (Saipan)," Medical Report, 6.
58. Richard, *United States Naval Administration*, Volume I, 568.
59. Department of the Navy, NTLF, "Operations Report Phase I (Saipan)," Narrative of Assault on Saipan, 34.
60. Richard, *United States Naval Administration*, Volume I, 482.
61. Department of the Navy, Office of the Military Governor for the Pacific Islands, Commander, Marianas Area; "First endorsement to Lt. Cdr. M.S. Buehler's Report of Observations in Forward Area, August 25 1944"; Box 38, Record Group 313: Records of Naval Operating Forces; National Archives at College Park, Maryland.
62. Meller, *Saipan's Camp Susupe*, 84.
63. Richard, *United States Naval Administration*, Volume I, 485.
64. Second Marine Division, "Saipan" (HM9-16), 14.
65. Department of the Navy, Office of the Military Governor for the Pacific Islands, Commander, Marianas Area; "Memorandum. Comments and Recommendations on Civil Affairs Based on Experience on Saipan and Tinian. 30 August 1944"; Box 38: A1—A2 1944—A17—A19 1944, Group 313: Records of Naval Operating Forces; National Archives at College Park, Maryland.
66. N.B. Kurnick, "War Edema in the Civilian Population of Saipan," *Annals of Internal Medicine* 28, no. 4 (1948): 784.
67. Petty, *Oral Histories*, 21.
68. Richard, *United States Naval Administration*, Volume I, 478.
69. Miller, "Beachhead Government," 42.
70. Stott, *Saipan Under Fire*, 12.
71. Stott, 12.
72. Wissolik et al., *There Was a War*, 122.
73. Embree, "Military Government," 9
74. Embree, 22.
75. Meller, *Saipan's Camp Susupe*, 20.
76. Embree, "Military Government," 31.
77. Meller, *Saipan's Camp Susupe*, 34.
78. Richard, *United States Naval Administration*, Volume I, 439.
79. Richard, 177, 441.
80. Department of the Navy, NTLF, "Operations Report Phase I (Saipan)," Administrative Orders 3-44 through 4-44, Enclosure (A), Appendix #1 to Annex Dog to Northern Troops and Landing Force Administrative Order Number 3-44, 1 May 1944, 5.
81. Richard, *United States Naval Administration*, Volume I, 567.
82. Rex Alan Smith and Gerald A. Meehl, *Pacific War*

Stories: In the Words of Those Who Survived (New York: Abbeville Press, 2004), 194.
83. Tuten-Puckett, "We Drank Our Tears," 108.
84. Meller, *Saipan's Camp Susupe*, 39.
85. Schlossenberg, "Jap Civilians on Tinian."

Chapter 10

1. Sherrod, *On to Westward*, 25.
2. Iitaka, "Remembering Nanyo from Okinawa," 131; Bōeichō Bōeikenshūjyo Senshishitsu: Senshi shōsho: Chūbu Taiheiyō rikugun sakusen (War history series: Japanese army operations in the Central Pacific area), vol. 1, Mariana gyokusai made (Fight to the death in the Marianas) (Tokyo: Asagumo Shinbun Sha, 1967), 508.
3. Toland, *The Rising Sun*, 519.
4. Richard Harwood, *A Close Encounter: The Marine Landing on Tinian* (Washington, D.C.: Marine Corps Historical Center, 1994), 29.
5. Higuchi, *Japanese Administration of Guam*, 112.
6. Higuchi, 120.
7. Higuchi, *Micronesia*, 64.
8. Imaizumi, "Mobilization and Perspectives," 8.
9. Department of the Navy, NTLF, "Operations Report Phase I (Saipan)," Civil Affairs Report, 3; Department of the Navy, NTLF, "Operations Report, Phase III (Tinian)," G-2 Periodic Report no. 49, 3 August 1944, 4.
10. Imaizumi, "Mobilization and Perspectives," 7.
11. George W. Garand and Truman R. Strobridge, *Western Pacific Operations*, Volume IV of "History of U.S. Marine Corps Operations in World War II," (Washington, D.C.: Government Printing Office, 1971), 445, 453; Imaizumi, "Mobilization and Perspectives," 6–7.
12. Crowl, *Campaign in the Marianas*, 120.
13. Cook, "Turning Women into Weapons," 251.
14. United States Strategic Bombing Survey (Pacific), *The Campaigns of the Pacific War*, 212.
15. Petty, *Oral Histories*, 41.
16. Petty, 26.
17. Department of the Navy, Office of the Chief of Naval Operations, "Memorandum, Report of Surrender and Occupation of Japan, Cincpac Confidential ltr. A6-5, Serial 0396, 11 February 1946, Commander in Chief, U.S. Pacific Fleet and Pacific Ocean Areas," Washington, D.C.: Department of the Navy, Office of the Chief of Naval Operations, 9 May 1946, 177.
18. Crowl, *Campaign in the Marianas*, 55; Department of the Navy, CINCPAC-CINCPOA Translations, "5th Special Base Force (Saipan) Situation Report."
19. Department of the Navy, NTLF, "Operations Report, Phase III (Tinian)," G-2 Periodic Report no. 48, 2 August 1944, 3.
20. Department of the Navy, NTLF, "Operations Report, Phase I (Saipan)," Civil Affairs Report, 3.
21. Department of the Navy, Office of the Chief of Naval Operations, "Memorandum, Report of Surrender and Occupation of Japan, Cincpac Confidential ltr. A6-5, Serial 0396, 11 February 1946, Commander in Chief, U.S. Pacific Fleet and Pacific Ocean Areas," Washington, D.C.: Department of the Navy, Office of the Chief of Naval Operations, 9 May 1946, 209.
22. Department of the Navy, "Memorandum, Report of Surrender and Occupation," 210.
23. Dorothy E. Richard, *United States Naval Administration of the Trust Territory of the Pacific Islands*, Volume II: *The Postwar Military Government Era, 1945–1947* (Washington, D.C.: Office of the Chief of Naval Operations, 1957), 22.
24. Richard, *United States Naval Administration*, Volume I, 444.
25. Hoffman, *Seizure of Tinian*, 7.
26. These numbers are approximations and do not factor in infant births and deaths after the censuses were taken. Furthermore, different numbers would be obtained based on the data provided by historian Yumiko Imaizumi. According to Imaizumi, there were 37,540 Japanese residents (24,761 on Saipan and 12,779 on Tinian) on the islands after the evacuations. It is unclear whether these figures included the Koreans on the islands.
27. Department of the Interior, National Park Service, "Marianas Memorial," https://www.nps.gov/amme/learn/historyculture/upload/Marianas-Memorial-Listing.pdf
28. Robert Trumbull, "Japanese Expect to Win, Poll Finds," *New York Times*, February 16, 1945.
29. National Park Service, Interview with Robert B. Sheeks.
30. Sherrod, *On to Westward*, 25.
31. Embree, "Military Government," 5.
32. Bosse, "Polling Civilian Japanese," 177.

Conclusion

1. Petty, *Oral Histories*, 21.
2. South Sea Islands Album Publication Committee, *Japanese Pioneers' Achievements*, 2
3. Beatrice Trefalt, "The Battle of Saipan in Japanese Civilian Memoirs: Non-combatants, Soldiers and the Complexities of Surrender," *The Journal of Pacific History* 53, no. 3 (2018): 260.
4. Cook, "Turning Women into Weapons," 254.
5. Cook, 240.
6. Yamashita, *Autumn of Emergencies*, 85.
7. Cook, "Turning Women into Weapons," 242.
8. Cook, 243.
9. Cook, 242.
10. Cook, 242.
11. Cook, 242.
12. Cook, 246.
13. Cook, 245, 257.
14. Cook, 246–247.
15. Rees, *Horror in the East*, Documentary.
16. Serge Viallet, *Kizu: The Untold Story of Unit 731*, Documentary, France: Marathon Media Group, 2004.
17. Earhart, *Certain Victory*, 399–400.
18. Imaizumi, "Mobilization and Perspectives," 13.
19. Porter, *Japanese Reflections*, 68–69.
20. Keiichiro Hoshino, "Okinawa man credits mother with saving family from WWII mass suicide," *The Japan Times*, May 15, 2015; McCormack and Norimatsu, *Resistant Islands*, 24–27; Matthew Allen, "A Story That Won't Fade Away: Compulsory Mass Suicide in the Battle of Okinawa," *The Asia-Pacific Journal: Japan Focus*, July 12, 2007.
21. Aniya Masaaki, "Compulsory Mass Suicide, the Battle of Okinawa, and Japan's Textbook Controversy," *The Asia-Pacific Journal: Japan Focus* 6, Issue 1 (January 2008): 1–13; Steve Rabson, "The Politics of Trauma: Compulsory Suicides During the Battle of Okinawa and Postwar Retrospective," *Intersections: Gender and Sexuality in Asia and the Pacific*, Issue 24 (June 2010); McCormack and Norimatsu, *Resistant Islands*, 31–34.
22. Matsumura and Wright, "Japanese Military Suicides," 3.
23. Satoshi, Kamata, "Shattering Jewels: 110,000 Okinawans Protest Japanese State Censorship of Compulsory Group Suicides," *The Asia-Pacific Journal: Japan*

Focus 6, Issue 1 (January 2008); McCormack and Norimatsu, *Resistant Islands*, 33.

24. *The Penguin Book of Japanese Verse*, trans. by Geoffrey Bownas and Anthony Thwaite (Baltimore, Maryland: Penguin Books, 1964), 197.

25. United States Strategic Bombing Survey, *The Effects of Bombing on Health and Medical Services in Japan*, Medical Division, Dates of Survey: 24 October–31, November 1945 (Washington, D.C.: Government Printing Office, June 1947), 142.

26. United States Strategic Bombing Survey, *Effects of Incendiary Bomb Attacks on Japan: A Report on Eight Cities*, Dates of Survey: 3 October 1945–1, December 1945, Physical Damage Division (Washington, D.C.: Government Printing Office April, 1947), 2, 67.

27. United States Strategic Bombing Survey, 94, 102.

28. United States Strategic Bombing Survey, *Medical Services in Japan*, 156.

29. United States Strategic Bombing Survey, 157.

30. Crowl, *Campaign in the Marianas*, 1.

31. Spector, *Eagle Against the Sun*, xvi.

32. Benis M. Frank and Henry I. Shaw Jr., *Victory and Occupation*, Volume V of "History of U.S. Marine Corps Operations in World War II," (Washington, D.C.: Government Printing Office, 1968), 449.

33. Department of the Navy, "Memorandum, Report of Surrender and Occupation," 180.

34. Richard, *United States Naval Administration*, Volume II, 30.

35. Department of the Navy, "Memorandum, Report of Surrender and Occupation," 209; Richard, *United States Naval Administration*, Volume II, 38–39.

36. Richard, *United States Naval Administration*, Volume II, 30.

37. Watt, *When Empire Comes Home*, 66.

38. Watt, 73–74.

39. Watt, 18.

40. Watt, 10.

41. Manako Ogawa, *Sea of Opportunity: The Japanese Pioneers of the Fishing Industry in Hawaii* (Honolulu: University of Hawaii Press, 2015), 133.

42. Camacho, *Cultures of Commemoration*, 111.

43. Farrell, *Northern Mariana Islands*, 475.

44. Hal M. Friedman, *Creating an American Lake: United States Imperialism and Strategic Security in the Pacific Basin, 1945-1947* (Westport, Connecticut: Greenwood Press, 2001), xxv, 4, 143.

45. Friedman, xi.

46. Friedman, xii.

47. United Nations Security Council, "Security Council Resolution 21 (1947) on the Trusteeship Agreement for the Trust Territory of the Pacific Islands," Official Records, Second Year, no. 31, 124th Meeting. Lake Success, New York, 2 April 1947.

48. Poyer, Falgout, and Carucci, *Typhoon of War*, 276; Joseph and Murray, *Chamorros and Carolinians of Saipan*, 1.

49. Beatrice Trefalt, *Japanese Army Stragglers and Memories of the War in Japan, 1950–1975* (New York: RoutledgeCurzon, 2003), 61–63.

50. Farrell, *Northern Mariana Islands*, 505–507.

51. Higuchi, *Micronesians and the Pacific War*, 48.

52. Poyer, Falgout, and Carucci, *Typhoon of War*, 431.

53. Wakako Higuchi, "Japan and War Reparations in Micronesia," *The Journal of Pacific History* 30, no. 1 (1995): 97.

54. Frank Quimby, "Americanised, Decolonised, Globalised and Federalised: *The Northern Mariana Islands since 1978*," *The Journal of Pacific History* 48, no. 4 (2013): 466.

55. CNMI, Second Northern Marianas Constitutional Convention, 1985, "Proposed Constitutional Amendment no. 43," Saipan: CNMI, 1985.

56. Emmanuel T. Erediano, "Santos honors designer of original NMI flag," *Marianas Variety* (Saipan, CNMI), January 22, 2012.

57. Quimby, "Americanised, Decolonised, Globalised," 466.

58. Camacho, *Cultures of Commemoration*, 18.

59. Quimby, "Americanised, Decolonised, Globalised," 464.

60. Iitaka, "Remembering Nanyo from Okinawa," 126–127.

61. Iitaka, 131–132.

62. Iitaka, 138.

63. Beatrice Trefalt, "Collecting Bones: Japanese Missions for the Repatriation of War Remains, and the Unfinished Business of the Asia-Pacific War," *Australian Humanities Review* 61 (2017): 145.

64. Denfeld, "Korean Laborers in Micronesia," 14.

65. Marine Corps Combat Correspondents, *Semper Fidelis: The U.S. Marines in the Pacific, 1942–1945* (New York: William Sloane Associates, 1947), 224.

66. Rees, *Horror in the East*, Documentary.

67. Wissolik et al., *There Was a War*, 415.

68. Gregg Stoner, *Hardcore 'Iron Mike': Conqueror of Iwo Jima* (Bloomington, Indiana: iUniverse, 2015).

69. Jeremy Hubbard, "November Hero of the Month: World War II veteran fighting stigma of PTSD," *KDVR*, Denver, November 5, 2017.

70. Chikako Maemori, "Saipan Survivor Recalls Mass Suicide Bids during the War," *The Japan Times*, July 6, 2015.

71. South Sea Islands Album Publication Committee, *Japanese Pioneers' Achievements*, 22.

Bibliography

Abbreviations

CINCPAC/POA: Commander in Chief, Pacific Fleet/ Pacific Ocean Areas
G-2: Military Intelligence
IJA: Imperial Japanese Army
IJM: Imperial Japanese Military
IJN: Imperial Japanese Navy
NTLF: Northern Troops and Landing Force

National Archives Documents

Department of the Army. The Adjutant General's Office. "Translation of the Diary of Japanese Serviceman Taroa Kawaguchi Detailing Combat Activity on Saipan." 1944. Identifier: 6922040. Record Group 407: Records of the Adjutant General's Office. National Archives at College Park, Maryland.

Department of the Navy. CINCPAC-CINCPOA Translations. Item #11,601. "5th Special Base Force (Saipan) Situation Report." 12 February 1944. Record Group 38: Records of the Office of the Chief of Naval Operations. National Archives at College Park, Maryland.

Department of the Navy. Engineer, Expeditionary Troops (Task Force 56). "Report on Japanese Defensive Plan for the Island of Saipan Southern Marianas." July 1944. Box 322. Record Group 127: Records of the United States Marine Corps. National Archives at College Park, Maryland.

Department of the Navy. Naval Photographic Center. "Invasion of Saipan: Civilian & Military Prisoners; Dead Japanese Women." Identifier: 77261. Record Group 428: General Records of the Department of the Navy. National Archives at College Park, Maryland.

Department of the Navy. Office of the Chief of Naval Operations. "Civil Affairs Handbook, Mandated Marianas Islands (OPNAV P22-8)." Washington, D.C.: Department of the Navy. Office of the Chief of Naval Operations, 15 April 1944.

Department of the Navy. Office of the Chief of Naval Operations. "Memorandum. Report of Surrender and Occupation of Japan. Cincpac Confidential ltr. A6-5. Serial 0396. 11 February 1946. Commander in Chief, U. S. Pacific Fleet and Pacific Ocean Areas." Washington, D.C.: Department of the Navy, Office of the Chief of Naval Operations, 9 May 1946. United States Department of Defense, Defense Technical Information Center, Fort Belvoir, VA.

Department of the Navy. Office of the Chief of Naval Operations. Northern Troops and Landing Force, Headquarters, In the Field. "Northern Troops and Landing Force Operations Report, Phase III (Tinian)." 12 August 1944. Record Group 38: Records of the Office of the Chief of Naval Operations. National Archives at College Park, Maryland.

Department of the Navy. Office of the Chief of Naval Operations. Office of Naval Records and Library. Northern Troops and Landing Force, Headquarters, In the Field. "Civil Affairs Report, Forager Phase I." 13 August 1944. Box 318. Record Group 127: Records of the United States Marine Corps. National Archives at College Park, Maryland.

Department of the Navy. Office of the Chief of Naval Operations. Office of Naval Records and Library. Northern Troops and Landing Force, Headquarters, In the Field. "Northern Troops and Landing Force Operations Report, Phase I (Saipan)." 12 August 1944. Record Group 38: Records of the Office of the Chief of Naval Operations. National Archives at College Park, Maryland.

Department of the Navy. Office of the Military Governor for the Pacific Islands. Commander, Marianas Area. "First endorsement to Lt. Cdr. M.S. Buehler's Report of Observations in Forward Area. August 25 1944." Box 38. Record Group 313: Records of Naval Operating Forces. National Archives at College Park, Maryland.

Department of the Navy. Office of the Military Governor for the Pacific Islands. Commander, Marianas Area. "Memorandum. Comments and Recommendations on Civil Affairs Based on Experience on Saipan and Tinian. 30 August 1944." Box 38: A1 - A2 1944—A17 - A19 1944. Group 313: Records of Naval Operating Forces. National Archives at College Park, Maryland.

Department of the Navy. Office of the Military Governor for the Pacific Islands. Commander, Marianas Area. "Saipan-Military Government (Civil Administration)-Report for month of May 1945. 1 June 1945." Box 40: A9 1944 (Folder 6 of 6)—L 1945. Group 313: Records of Naval Operating Forces. National Archives at College Park, Maryland.

Department of the Navy. Office of the Military Governor for the Pacific Islands. Commander, Marianas Area. "Shinozuka Kichitaro. Civilian Internee Interrogation Report. Interrogation by G-2 Section. 5 September 1944. Headquarters 27th Infantry Division. A.P.P. 27." Box 38: A1 - A2 1944—A17 - A19 1944. Group 313: Records of Naval Operating Forces. National Archives at College Park, Maryland.

Department of the Navy. Office of the Military Governor for the Pacific Islands. Commander, Marianas Area. "Standard Operating Procedure for Civilian Control. November, 1944." Box 38: A1 - A2 1944—A17 - A19 1944. Group 313: Records of Naval Operating Forces. National Archives at College Park, Maryland.

Department of the Navy. Office of the Military Governor for the Pacific Islands. Commander, Marianas Area. "Summary of Military Government Matters, Marianas. Period: 4–17. February 1945." Box 40: A9 1944 (Folder 6 of 6)—L 1945. Group 313: Records of Naval Operating Forces. National Archives at College Park, Maryland.

Department of the Navy. Office of the Military Governor for the Pacific Islands. Commander, Marianas Area.."Marianas Operation, Subject Report of Civil Affairs. 28 August 1944." Box 1: Administration 1944; Enclosure No.2. CINCPAC Civil Affairs Section. Record Group 313: Records of Naval Operating Forces. National Archives at College Park, Maryland.

Department of the Navy. Office of the Military Governor for the Pacific Islands. Commander, Marianas Area. Headquarters Camp Susupe. "Camp Susupe Duty Assignments. 15 November 1944." Box 1: Administration 1944; Enclosure No.2. CINCPAC Civil Affairs Section. Record Group 313: Records of Naval Operating Forces. National Archives at College Park, Maryland.

Department of the Navy. United States Marine Corps. "Second Marine Division Operations Report, Phase I Forager." Box 323. Record Group 127: Records of the United States Marine Corps. National Archives at College Park, Maryland.

Department of War. Office of the Director of Intelligence (G-2). "Project 1055, Behavior of Japanese Civilian Population On Saipan." 10 November 1944. Record Group 165: Records of the War Department General and Special Staffs. National Archives at College Park, Maryland.

Interviews

National Museum of the Pacific War. Interview with Arwin J. Bowden in San Antonio, Texas. March 9, 2000.

National Museum of the Pacific War. Interview with Burnes R. "B.R." Whitehead in Athens, Texas. July 26, 2011.

National Museum of the Pacific War. Interview with Carl Pettier in Fredericksburg, Texas. March 24, 2001.

National Museum of the Pacific War. Interview with Charles Pase. April 12, 2001.

National Museum of the Pacific War. Interview with Cleatus A. LeBow in Memphis, Texas. May 2, 2006.

National Museum of the Pacific War. Interview with Edward Bale. September 22, 2001.

National Museum of the Pacific War. Interview with George Gray. September 10, 2007.

National Museum of the Pacific War. Interview with H.L. Obermiller in Fredericksburg, Texas. April 30, 2004.

National Museum of the Pacific War. Interview with Jack Gilbreath in Fredericksburg, Texas. August 19, 2005.

National Museum of the Pacific War. Interview with Norman Delisle in Fredericksburg, Texas. March 15, 2001.

National Museum of the Pacific War. Interview with Olian T. Perry in Fort Worth, Texas. December 22, 2008.

National Museum of the Pacific War. Interview with Ray Harrison in Fredericksburg, Texas. September 17, 2006.

National Museum of the Pacific War. Interview with Robert Montgomery in San Antonio, Texas. August 28, 2010.

National Museum of the Pacific War. Interview with Warren S. Adams in Austin, Texas. September 18, 2002.

National Museum of the Pacific War. Interview with Wilson Allmand in Fredericksburg, Texas. November 12, 2010.

National Park Service. Interview with Robert B. Sheeks by Daniel Martinez at American Memorial Park, Saipan. June 14, 1994.

New York State Military Museum. Interview with Albert J. Harris at the Saratoga Armory, Saratoga Springs, New York. July 30, 2001.

New York State Military Museum. Interview with Gabriel J. Vertucci at Amsterdam Public Library, Amsterdam, New York. February 25, 2005.

New York State Military Museum. Interview with Joseph J. Meighan at New York National Guard Headquarters, Latham, New York. August 22, 2001.

New York State Military Museum. Interview with Joseph P. Fiore. February 18, 2004.

New York State Military Museum. Interview with Samuel Rocco Dinova in Troy, New York. February 11, 2003.

Sheeks, Robert B. Emails with author, 2017–2018.

The Veteran Voices of Pittsburgh Oral History Initiative. Interview with Bob Williams in Pittsburgh, Pennsylvania. March 12, 2014.

Veterans History Project, American Folklife Center, Library of Congress. Interview with George John Dorko on September 8, 2004.

Veterans History Project, American Folklife Center, Library of Congress. Interview with William B. Hoover. Undated.

Veterans History Project, Central Connecticut State University. Interview with Albert A. D'Amico in New Britain, Connecticut. November 27, 2006.

Veterans History Project. Central Connecticut State University. New Britain, Connecticut. Interview with Edwin P. DesRosiers at his home in Moodus, Connecticut. August 9, 2009.

Wisconsin Veterans Museum Research Center. Interview with Frank Urbanowicz. April 3, 2007.

Wisconsin Veterans Museum Research Center. Interview with Halley Young. February 9, 2000.

Period Articles

Associated Press. "Japanese Girl Had Grenades in Bloomers." *Amarillo Daily News*, August 9, 1944.
Associated Press. "Japs Killed Own Civilians Caught in Cave on Saipan." *The News* (Frederick, Maryland), July 17, 1944.
Associated Press. William Worden. "Youngsters Play but Internment Camp is a Tragic Scene of Human Misery." *The Abilene Reporter News* (Abilene, Texas), August 10, 1944.
Bosse, Paul C. "Polling Civilian Japanese on Saipan." *The Public Opinion Quarterly* 9, no. 2 (1945): 176–182.
Chicago Tribune. "America's Step Opens Way for Embargo Order." *Chicago Tribune*, July 27, 1939.
Chicago Tribune. "Tribune Writer Tells Lessons of Pacific War." *Chicago Tribune*, December 8, 1944.
Cochran, Raymond A. "Enquirer Man Photographs Mass Hara-Kiri of Japanese Soldiers, Families on Saipan." *The Cincinnati Enquirer*, Kentucky Edition, August 8, 1944.
Daily Herald Staff. "First Aid Men on Tinian Take Care of Natives Too." *Daily Herald* (Provo, Utah), September 11, 1944.
Dempsey, David. "Japs Kill Own Women, Children with Grenades in Saipan Cave." *Green Bay Press-Gazette*, July 17, 1944.
Dempsey, David. "Saipan Civilians Wailed as Japs Murdered Them in 'Cave of Horrors.'" *Des Moines Tribune*, July 17, 1944.
Gaffney Ledger Staff. "Randolph Sees Many Dead Japs on Saipan Isle." *The Gaffney Ledger* (Gaffney, South Carolina), August 1, 1944.
Graham, Cliff. "48 Hours at Tinian." *Coronet Magazine*, June 1945.
Handleman, Howard. International News Service. "Dying Jap Girl is Rushed to Hospital." *Moline Daily Dispatch* (Moline, Illinois), July 15, 1944.
Johann, Mary. "A Jap Jump Into Foxhole With Butler." *Des Moines Tribune*, November 7, 1944.
Johnston, Richard W. United Press. "Numbed Natives Glad to Get Out of Saipan Caves." *Medford Mail Tribune*, August 18, 1944.
Maryville Daily Forum. "Japanese Commit Mass Suicide on Saipan Isle." *The Maryville Daily Forum* (Maryville, Missouri), September 13, 1944.
McGaffin, William. "What the Japanese Civilian Fears Most." *The Saturday Evening Post* 217, no. 16 (October 14, 1944): 35–50.
Meyers, Lewis. "Japanese Civilians in Combat Zones." *Marine Corps Gazette* (February 1945): 11–16.
Miller, Bill. "Beachhead Government." *Marine Corps Gazette* (November 1944): 42–45.
San Bernardino County Sun Staff. "Frightened Saipan Civilians Feared Death from Americans." *The San Bernardino County Sun*, September 21, 1944.
Schlossenberg, Irving. "Jap Civilians on Tinian Surrender After Promised Water by Marines." *Harrisburg Telegraph*, December 23, 1944.
Sheeks, Robert B. "Civilians on Saipan." *Far Eastern Survey* 14, no. 9 (1945): 109–113.
Sherrod, Robert. "The Battle of Saipan: The Nature of the Enemy." *Time*, August 7, 1944.
Sherrod, Robert. "Saipan: Eyewitness Tells of Island Flight." *Life*, August 28, 1944.
Smith, Harold. "Tribune Writer Views Suicide of Jap Civilians." *Chicago Tribune*, August 13, 1944.
Tampa Morning Tribune. "A Message On War." *Tampa Morning Tribune*, August 7, 1944.
United Press. "Japs Commit Suicide in 'Cave of Horrors.'" *The Evening News* (Harrisburg, Pennsylvania), July 18, 1944.
United Press. "Mass Suicide Cave Named 'Cave of Horrors.'" *Daily World* (Opelousas, Louisiana), July 18, 1944.
Wheeler, Keith. "Jap Soldiers and Civilians Facing Capture, Chose Death." *The Arizona Daily Star*, November 11, 1944.

Other Publications

Aiko, Utsumi. "Japan's Korean Soldiers in the Pacific War." In *Asian Labor in the Wartime Japanese Empire, Unknown Histories*, edited by Paul H. Kratoska. New York: M.E. Sharpe, 2005.
Akagi, Roy Hidemichi. *Japan's Foreign Relations, 1542-1936, A Short History*. Tokyo: Hokuseido Press, 1936.
Alkire, William H. "The Carolinians of Saipan and the Commonwealth of the Northern Mariana Islands." *Pacific Affairs* 57, no. 2 (1984): 270–283.
Alkire, William H. *Lamotrek Atoll and Inter-island Socioeconomic Ties*. Urbana, Illinois: University of Illinois Press, 1965.
Allen, Matthew. *Idenity and Resistance in Okinawa*. Lanham, Maryland: Rowman & Littlefield Publishers, 2002.
Allen, Matthew. "A Story That Won't Fade Away: Compulsory Mass Suicide in the Battle of Okinawa." *The Asia-Pacific Journal: Japan Focus*, July 12, 2007.
Arcilla, Jose S. *An Introduction to Philippine History*. Third Edition. Quezon City: Ateneo de Manila University Press, 1984.
Asada, Sadao. *From Mahan to Pearl Harbor: The Imperial Japanese Navy and the United States*. Annapolis, Maryland: Naval Institute Press, 2006.
Asahi Shimbun. *Senso: The Japanese Remember the Pacific War; Letters to the Editor of Asahi Shimbun*. Expanded Edition, edited by Frank Gibney, translated by Beth Cary. New York: Routledge, 2015.
Atienza, David. "Indigenous Adaptive Resistance in the Mariana Islands: Rethinking Historical Eras." 3rd Marianas History Conference. Mangilao, Guam: Guampedia, 2017.
Atienza, David. "A Mariana Islands History Story: The Influence of the Spanish Black Legend in Mariana Islands Historiography." *Pacific Asia Inquiry* 4, no. 1 (2013): 13–29.
Atienza, David. "The Mariana Islands Militia and the Establishment of the 'Pueblos de Indios': Indigenous Agency in Guam from 1668 to 1758." 2nd Marianas History Conference. Mangilao, Guam: Guampedia, 2013.

Atienza, David. "Priests, Mayors and Indigenous Offices: Indigenous Agency and Adaptive Resistance in the Mariana Islands (1681 -1758)." *Pacific Asia Inquiry* 5, no. 1 (2014): 31–48.

Atienza, David, and Alexandre Coello De La Rosa. "Death Rituals and Identity in Contemporary Guam (Mariana Islands)." *The Journal of Pacific History* 47, no. 4 (2012): 459–473.

Bailey, Thomas A. "Japan's Protest Against the Annexation of Hawaii." *The Journal of Modern History* 3, no. 1 (1931): 46–61.

Barshaw, Andrew E. *The Gods Left First: The Captivity and Repatriation of Japanese POWs in Northeast Asia, 1945–1956*. Berkeley: University of California Pres, 2013.

Baumgart, Winfried. "German Imperialism in Historical Perspective." In *Germans in the Tropics, Essays in German Colonial History* 1987, edited by Arthur J. Knoll and Lewis H. Gann. New York: Greenwood Press, 1987.

Bayliss, Jeffrey Paul. *On the Margins of Empire: Buraku and Korean Identity in Prewar and Wartime Japan*. Cambridge, Massachusetts: Harvard University Asia Center, 2013.

Benesch, Oleg. *Inventing the Way of the Samurai: Nationalism, Internationalism, and Bushido in Modern Japan*. Oxford, United Kingdom: Oxford University Press, 2014.

Berry, Henry. *Semper Fi, Mac: Living Memories of the U.S. Marines in World War II*. New York: Arbor House, 1982.

Bingham, Marjorie Wall, and Susan Hill Gross. *Women in Japan: From Ancient Times to the Present*. St. Louis Park, Minnesota: Glenhurst Publications, 1987.

Blair Jr., Clay. *Silent Victory: The U.S. Submarine War against Japan*. Annapolis, Maryland: Naval Institute Press, 1975.

Bollinger, Edward E. *The Cross and the Floating Dragon: The Gospel in Ryukyu*. Pasadena, California: William Carey Library, 1983.

Boomhower, Ray E. *Dispatches from the Pacific: The World War II Reporting of Robert L. Sherrod*. Bloomington, Indiana: Indiana University Press, 2017.

Bowers, Neal M. "Problems of Resettlement on Saipan, Tinian and Rota, Mariana Islands." Ph.D. Dissertation, University of Michigan, 1950.

Bright, Richard Carl. *Pain and Purpose in the Pacific: True Reports of War*. Victoria, British Columbia, Canada: Trafford Publishing, 2010.

Brown, Delmer M. *Nationalism in Japan: An Introductory Historical Analysis*. Berkeley, University of California Press, 1955.

Camacho, Keith L. *Cultures of Commemoration: The Politics of War, Memory, and History in the Mariana Islands*. Honolulu: University of Hawaii Press, 2011.

Camacho, Keith L. "The Politics of Indigenous Collaboration: The Role of Chamorro Interpreters in Japan's Pacific Empire, 1914–45." *The Journal of Pacific History* 43, no. 2 (2008): 207–222.

Campbell, James. *The Color of War: How One Battle Broke Japan and Another Changed America*. New York: Crown Publishers, 2012.

Cant, Gilbert. *War on Japan*. I.P.R. Pamphlets No. 17. New York: American Council, Institute of Pacific Relations, 1945.

Carano, Paul, and Pedro C. Sanchez. *A Complete History of Guam*. Fifth Printing. Rutland, Vermont: Charles & Tuttle Company. 1969.

Carson, Mike T. *Archaeological Landscape Evolution: The Mariana Islands in the Asia-Pacific Region*. Switzerland: Springer, 2016.

Carson, Mike T. *First Settlement of Remote Oceania: Earliest Sites in the Mariana Islands*. New York: Springer, 2014.

Carson, Mike T., and Hsiao-chun Hung. *Substantive Evidence of Initial Habitation in the Remote Pacific: Archaeological Discoveries at Unai Bapot in Saipan, Mariana Islands*. Oxford, United Kingdom: Archaeopress Publishing Ltd, 2017.

Chapin, John C. *Breaching the Marianas: The Battle for Saipan*. "Marines in World War II Commemorative Series." Washington, D.C.: History and Museums Division, U.S. Marine Corps Headquarters, 1994.

Chatfield, Gail. *By Dammit, We're Marines!: Veterans' Stories of The Heroism, Horror, and Humor in World War II on The Pacific Front*. Paragould, Arkansas: Wyndham House, 2008.

China Daily. "Memoir of Comfort Woman Tells of 'Hell for Women.'" *China Daily*. July 6, 2007.

Cloud, Preston E., Robert George Schmidt, and Harold W. Burke. *Geology of Saipan, Mariana Islands. Part 1, General Geology*. United States Department of the Interior, Geological Survey Professional Paper 280-A. Washington, D.C.: United States Government Printing Office, 1956.

Clyde, Paul H. *Japan's Pacific Mandate*. New York: The Macmillan Company, 1935.

CNMI. Second Northern Marianas Constitutional Convention, 1985. Saipan.

Coello de la Rosa, Alexandre. *Jesuits at the Margins: Missions and Missionaries in the Marianas (1668–1769)*. New York: Routledge, 2016.

Coello de la Rosa, Alexandre. "Lights and Shadows: The Inquisitorial Process Against the Jesuit Congregation of Nuestra Señora de la Luz on the Mariana Islands (1758–1776)." *Journal of Religious History* 37, no. 2 (2013): 206–227.

Conrad, Sebastian. *German Colonialism: A Short History*. Cambridge, United Kingdom: Cambridge University Press, 2012.

Cook, Haruko Taya. "The Myth of the Saipan Suicides," *MHQ: The Quarterly Journal of Military History* 7, no. 3 (1995): 12–19.

Cook, Haruko Taya. "The Myth of the Saipan Suicides," In *No End Save Victory: Perspectives on World War II*, edited by Robert Cowley. New York: G.P. Putnam's Sons, 2001.

Cook, Haruko Taya. "Turning Women into Weapons: Japan's Women, the Battle of Saipan, and the 'Nature of the Pacific War.'" In *Women and War in the Twentieth Century: Enlisted With or Without Consent*, edited by Nicole Ann Dombrowski. New York: Garland Publishing, 1999.

Cook, Haruko Taya. "Women's Deaths as Weapons of War in Japan's 'Final Battle.'" In *Gendering Modern Japanese History*, edited by Barbara Molony and Kathleen Uno. Cambridge: Harvard University Asia Center, 2005.

Cook, Haruko Taya, and Theodore F. Cook. *Japan at War: An Oral History*. New York: The New Press, 1992.

Crowl, Philip A. *Campaign in the Marianas*. "The War in the Pacific, United States Army in World War II" Series. Washington, D.C.: Government Printing Office, 1959.

Cunningham, Lawrence J. *Ancient Chamorro Society*. Honolulu: The Bess Press, 1992.

Daniels, Roger. *The Politics of Prejudice: The Anti-Japanese Movement in California and the Struggle for Japanese Exclusion*. Berkeley: University of California Press, 1977.

Daws, Gavan. *Prisoners of the Japanese: POWS of World War II in the Pacific*. New York: William Morrow and Company, 1994.

Decker, John Alvin. *Labor Problems in the Pacific Mandates*. London: Oxford University Press, 1940.

Denfeld, D. Colt. "Korean Laborers in Micronesia during World War II." *Korea Observer* 15, no. 1 (Spring, 1984): 3–15.

Denoon, Donald. *The Cambridge History of the Pacific Islands*. Cambridge, United Kingdom: Cambridge University Press, 1997.

Department of Commerce. Bureau of Foreign and Domestic Commerce. *The Cane Sugar Industry: Agricultural, Manufacturing, and Marketing Costs in Hawaii, Porto Rico, Louisiana, and Cuba*. Miscellaneous Series no. 53. Washington, D.C.: Government Printing Office, 1917.

Department of the Interior, National Park Service. "Marianas Memorial." https://www.nps.gov/amme/learn/historyculture/upload/Marianas-Memorial-Listing.pdf

Department of the Interior, National Park Service. "National Register of Historic Places Registration Form for the Hachiman Jinja, Saipan, CNMI." NRIS Reference Number: 03000549. NPS Form 10-900. OMB No. 1024-0018. 2003.

Department of the Navy. *Civil Affairs Handbook. Administrative Organization and Personnel of the Japanese Mandated Islands*. OPNAV 50E-4. Washington, D.C.: Government Printing Office, 1 January 1944.

Department of War. "War Department Technical Manual TM-E 30-480, Handbook on Japanese Military Forces, 15 September 1944." Washington, D.C.: Government Printing Office, 1944.

De Vos, George, and Hiroshi Wagatsuma. *Japan's Invisible Race: Caste in Culture and Personality*. Berkeley, California: University of California Press, 1967.

Di Marco, Francesca. *Suicide in Twentieth-Century Japan*. New York: Routledge, 2016.

Dijk, Kees van. *Pacific Strife: The Great Powers and Their Political and Economic Rivalries in Asia and the Western Pacific, 1870-1914*. Amsterdam: Amsterdam University Press, 2015.

Directors System Company. Directed by Minoru Matsui. *Riben Guizi*. Documentary. Directors System Company, Japan, 2001.

Dixon, Boyd. "The Archaeology of Rural Settlement and Class in a Pre-WWII Japanese Plantation on Tinian, Commonwealth of the Northern Mariana Islands." *International Journal of Historical Archaeology* 8, no. 4 (December 2004): 281–299.

Dixon, Boyd. "Okinawa as Transported Landscape: Understanding Japanese Archaeological Remains on Tinian Using Ryukyu Ethnohistory and Ethnography." *Asian Perspectives: The Journal of Archaeology for Asia and the Pacific* 54, no. 2 (Fall 2015): 274–304.

Doan, David B. *Military Geology of Tinian, Mariana Islands*. Washington, D.C.: Department of the Army, 1960.

Dower, John W. *Embracing Defeat: Japan in the Wake of World War II*. New York: W.W. Norton & Company, 2000.

Dower, John W. *War Without Mercy: Race and Power in the Pacific War*. New York: Pantheon Books, 1993.

Drea, Edward J. *In the Service of the Emperor: Essays on the Imperial Japanese Army*. University of Nebraska Press: Lincoln, Nebraska, 1998.

Driver, Marjorie G., and Francis X. Hezel. *El Palacio: The Spanish Palace in Agana, 1668-1898*. Mangilao, Guam: Micronesian Area Research Center, 2004.

Dudden, Alexis. *Japan's Colonization of Korea: Discourse and Power*. Honolulu: University of Hawaii Press, 2005.

Dyer, George Carroll. *The Amphibians Came to Conquer: The Story of Admiral Richmond Kelly Turner*. Washington, D.C.: Government Printing Office, 1972.

Earhart, David C. *Certain Victory: Images of World War II in the Japanese Media*. Armonk, New York: M.E. Sharpe, 2008.

Elrod, Roy H. *We Were Going to Win, or Die There: With the Marines at Guadalcanal, Tarawa, and Saipan*. Edited by Fred H. Allison. Denton, Texas: University of North Texas Press, 2017.

Embree, John F. "Military Government in Saipan and Tinian: A Report on the Organization of Susupe and Churo." *Applied Anthropology* 5, no. 1 (1946): 1–39.

Erediano, Emmanuel T. "Santos honors designer of original NMI flag." *Marianas Variety* (Saipan, CNMI), January 22, 2012.

Evans, David C., and Mark R. Peattie. *Kaigun: Strategy, Tactics, and Technology in the Imperial Japanese Navy, 1887-1941*. Annapolis Maryland: Naval Institute Press, 1997.

Fahey, James J. *Pacific War Diary, 1942-1945*. Boston: Houghton Mifflin Company, 1991.

Farrell, Don A. *History of the Mariana Islands to Partition*. Saipan: CNMI Public School System, 2011.

Farrell, Don A. *History of the Northern Mariana Islands*. Saipan: CNMI Public School System, 1991.

Farrell, Don A. *Tinian: A Brief History*. Honolulu: Pacific Historic Parks, 2012.

Farrell, Don A., and Carmen Dela Cruz Farrell. *Saipan*. Saipan: Micronesian Productions, 1990.

Farrell, Don A., and Carmen Dela Cruz Farrell. *Tinian*. Saipan: Micronesian Productions, 1989.

Feifer, George. *Tennozan: The Battle of Okinawa and the Atomic Bomb*. New York: Ticknor & Fields, 1992.

Field, Norma. *In the Realm of a Dying Emperor*. New York: Vintage Books, 1993.

Frank, Benis M., and Henry I. Shaw, Jr. *Victory and Occupation*. Volume V of "History of U.S. Marine Corps Operations in World War II." Washington, D.C.: Government Printing Office, 1968.

Friedman, Hal M. *Creating an American Lake: United States Imperialism and Strategic Security in the Pacific Basin, 1945–1947*. Westport, Connecticut: Greenwood Press, 2001.

Friedman, Hal M. "The Limitations of Collective Security: The United States and the Micronesian Trusteeship, 1945–1947." *Isla*: A Journal of Micronesian Studies 3, no. 2 (1995): 339–370.

Fujitani, Takashi. *Race for Empire: Koreans as Japanese and Japanese as Americans during World War II*. Berkeley: University of California Press, 2011.

Gabaldon, Guy. *Saipan: Suicide Island*. Saipan: Guy Gabaldon, 1990.

Garand, George W., and Truman R. Strobridge. *Western Pacific Operations*. Volume IV of "History of U.S. Marine Corps Operations in World War II" Series. Washington, D.C.: Government Printing Office, 1971.

Gilmore, Allison B. *You Can't Fight Tanks with Bayonets: Psychological Warfare against the Japanese Army in the Southwest Pacific*. Lincoln, Nebraska: University of Nebraska Press, 1998.

Glacken, Clarence J. *The Great Loochoo: A Study of Okinawan Village Life*. Berkeley: University of California Press, 1955.

Goetzfridt, Nicholas J. *Guahan: A Bibliographic History*. Honolulu: University of Hawaii Press, 2011.

Goldberg, Harold J. *D-Day in the Pacific: The Battle of Saipan*. Bloomington: Indiana University Press, 2007.

Gregory, Charles Noble. "The Treaty as to Yap and the Mandated North Pacific Islands." *The American Journal of International Law* 16, no. 2 (1922): 248–51.

Hagimoto, Koichi. *Trans-Pacific Encounters: Asia and the Hispanic World*. Newcastle, United Kingdom: Cambridge Scholars Publishing, 2016.

Hane, Mikiso. *Peasants, Rebels, and Outcastes: The Underside of Modern Japan*. New York: Pantheon Books, 1982.

Hardach, Gerd. "Defining Separate Spheres: German Rule and Colonial Law in Micronesia." In *European Impact and Pacific Influence: British and German Colonial Policy in the Pacific Islands and the Indigenous Response 1997*, edited by Hermann Hiery and John M MacKenzie. London: I.B. Tauris Publishers, 1997.

Hardacre, Helen. *Shinto and the State, 1868–1988*. Princeton, New Jersey: Princeton University Press, 1989.

Harwood, Richard. *A Close Encounter: The Marine Landing on Tinian*. Washington, D.C.: Marine Corps Historical Center, 1994.

Hegi, Benjamin P. "Extermination Warfare?: The Conduct of The Second Marine Division at Saipan." Master's Thesis, University of North Texas, 2008.

Henderson, W. O. *The German Colonial Empire, 1884–1919*. London: Frank Cass & CO., 1993.

Henderson, W. O. *Studies in German Colonial History*. Chicago: Quadrangle Books, 1962.

Hezel, Francis X. *Before We Began Counting Years*. Documentary. Northern Marianas Humanities Council and Best Sunshine Enterprise. 2018.

Hezel, Francis X. "The Early Spanish Period in the Marianas, 1668–1698: Eight Theses." *San Vitores Theological Review*, Volume 1 (2014): 1–16.

Hezel, Francis X. "From Conquest to Colonization: Spain in the Mariana Islands 1690 to 1740." Saipan: Division of Historic Preservation, 1989.

Hezel, Francis X. "From Conversion to Conquest: The Early Spanish Mission in the Marianas." *Journal of Pacific History* 17, no. 3 (1982): 115–137.

Hezel, Francis X. *The History of Micronesia*. Documentary. Pohnpei: Micronesian Seminar Productions, 2008.

Hezel, Francis X. *Strangers in Their Own Land: A Century of Colonial Rule in the Caroline and Marshall Islands*. Honolulu: University of Hawai'i Press, 1995.

Hezel, Francis X. "When Cultures Clash: Revisiting the 'Spanish-Chamorro Wars.'" Saipan, CNMI: Northern Marianas Humanities Council, 2015.

Hibino, Yutaka. *Nippon Shindo Ron; or, The National Ideals of the Japanese People*. 1928. Reprint. Translated by A.P. McKenzie. Cambridge: Cambridge University Press, 2013.

Hicks, George. *The Comfort Women: Japan's Brutal Regime of Enforced Prostitution in the Second World War*. New York: W.W. Norton & Company, 1995.

Hiery, Hermann, and John M MacKenzie. *European Impact and Pacific Influence: British and German Colonial Policy in the Pacific Islands and the Indigenous Response*. London: I.B. Tauris Publishers, 1997.

Hiery, Hermann Joseph. *The Neglected War: The German South Pacific and the Influence of World War I*. Honolulu: University of Hawaii Press, 1995.

Higuchi, Wakako. "Japan and War Reparations in Micronesia." *The Journal of Pacific History* 30, no. 1 (1995): 87–98.

Higuchi, Wakako. *The Japanese Administration of Guam, 1941–1944: A Study of Occupation and Integration Policies, with Japanese Oral Histories*. Jefferson, North Carolina: McFarland, 2013.

Higuchi, Wakako. *Micronesia Under the Japanese Administration: Interviews with Former South Sea Bureau and Military Officials*. Mangilao, Guam: Micronesian Area Research Center, The University of Guam, 1987.

Higuchi, Wakako. *Micronesians and the Pacific War: The Palauans*. Mangilao, Guam: Micronesian Area Research Center, The University of Guam, 1986.

Higuchi, Wakako. "Pre-war Japanese Fisheries in Micronesia-Focusing on Bonito and Tuna Fishing in the Northern Mariana Islands." *Immigration Studies* 3 (2007): 49–68.

Hiraoka, Akitoshi. *Japanese Advance into the Pacific Ocean: The Albatross and the Great Bird Rush*. Singapore: Springer, 2018.

Hiroshi, Shimizu, and Hirakawa Hitoshi. *Japan and Singapore in the World Economy: Japan's Economic Advance into Singapore, 1870–1965*. New York: Routledge, 1999.

Hishida, Seiji. *Japan Among the Great Powers: A Survey of Her International Relations*. New York: Longmans, Green and Co., 1940.

Hoffman, Carl W. *Saipan: The Beginning of the End*. United States Marine Corps Historical Division Monograph. Washington, D.C.: Government Printing Office, 1950.

Hoffman, Carl W. *The Seizure of Tinian*. United States Marine Corps Historical Division Monograph. Washington, D.C.: Government Printing Office, 1951.

Holiday, Samuel, and Robert S. McPherson, *Under the Eagle: Samuel Holiday, Navajo Code Talker*. Norman: University of Oklahoma, 2013.

Horiguchi, Noriko J. *Women Adrift: The Literature of Japan's Imperial Body*. Minneapolis: University of Minnesota Press, 2012.

Hornfischer, James D. *The Fleet at Flood Tide: America at Total War in the Pacific, 1944-1945*. New York: Bantam, 2016.

Hornfischer, James D. *Neptune's Inferno: The U.S. Navy at Guadalcanal*. New York: Bantam Books, 2011.

Hoshino, Keiichiro. "Okinawa man credits mother with saving family from WWII mass suicide." *The Japan Times*, May 15, 2015.

Hoyt, Austin. *Victory in the Pacific*, "American Experience." Documentary. United States. WGBH Educational Foundation, PBS Distribution, 2005.

Hubbard, Jeremy. "November Hero of the Month: World War II veteran fighting stigma of PTSD." *KDVR*, Denver, November 5, 2017.

Hunter-Anderson, Rosalind. "An Anthropological Perspective on Marianas Prehistory, Including Guam." In *Guam History: Perspectives Volume Two*, edited by Carter, L.D., Wuerch, W.L. And Carter, R.R. Mangilao, Guam: Micronesian Area Research Center Educational Series 27, University of Guam, 2005: 20–59.

Hunter-Anderson, Rosalind L., and Joanne E. Eakin. "Chamorro Origins and the Importance of Archaeological Context." 3rd Marianas History Conference. Mangilao, Guam: Guampedia Foundation, 2016: 70–82.

Hunter-Anderson, Rosalind L. Gillian B. Thompson, and Darlene R. Moore. "Rice as a prehistoric valuable in the Mariana Islands, Micronesia." *Asian Perspectives* (1995): 69–89.

Ichiro, Tomiyama. "The 'Japanese' of Micronesia: Okinawans in the Nanyo Islands." In *Okinawan Diaspora 2002*, edited by Ronald Y. Nakasone. Honolulu: University of Hawaii Press, 2002.

Ienaga, Saburo. *The Pacific War, 1931–1945*. New York: Pantheon Books, 1978.

Iida, Akiko, Yoji Kurata, Satoshi Osawa, and Mikiko Ishikawa. "Industrial Development and its Impacts on the Environment of Micronesian Islands under the Japanese Administration: A Case Study of Babeldaob Island, Palau." *Pan-Japan: The International Journal of the Japanese Diaspora* 10, no. 1 & 2 (2014): 28–56.

Iitaka, Shingo. "Remembering Nanyo from Okinawa: Deconstructing the Former Empire of Japan through Memorial Practices." *History & Memory* 27, no. 2 (2015): 126–151.

Ikegami, Eiko. *The Taming of the Samurai: Honorific Individualism and the Making of Modern Japan*. Cambridge, Massachusetts: Harvard University Press, 1995.

Imaizumi, Yumiko. "Mobilization and Perspectives by the Japanese Army on Japanese Civilians and Local People during the Pacific War in Saipan and Tinian." 3rd Marianas History Conference. Mangilao, Guam: Guampedia, 2017.

Imaizumi, Yumiko. "Northern Marianas Under Japanese Navy Administration (1914–1922)." 2nd Marianas History Conference. Mangilao, Guam: Guampedia, 2013: 287–300.

Iritani, Toshio. *Group Psychology of the Japanese in Wartime*. New York: Kegan Paul International, 1991.

Itoh, Mayumi. *Japanese War Orphans in Manchuria: Forgotten Victims of World War II*. New York: Palgrave Macmillan, 2010.

Japan Broadcasting Corporation, Nippon Hoso Kyokai. NHK. Directed by Seijo Naito, Hideki Yamagishi, and Izuru Yamamoto. *The Island of Death*. Iwo Jima Documentary. Japan. NHK. 2006.

Japan Broadcasting Corporation, Nippon Hoso Kyokai. NHK. Directed by Yasuhiro Miyamoto and Naoki Yonemoto. *The Pacific War: Despair on the Battlefield*. Documentary. Japan, NHK, 2013.

Japanese Government. *Annual Report to the League of Nations on the Administration of the South Sea Islands under Japanese Mandate for the Year 1925*. Tokyo, Japan: Japanese Government, 1925.

Japanese Government. *Annual Report to the League of Nations on the Administration of the South Sea Islands under Japanese Mandate for the Year 1930*. Tokyo, Japan: Japanese Government, 1930.

Japanese Government. *Report to the League of Nations on the Administration of the South Sea Islands under Japanese Mandate for the Year 1937*. Tokyo, Japan: Japanese Government, 1937.

Japanese Ministry of Education. *Kokutai No Hongi: Cardinal Principles of the National Entity of Japan*. Translated by John Owen Gauntlett. Cambridge, Massachusetts: Harvard University Press, 1949.

Jones, Don. *Oba, The Last Samurai: Saipan 1944–45*. Novato, California: Presidio Press, 1986.

Joseph, Alice, and Veronica F. Murray. *Chamorros and Carolinians of Saipan: Personality Studies*. Cambridge, Massachusetts: Harvard University Press. 1951.

Kang, Wi Jo. "Church and State Relations in the Japanese Colonial Period." In *Christianity in Korea 2006*, edited by Robert E. Buswell Jr., and Timothy S. Lee, 97–115. Honolulu: University of Hawaii Press, 2006.

Kawamura, Noriko. *Emperor Hirohito and The Pacific War*. Seattle: University of Washington Press, 2015.

Kerr, George H. *Okinawa: The History of an Island People*, Revised Edition. Rutland, Vermont: Tuttle Publishing, 2000.

Kim, Sebastian C. H., and Kirsteen Kim. *A History of Korean Christianity*. New York: Cambridge University Press. 2015.

Kleber, Brooks E., and Dale Birdsell. *The Chemical Warfare Service: Chemicals in Combat*. The Technical Services, "United States Army in World War II" Series. Washington, D.C.: Office of the Chief of Military History, Department of the Army, 1966.

Knoll, Arthur J., and Lewis H. Gann. *Germans in the Tropics: Essays in German Colonial History*. New York: Greenwood Press, 1987.

Kurnick, N.B. "War Edema in the Civilian Population of Saipan." *Annals of Internal Medicine* 28, no. 4 (1948): 782–791.

Kushner, Barak. *The Thought War: Japanese Imperial Propaganda*. Honolulu: University of Hawaii, 2006.

Kwak, Jun-Hyeok and Melissa Nobles. *Inherited Responsibility and Historical Reconciliation in East Asia*. New York: Routledge, 2013.

Ladd, Dean and Steven Weingartner. *Faithful Warriors: A Combat Marine Remembers the Pacific War*. Annapolis, Maryland: Naval Institute Press, 2009.

Lebra, William P. *Okinawan Religion: Belief, Ritual, and Social Structure*, Second Printing. Honolulu: University of Hawaii Press, 1985.

Lee, John M. "Japanese Search Pacific Isles for Bones of War Dead." *The New York Times*, March 15, 1972.

Levesque, Rodrigue. *History of Micronesia: A Collection of Source Documents. Volume 7-More Turmoil in the Marianas, 1679-1683*. Gatineau, Canada: Levesque Publications, 1996.

Lewis, Jonathan. *Hell in the Pacific*. Documentary. United Kingdom, ITV Studios Global Entertainment, 2001.

Maemori, Chikako. "Saipan Survivor Recalls Mass Suicide Bids during the War." *The Japan Times*, July 6, 2015.

Marine Corps Combat Correspondents. *Semper Fidelis: The U.S. Marines in the Pacific, 1942–1945*. New York: William Sloane Associates, 1947.

Marsden, Lawrence A. *Attack Transport: The Story of the U.S.S Doyen*. Minneapolis, Minnesota: University of Minnesota Press, 1946.

Masaaki, Aniya. "Compulsory Mass Suicide, the Battle of Okinawa, and Japan's Textbook Controversy." *The Asia-Pacific Journal: Japan Focus* 6, Issue 1 (January 2008): 1–13.

Masahide, Ota. "Ryukyu Shimpo, Ota Masahide, Mark Ealey and Alastair McLauchlan, Descent into Hell: The Battle of Okinawa." *The Asia-Pacific Journal* 12, Issue 48, no. 4 (2014): 1–22.

Masaie, Ishihara. "Memories of War and Okinawa." Translated by Douglas Driestadt. In *Perilous Memories: The Asia-Pacific War(s)*. Durham, North Carolina: Duke University Press, 2001.

Matsumura, Janice and Diana Wright. "Japanese Military Suicides During the Asia-Pacific War: Studies of the Unauthorized Self-killings of Soldiers." *The Asia-Pacific Journal: Japan Focus* 13, Issue 25, Number 2 (June 2015): 1–20.

Mawson, Stephanie. "Rebellion and Mutiny in the Mariana Islands, 1680–1690." *The Journal of Pacific History* 50, no. 2 (2015): 128–148.

McAuliffe, Josh. "South Scranton man saw horrors of World War II treating wounded Marines in Pacific Theater." *The Times-Tribune* (Scranton, Pennsylvania), May 26, 2013.

McCormack, Gavan and Satoko Oka Norimatsu. *Resistant Islands: Okinawa Confronts Japan and the United States*. New York: Rowman & Littlefield Publishers, 2012.

McLauchlan, Alastair A. "War Crimes and Crimes Against Humanity on Okinawa: Guilt on Both Sides." *Journal of Military Ethics* 13, no. 4 (2014): 363–380.

Meehl, Gerald A. *One Marine's War: A Combat Interpreter's Quest for Humanity in the Pacific*. Annapolis, Maryland: Naval Institute Press, 2012.

Meller, Norman. *Saipan's Camp Susupe*. Honolulu: Center for Pacific Island Studies, University of Hawaii, 1999.

Metzer, Steve. "Relatives Tried to Drown Child Before Killing Selves." *The Lawton Constitution*, December 10, 2017.

Miako, Ichikawa. "Child survivor of forced mass suicide in Manchuria still loves hero who saved her." *The Asia-Pacific Journal: Japan Focus* 3, Issue 8 (August 2005): 1–2.

Military Government Section, United States Navy. *Camp Susupe: A Photographic Record of The Operation of Military Government on Saipan. June 1944 to December 1945*. United States Naval Military Government on Saipan. Navy Number 3245 (Saipan Island, Marianas Islands). FPO San Francisco, 1945.

Miller, Edward S. *War Plan Orange: The U.S. Strategy to Defeat Japan, 1897–1945*. Annapolis, Maryland: Naval Institute Press, 1991.

Miyake, Yoshiko. "Doubling Expectations: Motherhood and Women's Factory Work Under State Management in Japan in the 1930s and 1940s." In *Recreating Japanese Women, 1600–1945*, edited by Gail Lee Bernstein, 267–295. Berkeley: University of California Press, 1991.

Moore, Darlene R. "Archaeological Evidence of a Prehistoric Farming Technique on Guam." *Micronesica* 38, no. 1 (2005): 93–120.

Moore, Darlene R., and R. L. Hunter-Anderson. "Pots and pans in the intermediate pre–Latte (2500–1600 bp) Mariana Islands, Micronesia." In J-C Galipaud and I. Lilley (eds), *The Pacific from 5000 to 2000 BP, Colonisation and Transformations*. Paris: IRD (1999): 487–503.

Moore, Don. "John Barrow saw Japanese women at Saipan throw babies off cliff then jump themselves." *Charlotte Sun*, December 21, 2015.

Morison, Samuel Eliot. *Aleutians, Gilberts and Marshalls, June 1942–April 1944*. Volume VII of "History of United States Naval Operations in World War II." Boston: Little, Brown and Company, 1951.

Morison, Samuel Eliot. *New Guinea and the Marianas, March 1944-August 1944*. Volume VIII of "History of United States Naval Operations in World War II Series." Boston: Little, Brown and Company, 1953.

Morison, Samuel Eliot. *The Two-Ocean War: A Short History of the United States Navy in the Second World War*. Boston: Little, Brown and Company, 1963.

Morton, Louis. *Strategy and Command: The First Two Years*. "The War in the Pacific, United States Army in World War II" Series. Washington, D.C.: Office of the Chief of Military History, Department of the Army, 1962.

Myers, Ramon Hawley, Mark R. Peattie, and Jingzhi Zhen. *The Japanese Colonial Empire, 1895–1945*. Princeton, New Jersey: Princeton University Press, 1984.

Nagata, Yuriko. "The Japanese in Torres Strait." In *Navigating Boundaries: The Asian Diaspora in Tor-*

res Strait. Canberra. Australia: Pandanus Books, 2004.

Nakajima, Michio. "Shinto Deities that Crossed the Sea: Japan's 'Overseas Shrines,' 1868 to 1945." *Japanese Journal of Religious Studies* 37, no. 1 (2010): 21-46.

Nakasone, Ronald Y. "An Impossible Possibility." In *Okinawan Diaspora 2002*, edited by Ronald Y. Nakasone, 3-25. Honolulu: University of Hawaii Press, 2002.

Nakasone, Ronald Y. *Okinawan Diaspora*. Honolulu: University of Hawaii Press, 2002.

Ngo, Ti. "Mapping Economic Development: The South Seas Government and Sugar Production in Japan's South Pacific Mandate, 1919-1941." *Cross-Currents: East Asian History and Culture Review*, University of California Berkeley, 2 (March 2012): 1-23.

O'Brien, Francis A. *Battling for Saipan*. New York: Ballantine Books, 2003.

O'Day, Patrick and Nicole Vernon. "The Archaeology of Landscape Transformation in Colonization and Conflict: Historic Japanese Cultural Resources of the Carolinas Heights Region of Tinian Island, Commonwealth of the Northern Marianas Islands." *Pan-Japan* 11, no. 1 & 2 (2015): 1-20.

Odo, Franklin. *Voices from the Cane Fields: Folk Songs from Japanese Immigrant Workers in Hawaii*. New York: Oxford University Press, 2013.

Ogawa, Manako. *Sea of Opportunity: The Japanese Pioneers of the Fishing Industry in Hawaii*. Honolulu: University of Hawaii Press, 2015.

Ohnuki-Tierney, Emiko. *Kamikaze, Cherry Blossoms, and Nationalisms: The Militarization of Aesthetics in Japanese History*. Chicago: The University of Chicago Press, 2002.

Okinawa Prefectural Government. *Keys to Okinawan Culture*. Okinawa, Japan: Okinawa Prefectural Government, 1992.

Oliver, Douglas L. *The Pacific Islands*. Third Edition. Honolulu: University of Hawaii Press, 1989.

Ono, Keiko, John P. Lea, and Tetsuya Ando. "A Study of Urban Morphology of Japanese Colonial Towns in Nanyo Gunto: Part 1 Garapan, Tinian and Chalan Kanoa in Northern Marianas." *Journal of Architecture, Planning, and Environmental Engineering*. Architectural Institute of Japan, no. 556 (2002): 333-339.

Orbell, John, and Tomonori Morikawa. "An Evolutionary Account of Suicide Attacks: The Kamikaze Case," *Political Psychology* 32, no. 2 (2011): 297-322.

Owens, Donald Dean. "Korean Shamanism: Its Components, Context, and Functions." Doctoral Dissertation, University of Oklahoma Graduate College, 1975.

Pash, Sidney. *The Currents of War: A New History of American-Japanese Relations, 1899-1941*. Lexington, Kentucky: The University Press of Kentucky, 2014.

Pawley, Andrew, and Roger Green. "Dating the Dispersal of the Oceanic Languages." *Oceanic Linguistics* 12, no. 1/2 (1973): 1-67.

Peattie, Mark R. *The Japanese Colonial Empire, 1895-1945*. Edited by Ramon Hawley Myers, Mark R. Peattie, and Jingzhi Zhen. Princeton, New Jersey: Princeton University Press, 1984.

Peattie, Mark R. "The Nanyo: Japan in the South Pacific, 1885-1945." In *The Japanese Colonial Empire, 1895-1945*, edited by Ramon Hawley Myers, Mark R. Peattie, and Jingzhi Zhen. Princeton, New Jersey: Princeton University Press, 1984.

Peattie, Mark R. *Nanyo: The Rise and Fall of the Japanese in Micronesia, 1885-1945* (Honolulu: University of Hawaii Press, 1988

Penguin Books. *The Penguin Book of Japanese Verse*. Translated by Geoffrey Bownas and Anthony Thwaite. Baltimore, Maryland: Penguin Books, 1964.

Petty, Bruce M. *Saipan: Oral Histories of the Pacific War*. Jefferson, North Carolina: McFarland, 2002.

Pharr, Susan J. *Political Women in Japan: The Search for a Place in Political Life*. Berkeley: University of California Press, 1981.

Pierard, Richard V. "The German Colonial Society." In *Germans in the Tropics, Essays in German Colonial History* 1987, edited by Arthur J. Knoll and Lewis H. Gann. New York: Greenwood Press, 1987.

Pinguet, Maurice. *Voluntary Death in Japan*. Translated by Rosemary Morris. Padstow, Cornwall, United Kingdom: Polity Press, 1993.

Porter, Edgar A., and Ran Ying Porter. *Japanese Reflections on World War II and the American Occupation*. Amsterdam, Netherlands: Amsterdam University Press, 2017.

Poyer, Lin, Suzanne Falgout, and Laurence Marshall Carucci. *The Typhoon of War: Micronesian Experiences of the Pacific War*. Honolulu: University of Hawai'i, 2001.

Price, Willard. *The South Sea Adventure: Through Japan's Equatorial Empire*. Tokyo: The Hokuseido Press, 1936.

Purcell, Jr., David Campbell. "The Economics of Exploitation: The Japanese in the Mariana, Caroline and Marshall Islands, 1915-1940." *The Journal of Pacific History* 11, no. 3 (1976): 189-211.

Purcell, Jr., David Campbell. "Japanese Expansion in the South Pacific, 1890-1935." Ph.D. History Dissertation, University of Pennsylvania, 1967.

Purcell, Jr., David Campbell. "Suicide in Micronesia: The 1920s and 1930s." *Pacific Studies* 14, no. 2 (1991): 71-86.

Quimby, Frank. "The Hierro Commerce: Culture Contact, Appropriation and Colonial Entanglement in the Marianas, 1521-1668." *The Journal of Pacific History* 46, no. 1 (June 2011): 1-26.

Rabson, Steve. "The Politics of Trauma: Compulsory Suicides During the Battle of Okinawa and Postwar Retrospectives." *Intersections: Gender and Sexuality in Asia and the Pacific*, Issue 24 (June 2010).

Rainbird, Paul. *The Archaeology of Micronesia*. Cambridge, United Kingdom: Cambridge University Press, 2004.

Rees, Laurence. *Horror in the East*. Book. London: BBC Worldwide, 2001.

Rees, Laurence. *Horror in the East*. Documentary. United Kingdom. British Broadcasting Corporation. 2000.

Reider, Noriko T. *Japanese Demon Lore: Oni from Ancient Times to the Present*. Logan, Utah: Utah State University Press, 2010.

Rhee, M. J. *The Doomed Empire: Japan in Colonial*

Korea. Brookfield, Vermont: Ashgate Publishing, 1997.

Richard, Dorothy E. *United States Naval Administration of the Trust Territory of the Pacific Islands, Volume I: The Wartime Military Government Period, 1942–1945*. Washington, D.C.: Office of the Chief of Naval Operations, 1957.

Richard, Dorothy E. *United States Naval Administration of the Trust Territory of the Pacific Islands, Volume II: The Postwar Military Government Era, 1945–1947*. Washington, D.C.: Office of the Chief of Naval Operations, 1957.

Roberts, Stephen H. *Population Problems of the Pacific*. London: George Routledge & Sons, Ltd., 1927.

Robinson, James C. *Okinawa: A People and Their Gods*. Rutland, Vermont: Charles E. Tuttle Company Publishers, 1969.

Rogal, William P. *Guadalcanal, Tarawa, and Beyond: A Mud Marine's Memoir of the Pacific Island War*. Jefferson, North Carolina: McFarland, 2010.

Rogers, Robert F. *Destiny's Landfall: A History of Guam*. Honolulu: University of Hawaii Press, 1995.

Rosario, Frank and Floyd Takeuchi. "Saipanese Recall a Day in June When Thousands Leapt to Death." *Pacific Islands Monthly* 45, no. 9 (September, 1974): 57–58.

Rothman, Lily and Liz Ronk. "What One Photographer Saw at the Battle of Saipan." *Time*, June 15, 2016.

Roush, Roy William. *Open Fire!* Marceline, Missouri: Walsworth Publishing Company, 2003.

Ruoff, Kenneth J. *Imperial Japan at Its Zenith: The Wartime Celebration of the Empire's 2,600th Anniversary*. Ithaca: Cornell University Press, 2010.

Russell, Scott. *From Arabwal to Ashes: A Brief History of Garapan Village, 1818 to 1945*. Micronesian Archaeological Survey Report Number 19. Saipan, CNMI: Department of Education, 1984.

Russell, Scott. "From Company Town to Capital Village: A Brief History of Chalan Kanoa, Saipan, CNMI." Saipan: CNMI Division of Historic Preservation, 2018.

Russell, Scott. *Rising Sun over the Northern Marianas: Life and Culture Under the Japanese Administration (1914–1944)*. Saipan: CNMI Department of Education, 1983.

Russell, Scott. *Tiempon Aleman: A Look Back at German Rule of the Northern Mariana Islands, 1899–1914*. Saipan: CNMI Division of Historic Preservation, 1998.

Russell, Scott. *Tiempon I Manmofo'na: Ancient Chamorro Culture and History of the Northern Mariana Islands*. Saipan: CNMI Division of Historic Preservation, 1998.

Russell, Scott. *Tinian, the Final Chapter*. Saipan: CNMI Division of Historic Preservation, 1995.

Russell, Scott and Genevieve S. Cabrera. "An Archaeological Survey of the *Hachiman Jinja* Site, Kannat Taddong Papago, Saipan." Saipan: CNMI Division of Historic Preservation, 2003.

Salaberria, Maria Angelica. *A Time of Agony: The War in the Pacific in Saipan, The Personal Account of Sister Maria Angelica Salaberria*. 1944. Reprint. Translated by Marjorie G. Driver and Omaira Brunal-Perry. Saipan: Committee on the Commemoration of the 50th Anniversary of World War II, 1994.

Satoshi, Kamata. "Shattering Jewels: 110,000 Okinawans Protest Japanese State Censorship of Compulsory Group Suicides." *The Asia-Pacific Journal: Japan Focus* 6, Issue 1 (January 2008).

Schickel, Richard. *Shooting War: World War II Combat Cameramen*. Documentary. DreamWorks L.L.C. 2000.

Schattschneider, Ellen. "The Bloodstained Doll: Violence and the Gift in Wartime Japan." *The Journal of Japanese Studies* 31, no. 2 (2003): 329–356.

Schmidt, David Andrew. *Ianfu: The Comfort Women of The Japanese Imperial Army of The Pacific War*. New York: The Edwin Mellen Press, 2000.

Second Armored Amphibian Battalion Association. *2nd Armored Amphibian Battalion USMC WWII, Saipan, Tinian, Iwo Jima*. Washington, D.C., Second Armored Amphibian Battalion Association, 1991.

Second Marine Division. "Saipan" (HM9-16). Pearl Harbor, Hawaii, 1944. https://www.ibiblio.org/hyperwar/USMC/ref/Saipan-HB/index.html

Sherrod, Robert. *On to Westward: War in the Central Pacific*. New York: Duell, Sloan, and Pearce, 1945.

Shizuoka Broadcasting System. SBS. Directed by Tatsuya Kishimoto. *Message from a Japanese Soldier*. Iwo Jima Documentary. Japan. SBS. 2009.

Shuster, Donald R. *Major Patterns of Social Change Instituted in Micronesia during Japanese Colonial Rule, 1914–1940*. Honolulu: Department of Educational Foundations, University of Hawaii, 1978.

Shuster, Donald R. "State Shinto in Micronesia during Japanese Rule, 1914–1945." *Pacific Studies* 5, no. 2 (1982): 20–43.

Sims, Lynn L. *"They Have Seen the Elephant," Veterans Remembrances from World War II for the 40th Anniversary of V-E Day*. Fort Lee, Virginia: United States Army Logistics Center, 1985.

Sloan, Bill. *Their Backs Against the Sea: The Battle of Saipan and the Largest Banzai Attack of World War II*. New York: Da Capo Press, 2017.

Smith, Holland M., and Percy Finch. *Coral and Brass*. New York: Charles Scribner's Sons, 1949.

Smith, Rex Alan and Gerald A. Meehl. *Pacific War Stories: In the Words of Those Who Survived*. New York: Abbeville Press, 2004.

Smith, W. Eugene. *W. Eugene Smith: His Photographs and Notes*. New York: Aperture Foundation, 1993.

South Sea Islands Album Publication Committee. *A Record of the Japanese Pioneers' Achievements Obliterated by the War: Photographic Collections of Saipan, Tinian, Rota*. Tokyo: South Sea Islands Album Publication Committee, 1985.

Spector, Ronald H. *Eagle Against the Sun: The American War with Japan*. New York: Random House, 1985.

Spennemann, Dirk H. R., *Aurora Australis: The German Period in the Mariana Islands 1899–1914*. Saipan: CNMI Division of Historic Preservation, 1999.

Spennemann, Dirk H.R., *Edge of Empire: The German Colonial Period in the Mariana Islands, 1899–1914*. Albury, NSW, Australia: Retrospect Imprint, HeritageFutures International, 2007.

Spoehr, Alexander. *Marianas Prehistory: Archaeological Survey and Excavations on Saipan, Tinian, and Rota.* Chicago: Chicago Natural History Museum, 1957.

Spoehr, Alexander. *Saipan: The Ethnology of a War-devastated Island.* Chicago: Chicago Natural History Museum, 1954.

Stanlaw, James. "Japanese emigration and immigration: From the Meiji to the modern." In *Japanese Diasporas: Unsung pasts, conflicting presents, and uncertain futures 2006*, edited by Nobuko Adachi, 35–51. New York: Routledge, 2006.

Stanley, David. *South Pacific Handbook.* Chico, California: Moon Publications, 1985.

Stoner, Gregg. *Hardcore 'Iron Mike': Conqueror of Iwo Jima.* Bloomington, Indiana: iUniverse, 2015.

Stott, Frederic A. *Saipan Under Fire.* Andover, Massachusetts. 1945.

Strasser, Ulrike. "Copies with Souls: The Late Seventeenth-century Marianas Martyrs, Francis Xavier, and the Question of Clerical Reproduction." *Journal of Jesuit Studies* 2 (2015): 558–585.

Straus, Ulrich. *The Anguish of Surrender: Japanese POWs of World War II.* Seattle: University of Washington Press, 2003.

Stubbs, William C., and D. G. Purse. *Cultivation of Sugar Cane.* Savannah, Georgia: The Morning News Print, 1900.

Sudo, Naoto. *Nanyo-orientalism: Japanese Representations of the Pacific.* Amherst, New York: Cambria Press, 2010.

Takenaka, Akiko. *Yasukuni Shrine: History, Memory, and Japan's Unending Postwar.* Honolulu: University of Hawaii Press, 2015.

Takizawa, Karen Ann. "War Stories (1): The Battle of Saipan (June 15–July+α, 1944)." *Honsei Journal of Sociology and Social Sciences* 59.1, 211 (2012): 1–33.

Tamanoi, Mariko Asano. *Memory Maps: The State and Manchuria in Postwar Japan.* Honolulu: University of Hawaii Press, 2009.

Tanaka, Yuki. *Hidden Horrors: Japanese War Crimes in World War II.* Boulder, Colorado: Westview Press, 1996.

Tanaka, Yuki. *Japan's Comfort Women: Sexual Slavery and Prostitution during World War II and the US Occupation.* New York: Routledge, 2002.

Thompson, Laura. *Guam and its People.* Reprint. New York: Greenwood Press, 1969.

Tierney, Robert Thomas. *Tropics of Savagery: The Culture of Japanese Empire in Comparative Frame.* Berkeley: University of California Press, 2010.

Toland, John. *The Rising Sun: The Decline and Fall of the Japanese Empire, 1936–1945.* New York: Random House, 1970.

Tolischus, Otto D. *Through Japanese Eyes.* New York: Reynal & Hitchcock, 1945.

Townsend, Mary Evelyn. *Origins of Modern German Colonialism, 1871–1885.* New York: Columbia University Press, 1921.

Trefalt, Beatrice. "After the Battle for Saipan: The Internment of Japanese Civilians at Camp Susupe, 1944–1946." *Japanese Studies* 29, no. 3 (2009): 337–352.

Trefalt, Beatrice. "Collecting Bones: Japanese Missions for the Repatriation of War Remains, and the Unfinished Business of the Asia-Pacific War." *Australian Humanities Review* 61 (2017): 145–159.

Trefalt, Beatrice. "Fanaticism, Japanese soldiers and the Pacific War, 1937–45." In *Fanaticism and Conflict in the Modern Age*, edited by Matthew Hughes and Gaynor Johnson. New York: Frank Cass, 2005.

Trefalt, Beatrice. *Japanese Army Stragglers and Memories of the War in Japan, 1950–1975.* New York: RoutledgeCurzon, 2003.

Trefalt, Beatrice. "The Battle of Saipan in Japanese Civilian Memoirs: Non-combatants, Soldiers and the Complexities of Surrender." *The Journal of Pacific History* 53, no. 3 (2018): 252–267.

Trumbull, Robert. "Japanese Expect to Win, Poll Finds." *New York Times*, February 16, 1945.

Tuggle, Dave. "The Archaeological Landscape of Japanese-Era Tinian, Mariana Islands." *Pan-Japan* 11, no. 1 & 2 (2015): 74–114.

Tuggle, Dave and Wakako Higuchi. "Concrete Terraces and Japanese Agricultural Production on Tinian, Mariana Islands." 1st Marianas History Conference. Late Colonial History (Mangilao, Guam: Guampedia Foundation, 2012): 63–75.

Tuten-Puckett, Katharyn. *"We Drank Our Tears": Memories of the Battles for Saipan and Tinian as Told by Our Elders.* Saipan, CNMI: Pacific Star Young Writers Foundation, 2004.

Uchida, Jun. *Brokers of Empire: Japanese Settler Colonialism in Korea, 1876–1945.* Cambridge, Massachusetts: Harvard University Asia Center, 2011.

Ueno, Chizuko. *Nationalism and Gender.* Translated by Beverley Yamamoto. Melbourne, Trans Pacific Press, 2004.

United Nations Security Council. "Security Council Resolution 21 (1947) on the Trusteeship Agreement for the Trust Territory of the Pacific Islands." Official Records, Second Year, no. 31. 124th Meeting. Lake Success, New York. 2 April 1947.

United States Pacific Fleet and Pacific Ocean Areas. "Psychological Warfare, Part 1." Pearl Harbor, Hawaii. United States Pacific Fleet and Pacific Ocean Areas. 1944.

United States Strategic Bombing Survey. *The Effects of Bombing on Health and Medical Services in Japan.* Medical Division. Dates of Survey: 24 October-31, November 1945. Washington, D.C.: Government Printing Office, June, 1947.

United States Strategic Bombing Survey. *Effects of Incendiary Bomb Attacks on Japan: A Report on Eight Cities.* Dates of Survey: 3 October 1945–1 December 1945. Physical Damage Division. Washington, D.C.: Government Printing Office, April, 1947.

United States Strategic Bombing Survey (Pacific). Naval Analysis Division. *The Campaigns of the Pacific War.* Washington, D.C.: Government Printing Office, 1946.

Uno, Kathleen S. "Women and Changes in the Household Division of Labor." In *Recreating Japanese Women, 1600–1945*, edited by Gail Lee Bernstein. Berkeley: University of California Press, 1991.

Viallet, Serge. *Kizu: The Untold Story of Unit 731.* France: Marathon Media Group, 2004.

Viana, Augusto. "Belgian Missionaries in 17th Century Marianas: The Role of Fr. Peter Coomans and

Fr. Gerard Bouwens." *Philippiniana Sacra* 46, no. 136 (2011): 365-389.

Viana, Augusto. "Filipino Natives in Seventeenth Century Marianas: Their Role in the Establishment of the Spanish Mission in the Islands." *Micronesian Journal of the Humanities and Social Sciences* 3, no. 1-2 (2004): 19-26.

Viana, Augusto. *In the Far Islands: The Role of Natives from the Philippines in the Conquest, Colonization and Repopulation of the Mariana Islands, 1668-1903*. Manila, University of Santo Tomas Publishing House, 2004.

Viana, Augusto. "The Pampangos in the Mariana Mission 1668-1684." *Micronesian Journal of the Humanities and Social Sciences* 4, no.1 (2005): 1-16.

Vilar, Miguel G. et al. "The Origins and Genetic Distinctiveness of the Chamorros of the Marianas Islands: An mtDNA Perspective." *American Journal of Human Biology* 25, no.1 (2013): 116-122.

Villella, Peter B. *Indigenous Elites and Creole Identity in Colonial Mexico, 1500-1800*. New York: Cambridge University Press, 2016.

Walth, Cherie K. "Naton Beach Site, Guam: A Look Back in Time." 3rd Marianas History Conference. Mangilao, Guam: Guampedia, 2017.

Walther, Daniel J. *Sex and Control: Venereal Disease, Colonial Physicians, and Indigenous Agency in German Colonialism, 1884-1914*. New York: Berghahn, 2015.

Ward, Geoffrey C., and Ken Burns. *The War: An Intimate History, 1941-1945*. New York: Alfred A. Knopf, 2007.

Warren, James Francis. *Ah Ku and Karayuki-san: Prostitution in Singapore, 1870-1940*. Singapore: Oxford University Press, 1993.

Watt, Lori. *When Empire Comes Home: Repatriation and Reintegration in Postwar Japan*. Cambridge, Massachusetts: Harvard University Press, 2009.

Weiner, Michael. *Race and Migration in Imperial Japan*. New York: Routledge, 1994.

Wenkam, Robert, and Byron Baker. *Micronesia: The Breadfruit Revolution*. Honolulu: East-West Center, 1971.

Westfall, Douglas, and Ryozo Kimihira. *The Taking of Saipan: Two Sides to Every Battle in WWII. The Memoirs of Cpl. Richard Meadows & Cpl. Genkichi Ichikawa*. Orange, California: The Paragon Agency Publishers, 2014.

Wetherall, William. "Japan's Anti-Suicide Traditions." In International Cultural Association of Kyoto Essays on Japanology, 1978-1982 (Kyoto: Bunrikaku, 1983): 105-123.

Willens, Howard P. *An Honorable Accord: The Covenant between the Northern Mariana Islands and the United States*. Honolulu: University of Hawaii Press, 2002.

Winkler, Allan M. *The Politics of Propaganda: The Office of War Information 1942-1945*. New Haven, Connecticut: Yale University Press, 1978.

Wissolik, Richard David et al. *They Say There Was a War*. Latrobe, Pennsylvania: Center for Northern Appalachian Studies, Saint Vincent College, 2005.

Wong, Michael F., and Barry R. Hill. *Reconnaissance of Hydrology and Water Quality of Lake Susupe, Saipan, Commonwealth of the Northern Mariana Islands, 1990*. United States Geological Survey, Water-Resources Investigations Report 00-4054. Honolulu: United States Geological Survey, 2000.

Wuerch, William L., and Dirk Anthony Ballendorf. *Historical Dictionary of Guam and Micronesia*. Metuchen, N.J.: The Scarecrow Press, 1994.

Yamashita, Samuel Hideo. *Leaves from an Autumn of Emergencies: Selections from the Wartime Diaries of Ordinary Japanese*. Honolulu: University of Hawaii Press, 2005.

Yoshiaki, Yoshimi. *Comfort Women: Sexual Slavery in the Japanese Military During World War II*. New York: Columbia University Press, 2000.

Young, Louise. *Japan's Total Empire: Manchuria and the Culture of Wartime Imperialism*. Berkeley: University of California Press, 1998.

Zotomayor, Alexie Villegas. "Japanese Shrine in Chinatown to Mark Centennial." *Marianas Variety* (Saipan, CNMI), July 23, 2014.

Zotomayor, Alexie Villegas. "Tan Felisa's Story." *Marianas Variety* (Saipan, CNMI), March 21, 2011.

Index

Abadilla, Benjamin Quinzon 152
Absolute National Defense Sphere 67
Acapulco 19
acid 50, 88
Adams, Warren S. 134
Adolf von Hansemann's New Guinea Company 25
Adolph Capelle & Company 25
Africa 26–27
Agana 21–22
Agingan Point 16
agrarian celebrations 47
Agrihan 15, 25, 38
Aguiguan 15, 166
Agulto, Rosa Reyes 152
air defense 69
airfield 65, 67, 69, 75, 79, 82, 155
airway beacons 65
Aizuwakamatsu 36
Akata, Reiko 171
Akikusa, Tsuruji 119
Akiyama, Victoria 55, 75, 77, 107, 147–148, 157, 161, 169
Alamagan 15, 38
Alaska 30, 125
alcohol 36, 38, 48, 76
alcoholism 178
Aleutian Islands 67, 125
All Saints' Day 22
ambushes 133
America Maru 165
American Indian Wars 30
American Memorial Park 166, 177
ammunition carriers 135
ammunition dump 76
amputations 95, 159
Anatahan 15, 38
ancestor worship 17, 22, 24, 46–47
ancestral memorial tablets 46
anchovy 55
Anglo-Japanese Alliance 31, 33
Anglo-Japanese Friendship Treaty 30
animism 17, 24, 46–47
Ansei Five-Power Treaties 30
Aono, Chieko 139–140
Arabwal 24

Armistice of Compiegne 33
Arnold, Henry H. 74
Asahi Shimbun 170
Asahigraph's Great East Asia War Report 106
Asian Exclusion Act 63
Asiga 16, 45, 84
Aslito Airfield 67, 79, 82
asthma 160
Asuncion 15
Aulick 106
Australia 34, 60, 64, 73
awamori 60
Azumino 122

Babauta, Francisco Igwer 141
Baker Island 30
bakeries 42
Bale, Edward 106, 109
bamboo 17, 124, 126, 135, 138
Banana Wars 30, 97
bananas 17, 48, 55, 66
banks 42
banzai attacks 82, 84, 138
Banzai Cliff 85, 94, 130, 177
baptism 22
barmaids 60
barns 42, 146
barracks 69
Barrow, John 106
bars 42, 60
baseball 47, 82
bathhouses 42
Battle of Attu 96, 125
Battle of Iwo Jima 79, 96, 164
Battle of Makin 74–75
Battle of Midway 65
Battle of Tarawa 74–75, 78, 96, 102
Battle of the Coral Sea 74
Battle of the Philippine Sea 80
Battle of Tulagi 75
battleships 44, 75–76
bauxite 67
bayonets 56, 88, 109, 137–138
Baza, Felisa Chargualaf 105
beachcombers 22

Index

beans 22
beef 24, 27, 48, 55, 129
beer 129
Beijing 63
Belgium 33
Benavente, Antonio 86
beri-beri 160–161
betel nut 17
bicycle shops 42
Bidwell, M. Oakley 139
Bird Island 16
birds 15, 17, 125
biscuits 41
Bismarck Archipelago 16, 25–27, 34
blackbirders 22
Blanco, Juan 151
blockhouses 68, 79
board games 47
Bodhisattva statues 46
body count 7
Boeing B-29 heavy bombers 74, 171
bombers 74, 82, 171
bone collecting missions 178
Bonin Islands 31, 36, 67
bonito 41–42
bonsai 47
booby traps 75, 124, 141, 169
Borja, Victoria Tudela 77
Borneo 65
Borta, Frank W. 81, 124, 146
Bosse, Paul C. 167
Bougainville 65
Bowden, Arwin J. 131
Boys' Day 47
breadfruit 17, 48
breastfeeding (breast milk) 92, 130
British Empire 23, 25–26, 30–31, 33–34
brothels 29, 60, 70–71
Browner, Ralph L. 79
Buddha's Birthday 47
Buddhism 46–47, 49; shrines 46; temples 46
bulldozers 38, 144
bunraku 42
Burakumin 54–55
Burma 26, 53, 65, 67
burns 147, 160, 172
Busan 41, 172
Butler, Richard J. 109
Buzzard, Glenn L. 110, 133

Cabrera, Alejandro 50
Cabrera, Escolastica Tudela 49–50, 55, 67, 107, 109, 165
Cabrera, Gregorio C. 48, 75, 130, 146
cafes 42
Cairo Conference 74
California 40, 62, 97, 102
calisthenics 49
calligraphy 47, 119
cameramen 85
cameras 42, 90
Camp Elliott Marine Corps Base 102
candies 42, 129
cane borer 38
canneries 41

cannibals (cannibalism) 106
canoes 16–17
canteen 55, 95
carabao 22
cardiac failure 160
Cardinal Principles of the National Polity 52
cards 47
cargo 32–33, 37, 41
Caribbean 30
Carter, Winton W. 86
Casablanca Conference 73
cassava 37, 66
castaways 18, 22
castor oil plants 37
Castro, Marie Soledad 50, 69, 108, 128, 131, 150, 156
cathedral 22
Catholic missions and missionaries 18–23, 25, 27, 28, 51
cats 22
cattle 17, 22, 55, 129
cave of horrors 111
cave pictographs and petroglyphs 17
cemeteries 46
censorship 50, 142
Central America 30
Central Pacific drive 73–75
cerebral contusion 160
cerebral hemorrhage 160
Chambers, Justice M. 104, 111
chants 17, 24, 47, 110
Chapin, John C. 79, 128
charcoal 37
chemists 40
chess 47
Chicago Tribune 83, 87, 143, 170
chickens 48, 66, 161
Chief 96
Chief of Naval Operations 74
Chief of Staff of the United States Army 74
Chief of the United States Army Air Forces 74
chiefs 17, 18, 20–21, 24–25, 35
childbirth 59
childcare 18, 57
Chiyo Maru 165
Christian missions and missionaries 18–23, 25, 27, 28, 51
Christians 47, 50–51
Christmas 22, 47
Chungking 63
churches 20–22, 51
Chuseok 47
Chuuk 33, 35, 65, 75
cigarettes 41–42, 48, 104
cisterns 42, 147
Civil Affairs Bureau 34
civilian contractors 65, 77
civilian volunteer corps 69
clams 17
clans 17–24
Class "C" mandate 34
Cleaves, Emery 96
clocks 42
clothing 17, 22, 41, 48, 61, 82, 86, 96, 99, 100, 133, 139, 140, 143, 151–152, 155–156, 173
Cochran, Ran 86

coconut beetle 27
coconuts 1, 17, 24–25, 27, 36–37, 79
coffee 24, 37, 106
collaborators 21, 67
coma 130
comb 150, 90
Combined Chiefs of Staff (CCS) 73–74
comfort stations 70
comfort women 70–71, 98, 156, 166, 174
Commander Amphibious Forces Pacific 75
Commander Forward Area Central Pacific 153
Commander in Chief of the Pacific Ocean Areas 74, 172
Commander in Chief of the United States Fleet 74
Commander in Chief of the United States Pacific Fleet 74
Commander Joint Expeditionary Force 75
Commander Marianas 53, 172
Commander of the United States Navy Fifth Fleet 75
Commonwealth of the Northern Mariana Islands 176–177
communal lands 21, 26
communication facilities 65
Communism 175
community volunteer organizations 49
composting facilities 42
conches 17
concrete 41–42, 44, 68, 70–71
condoms 71
confectionaries 42
Confucianism 47
conscription 53, 58, 68, 69, 164
constables 35, 67
cooks 67
Cooper, Paul E. 132
copper 67
copra 25, 27, 38, 41
coral reefs 15
corn 22, 48, 55, 66
corn meal 48
corruption 22
cosmetics 42, 48, 61
cotton 25, 37, 48, 76
Council of the Indies 21
counterattacks 82, 84, 138
courts 27, 35
Cox, Floyd R. 150
crab 17, 82, 129
cremations 46
criminals 23
crops 20, 24, 27, 37–38, 66; failure 17, 37; neglect 67
cruisers 75–77, 85, 88, 92
Cruz, Cristino Dela 109
Cuba 30, 40
cyanide 89

Daejonggyo 47
D'Amico, Albert Anthony 110
dance 22, 47, 50; halls 42
death rituals (funeral) 18, 23, 46
Death Valley 81
decoys 80, 133–134, 136
deer 22

defense facilities 67
defense structures 75
dehydration 105, 127, 130
deities 44, 46–47
Delisle, Norman 85
DeMarino, Sante 106, 110, 124, 137
demons 105
Dempsey, David 111
dengue 131, 160
Department of Civil Administration 34
deportations 28, 30
Desrosiers, Edwin P. 90, 141
destroyers 75–76, 85, 92, 106
dialects 44
diarrhea 82, 160
Diaz, Juan Camacho 106
dice 47
Dinova, Samuel R. 138
discrimination 36, 43, 48, 50–56
dishes 41, 46
distillery 38
divorce 60
dogs 22
Dolan, Kenneth J. 77
dolls 42, 59
Dominican Republic 30
Doolittle Raid 105
Dorko, George J. 124, 132
Dowdakin, David 92
Doyen 158
Drea, Edward 120
dresses 48, 57
drills 49, 51, 59
drownings 43
drugs 19, 70
Druiding, P. 160
ducks 17, 161
duckweed 17
Duenas, Lucia Aldan 55
dumplings 48
dungarees 82
Dutch 30, 64
Dutch East Indies (Netherlands Indies) 60, 65, 67, 171
dysentery 43, 160

earthquakes 15
East Honganji Temple 46
Easter 22, 47
eels 17
eggs 17, 36, 48, 131
Ellis, Stan 137
Elrod, Roy H. 124, 139, 143, 148
embargoes 64
Embree, John F. 88, 143, 158
embroidery 47
emperor's portrait 49
Empire of Japan national anthem 49
engineers and engineering 40–41, 65, 69, 86, 139, 153, 163
Eniwetok (Enewetak) 26, 74
Enomoto, Masayo 124–125
Ensuiko Sugar Company 37
epilepsy 160
ethanol 38

evacuations 80, 126, 164–165, 172
executions 20, 124
exhaustion 22, 82
Export Control Act 64
exposure 160

F. & W. Hennings 25
factories 36–38, 42, 52, 68, 77, 100, 169, 177; workers 37, 40
fading nuts 17
Fahey, James J. 76, 85
famine 17, 20, 37
Fanonchuluyan Bay 16
fans 42
Farallon de Medinilla 15
farmers 24, 37, 39, 42, 45, 48, 61, 68, 94
farmhouse 83, 119, 146, 151
feasts 18, 22, 24
feces 1, 131, 158, 163
fever 130–131, 160
Field Service Code 82, 121
fiestas 23
Fiji 25
Filipinos 20, 23, 26, 30, 177
Fiore, Joseph P. 148
fire god (hinukan) 46
firebombing 5, 166, 171–172
firefighting drills 59
First Sino-Japanese War 31
fisheries 41–42
fishermen 41–42, 48, 61
fishing 11, 17–18, 24, 28, 32, 35, 41–42, 47, 50, 61, 65–66, 154, 161
flags 34, 47, 71, 96, 109–110, 133–134, 140, 170, 176
flame tanks 145, 147
flamethrowers 144, 147–148
Flier 165
flies 77, 83, 88, 110, 127, 131, 158
floating bodies 85, 98
flooding 36
flowers 17, 46–47, 170, 178; arrangements 47
folk costumes 47
folk festivals 47
food crisis 66
forced labor 11, 22, 53, 56, 66–68
Formosan koa 38
fortifications 34, 67, 147, 175
forts 19–20
fortune tellers 46–47
foxhole 77, 81, 104
France 26, 31
freight 28, 32, 40
French 30
fruit bats 15, 17
Fujimoto, Shigekazu 54
Fukushima Prefecture 36
Fumi, Saito 170
funerals 18, 23
futons 42

Gabaldon, Guy L. 71, 97–98, 135, 138, 143
galleons 19, 21, 23
gambling 47
games 22, 47
gangrene 104, 160

gardens 42, 156
gas bacillus 131
gas stations 42
gastrointestinal infections 127
Gates, Michael 79, 86, 106, 161
geisha 42, 60, 71, 107; houses 71
General Survey of the South Seas Islands 164
Geneva 34
Geneva Convention 124
geography 41, 49
German Colonial Office 26
German Colonial Society 25
German Foreign Office 26
German Pacific Protectorate 26
germs 160
Geruma 171
Gilbert Islands (Kiribati) 15, 65, 67, 74, 97, 102
Gilberts 15, 65, 67, 74, 97
Gilbreath, Jack V. 71, 99, 133, 148
glassware 42
goats 22, 129
Goeku, Sumiko 93
gold teeth 106
gonorrhea 29, 75, 143
gourds 55
gowns 48, 57, 82
Graf, Robert F. 130, 144
Graham, Cliff 86–87, 119
grave goods 17
graves 43, 139, 169
Gray, George E. 132
Great Britain 23, 25–26, 30–31, 33–34
Great Japan Women's Association 59
Great Kanto Earthquake 38, 53, 63
Great Marianas Turkey Shoot 80
Greater East Asian CoProsperity Sphere 65, 68
Greider, Carlton B. 91
Guadalcanal 73–75
Guano Islands Act 30
Guantanamo Bay 30
Guerrero, Mariano 56
Guguan 15
Gurguan Point 16
gyokusai 93, 125–126, 169

Haberman, Harold F. 79
Hachiman Shrine 44
hair (hairstyles) 22, 42, 48, 87, 90–91, 96–97, 144, 157, 170
Haiti 30
Hakusan Maru 165
Hanbok 48
handicrafts 47, 57, 59
hand-to-hand combat 81
Handleman, Howard 83, 130
hanging 43
Hansen, Arthur G. 146
Harris, Albert J. 88
Haruji, Matsue 36
Harvard University 102
Hatsumiyamairi 45
Hawaii (Hawaiian Islands) 30, 40, 47, 62, 73–75, 98, 103, 156, 163
Hazard, Benjamin H. 79, 107, 141
hearth 46

hepatitis 160
herbal medicine shops 42
hibiscus 17
Hiki South Seas Trading Company Limited 32
Hill, George C. 136
Hinamatsuri 47
Hinode Shrine 45
Hirakushi, Takashi 126
Hiroshima Prefecture 171
Hoffman, Carl W. 82, 84, 90, 141
Hoffschlaeger & Stapenhorst 25
holdouts 5, 84, 103, 140, 163, 175
Holiday, Samuel T. 91, 148
holidays 22, 47–48
Home Guard 68, 109
homesteads 37, 177
Hong Kong 60, 65
Honolulu 16, 71, 163
Honolulu 88
Hoover, John H. 153
Hoover, William B. 145
Horiguchi, Mitsusada 48
horse mackerel 41
horses 22
hospital ships 106
hostages 104, 134–135
Howe, Clifford W. 86
Howland Island 30
human shields 80, 132–133, 136
human waste 103
huts 17–18, 131

ice cream parlors 42
ice plants 41
Ichikawa, Genkichi 57, 75, 119
Iejima 171
IJN Provisional South Sea Islands Defense Force 33
IJN Second South Seas Squadron 33
immigration 23, 38, 55, 164
immunities 20, 29, 160
immunization 29
imon ningyo 59
Imperial General Headquarters 126, 169–170
Imperial German Navy 25
Imperial Japanese Army Airfield Construction Units 69
Imperial Japanese Army Construction Duty Companies 69
Imperial Japanese Army Criminal Code 120
Imperial Japanese Army Labor Units 69
Imperial Japanese Army Land Duty Companies 69
Imperial Japanese Army Mobile Lumber Squads 69
Imperial Japanese Army Sea Duty Companies 69
Imperial Japanese Army Special Volunteer System Law 68
Imperial Japanese Army 31st Army 68
Imperial Japanese Navy Central Pacific Area Fleet 68
Imperial Japanese Navy Civil Engineering and Construction Units 69
Imperial Japanese Navy 5th Special Base Force 65–66, 69
Imperial Japanese Navy 4th Fleet 65, 69
Imperial Japanese Navy Mobile Fleet 80
Imperial Japanese Navy Naval Land and Guard forces 65
Imperial Japanese Navy Pioneer Units 69
Imperial Japanese Navy Special Volunteer Law 69
Imperial Japanese Navy tunneling companies 69
Imperial Japanese Navy Yokosuka 1st Special Naval Landing Force 65
Imperial National Defense Policy 62
imperial ordinances 34–35, 68–69
imperial palace 49
Imperial Rescript on Education 49
Imperial Rule Assistance Association 59
imports 41, 48, 64, 66, 129
incendiaries 77, 147, 171–172
incense 45–46
Indalecio, Henry Taimanao 163
India 26
Indian removals 30
Indianapolis 92
indigenous Americans 20
indigo 25
Indochina 26, 60, 64
Indonesia 60, 65, 67, 171
infections 127, 131, 140, 159–160
infertility 70
infrastructure 26, 33, 41–42, 55, 158
ink art 47
Inner South Seas 64
inns 42
insects 36, 66, 131
International Electronic Communication Company 77
International News Service 83, 130
intestinal parasites 160
Investigation of Global Policy with the Yamato Race as Nucleus 52
iron 18, 20
ironwood trees 38
Island Commander of Saipan 153, 172
Island Commander of Tinian 153
Island Southeast Asia 15–17, 19, 22, 32, 41, 64
Italy 64
Iwo Jima 31, 79, 96, 164
Izumi Shrine 45

Jaluit 26, 33, 35
Jaluit Company 25
Japan Hygiene Association 52
Japan Industry and Economics Newspaper 105
Japan Mail Steamship Company 41
Japan Military Service Law 69
Japan Sugar Company 36
Japanese High Command 67, 74, 125, 126, 165, 171
Japanese Ministry of Education 49, 57
Japanese Ministry of Welfare 59
Japanese Navy Ministry 33
Japanese Office of Colonial Affairs 34
Japanese South Sea Islands Mandate 34
Japaneseness (Nihon rashisa) 45
Jarman, Sanderford 153
Jarvis Island 30
jaundice 160
Java 39
J.C. Godeffroy & Sohn 25

jeeps 96–97, 100
jewelry 17, 24, 42
jewels 19, 125
Jiazhou (Kiautschou) Bay 26
Johnson, Orvel E. 140
Johnson, Wallace 145
Johnston, Richard W. 158
Johnston Atoll 30
Joint Chiefs of Staff 73
Jones, Louis R. 111
Judd, Steve 110, 143
Julian, Tony 131
jungle of skeletons 86
jungle rot 130

Kabayama, Hisao 39, 52
Kabuki 42
Kagman Peninsula 16, 44, 81
Kagoshima Prefecture 37
Kahi 43, 45
kami shelf 45
Kamikaze 7
kaminchu 46
Kanagawa Prefecture 88
Kanagawa Treaty 30
Kantoshu 31
Kapingamarangi 26
Karafuto 35, 175
Karashima, Toyoshige 124
karayuki-san 60
Katori 44
Kawaguchi, Taroa 77, 119, 123
Kazuo, Kawamura 121, 148
Kellogg-Briand Pact 63
Kempeitai 56
Kensuke, Tamayama 55
kerosene lamps 41
Kichitaro, Shinozuka 107
Kigensetsu 47
Kikuchi, Akiko 1, 44, 47, 104, 178
Kikuchi, Hiroshi 93–94
kill-or-be-killed psychology 124
Kimble, Frederick V.H. 153
kimchi 48
kimono 48, 95, 156
kindness 95, 119, 148
kin-groups 19
King, Ernest J. 74
Kingdom of Hawaii 30
Kiribati 15, 65, 67, 74, 97
Kita Iwo Jima 31
kite flying 47
Kiyochi, Ogata 68, 84
Kiyoshi, Hiraizumi 170
knife (knives) 40, 81, 88, 91–92, 108, 124, 128, 138
Kokopo 26
Kondo, Hajime 124
Korean Memorial Service Association 178
Korean military laborers (Korean troops) 5, 11, 69, 83, 98–100, 135, 139, 156, 166
Korean National Association 163
Korean Shamanism 47
Korean War 174
Koror 34–35, 45
Kubo, Hoichi 103–104

Kuniyoshi, Shinsho 93, 278
Kurihara, Tokuichi 88
Kuril Islands 67, 175
Kurnick, N.B. 161
kut rituals 47
Kwajalein 74–75
Kwantung Army 63
Kwantung Leased Territory 31
Kyoto 169
Kyushu 31

labor parties 69
lacquerware 42
Ladd, Dean 86, 150
Lake Susupe 16, 79, 150, 156
Lalo Point 16, 84–85
lamb 48
land claims 25
land grants 21
land rights 26
land-tenure 18, 37
landing craft infantry gunboats 144
landing ship tank 90, 110
Landing Vehicle Tracked (LVT) 79, 90, 134
landmines 79
Lansing-Ishii Agreement 63
lanterns 42, 44
Lasso Shrine 45
latrines 131, 158
latte stones 17, 169
Laulau Bay 16
laundresses 57
League of Nations 33–34, 48, 50, 63–64
Leahy, William D. 74
LeBow, Cleatus A. 92
Lee, Taeki 50
legumes 48
leprosy colony 23
Levin, Dan 109
Lexington 74
Liaotung Peninsula 31
Lieb, Rita Titibau 109
life saving guarantee 99–100
Lifestyle Reform Movement 55
limestone 15, 44
lion-dog guardian statues 44
liquor 22, 32, 41
liver oil 42
livestock 22, 24, 27, 35, 37, 66, 129, 161
Lizama, Primitiva Reyes 130
Lloyd, Russell 107, 137
lobster 17, 41
local militia 27
logistics 77, 154
loudspeakers 88, 91, 100, 146
Louisiana State University 36
Louisiana Sugar Experiment Station 40
Lucas, Jim G. 90, 99, 109, 127, 133, 178
lumber yards 42
lunar calendar 46
Lunar New Year 47
LVT *see* Landing Vehicle Tracked

MacArthur, Douglas 73
machine gun 79

machinery 41
mackerel 41
magazines 32, 42, 50, 96
Magicienne Bay 16
Mahdist War 26
maids 60, 57
mail 32, 40
Mainichi Shimbun 170
makeup 42, 48, 61
Makin 74–75
Makunsha 138
Malaya 60, 65
managed forests 17
Manchurian Incident 63
Manganese 67
Maniagassa Island (Managaha Island) 16
Manifest Destiny 30
Manila 16
manure 39
marble 67
Marco Polo Bridge Incident 63
Marcus Island 32
Mariana of Austria 21
Marianas Evacuation and Occupation Command 172
Marianas Trench 15
Marpo Point 16, 84–86
Marpo Valley 16
Marpo Village 45
Marsden, Lawrence A. 158
Marshall, George C. 74
martial arts 47
Masalog Point 16
masks 47
massacres 111
matriclans 17
Matsujiro, Chodo 37
Matsumoto 150th Infantry Regiment 121, 148
Matthews, Carl W. 146–147
Maug 15
McCarthy, Edward 138
McGaffin, William 107, 142
Meadows, Richard 79
measles 160
medical supplies 140, 158–159
medicine 17, 42, 61, 100, 154, 158–159, 161
Megumi, Komatsu 127, 131
Meighan, Joseph J. 137–138, 140
Meiji Sugar Company 37
Meijisetsu 47
Meller, Norman 154, 159–161
merchant marine vessels 66, 172
mercy killings 5, 125
Mesoamerica 18
mess kits 131
Mestizos 20
metals 19, 22, 64, 67
meteorological observation stations 42
methamphetamine hydrochloride 70
Mexican-American War 30
Mexico 19, 21, 23
Mexico City 21
Meyers, Lewis 80
Mica 67
Michalak, Henry C. 78

Micronesian Claims Commission 176
Micronesian Repatriation Association 177
Midway 30, 65, 74
Military Administration of the South Sea Islands 65
military facilities 67
Miller, Bill 71, 107, 161
Minami Iwo Jima 31
Minami-Torishima 32
mining 27–28, 65, 67, 146, 175
Ministry of Colonization 34
Ministry of Greater East Asia 34
miscarriages 142
miso 41, 48, 55
mission schools 22, 49
Mita, Haruji 121
Mitsuharu, Kaneko 172
Miura, Shizuko 94, 106
Miyagi Prefecture 105
Mokpo 41
molasses 38, 40
monpe 48
Monroe Doctrine 31
Montgomery, Robert R. 110
Montpelier 76
Moon Viewing Island 16
moral embargo 64
More, William L. 88
Morison, Samuel Eliot 77, 88–89, 125
mortars 79, 84, 155
Mother-Child Protection Law 59
motion pictures 50
Mt. Donnay 94–95
Mt. Kastiyu 16
Mt. Lasso 16, 84, 144
Mt. Maga 16, 84
Mt. Marpi 85
Mt. Tapochau 16, 44, 93–94, 137, 152
mountain spirits 47
movie theaters 42
Mukden 63
Muna, Nicolas Q. 50
Murayama, Kakuichiro 66
Murayama South Seas Trading Company Unlimited 32
Murray, George D. 172
music 50, 75
mussels 17
Mutcho Point 16, 138
mythology recitations 47
myths 8, 17, 22, 49, 172

Nafutan Point 16, 80, 82, 119, 131
Nagano, Osami 172
Nagasaki 172
Nagumo, Chuichi 68, 126
Naha 172
Nakano, Jiro 171
Nanking 63–64; Massacre 64
Nanko 37, 41–42, 45
Nanko Marine Production Company 41
Nanko Shrine 45
Nanshin (southward advance) 31–32
Nanyo Shrine 45
Naokata, Sasaki 105

Index

napalm 77
narcotics 19, 70
National Mobilization Law 66
nationalism 7, 13, 49, 51, 53
Nauru 26
Nautilus 165
Navajo Code Talker 91, 148
Nazi Germany 64
NBK, South Seas Trading Company 32, 36, 40–41
Near Oceania 16
neighborhood associations 50
New Britain 26, 65
New Spain 19, 21, 23
New Year 47
New York Times 167
New Zealand 34, 74
newspapers 2, 42, 49–50, 85, 87, 105, 170
Nicaragua 30
nickel 67
night soil 40
Nihei, Torayoshi 95
Nii, Seiichi 77
Nimitz, Chester W. 74–75, 153
ningyo joruri 42
Nisei 71
Nishikawa, Kimiko 130, 150, 157
Nishimura Development Company 36
nitrate of soda 39
noh 42
noodles 48
nuclear testing 175
Nukuoro 26
nurses 94, 137, 139, 141, 158

Oakland 85
Oba, Sakae 119, 140
Obermiller, H.L. 90, 150
Obon Festival 47
octopus 17
Office of Naval Intelligence 102
Office of War Information 88, 98, 143, 158
Ogasawara Islands 31
Ojeda, Joe E. 79, 88
Okae, Shiro 70
Okoshi, Harunori 120
Okunoshima Island 171
Okuyama, Ryoko 92
onarigami 46
Operation Forager 75
opium 70
Order for Labor Coordination 66
Order for National Labor Services Cooperation 66
Oriental Development Company 37
ornaments 17, 24, 42
orphans 94, 156, 159
Osaka 41, 49
Osamu, Yoshida 121
Oshima Soap Factory 130
Outline for Economic Policies for the Southern Areas 67
Outline of Food Policies for the South Sea Islands 66
Overall Plan for the Defeat of Japan 74
Oya, Goichi 68
oysters 17

Pagan 15, 38, 66, 75
painting 47
Palau 27, 33–35, 45, 65
pamphlets 32, 50, 99
Panama 21
Panama Canal 30, 62
pandanus 17
Pangelinan, Henry Sablan 43, 49, 52, 60, 70
papaya 37, 55
paper cutting and folding 47
parades 47, 59
paramilitary 8; drills 51
parks 42
parties 36, 59, 70
Pase, Charles 84, 100, 111, 146, 156
passenger transportation 32
patriotism 7, 49, 53, 170, 174; organizations 69; societies 49, 59; songs 108
patrolmen 35
peanuts 55
peasants 20, 37
Peking 63
penal colony 23, 28
peppers 22
perfume 71
peritonitis 160
Permanent Mandates Commission 34, 48, 50
Perry, Olian T. 90
Pescadores (Penghu) Islands 31
Pettier, Carl 89
pharmacies 42, 140
Philippine-American War 30
Philippine Sea 15, 42, 80
Philippines 7
phosphate 38, 67
Photographic Weekly Report 105
pigpens 42
pigs 17, 22, 48, 55, 66, 79, 158, 161
pillboxes 68, 79, 88
pineapples 25, 37
pirates 22
Pittmann, Alvy Ray 106
plantations 25, 27–28, 32
plays 47
Pleasant Island 26
pleasure quarters 42, 61
pneumonia 160
poetry 47
Pohnpei 26–27, 33, 36, 65
poisons 43, 88
Polynesia 25–26
Ponape 26–27, 33, 36, 65
porcelain 19
pork 24, 48
Portugal 21
post-traumatic stress disorder 70
potatoes 55, 66
pots 41
pottery 17, 46–47
poverty 37
power plants 42
POWS 119, 120, 124, 135, 156
prayer vigils 22
pregnancy 34, 94, 142, 152, 160
prejudice 28, 46, 50, 162

premature birth 160
Price, Willard 39, 51
principalia 21–23, 27, 36
privateers 22
prostitutes 20, 29, 60–61, 70–71
Prussian-Japanese Treaty 31
Public Peace Police Law 60
public works 21, 27, 29
Puerto Rico 24
pulmonary edema 160
puppet shows 42
purses 42
Pusan 41, 172a

quail 22
quarantine 172–173
Quebec Conference 73
Quitugua, Gregorio Muna 129, 135

Rabaul 26, 75
racial animosity 140
Racial Equality Proposal 63
radios 42; broadcasts 50
railcars 40
railroads 76
railways 38, 40, 63
Rainbow Plans 73
Ralph Talbot 92
ranches 21
Randolph, H.C. 131
rape 20, 22, 34, 64, 67, 69–70, 141–143, 174
Rape of Nanking 64
rashes 82
rationing 59, 66, 152
rats 17
reconnaissance 25, 32, 75–76
record players 42
Red Cross 95, 155
Remote Oceania 16–17
Rempke, John R. 87
Renstrom, Keith A. 137
reparations 172, 176
Repeki, Soledad 50
respiratory diseases 160
restaurants 42, 60
Reyes, Margarita Pia Tudela 130
rice wine cups 46
rings 106
ritual purifications 47
Robertson & Hernsheim 25
Rogal, William W. 86, 131, 133, 148
Rogers, Charles B. 90
Roosevelt, Franklin D. 74, 153
Root-Takahira Agreement 31
rosary services 22
Roush, Roy William 79, 86, 90, 137, 145
Roush, William 79, 86, 90, 137, 145
Ruak, Felipe Iguel 67, 145
Ruak, Jesus Ubet 67
rubber 64
rugs 19
Rules for Native Village Officials 35
Russian Empire 31, 62
Russians 8, 30
Russo-Japanese War 31, 62

ryosai kenbo 57
Ryu, Saito 170
Ryukyu Islands 31, 178
ryuso 48

Sablan, Benigno 56
Sablan, David 56, 106, 165
Sablan, Joaquin Oma 146
Sablan, Manuel T. 56, 77, 157
sacraments 22
sacrificial offerings 47
sago palm 37
saint feast days 22
Saipan and Tinian Evacuation Task Unit 172
Saipan Business School 51
Saipan intelligence pamphlet 77, 138, 141, 160
Saipan Vocational School 43
sake 45, 60, 82, 104, 178
Sakhalin 35, 175
Salaberria, Maria Angelica 127–128
salt 17, 40, 46
Samoa 25–26, 28, 30, 34, 71
San Diego 64, 98, 102
San Francisco 40
sandbags 65
Sandburg, Rod 82, 131, 133
Sanhalom 16, 24
sanitation 37, 158, 159, 162–163
Sankyu Corporation 69
sardines 55
Sarigan 15
satchel charge 111, 144, 146
Sato, Tatsu 42, 55, 151, 169
Satsunan Islands 37
Saturday Evening Post 107, 142
savages 28, 53–54, 98
Schlossenberg, Irving 127, 156, 163
Schmidt, Harry 84, 143
Schroeder, Karl B. 85, 144
scientists 7, 25, 36, 39–40, 48
scouts 67, 135
sculpture 47
scurvy 161
sea cucumber 17, 41
sea products 24, 38, 41
Seabees (construction battalions) 85, 106, 144, 157
seafood 17, 48
seamstresses 57
seaplane stations 65
seashell 17
seasickness 37
seaweed 17
Second London Naval Disarmament Conference 63
Second Sino-Japanese War 55, 138
secret police 56, 67
secretaries 56, 67
segregation 51
senninbari 59
Seollal 47
Setsubun 47
sewage systems 42
sewing machines 41
sex workers 60
sexism 56

sexual assault 67
sexual slavery 53, 61, 70, 174
sexually transmitted diseases 20, 29, 61, 71, 75, 143
shamanism 17, 24, 46–47
Shanghai Incident 63
Shantung Peninsula 26, 33, 63
Shantung Treaty 63
Shark 165
shark 41–42, 165; fins 42
shaved ice 42
Sheeks, Robert 69, 99, 104, 106, 108, 120, 127, 141, 147, 152, 163
Sherrod, Robert 16, 68, 71, 77, 80, 82, 90, 96–97, 100, 109, 137, 151, 156, 164, 167, 170, 174
Shichi-Go-San 45
Shinsho, Miyagi 106
shipwreck 18–19
Shiroma, Koyu 94, 106
Shirota, Suzuko 70
shore facilities 65
shrimp 17
Siege of Tsingtao 33
silk 19, 37
silver 19
Singapore 65
slaves 19
smallpox 23, 29
Smith, Harold 87, 143
Smith, Holland M. 75, 84
Smith, Kenneth E. 88
Smith, W. Eugene 146, 148
snails 17, 129
snipers 79, 83, 103, 109–110, 135, 150
Snowden, Lawrence F. 131
soap 130, 155, 158, 163
soapstone 67
social unrest 37
Sokehs Rebellion 27
Solomons 16, 26, 34, 67, 74, 80
song 22, 47, 108, 125, 171–172
soups 48
South Manchuria Railway 63
South Sea Marine Transportation Company 41
South Seas Bureau 34
South Seas Colonization Company 41, 65
South Seas Development Company (Nanyo Kohatsu) 37
South Seas Islanders 53
South Seas Islands Territory 65
South Seas Mandate 34, 38, 41–42, 63, 175
South Seas Production Company 36
South Seas Trading Company Limited 32, 36, 40–41
souvenirs 71, 106, 143
Soviet Union 8, 172, 175
soy sauce 41, 55
Spanish-American War 24, 30
Spanish mackerel 41
Sperling, Milton 90
spices 19
spider holes 79
spies 51, 56, 135
spirit-consoling services 177
sports 47, 49
Spruance, Raymond A. 75, 172

squid 17
Steck, Lewis J. 110, 137, 178
Stein, Richard R. 86
stockings 48
Stott, Frederic A. 78, 104, 110, 130, 133, 150, 161
stoves 46
Strategic Plan for the Defeat of Japan 74
street vendors 42
striped mullet 41
Stubbs, William Carter 40
submarines 66, 165
sugar factory 38
sugar manufacturing 36, 38–40
sugar mill 38, 77
Suicide Cliff: Saipan 85–86, 110, 177; Tinian 85–86, 92, 177
suits 48
Sumiyoshi Shrine 45
sumo 47
sun umbrellas 42
Sunda Islands 67
Sunharon 16, 41
surgeons 94–95
surrender leaflets 98, 124
Suzuki Brothers Trading Company 36
Suzuko Shirota 70
sweet potatoes 48, 66
Switzerland 34
swords 20, 71, 82, 88, 109, 138
syphilis 29, 75
Szech, Chester J. 77, 90

Tachibana Shrine 45
tachinid fly 38
Taft-Katsura Memorandum 31
tailors 42
Taiwan 31, 35–36, 38–41, 46, 49, 69, 70
Taiwan blackbird 38
Takao 41
Takeo, Yamauchi 111, 148
Takoyama Hill 140
Tanapag Harbor 16, 24, 41, 82, 88, 95
Tangono-sekku 47
tankers 80
Taoism 46–47
tapioca 37, 66
Tarawa 74–75, 78, 96, 102
Taro 17, 24, 55, 66
tattoos 24
taxes 21
tea 16, 41, 48; ceremony 47; houses 42
teachers 35, 49–51, 55
telecommunications 42, 77
Ten-year Development Plan of the South Sea Islands 65
tenant farmers 37
Tenchosetsu 47
tennis courts 42
tetanus 131, 160
textbooks 49, 171
textiles 19, 41
theaters 42, 47, 50
Third Washington Conference 73
thousand stitch belts 59
Tianjin 63

tin 64
Tinian Gesellschaf 27
Tinian Shrine 45
Tinian Town 24, 40, 42, 45, 60, 78, 84, 156, 169, 176
tobacco 22, 24–25, 41, 100
Tokashiki 171
Tokugawa Shogun 31
Tokyo Express 80
Tokyo Imperial University 170
Tokyo Industrial College 36
Tokyo Liaison Office 34, 66
Tokyo Liaison Office of the South Seas Government 34, 66
Tokyo Rose 75
Toland, John 3, 164
tomatoes 22
tonarigumi 50
tools 17, 24, 39, 125, 138
Torgerson, Albert C. 77, 86
torii gate 44
Torres Strait Islands 60
tortillas 48
tortoiseshell 41
towels 41
toxemia 160
toy stores 42
track and field 47
trains 76
transport ships 77
Treaty of Commerce and Navigation 64
Treaty of Paris 24, 30
Treaty of Shimoda 30
Treaty of Tordesillas 21
Treaty of Versailles 33
Treaty of Zaragoza 21
trenches 68, 79, 158
trepang 41
Tripartite Convention 30
Tripartite Pact 64
Tropical Industries Research Institute 65
Tropical Industry Laboratory 36
tropical storms 15, 32, 38
trousers 48, 96–97
trucks 76, 107
Truk 33, 35, 65, 75
Trust Territory of the Pacific Islands 175
Tsuguharu, Fujita 171
tsunamis 17
Tsunejiro, Tamura 169
Tsuyoshi, Ebato 124
tuberculosis 43, 61, 160–161
tuna 41
Turner, Richmond Kelly 75
turtle 17, 42
Twenty-One Demands 63
typhoid 43
typhoons 15, 17, 24, 27, 28, 32

uganju 46
Ujelang 26
ultranationalism 51
umbrellas 42
Underhill, James L. 153
United Kingdom 23, 25–26, 30–31, 33–34
United Nations 175

United States Army Air Forces: airdromes 171; bombing groups 74
United States Department of the Interior 175, 177
United States Joint Army and Navy Board 62
United States National Park Service 177
United States National Register of Historic Places 177
United States Navy Fifth Fleet 75, 80, 97, 153
United States Navy Japanese Language School 102
United States Navy Seabees (Construction Battalions) 85, 106, 144, 157
United States Navy Task Force 58 75–76
United States Navy Task Force 94 172
United States Pacific Fleet 62, 64, 74, 172
United States Strategic Bombing Survey 82, 165, 171
United States War Department 96
Universal Manhood Suffrage Law 60
University of California–Berkeley 102
University of Colorado–Boulder 102
University of Georgia 96
Uraga 172
Urbanowicz, Frank 91–92
Ushi Point 16, 155
ushinchi 48
utaki 46

venereal diseases 20, 29, 61, 71, 75, 143
Versailles Peace Conference 63
Vertucci, Gabriel J. 88, 137
Vietnam War 174
Virgin Mary 21, 23
Volcano Islands 31, 97
volcanoes 15

Wabol, Jesus Taisakan 129
Wabol, Mariana 147
Wachsmuth, Jerome C. 79, 138, 143
Wake Island 30
war brides 20
War Plan Orange 62, 73
war scares 62
Washington Naval Conference 63
Washington Naval Treaties 63
watches 41, 106
waterworks 42
Watson, Thomas E. 99
wax 40–41
weather stations 65
weaving 47
wedding 45, 82
Western Pacific Base Command 107, 167
whalers 22
Wheeler, Keith 83, 89, 127
white phosphorous 147
Whitehead, Burnes R. 133
Whiting, Francis Eliot Maynard 172
Williams, Dan 71
Williams, Robert L. 137
Wilson P. Allmand 86
Witowich, Michael 92, 178
wives 33, 42, 57, 90, 95
Wollin, Robert E. 88
women's patriotic associations 59
Wood, Phil 104

Worden, William L. 158
World War I 29, 32–33, 36, 40–41, 60, 97

Yamagata Prefecture 94
Yamamoto, Shintaro 56, 70
yams 17
Yap 23, 26–27, 33, 35, 63
Yap Treaty 63
Yasukuni Shrine 123
Yasutake, Seitaro 34, 52
Yokohama 41, 53, 172
Yokosuka 165
Yokosuka 1st Special Naval Landing Force 65
Yokosuka Naval Civil Engineering Department 65

Yokota, Chiyoko 107
Yomiuri Hochi 170
Yorktown 74
Yoshitaro, Shinozuka 69, 106, 111, 122, 169
Yoshitsugu, Saito 68, 82, 126
Young, Halley 143
Young Men's Association 152
Young Men's Corps 69
Young Women's Corps 69
youth associations 108
yukata 48
yuta 46

Zamami 171

www.ingramcontent.com/pod-product-compliance
Lightning Source LLC
Chambersburg PA
CBHW081553300426
44116CB00015B/2872